Jean Ingelow

The Complete Poems of Jean Ingelow

Jean Ingelow
The Complete Poems of Jean Ingelow
ISBN/EAN: 9783744713122
Printed in Europe, USA, Canada, Australia, Japan
Cover: Foto ©Thomas Meinert / pixelio.de

More available books at **www.hansebooks.com**

THE

COMPLETE POEMS

OF

JEAN INGELOW.

TORONTO:
RUSSELL WILKINSON, PUBLISHER, 25 COLBORNE ST.
1872.

TORONTO:
HUNTER, ROSE & CO., PRINTERS.

Dedication.

TO

GEORGE K. INGELOW.

YOUR LOVING SISTER
OFFERS YOU THESE POEMS, PARTLY AS
AN EXPRESSION OF HER AFFECTION, PARTLY FOR THE
PLEASURE OF CONNECTING HER EFFORT
WITH YOUR NAME.

KENSINGTON, June, 1863.

Contents.

	PAGE
Divided	1
Honors.—Part I.	3
Honors.—Part II.	6
Requiescat in Pace!	10
Supper at the Mill	13
Scholar and Carpenter	16
The Star's Monument	20
A Dead Year	28
Reflections	30
The Letter L	32
The High Tide on the Coast of Lincolnshire	40
Afternoon at a Parsonage	42
Songs of Seven	45
A Cottage in a Chine	48
Persephone	50
A Sea Song	52
Brothers, and a Sermon	53
A Wedding Song	61
The Four Bridges	62
A Mother showing the Portrait of her Child	70
Strife and Peace	72

A STORY OF DOOM AND OTHER POEMS.

	PAGE
The Dreams that came True	75
Songs on the Voices of Birds.	
Introduction.—Child and Boatman	81
The Nightingale heard by the Unsatisfied Heart	81
Sand Martins	82
A Poet in his Youth, and the Cuckoo-Bird	82
A Raven in a White Chine	84
The Warbling of Blackbirds	84
Sea-Mews in Winter-Time	85
Laurance	86
Songs of the Night Watches.	
Introductory—Evening	97
The First Watch.—Tired	97
The Middle Watch	99
The Morning Watch	100
Concluding.—Early Dawn	100
A Story of Doom	102
Contrasted Songs.	
Sailing beyond Seas	128
Remonstrance	128
Song for the Night of Christ's Resurrection	128
Song of Margaret	130
Song of the Going Away	131
A Lily and a Lute	131
Gladys and her Island	134
Songs with Preludes.	
Wedlock	143
Regret	144
Lamentation	144
Dominion	145
Friendship	145
Winstanley	147
The Monitions of the Unseen	152
A Birthday Walk	158
Not in vain I waited	158
A Gleaning Song	159
With a Diamond	159
Fancy	159
Compensation	159
Looking Down	159

CONTENTS.

	PAGE		PAGE
Married Lovers	160	Though all Great Deeds	167
A Winter Song	160	The Long White Seam	167
Binding Sheaves	160	An Old Wife's Song	167
Work	161	Cold and Quiet	168
Wishing	161	A Snow Mountain	168
To ———	161	Sleep (a Woman Speaks)	168
On the Borders of Cannock Chase	161	Promising (a Man Speaks)	168
The Mariner's Cave	161	Love	169
A Reverie	165	Poems on the Deaths of Three Lovely Children	170
Defton Wood	165		
The Snowdrop Monument (in Lichfield Cathedral	166	The two Margarets.	
		I. Margaret by the Mere Side	174
An Ancient Chess-King dug from some Ruins	166	II. Margaret in the Xebec	178
Comfort in the Night	166	Notes	185

POEMS.

DIVIDED.

I.

N empty sky, a world of heather,
  Purple of foxglove, yellow of
    broom;
We two among them wading to-
    gether,
  Shaking out honey, treading per-
    fume.

Crowds of bees are giddy with clover,
  Crowds of grasshoppers skip at our feet,
Crowds of larks at their matins hang over,
  Thanking the Lord for a life so sweet.

Flusheth the rise with her purple favor,
  Gloweth the cleft with her golden ring,
'Twixt the two brown butterflies waver
  Lightly settle and sleepily swing.

We two walk till the purple dieth
  And short dry grass under foot is brown,
But one little streak at a distance lieth
  Green like a ribbon to prank the down.

II.

Over the grass we stepped unto it,
  And God He knoweth how blithe we were!
Never a voice to bid us eschew it:
  Hey the green ribbon that showed so fair!

Hey the green ribbon! we kneeled beside it,
  We parted the grasses dewy and sheen;
Drop over drop there filtered and slided
  A tiny bright beck that trickled between.

Tinkle, tinkle, sweetly it sung to us,
  Light was our talk as of faëry bells—
Faëry wedding-bells faintly rung to us
  Down in their fortunate parallels.

Hand in hand, while the sun peered over,
  We lapped the grass in that youngling spring;
Swept back its rushes, smoothed its clover,
  And said, "Let us follow it westering."

III.

A dappled sky, a world of meadows,
  Circling above us the black rooks fly
Forward, backward; lo, their dark shadows
  Flit on the blossoming tapestry—

Flit on the beck, for her long grass parteth
  As hair from a maid's bright eyes blown back;
And, lo, the sun like a lover darteth
  His flattering smile on her wayward track.

Sing on! we sing in the glorious weather
  Till one steps over the tiny strand,
So narrow, in sooth, that still together
  On either brink we go hand in hand.

The beck grows wider, the hands must sever,
  On either margin, our songs all done,
We move apart, while she singeth ever,
  Taking the course of the stooping sun.

He prays, "Come over"—I may not follow;
  I cry, "Return"—but he cannot come:
We speak, we laugh, but with voices hollow;
  Our hands are hanging, our hearts are numb.

IV.

A breathing sigh, a sigh for answer,
  A little talking of outward things:
The careless beck is a merry dancer,
  Keeping sweet time to the air she sings.

A little pain when the beck grows wider;
  "Cross to me now—for her wavelets swell:"
"I may not cross"—and the voice beside her
  Faintly reacheth, though heeded well.

No backward path; ah! no returning;
  No second crossing that ripple's flow;
"Come to me now, for the west is burning;
  Come ere it darkens;"—"Ah, no! ah no!"

Then cries of pain, and arms outreaching—
  The beck grows wider and swift and deep:
Passionate words as of one beseeching—
  The loud beck drowns them; we walk, and
    weep.

V.

A yellow moon in splendor drooping,
   A tired queen with her state oppressed,
Low by rushes and swordgrass stooping,
   Lies she soft on the waves at rest.

The desert heavens have felt her sadness;
   Her earth will weep her some dewy tears;
The wild beck ends her tune of gladness,
   And goeth stilly as soul that fears.

We two walk on in our grassy places
   On either marge of the moonlit flood,
With the moon's own sadness in our faces,
   Where joy is withered, blossom and bud.

VI.

A shady freshness, chafers whirring,
   A little piping of leaf-hid birds;
A flutter of wings, a fitful stirring,
   A cloud to the eastward snowy as curds.

Bare glassy slopes, where kids are tethered;
   Round valleys like nests all ferney-lined;
Round hills, with fluttering tree-tops feathered,
   Swell high in their freckled robes behind.

A rose-flush tender, a thrill, a quiver,
   When golden dreams to the tree-tops glide;
A flashing edge for the milk-white river,
   The beck, a river—with still sleek tide.

Broad and white, and polished as silver,
   On she goes under fruit-laden trees;
Sunk in leafage cooeth the culver,
   And 'plaineth of love's disloyalties.

Glitters the dew and shines the river,
   Up comes the lily and dries her bell;
But two are walking apart for ever,
   And wave their hands for a mute farewell.

VII.

A braver swell, a swifter sliding;
   The river hasteth, her banks recede:
Wing-like sails on her bosom gliding
   Bear down the lily and drown the reed.

Stately prows are rising and bowing
   (Shouts of mariners winnow the air),
And level sands for banks endowing
   The tiny green ribbon that showed so fair.

While, O my heart! as white sails shiver,
   And crowds are passing, and banks stretch wide,
How hard to follow, with lips that quiver,
   That moving speck on the far-off side!

Farther, farther—I see it—know it—
   My eyes brim over, it melts away:
Only my heart to my heart shall show it
   As I walk desolate day by day.

VIII.

And yet I know past all doubting, truly—
   A knowledge greater than grief can dim—
I know, as he loved, he will love me duly—
   Yea, better—e'en better than I love him.

And as I walk by the vast calm river,
   The awful river so dread to see,
I say, "Thy breadth and thy depth for ever
   Are bridged by his thoughts that cross to me.

HONORS.—PART I.

A Scholar is musing on his Want of Success.

O strive—and fail. Yes, I did strive and fail.
I set mine eyes upon a certain night
To find a certain star—and could not hail
With them its deep-set light.

Fool that I was! I will rehearse my fault:
I, wingless, thought myself on high to lift
Among the winged—I set these feet that halt
To run against the swift.

And yet this man, that loved me so, can write—
That loves me, I would say, can let me see;
Or fain would have me think he counts but light
These Honors lost to me.

[*The Letter of his Friend.*]

" What are they? that old house of yours which gave
Such welcomes oft to me, the sunbeams fall
Still down the squares of blue and white which pave
Its hospitable hall.

"A brave old house! a garden full of bees,
Large dropping poppies, and queen hollyhocks,
With butterflies for crowns—tree peonies
And pinks and goldilocks.

"Go, when the shadow of your house is long
Upon the garden—when some new waked bird,
Pecking and fluttering, chirps a sudden song,
And not a leaf is stirred;

"But every one drops dew from either edge
Upon its fellow, while an amber ray
Slants up among the tree-tops like a wedge
Of liquid gold—to play

"Over and under them, and so to fall
Upon that lane of water lying below—
That piece of sky let in, that you do call
A pond, but which I know

"To be a deep and wondrous world; for I
Have seen the trees within it—marvellous things:

So thick no bird betwixt their leaves could fly
But she would smite her wings;—

" Go there, I say; stand at the water's brink,
And shoals of spotted grayling you shall see
Basking between the shadows—look, and think
'This beauty is for me;

"' For me this freshness in the morning hours;
For me the water's clear tranquility;
For me that soft descent of chestnut flowers;
The cushat's cry for me.

"'The lovely laughter of the wind-swayed wheat;
The easy slope of yonder pastoral hill;
The sedgy brook whereby the red kine meet
And wade and drink their fill.'

" Then saunter down that terrace whence the sea
All fair with wing-like sails you may discern;
Be glad, and say 'This beauty is for me—
A thing to love and learn.

"' For me the bounding in of tides; for me
The laying bare of sands when they retreat;
The purple flush of calms, the sparkling glee
When waves and sunshine meet.'

" So, after gazing, homeward turn, and mount
To that long chamber in the roof; there tell
Your heart the laid-up lore it holds to count
And prize and ponder well.

" The lookings onward of the race before
It had a past to make it look behind;
Its reverent wonders, and its doubtings sore,
Its adorations blind.

" The thunder of its war-songs, and the glow
Of chants to freedom by the old world sung;
The sweet love cadences that long ago
Dropped from the old-world tongue.

" And then this new-world lore that takes account
Of tangled star-dust; maps the triple whirl
Of blue and red and argent worlds that mount
And greet the IRISH EARL;

" Or float across the tube that HERSCHEL sways,
Like pale-rose chaplets, or like sapphire mist;
Or hang or droop along the heavenly ways,
Like scarfs of amethyst.

"O strange it is and wide the new-world lore,
   For next it treateth of our native dust !
Must dig out buried monsters and explore
      The green earth's fruitful crust ;

"Must write the story of her seething youth—
   How lizards paddled in her lukewarm seas;
Must show the cones she ripened, and forsooth
      Count seasons on her trees ;

"Must know her weight, and pry into her age,
   Count her old beach lines by her tidal swell;
Her sunken mountains name, her craters gauge,
      Her cold volcanoes tell ;

"And treat her as a ball that one might pass
   From this hand to the other—such a ball
As he could measure with a blade of grass,
      And say it was but small !

"Honors! O friend, I pray you bear with me;
   The grass hath time to grow in meadow lands,
And leisurely the opal murmuring sea
      Breaks on her yellow sands ;

"And leisurely the ring-dove on her nest
   Broods till her tender chick will peck the shell;
And leisurely down fall from ferny crest
      The dew-drops on the well ;

"And leisurely your life and spirit grew,
   With yet the time to grow and ripen free :
No judgment past withdraws that boon from you,
      Nor granteth it to me.

"Still must I plod, and still in cities moil ;
   From precious leisure, learned leisure far,
Dull my best self with handling common soil ;
      Yet mine those honors are.

"Mine they are called ; they are a name which means,
   This man had steady pulses, tranquil nerves ;
Here, as in other fields, the most he gleans
      Who works and never swerves.

"'We measure not his mind; we cannot tell
   What lieth under, over, or beside
The test we put him to ; he doth excel
      We know where he is tried ;

"'But, if he boast some further excellence—
   Mind to create as well as to attain ;
To sway his peers by golden eloquence,
      As wind doth shift a fane ;

"'To sing among the poets—we are nought :
   We cannot drop a line into that sea
And read its fathoms off, nor gauge a thought,
      Nor map a simile.

"'It may be of all voices sublunar
   The only one he echoes we did try;
We may have come upon the only star
      That twinkles in his sky.'

" And so it was with me."
                              O false my friend !
    False, false, a random charge, a blame undue ;
Wrest not fair reasoning to a crooked end :
         False, false, as you are true !

But I read on : " And so it was with me ;
   Your golden constellations lying apart
They neither hailed nor greeted heartily,
      Nor noted on their chart.

"And yet to you and not to me belong
   Those finer instincts that, like second sight
And hearing, catch creation's undersong,
      And see by inner light.

"You are a well, whereon I, gazing, see
   Reflections of the upper heavens—a well
From whence come deep, deep echoes up to me—
      Some underwave's low swell.

"I cannot soar into the heights you show,
   Nor dive among the deeps that you reveal ;
But it is much that high things are to know,
      That deep things ARE to feel.

"'Tis yours, not mine, to pluck out of your breast
   Some human truth, whose workings recondite
Were unattired in words, and manifest
      And hold it forth to light,

"And cry, 'Behold this thing that I have found.'
   And though they knew not of it till that day,
Nor should have done with no man to expound
      Its meaning, yet they say,

"'We do accept it : lower than the shoals
   We skim, this diver went, nor did create,
But find it for us deeper in our souls
      That we can penetrate.'

"You were to me the world's interpreter,
   The man that taught me nature's unknown tongue,
And to the notes of her wild dulcimer
      First set sweet words and sung.

"And what am I to you ? A steady hand
   To hold, a steadfast heart to trust withal ;
Merely a man that loves you and will stand
      By you, whate'er befall.

"But need we praise his tendance tutelar
   Who feeds a flame that warms him ? Yet 'tis true
I love you for the sake of what you are,
      And not of what you do :—

"As heaven's high twins, whereof in Tyrian blue
   The one revolveth ; through his course immense
Might love his fellow of the damask hue,
      For like, and difference.

"For different pathways ever more decreed
  To intersect, but not to interfere ;
For common goal, two aspects, and one speed,
    One centre and one year ;

"For deep affinities, for drawings strong,
  That by their nature each must needs exert ;
For loved alliance, and for union long,
    That stands before desert.

"And yet desert makes brighter not the less,
  For nearest his own star he shall not fail
To think those rays unmatched for nobleness,
    That distance counts but pale.

"Be pale afar, since still to me you shine,
  And must while Nature's eldest law shall hold ;"—
Ah, there's the thought which makes his random line
    Dear as refinèd gold!

Then shall I drink this draught of oxymel,
  Part sweet, part sharp? Myself o'erprized to know

Is sharp ; the cause is sweet, and truth to tell
  Few would that cause forego,

Which is, that this of all the men on earth
  Doth love me well enough to count me great—
To think my soul and his of equal girth—
    O liberal estimate!

And yet it is so ; he is bound to me,
  For human love makes aliens near of kin ;
By it I rise, there is equality :
    I rise to thee, my twin.

"Take courage,"—courage! ay, my purple peer,
  I will take courage: for thy Tyrian rays
Refresh me to the heart, and strangely dear
    And healing is thy praise.

"Take courage," quoth he, "and respect the mind
Your Maker gave, for good your fate fulfil ;
The fate round many hearts your own to wind."
    Twin soul, I will! I will!'

HONORS.—PART II.

The Answer.

AS one who, journeying, checks the
    rein in haste
Because a chasm doth yawn
    across his way
Too wide for leaping, and too
    steeply faced
For climber to essay—

As such an one, being brought to sudden stand,
  Doubts all his foregone path if 'twere the true,
And turns to this and then to the other hand
  As knowing not what to do,—

So I, being checked, am with my path at strife
  Which led to such a chasm, and there doth
    end.
False path! it cost me priceless years of life,
  My well-beloved friend.

There fell a flute when Ganymede went up—
  The flute that he was wont to play upon:
It dropped beside the jonquil's milk-white cup,
  And freckled cowslips wan—

Dropped from his heedless hand when, dazed
    and mute,
He sailed upon the eagle's quivering wing,
Aspiring, panting—ay, it dropped—the flute
  Erewhile a cherished thing.

Among the delicate grasses and the bells
  Of crocuses that spotted a rill side,
I picked up such a flute, and its clear swells
  To my young lips replied.

I played thereon, and its response was sweet;
  But, lo, they took from me that solacing reed.
"O shame!" they said; "such music is not
    meet;
Go up like Ganymede.

"Go up, despise these humble grassy things,
  Sit on the golden edge of yonder cloud."
Alas! though ne'er for me those eagle wings
  Stooped from their eyrie proud.

My flute! and flung away its echoes sleep;
  But as for me, my life-pulse beateth low;
And like a last-year's leaf enshrouded deep
  Under the drifting snow.

Or like some vessel wrecked upon the sand
  Of torrid swamps, with all her merchandise,
And left to rot betwixt the sea and land,
  My helpless spirit lies.

Ruing, I think for what then was I made;
  What end appointed for—what use designed?
Now let me right this heart that was bewrayed—
  Unveil these eyes gone blind.

My well-beloved friend, at noon to-day
  Over our cliffs a white mist lay unfurled,
So thick, one standing on their brink might say,
  Lo, here doth end the world.

A white abyss beneath, and nought beside;
  Yet, hark! a cropping sound not ten feet down;
Soon I could trace some browsing lambs that hied
  Through rock-paths cleft and brown.

And here and there green tufts of grass peered
    through,
Salt lavender, and sea thrift; then behold,
The mist, subsiding ever, bared to view
  A beast of giant mould.

She seemed a great sea monster lying content
  With all her cubs about her: but deep—deep—
The subtile mist went floating; its descent
  Showed the world's end was steep.

It shook, it melted, shaking more, till, lo,
  The sprawling monster was a rock; her brood
Were boulders, whereon seamews white as snow
  Sat watching for their food.

Then once again it sank, its day was done:
  Part rolled away, part vanished utterly,
And glimmering softly under the white sun,
  Behold! a great white sea.

O that the mist which veileth my To-come
  Would so dissolve and yield unto mine eyes
A worthy path! I'd count not wearisome
  Long toil nor enterprise.

But strain to reach it; ay, with wrestlings stout
  And hopes that even in the dark will grow
(Like plants in dungeons, reaching feelers out),
  And ploddings wary and slow.

Is there such path already made to fit
  The measure of my foot? It shall atone
For much, if I at length may light on it
  And know it for mine own.

But is there none? why, then 'tis more than
       well:
  And glad at heart myself will hew one out,
  Let me be only sure; for, sooth to tell,
       The sorest dole is doubt—

Doubt, a blank twilight of the heart, which mars
  All sweetest colors in its dimness same;
A soul-mist, through whose rifts familiar stars
       Beholding, we misname.

A ripple on the inner sea, which shakes
  Those images that on its breast reposed;
A fold upon the wind-swayed flag, that breaks
       The motto it disclosed.

O doubt! O doubt! I know my destiny;
  I feel thee fluttering bird-like in my breast;
I cannot loose, but I will sing to thee,
       And flatter thee to rest.

There is no certainty, "my bosom's guest,"
  No proving for the things whereof ye wot;
For, like the dead to sight unmanifest,
       They are, and they are not.

But surely as they are, for God is truth,
  And as they are not, for we saw them die,
So surely from the heaven drops light for youth,
       If you will walk thereby.

And can I see this light? It may be so;
  "But see it thus and thus," my fathers said.
The living do not rule this world; ah, no!
       It is the dead, the dead.

Shall I be slave to every noble soul,
  Study the dead, and to their spirits bend;
Or learn to read my own heart's folded scroll,
       And make self-rule my end?

Thought from *without*—O shall I take on trust
  And life from other modelled steal or win;
Or shall I heave to light, and clear of rust
       My true life from *within*.

O, let me be myself! But where, O where,
  Under this heap of precedent, this mound
Of customs, modes, and maxims, cumbrance
       rare,
  Shall the Myself be found?

O thou *Myself*, thy fathers thee debarred
  None of their wisdom, but their folly came
Therewith; they smoothed thy path, but made
       it hard
  For thee to quit the same.

With glosses they obscured God's natural truth,
  And with tradition tarnished His revealed;
With vain protections they endangered youth,
       With layings bare they sealed.

What aileth thee, myself? Alas! thy hands
  Are tired with old opinions—heir and son,
Thou hast inherited thy father's lands
       And all his debts thereon.

O that some power would give me Adam's eyes!
  O for the straight simplicity of Eve!
For I see nought, or grow, poor fool, too wise
       With seeing to believe.

Exemplars may be heaped until they hide
  The rules that they were made to render plain;
Love may be watched, her nature to decide,
       Until love's self doth wane.

Ah me! and when forgotten and foregone
  We leave the learning of departed days,
And cease the generations past to con,
       Their wisdom and their ways—

When fain to learn we lean into the dark,
  And grope to feel the floor of the abyss,
Or find the secret boundary lines which mark
       Where soul and matter kiss—

Fair world! these puzzled souls of ours grow
       weak
  With beating their bruised wings against the
       rim
That bounds their utmost flying, when they seek
       The distant and the dim.

We pant, we strain like birds against their wires;
  Are sick to reach the vast and the beyond;—
And what avails, if still to our desires
       Those far-off gulfs respond?

Contentment comes not therefore; still there
       lies
An outer distance when the first is hailed,
And still for ever yawns before our eyes
       An UTMOST—that is veiled.

Searching those edges of the universe,
  We leave the central fields a fallow part;
To find the eye more precious things amerce,
       And starve the darkened heart.

Then all goes wrong: the old foundations rock;
  One scorns at him of old who gazed unshod;
One striking with a pickaxe thinks the shock
       Shall move the seat of God.

A little way, a very little way
  (Life is so short), they dig into the rind,
And they are very sorry, so they say,—
       Sorry for what they find.

But truth is sacred—ay, and must be told:
  There is a story long beloved of man;
We must forego it, for it will not hold—
       Nature had no such plan.

And then, "if God hath said it," some should
    cry,
"We have the story from the fountain-head:"
Why, then, what better than the old reply,
    The first "Yea, HATH God said?"

The garden, O the garden, must it go,
    Source of our hope and our most dear regret?
The ancient story, must it no more show
    How men may win it yet?

And all upon the Titan child's decree,
    The baby science, born but yesterday,
That in its rash unlearned infancy
    With shells and stones at play,

And delving in the outworks of this world,
    And little crevices that it could reach,
Discovered certain bones laid up, and furled
    Under an ancient beach,

And other waifs that lay to its young mind
    Some fathoms lower than they ought to lie,
By gain whereof it could not fail to find
    Much proof of ancientry,

Hints at a pedigree withdrawn and vast,
    Terrible deeps, and old obscurities,
Or soulless origin, and twilight passed
    In the primeval seas,

Whereof it tells, as thinking it hath been
    Of truth not meant for man inheritor;
As if this knowledge Heaven had ne'er foreseen
    And not provided for!

Knowledge ordained to live! although the fate
    Of much that went before it was—to die,
And be called ignorance by such as wait
    Till the next drift comes by.

O marvellous credulity of man!
    If God indeed kept secret, couldst thou know
Or follow up the mighty Artisan
    Unless He willed it so?

And canst thou of the Maker think in sooth
    That of the Made He shall be found at fault,
And dream of wresting from Him hidden truth
    By force or by assault?

But if He keeps not secret—if thine eyes
    He openeth to His wondrous work of late—
Think how in soberness thy wisdom lies,
    And have the grace to wait.

Wait, nor against the half-learned lesson fret,
    Nor chide at old belief as if it erred,
Because thou canst not reconcile as yet
    The Worker and the word.

Either the Worker did in ancient days
    Give us the word, His tale of love and might;
(And if in truth He gave it us, who says
    He did not give it right?)

Or else He gave it not, and then indeed
    We know not if HE IS—by whom our years
Are portioned, who the orphan moons doth lead,
    And the unfathered spheres.

We sit unowned upon our burial sod,
    And know not whence we come or whose
        we be,
Comfortless mourners for the mount of God,
    The rocks of Calvary:

Bereft of heaven, and of the long-loved page
    Wrought us by some who thought with death
        to cope;
Despairing comforters, from age to age
    Sowing the seeds of hope:

Gracious deceivers who have lifted us
    Out of the slough where passed our unknown
        youth;
Beneficent liars, who have gifted us
    With sacred love of truth!

Farewell to them: yet pause ere thou unmoor
    And set thine ark adrift on unknown seas;
How wert thou bettered so, or more secure
    Thou, and thy destinies?

And if thou searchest, and art made to fear
    Facing of unread riddles dark and hard,
And mastering not their majesty austere,
    Their meaning locked and barred:

How would it make the weight and wonder less,
    If, lifted from immortal shoulders down,
The worlds were cast on seas of emptiness
    In realms without a crown,

And (if there were no God) were left to rue
    Dominion of the air and of the fire?
Then if there be a God, "Let God be true,
    And every man a liar."

But as for me, I do not speak as one
    That is exempt: I am with life at feud:
My heart reproacheth me, as there were none
    Of so small gratitude.

Wherewith shall I console thee, heart o' mine,
    And still thy yearning and resolve thy doubt?
That which I know, and that which I divine,
    Alas! have left thee out.

I have aspired to know the might of God,
    As if the story of His love was furled,
Nor sacred foot the grasses e'er had trod
    Of this redeemèd world:—

Have sunk my thoughts as lead into the deep,
    To grope for that abyss whence evil grew,
And spirits of ill, with eyes that cannot weep,
    Hungry and desolate flew;

As if their legions did not one day crowd
   The death-pangs of the Conquering Good to
      see!
As if a sacred head had never bowed
   In death for man—for me;

Nor ransomed back the souls beloved, the sons
   Of men, from thraldom with the nether kings
In that dark country where those evil ones
      Trail their unhallowed wings.

And didst Thou love the race that loved not
      Thee,
   And didst Thou take to heaven a human brow?
Dost plead with man's voice by the marvellous
      sea?
   Art Thou his kinsman now?

O God, O kinsman loved, but not enough!
   O man, with eyes majestic after death,
Whose feet have toiled along our pathways
      rough,
   Whose lips drawn human breath!

By that one likeness which is ours and Thine,
   By that one nature which doth hold us kin,
By that high heaven where, sinless, Thou dost
      shine
   To draw us sinners in,

By Thy last silence in the judgment-hall,
   By long foreknowledge of the deadly tree,
By darkness, by the wormwood and the gall,
   I pray Thee visit me.

Come, lest this heart should, cold and cast away,
   Die ere the guest adored she entertain—

Lest eyes which never saw Thine earthly day
   Should miss Thy heavenly reign.

Come weary-eyed from seeking in the night
   Thy wanderers strayed upon the pathless wold,
Who wounded, dying, cry to Thee for light,
   And cannot find their fold.

And deign, O Watcher, with the sleepless brow,
   Pathetic in its yearning—deign reply:
Is there, O is there aught that such as Thou
      Wouldst take from such as I?

Are there no briars across Thy pathway thrust?
   Are there no thorns that compass it about?
Nor any stones that Thou wilt deign to trust
      My hands to gather out?

O, if Thou wilt, and if such bliss might be,
   It were a cure for doubt, regret, delay—
Let my lost pathway go—what aileth me?—
      There is a better way.

What though unmarked the happy workman
      toil,
   And break unthanked of man the stubborn
      clod?
It is enough, for sacred is the soil,
   Dear are the hills of God.

Far better in its place the lowliest bird
   Should sing aright to Him the lowliest song,
Than that a seraph strayed should take the word
   And sing His glory wrong.

Friend, it is time to work. I say to thee,
   Thou dost all earthly good by much excel;
Thou and God's blessing are enough for me:
      My work, my work—farewell!

REQUIESCAT IN PACE!

MY heart, my heart is sick awishing and awaiting:
The lad took up his knapsack, he went, he went his way;
And I looked on for his coming, as a prisoner through the grating
Looks and longs and longs and wishes for its opening day.

On the wild purple mountains, all alone with no other,
The strong terrible mountains, he longed, he longed to be;
And he stooped to kiss his father, and he stooped to kiss his mother,
And till I said "Adieu, sweet Sir," he quite forgot me.

He wrote of their white raiment, the ghostly capes that screen them,
Of the storm winds that beat them, their thunder-rents and scars,
And the paradise of purple, and the golden slopes atween them,
And fields, where grow God's gentian bells, and His crocus stars.

He wrote of frail gauzy clouds, that drop on them like fleeces,
And make green their fir forests, and feed their mosses hoar;
Or come sailing up the valleys, and get wrecked and go to pieces,
Like sloops against their cruel strength: then he wrote no more.

O the silence that came next, the patience and long aching!
They never said so much as "He was a dear loved son;"
Not the father to the mother moaned, that dreary stillness breaking:
"Ah! wherefore did he leave us so—this, our only one?"

They sat within, as waiting, until the neighbors prayed them,
At Cromer, by the sea-coast, 'twere peace and change to be;
And to Cromer, in their patience, or that urgency affrayed them,
Or because the tidings tarried, they came, and took me.

It was three months and over since the dear lad had started:
On the green downs at Cromer I sat to see the view;
On an open space of herbage, where the ling and fern had parted,
Betwixt the tall white light house towers, the old and the new.

Below me lay the wide sea, the scarlet sun was stooping,
And he dyed the waste water, as with a scarlet dye;
And he dyed the lighthouse towers; every bird with white wing swooping
Took his colors, and the cliffs did, and the yawning sky.

Over grass came that strange flush, and over ling and heather,
Over flocks of sheep and lambs, and over Cromer town;
And each filmy cloudlet crossing drifted like a scarlet feather
Torn from the folded wings of clouds, while he settled down.

When I looked, I dared not sigh:—In the light of God's splendor,
With His daily blue and gold, who am I? what am I?
But that passion and outpouring seemed an awful sign and tender,
Like the blood of the Redeemer, shown on earth and sky.

O for comfort, O the waste of a long doubt and trouble!
On that sultry August eve trouble had made me meek;
I was tired of my sorrow—O so faint, for it was double
In the weight of its oppression, that I could not speak!

And a little comfort grew, while the dimmed eyes were feeding,
And the dull ears with murmur of waters satisfied;
But a dream came slowly nigh me, all my thoughts and fancy leading
Across the bounds of waking life to the other side.

And I dreamt that I looked out, to the waste waters turning,
And saw the flakes of scarlet from wave to wave tossed on;

And the scarlet mix with azure, where a heap
    of gold lay burning
  On the clear remote sea reaches; for the sun
    was gone.

Then I thought a far-off shout dropped across
    the still water—
  A question as I took it, for soon an answer
    came
From the tall white ruined lighthouse: "If it
    be the old man's daughter
  That we wot of," ran the answer, "what
    then—who's to blame?"

I looked up at the lighthouse all roofless and
    storm-broken:
  A great white bird sat on it, with neck
    stretched to sea;
Unto somewhat which was sailing in a skiff
    the bird had spoken,
  And a trembling seized my spirit, for they
    talked of me.

I was the old man's daughter, the bird went on
    to name him;
  "He loved to count the starlings as he sat
    in the sun;
Long ago he served with Nelson, and his story
    did not shame him:
  Ay, the old man was a good man—and his
    work was done."

The skiff was like a crescent, ghost of some
    moon departed,
  Frail, white, she rocked and curtseyed as the
    red wave she crossed,
And the thing within sat paddling, and the
    crescent dipped and darted,
  Flying on, again was shouting, but the words
    were lost.

I said, "That thing is hooded; I could hear
    but that floweth
  The great hood below its mouth:" then the
    bird made reply,
"If they know not, more's the pity, for the
    little shrewmouse knoweth,
  And the kite knows, and the eagle, and the
    glead and pye."

And he stooped to whet his beak on the stones
    of the coping;
  And when once more the shout came, in
    querulous tones he spake,
"What I said was 'more's the pity;' if the
    heart be long past hoping,
  Let it say of death, 'I know it,' or doubt
    on and break.

"Men must die—one dies by day, and near
    him moans his mother,
  They dig his grave, tread it down, and go
    from it full loth:

And one dies about the midnight, and the
    wind moans, and no other,
  And the snows give him a burial—and God
    loves them both.

"The first hath no advantage—it shall not
    soothe his slumber
  That a lock of his brown hair his father aye
    shall keep;
For the last, he nothing grudgeth, it shall
    nought his quiet cumber,
  That in a golden mesh of HIS callow eaglets
    sleep.

"Men must die when all is said, e'en the kite
    and glead know it,
  And the lad's father knew it, and the lad,
    the lad too;
It was never kept a secret, waters bring it and
    winds blow it,
  And he met it on the mountain—why then
    make ado?"

With that he spread his white wings, and
    swept across the water,
  Lit upon the hooded head, and it and all
    went down;
And they laughed as they went under, and I
    woke, "the old man's daughter,"
  And looked across the slope of grass, and at
    Cromer town.

And I said, "Is that the sky, all grey and
    silver suited?"
  And I thought, "Is that the sea that lies
    so white and wan?
I have dreamed as I remember: give me
    time—I was reputed
  Once to have a steady courage—O, I fear
    'tis gone!"

And I said, "Is this my heart? if it be, low
    'tis beating,
  So he lies on the mountain, hard by the
    eagles' brood;
I have had a dream this evening, while the
    white and gold were fleeting,
  But I need not, need not tell it—where
    would be the good?

"Where would be the good to them, his father
    and his mother?
  For the ghost of their dead hope appeareth
    to them still.
While a lonely watch-fire smoulders, who its
    dying red would smother,
  That gives what little light there is to a
    darksome hill?"

I rose up, I made no moan, I did not cry nor
    falter,
  But slowly in the twilight I came to Cromer
    town.

What can wringing of the hands do that which is ordained to alter?
He had climbed, had climbed the mountain, he would ne'er come down.

But, O my first, O my best, I could not choose but love thee!
O, to be a wild white bird, and seek thy rocky bed!
From my breast I'd give thee burial, pluck the down and spread above thee;
I would sit and sing thy requiem on the mountain head.

Fare thee well, my love of loves! would I had died before thee!
O, to be at least a cloud, that near thee I might flow,
Solemnly approach the mountain, weep away my being o'er thee,
And veil thy breast with icicles, and thy brow with snow!

SUPPER AT THE MILL.

MOTHER.

WELL, Frances.

FRANCES.
Well, good mother, how are you?
M. I'm hearty, lass, but warm; the weather's warm: I think 'tis mostly warm on market days.
I met with George behind the mill : said he, "Mother, go in and rest awhile."
F. Ay, do,
And stay to supper ; put your basket down.
M. Why, now, it is not heavy?
F. Willie, man,
Get up and kiss your Granny. Heavy, no!
Some call good churning luck; but luck or skill,
Your butter mostly comes as firm and sweet
As if 'twas Christmas. So you sold it all?
M. All but this pat that I put by for George;
He always loved my butter.
F. That he did
M. And has your speckled hen brought off her brood?
F. Not yet ; but that old duck I told you of,
She hatched eleven out of twelve to-day.
Child. And, Granny, they're so yellow.
M. Ay, my lad,
Yellow as gold—yellow as Willie's hair.
C. They're all mine, Granny—father says they're mine.
M. To think of that !
F. Yes, Granny, only think !
Why, father means to sell them when they're fat,
And put the money in the savings bank,
And all against our Willie goes to school :
But Willie would not touch them—no, not he;
He knows that father would be angry else.
C. But I want one to play with—O, I want
A little yellow duck to take to bed !
M. What ! would ye rob the poor old mother, then ? [*awhile* ;
F. Now, Granny, if you'll hold the babe
'Tis time I took up Willie to his crib.
[*Exit* FRANCES.

[*Mother sings to the infant.*]

Playing on the virginals,
  Who but I? Sae glad, sae free,
Smelling for all cordials,
  The green mint and marjorie ;
Set among the budding broom,
  Kingcup and daffodilly,

By my side I made him room :
  O love my Willie !

"Like me, love me, girl o' gowd,"
  Sang he to my nimble strain ;
Sweet his ruddy lips o'erflowed
  Till my heartstrings rang again :
By the broom, the bonny broom,
  Kingcup and daffodilly,
In my heart I made him room :
  O love my Willie !

"Pipe and play, dear heart," sang he,
  "I must go, yet pipe and play ;
Soon I'll come and ask of thee
  For an answer yea or nay ;"
And I waited till the flocks
  Panted in yon waters stilly,
And the corn stood in the shocks :
  O love my Willie !

I thought first when thou didst come
  I would wear the ring for thee,
But the year told out its sum
  Ere again thou sat'st by me ;
Thou hadst nought to ask that day
  By kingcup and daffodilly ;
I said neither yea nor nay :
  O love my Willie !

Enter GEORGE.

G. Well, mother, 'tis a fortnight now, or more,
Since I set eyes on you.
M. Ay, George, my dear,
I reckon you've been busy : so have we.
G. And how does father ?
M. He gets through his work,
But he grows stiff, a little stiff, my dear ;
He's not so young, you know, by twenty years,
As I am—not so young by twenty years,
And I'm past sixty.
G. Yet he's hale and stout,
And seems to take a pleasure in his pipe ;
And seems to take a pleasure in his cows,
And a pride, too.
M. And well he may, my dear.
G. Give me the little one, he tires your arm;
He's such a kicking, crowing, wakeful rogue,
He almost wears our lives out with his noise
Just at day-dawning, when we wish to sleep.
What ! you young villain, would you clench your fist
In father's curls ? a dusty father, sure,
And you're as clean as wax.
Ay, you may laugh

But if you live a seven years more or so,
These hands of yours will all be brown and scratched
With climbing after nest-eggs. They'll go down
As many rat-holes as are round the mere ;
And you'll love mud, all manner of mud and dirt
As your father did afore you, and you'll wade
After young water-birds ; and you'll get bogged
Setting of eel-traps, and you'll soil your clothes,
And come home torn and dripping ; then, you know,
You'll feel the stick—you'll feel the stick, my lad !

Enter FRANCES.

F. You should not talk so to the blessed babe—
How can you, George? why, he may be in heaven
Before the time you tell of.
    M.   Look at him :
So earnest, such an eager pair of eyes !
He thrives my dear.
    F.   Yes, that he does, thank God
My children are all strong.
    M.   'Tis much to say :
Sick children fret their mothers' hearts to shreds,
And do no credit to their keep nor care ;
Where is your little lass?
    F.   Your daughter came
And begged her of us for a week or so.
    M. Well, well, she might be wiser, that she might,
For she can sit at ease and pay her way ;
A sober husband, too—a cheerful man—
Honest as ever stepped, and fond of her ;
Yet she is never easy, never glad,
Because she has not children. Well-a-day !
If she could know how hard her mother worked,
And what ado I had, and what a moil
With my half-dozen ! Children, ay, forsooth,
They bring their own love with them when they come,
But if they come not there is peace and rest ;
The pretty lambs ! and yet she cries for more :
Why, the world's full of them, and so is heaven—
They are not rare.
    G.   No, mother, not at all ;
But Hannah must not keep our Fanny long—
She spoils her.
    M.   Ah ! folks spoil their children now ;
When I was a young woman 'twas not so ;
We made our children fear us, made them work,
Kept them in order.
    G.   Were not proud of them—
Eh, mother ?
    M.   I set store by mine, 'tis true,
But then I had good cause.
    G.   My lad, d'ye hear?
Your Granny was not proud, by no means proud !
She never spoilt your father—no, not she,
Nor never made him sing at harvest-home,
Nor at the forge, nor at the baker's shop,
Nor to the doctor while she lay abed
Sick, and he crept up stairs to share her broth,

M. Well, well, you were my youngest, and, what's more,
Your father loved to hear you sing—he did,
Although, good man, he could not tell one tune
From the other.
    F.   No, he got his voice from you :
Do use it, George, and send the child to sleep.
    G. What must I sing?
    F.   The ballad of the man
That is so shy he cannot speak his mind.
    G. Ay, of the purple grapes and crimson leaves ;
But, mother, put your shawl and bonnet off.
And, Frances, lass, I brought some cresses in :
Just wash them, toast the bacon, break some eggs,
And let's to supper shortly.

[*Sings.*]

My neighbor White—we met to-day—
He always had a cheerful way,
    As if he breathed at ease ;
My neighbor White lives down the glade,
And I live higher, in the shade
    Of my old walnut-trees.

So many lads and lasses small,
To feed them all, to clothe them all,
    Must surely tax his wit ;
I see his thatch when I look out,
His branching roses creep about,
    And vines half smother it.

There white-haired urchins climb his eaves,
And little watch-fires heap with leaves,
    And milky filberts hoard ;
And there his oldest daughter stands
With downcast eyes and skilful hands
    Before her ironing-board.

She comforts all her mother's days,
And with her sweet obedient ways
    She makes her labor light ;
So sweet to hear, so fair to see !
O, she is much too good for me,
    That lovely Lettice White !

'Tis hard to feel oneself a fool !
With that same lass I went to school—
    I then was great and wise ;
She read upon an easier book,
And I—I never cared to look
    Into her shy blue eyes.

And now I know they must be there,
Sweet eyes, behind those lashes fair
    That will not raise their rim :
If maids be shy, he cures who can ;
But if a man be shy—a man—
    Why then the worse for him !

My mother cries, "For such a lad
A wife is easy to be had
    And always to be found ;
A finer scholar scarce can be,
And for a foot and leg," says she,
    "He beats the country round !

"My handsome boy must stoop his head
  To clear her door whom he would wed."
    Weak praise, but fondly sung!
"O mother! scholars sometimes fail—
  And what can foot and leg avail
    To him that wants a tongue?"

When by her ironing-board I sit,
Her little sisters round me flit,
  And bring me forth their store;
Dark cluster grapes of dusty blue,
And small sweet apples, bright of hue
  And crimson to the core.

But she abideth silent, fair;
All shaded by her flaxen hair
  The blushes come and go;
I look, and I no more can speak
Than the red sun that on her cheek
  Smiles as he lieth low.

Sometimes the roses by the latch,
Or scarlet vine-leaves from her thatch,
  Come sailing down like birds;
When from their drifts her board I clear,
She thanks me, but I scarce can hear
  The shyly uttered words.

Oft have I wooed sweet Lettice White
By daylight and by candlelight
  When we two were apart.
Some better day come on apace,
And let me tell her face to face,
  "Maiden, thou hast my heart."

How gently rock yon poplars high
Against the reach of primrose sky
  With heaven's pale candles stored!
She sees them all, sweet Lettice White;
I'll e'en go sit again to-night
  Beside her ironing-board!

Why, you young rascal! who would think it now?
No sooner do I stop than you look up.
What would you have your poor old father do?
'Twas a brave song, long-winded, and not loud.
  M. He heard the bacon sputter on the fork.
And heard his mother's step across the floor.
Where did you get that song?—'tis new to me.
  G. I bought it of a pedler.
  M.   Did you so?
Well, you were always for the love songs, George.
  F. My dear, just lay his head upon your arm,
And if you'll pace and sing two minutes more
He needs must sleep—his eyes are full of sleep.

G. Do you sing, mother.
F.   Ay, good mother, do;
'Tis long since we have heard you.
  M.   Like enough;
I'm an old woman, and the girls and lads
I used to sing to sleep o'ertop me now.
What should I sing for?
  G.   Why, to pleasure us.
Sing in the chimney corner, where you sit,
And I'll pace gently with the little one.

[*Mother sings.*]

When sparrows build, and the leaves break forth,
  My old sorrow wakes and cries,
For I know there is dawn in the far, far north,
  And a scarlet sun doth rise;
Like a scarlet fleece the snow-field spreads,
  And the icy founts run free,
And the bergs begin to bow their heads,
  And plunge, and sail in the sea.

O my lost love, and my own, own love,
  And my love that loved me so!
Is there never a chink in the world above
  Where they listen for words from below?
Nay, I spoke once, and I grieved thee sore,
  I remember all that I said,
And now thou wilt hear me no more—no more
  Till the sea gives up her dead.

Thou didst set thy foot on the ship and sail
  To the ice-fields and the snow;
Thou wert sad, for thy love did nought avail,
  And the end I could not know;
How could I tell I should love thee to-day,
  Whom that day I held not dear?
How could I know I should love thee away
  When I did not love thee anear?

We shall walk no more through the sodden plain
  With the faded bents o'erspread,
We shall stand no more by the seething main
  While the dark wrack drives o'erhead;
We shall part no more in the wind and the rain,
  Where thy last farewell was said:
But perhaps I shall meet thee and know thee again
  When the sea gives up her dead.

F. Asleep at last, and time he was, indeed.
Turn back the cradle-quilt, and lay him in;
And, mother, will you please to draw your chair?—
The supper's ready.

SCHOLAR AND CARPENTER.

WHILE ripening corn grew thick
    and deep,
And here and there men stood
    to reap,
One morn I put my heart to
    sleep,
    And to the lanes I took my
        way.
The goldfinch on a thistle-head
Stood scattering seedlets while she fed ;
The wrens their pretty gossip spread,
    Or joined a random roundelay.

On hanging cobwebs shone the dew,
And thick the way-side clovers grew ;
The feeding bee had much to do,
    So fast did honey-drops exude :
She sucked and murmured, and was gone,
And lit on other blooms anon,
The while I learned a lesson on
    The source and sense of quietude.

For sheep-bells chiming from a wold,
Or bleat of lamb within its fold,
Or cooing of love-legends old
    To dove-wives make not quiet less ;
Ecstatic chirp of wingèd thing
Or bubbling of the water-spring,
Are sounds that more than silence bring
    Itself and its delightsomeness.

While thus I went to gladness fain,
I had but walked a mile or twain
Before my heart woke up again,
    As dreaming she had slept too late ;
The morning freshness that she viewed
With her own meanings she endued,
And touched with her solicitude
    The natures she did meditate.

"If quiet is, for it I wait ;
To it, ah! let me wed my fate,
And, like a sad wife, supplicate
    My roving lord no more to flee ;
If leisure is—but, ah ! 'tis not—
'Tis long past praying for, God wot ;
The fashion of it men forgot,
    About the age of chivalry.

"Sweet is the leisure of the bird ;
She craves no time for work deferred ;
Her wings are not to aching stirred
    Providing for her helpless ones.

Fair is the leisure of the wheat ;
All night the damps about it fleet ;
All day it basketh in the heat,
    And grows, and whispers orisons.

" Grand is the leisure of the earth ;
She gives her happy myriads birth,
And after harvest fears not dearth,
    But goes to sleep in snow-wreaths dim.
Dread is the leisure up above
The while He sits whose name is Love,
And waits, as Noah did, for the dove,
    To wit if she would fly to him.

" He waits for us, while, houseless things,
We beat about with bruisèd wings
On the dark floods and water-springs,
    The ruined world, the desolate sea ;
With open windows from the prime
All night, all day, He waits sublime,
Until the fulness of the time
    Decreed from His eternity.

"Where is OUR leisure?—Give us rest.
Where is the quiet we possessed?
We must have had it once—were blest
    With peace whose phantoms yet entice.
Sorely the mother of mankind
Longed for the garden left behind ;
For we still prove some yearnings blind
    Inherited from Paradise."

" Hold, heart !" I cried ; " for trouble sleeps ;
I hear no sound of aught that weeps ;
I will not look into thy deeps—
    I am afraid, I am afraid !"
"Afraid !" she saith ; "and yet 'tis true
That what man dreads he still should view—
Should do the thing he fears to do,
    And storm the ghosts in ambuscade."

"What good ?" I sigh. " Was reason meant
To straighten branches that are bent,
Or soothe an ancient discontent,
    The instinct of a race dethroned ?
Ah ! doubly should that instinct go
Must the four rivers cease to flow,
Nor yield those rumors sweet and low
    Wherewith man's life is undertoned."

"Yet had I but the past," she cries,
" And it was lost, I would arise
And comfort me some otherwise.
    But more than loss about me clings :
I am but restless with my race ;
The whispers from a heavenly place,
Once dropped among us, seem to chase
    Rest with their prophet-visitings.

"The race is like a child, as yet
Too young for all things to be set
Plainly before him with no let
   Or hindrance meet for his degree ;
But ne'ertheless by much too old
Not to perceive that men withhold
More of the story than is told,
   And so infer a mystery.

"If the Celestials daily fly
With messages on missions high,
And float, our masts and turrets nigh,
   Conversing on Heaven's great intents ;
What wonder hints of coming things,
Whereto man's hope and yearning clings,
Should drop like feathers from their wings,
   And give us vague presentiments ?

"And as the waxing moon can take
The tidal waters in her wake
And lead them round and round to break
   Obedient to her drawings dim ;
So may the movements of His mind,
The first Great Father of mankind,
Affect with answering movements blind,
   And draw the souls that breathe by Him.

"We had a message long ago,
That like a river peace should flow,
And Eden bloom again below.
   We heard, and we began to wait :
Full soon that message men forgot ;
Yet waiting is their destined lot,
And waiting for they know not what
   They strive with yearnings passionate.

"Regret and faith alike enchain ;
There was a loss, there comes a gain ;
We stand at fault betwixt the twain,
   And that is veiled for which we pant.
Our lives are short, our ten times seven ;
We think the councils held in Heaven
Sit long, ere yet that blissful leaven
   Work peace amongst the militant.

"Then we blame God that sin should be :
   Adam began it at the tree,
'The woman whom THOU gavest me ;'
   And we adopt his dark device.
O long Thou tarriest ! come and reign,
And bring forgiveness in Thy train,
And give us in our hands again
   The apples of Thy Paradise."

"Far-seeing heart ! if that be all,
The happy things that did not fall,"
I sighed, "from every coppice call
   They never from that garden went.
Behold their joy, so comfort thee,
Behold the blossom and the bee,
For they are yet as good and free
   As when poor Eve was innocent.

"But reason thus : 'If we sank low,
If the lost garden we forego,
Each in his day, nor ever know

But in our poet souls his face ;
Yet we may rise until we reach
A height untold of in its speech—
   A lesson that it could not teach
   Learn in this darker dwelling-place.'

"And reason on : 'We take the spoil ;
Loss made us poets, and the soil
Taught us great patience in our toil,
   And life is kin to God through death.
Christ were not One with us but so,
And if bereft of Him we go ;
Dearer the heavenly mansions grow,
   His home, to man that wandereth.'

"Content thee so, and ease thy smart."
With that she slept again, my heart,
And I admired and took my part
   With crowds of happy things the while :
With open velvet butterflies
That swung and spread their peacock eyes,
As if they cared no more to rise
   From off their beds of camomile.

The blackcaps in an orchard met,
Praising the berries while they ate :
The finch that flew her beak to whet
   Before she joined them on the tree ;
The water-mouse among the reeds—
His bright eyes glancing black as beads,
So happy with a bunch of seeds—
   I felt their gladness heartily.

But I came on, I smelt the hay,
And up the hills I took my way,
And down them still made holiday,
   And walked, and wearied not a whit ;
But ever with the lane I went
Until it dropped with steep descent,
Cut deep into the rock, a tent
   Of maple branches roofing it.

Adown the rocks small runlets wept,
And reckless ivies leaned and crept,
And little spots of sunshine slept
   On its brown steeps and made them fair ;
And broader beams athwart it shot,
Where martins cheeped in many a knot,
For they had ta'en a sandy plot
   And scooped another Petra there.

And deeper down, hemmed in and hid
From upper light and life amid
The swallows gossiping, I thrid
   Its mazes, till the dipping land
Sank to the level of my lane :
That was the last hill of the chain,
And fair below I saw the plain
   That seemed cold cheer to reprimand.

Half drowned in sleepy peace it lay,
As satiate with the boundless play
Of sunshine on its green array.
   And clear-cut hills of gloomy blue
To keep it safe rose up behind,
As with a charmèd ring to bind

The glassy sea, where clouds might find
  A place to bring their shadows to.

I said, and blest that pastoral grace,
"How sweet thou art, thou sunny place!
Thy God approves thy smiling face;"
  But straight my heart put in a word;
  She said, "Albeit thy face I bless,
There have been times, sweet wilderness,
When I have wished to love thee less,
  Such pangs thy smile administered."

But, lo! I reached a field of wheat,
And by its gate full clear and sweet
A workman sang, while at his feet
  Played a young child, all life and stir—
A three years' child, with rosy lip,
Who in the song had partnership,
Made happy with each falling chip
  Dropped by the busy carpenter.

This, reared a new gate for the old,
And loud the tuneful measure rolled,
But stopped as I came up to hold
  Some kindly talk of passing things.
Brave were his eyes, and frank his mien;
Of all men's faces, calm or keen,
A better I have never seen
  In all my lonely wanderings.

And how it was I scarce can tell,
We seemed to please each other well;
I lingered till a noonday bell
  Had sounded, and his task was done.
An oak had screened us from the heat;
And 'neath it in the standing wheat,
A cradle and a fair retreat,
  Full sweetly slept the little one.

The workman rested from his stroke,
And manly were the words he spoke,
Until the smiling babe awoke
  And prayed to him for milk and food.
Then to a runlet forth he went,
And brought a wallet from the bent,
And bade me to the meal, intent
  I should not quit his neighborhood.

"For here," said he, "are bread and beer,
And meat enough to make good cheer;
Sir, eat with me, and have no fear,
  For none upon my work depend,
Saving this child; and I may say
That I am rich, for every day
I put by somewhat; therefore stay,
  And to such eating condescend."

We ate. The child—child fair to see—
Began to cling about his knee,
And he down leaning fatherly
  Received some softly-prattled prayer;
He smiled as if to list were balm,
And with his labor-hardened palm
Pushed from the baby-forehead calm
  Those shining locks that clustered there.

The rosy mouth made fresh essay—
"O would he sing or would he play?"
I looked, my thought would make its way—
  "Fair is your child of face and limb,
The round blue eyes full sweetly shine."
He answered me with glance benign—
"Ay, Sir; but he is none of mine,
  Although I set great store by him."

With that, as if his heart was fain
To open—nathless not complain—
He let my quiet questions gain
  His story: "Not of kin to me,"
Repeating; "but asleep, awake,
For worse, for better, him I take,
To cherish for my dead wife's sake,
  And count him as her legacy.

"I married with the sweetest lass
That ever stepped on meadow grass;
That ever at her looking-glass
  Some pleasure took, some natural care;
That ever swept a cottage floor
And worked all day, nor e'er gave o'er
Till eve, then watched beside the door
  Till her good man should meet her there.

"But I lost all in its fresh prime;
My wife fell ill before her time—
Just as the bells began to chime
  One Sunday morn. By next day's light
Her little babe was born and dead,
And she, unconscious what she said,
With feeble hands about her spread,
  Sought it with yearnings infinite.

"With mother-longing still beguiled,
And lost in fever-fancies wild,
She piteously bemoaned her child
  That we had stolen, she said, away.
And ten sad days she sighed to me,
'I cannot rest until I see
My pretty one! I think that he
  Smiled in my face but yesterday.'

"Then she would change, and faintly try
To sing some tender lullaby;
And 'Ah!' would moan, 'if I should die,
  Who, sweetest babe, would cherish thee?'
Then weep, 'My pretty boy is grown;
With tender feet on the cold stone
He stands, for he can stand alone,
  And no one leads him motherly.'

"Then she with dying movements slow
Would seem to knit, or seem to sew:
'His feet are bare, he must not go
  Unshod:' and as her death drew on,
'O little baby,' she would sigh;
'My little child, I cannot die
Till I have you to slumber nigh—
  You, you to set mine eyes upon.'

"When she spake thus, and moaning lay,
They said, 'She cannot pass away,
So sore she longs:' and as the day

Broke on the hills, I left her side.
Mourning along this lane I went;
Some travelling folk had pitched their tent
Up yonder: there a woman, bent
    With age, sat meanly canopied.

"A twelvemonths' child was at her side:
'Whose infant may that be?' I cried.
'His that will own him,' she replied;
    'His mother's dead, no worse could be.'
'Since you can give—or else I erred—
See, you are taken at your word,'
Quoth I; 'That child is mine; I heard,
    And own him! Rise, and give him me.'

"She rose amazed, but cursed me too;
She could not hold such luck for true,
But gave him soon, with small ado.
    I laid him by my Lucy's side:
Close to her face that baby crept,
And stroked it, and the sweet soul wept;
Then, while upon her arm he slept,
    She passed, for she was satisfied.

"I loved her well, I wept her sore,
And when her funeral left my door
I thought that I should never more
    Feel any pleasure near me glow;
But I have learned, though this I had,
'Tis sometimes natural to be glad,
And no man can be always sad
    Unless he wills to have it so.

"Oh, I had heavy nights at first,
And daily wakening was the worst:
For then my grief arose, and burst
    Like something fresh upon my head;
Yet when less keen it seemed to grow,
I was not pleased—I wished to go
Mourning adown this vale of woe,
    For all my life uncomforted.

"I grudged myself the lightsome air,
That makes man cheerful unaware;
When comfort came, I did not care
    To take it in, to feel it stir:
And yet God took with me His plan,
And now for my appointed span
I think I am a happier man
    For having wed and wept for her.

"Because no natural tie remains,
On this small thing I spend my gains;
God makes me love him for my pains,
    And binds me so to wholesome care:
I would not lose from my past life
That happy year, that happy wife!
Yet now I wage no useless strife
    With feelings blithe and debonair.

"I have the courage to be gay,
Although she lieth lapped away
Under the daisies, for I say,
    'Thou wouldst be glad if thou couldst see:'
My constant thought makes manifest
I have not what I love the best,
But I must thank God for the rest
    While I hold heaven a verity."

He rose, upon his shoulder set
The child, and while with vague regret
We parted, pleased that we had met,
    My heart did with herself confer;
With wholesome shame she did repent
Her reasonings idly eloquent,
And said, "I might be more content:
    But God go with the carpenter."

THE STAR'S MONUMENT.

IN THE CONCLUDING PART OF A DISCOURSE ON FAME.

[*He thinks.*]

IF there be memory in the world to come,
  If thought recur to SOME THINGS silenced here,
Then shall the deep heart be no longer dumb,
  But find expression in that happier sphere;
  It shall not be denied their utmost sum
Of love, to speak without fault or fear,
But utter to the harp with changes sweet
Words that, forbidden still, then heaven were incomplete.

[*He speaks.*]

Now let us talk about the ancient days,
  And things which happened long before our birth:
It is a pity to lament that praise
  Should be no shadow in the train of worth.
What is it, Madam, that your heart dismays?
  Why murmur at the course of this vast earth?
Think rather of the work than of the praise;
Come, we will talk about the ancient days.

There was a Poet, Madam, once (said he);
  I will relate his story to you now,
While through the branches of this apple-tree
  Some spots of sunshine flicker on your brow;
While every flower hath on its breast a bee,
  And every bird in stirring doth endow
The grass with falling blooms that smoothly glide,
As ships drop down a river with the tide.

For telling of his tale no fitter place
  Than this old orchard, sloping to the west;
Through its pink dome of blossom I can trace
  Some overlying azure; for the rest,
These flowery branches round us interlace;
  The ground is hollowed like a mossy nest:
Who talks of fame while the religious spring
Offers the incense of her blossoming?

There was a Poet, Madam, once (said he),
  Who, while he walked at sundown in a lane,
Took to his heart the hope that destiny
  Had singled him this guerdon to obtain,
That by the power of his sweet minstrelsy
  Some hearts for truth and goodness he should gain,
And charm some grovellers to uplift their eyes
And suddenly wax conscious of the skies.

"Master, good e'en to ye!" a woodman said,
  Who the low hedge was trimming with his shears.
"This hour is fine"—the Poet bowed his head.
  "More fine," he thought, "O friend! to me appears
The sunset than to you; finer the spread
  Of orange lustre through these azure spheres,
Where little clouds lie still, like flocks of sheep,
Or vessels sailing in God's other deep.

"O finer far! What work so high as mine,
  Interpreter betwixt the world and man,
Nature's ungathered pearls to set and shrine,
  The mystery she wraps her in to scan;
Her unsyllabic voices to combine,
  And serve her with such love as poets can;
With mortal words, her chant of praise to bind,
Then die, and leave the poem to mankind?

"O fair, O fine, O lot to be desired!
  Early and late my heart appeals to me,
And says, 'O work, O will—Thou man be fired
  To earn this lot,'—she says, 'I would not be
A worker for mine OWN bread, or one hired
  For mine OWN profit. O, I would be free
To work for others; love so earned of them
Should be my wages and my diadem.

"'Then when I died I should not fall,' says she,
  'Like dropping flowers that no man noticeth,
But like a great branch of some stately tree
  Rent in a tempest, and flung down to death,
Thick with green leafage—so that piteously
  Each passer by that ruin shuddereth,
And saith, The gap this branch hath left is wide;
The loss thereof can never be supplied.'"

But, Madam, while the Poet pondered so,
  Toward the leafy hedge he turned his eye,
And saw two slender branches that did grow,
  And from it rising spring and flourish high;
Their tops were twined together fast, and, lo,
  Their shadow crossed the path as he went by—

The shadow of a wild rose and a briar,
And it was shaped in semblance like a lyre.

In sooth, a lyre! and as the soft air played,
  Those branches stirred, but did not disunite.
"O emblem meet for me!" the Poet said;
  "Ay, I accept and own thee for my right;
The shadowy lyre across my feet is laid,
  Distinct though frail, and clear with crimson
    light:
Fast is it twined to bear the windy strain,
And, supple, it will bend and rise again.

"This lyre is cast across the dusty way,
  The common path that common men pursue;
I crave like blessing for my shadowy lay,
  Life's trodden paths with beauty to renew,
And cheer the eve of many a toil-stained day.
  Light it, old sun, wet it, thou common dew,
That 'neath men's feet its image still may be
While yet it waves above them, living lyre,
  like thee!"

But, even as the Poet spoke, behold
  He lifted up his face toward the sky;
The ruddy sun dipt under the grey wold,
  His shadowy lyre was gone; and, passing by,
The woodman lifting up his shears, was bold
  Their temper on those branches twain to try,
And all their loveliness and leafage sweet
Fell in the pathway, at the Poet's feet.

"Ah! my fair emblem that I chose," quoth he,
  "That for myself I coveted but now,
Too soon, methinks, thou hast been false to me;
  The lyre from pathway fades, the light from
    brow."
Then straightway turned he from it hastily,
  As dream that waking sense will disallow;
And while the highway heavenward paled
    apace,
He went on westward to his dwelling-place.

He went on steadily, while far and fast
  The summer darkness dropped upon the
    world,
A gentle air among the cloudlets passed
  And fanned away their crimson; then it
    curled
The yellow poppies in the field, and cast
  A dimness on the grasses, for it furled
Their daisies, and swept out the purple stain
That eve had left upon the pastoral plain.

He reached his city. Lo! the darkened street
  Where he abode was full of gazing crowds;
He heard the muffled tread of many feet;
  A multitude stood gazing at the clouds.
"What mark ye there," said he, "and where-
    fore meet?"
  Only a passing mist the heaven o'ershrowds;
It breaks, it parts, it drifts like scattered spars—
What lies beyond it but the nightly stars?"

Then did the gazing crowd to him aver
  They sought a lamp in heaven whose light
    was hid;
For that in sooth an old Astronomer
  Down from his roof had rushed into their
    mid,
Frighted, and fain with others to confer,
  That he had cried, "O sirs!"—and upward
    bid
Them gaze—"O sirs, a light is quenched afar;
Look up, my masters, we have lost a star!"

The people pointed, and the Poet's eyes
  Flew upward, where a gleaming sisterhood
Swam in the dewy heaven. The very skies
  Were mutable; for all amazed he stood
To see that truly not in any wise
  He could behold them as of old, nor could
His eyes receive the whole whereof he wot,
But when he told them over, one WAS NOT.

While yet he gazed and pondered reverently,
  The fickle folk began to move away.
"It is but one star less for us to see;
  And what does one star signify?" quoth
    they;
"The heavens are full of them." "But,
    ah!" said he,
  "That star was bright while yet she lasted."
    "Ay!"
They answered: "praise her, Poet, an' ye
    will;
Some are now shining that are brighter still."

"Poor star! to be disparagèd so soon
  On her withdrawal," thus the Poet sighed;
"That men should miss, and straight deny her
    noon
  Its brightness!" But the people in their
    pride
Said, "How are we beholden? 'twas no boon
  She gave. Her nature 'twas to shine so wide:
She could not choose but shine, nor could we
    know
Such star had ever dwelt in heaven but so."

The Poet answered sadly, "That is true!"
  And then he thought upon unthankfulness;
While some went homeward; and the residue,
  Reflecting that the stars are numberless,
Mourned that man's daylight hours should be
    so few,
  So short the shining that his path may bless;
To nearer themes then tuned their willing lips,
And thought no more upon the star's eclipse.

But he, the Poet, could not rest content
  Till he had found that old Astronomer;
Therefore at midnight to his house he went,
  And prayed him to be his tale's interpreter.
And yet upon the heaven his eyes he bent,
  Hearing the marvel; yet he sought for her
That was awanting, in the hope her face
Once more might fill its reft abiding-place.

Then said the old Astronomer: "My son,
  I sat alone upon my roof to-night;
I saw the stars come forth, and scarcely shun
  To fringe the edges of the western light;
I marked those ancient clusters one by one,
  The same that blessed our old forefather's sight:
For God alone is older—none but He
Can charge the stars with mutability:

"The elders of the night, the steadfast stars,
  The old, old stars which God has let us see,
That they might be our soul's auxiliars,
  And help us to the truth how young we be—
God's youngest, latest born, as if, some spars
  And a little clay being over of them—He
Had made our world and us thereof, yet given,
To humble us, the sight of His great heaven.

"But ah! my son, to-night mine eyes have seen
  The death of light, the end of old renown;
A shrinking back of glory that had been,
  A dread eclipse before the Eternal's frown.
How soon a little grass will grow between
  These eyes and those appointed to look down
Upon a world that was not made on high
Till the last scenes of their long empiry!

"To-night that shining cluster now despoiled
  Lay in day's wake a perfect sisterhood;
Sweet was its light to me that long had toiled,
  It gleamed and trembled o'er the distant wood;
Blown in a pile the clouds from it recoiled,
  Cool twilight up the sky her way made good;
I saw, but not believed—it was so strange—
That one of those same stars had suffered change.

"The darkness gathered, and methought she spread,
  Wrapped in a reddish haze that waxed and waned;
But notwithstanding to myself I said—
  'The stars are changeless; sure some mote hath stained
Mine eyes, and her fair glory minishèd.'
  Of age and failing vision I complained,
And thought 'some vapor in the heavens doth swim,
That makes her look so large and yet so dim.'

"But I gazed round, and all her lustrous peers
  In her red presence showed but wan and white;
For like a living coal beheld through tears
  She glowed and quivered with a gloomy light;
Methought she trembled, as all sick through fears,
  Helpless, appalled, appealing to the night;
Like one who throws his arms up to the sky
And bows down suffering, hopeless of reply.

"At length, as if an everlasting Hand
  Had taken hold upon her in her place,
And swiftly, like a golden grain of sand,
  Through all the deep infinitudes of space
Was drawing her—God's truth as here I stand—
  Backward and inward to itself; her face
Fast lessened, lessened, till it looked no more
Than smallest atom on a boundless shore.

"And she that was so fair, I saw her lie,
  The smallest thing in God's great firmament,
Till night was at the darkest, and on high
  Her sisters glittered, though her light was spent;
I strained, to follow her, each aching eye,
  So swiftly at her Maker's will she went;
I looked again—I looked—the star was gone,
And nothing marked in heaven where she had shone."

"Gone!" said the Poet, "and about to be
  Forgotten: O, how sad a fate is hers!"
"How is it sad, my son?" all reverently
  The old man answered; "though she ministers
No longer with her lamp to me and thee,
  She has fulfilled her mission. God transfers
Or dims her ray; yet was she blest as bright,
For all her life was spent in giving light."

"Her mission she fulfilled assuredly,"
  The Poet cried: "but, O unhappy star!
None praise and few will bear in memory
  The name she went by. O, from far, from far
Comes down, methinks, her mournful voice to me,
  Full of regrets that men so thankless are."
So said, he told that old Astronomer
All that the gazing crowd had said of her.

And he went on to speak in bitter wise,
  As one who seems to tell another's fate,
But feels that nearer meaning underlies,
  And points its sadness to his own estate:
"If such be the reward," he said with sighs,
  "Envy to earn for love, for goodness hate—
If such be thy reward, hard case is thine!
It had been better for thee not to shine.

"If to reflect a light that is divine
  Makes that which doth reflect it better seen,
And if to see is to contemn the shrine,
  'Twere surely better it had never been:
It had been better for her NOT TO SHINE,
  And for me NOT TO SING. Better, I ween,
For us to yield no more that radiance bright,
For them, to lack the light than scorn the light."

Strange words were those from Poet lips (said he);
  And then he paused, and sighed, and turned to look
Upon the lady's downcast eyes, and see

How fast the honey bees in settling shook
Those apple blossoms on her from the tree;
He watched her busy fingers as they took
And slipped the knotted thread, and thought how much
He would have given that hand to hold—to touch.

At length, as suddenly become aware
Of this long pause, she lifted up her face,
And he withdrew his eyes—she looked so fair
And cold, he thought, in her unconscious grace.
"Ah! little dreams she of the restless care,"
He thought, "that makes my heart to throb apace:
Though we this morning part, the knowledge sends
No thrill to her calm pulse—we are but FRIENDS."

Ah! turret clock (he thought), I would thy hand
Were hid beyond yon towering maple trees!
Ah! tell-tale shadow, but one moment stand—
Dark shadow—fast advancing to my knees;
Ah! foolish heart (he thought), that vainly planned
By feigning gladness to arrive at ease;
Ah! painful hour, yet pain to think it ends;
I must remember that we are but friends.

And while the knotted thread moved to and fro,
In sweet regretful tones that lady said:
"It seemeth that the fame you would forego
The Poet whom you tell of coveted;
But I would fain, methinks, his story know.
And was he loved?" said she, "or was he wed?
And had he friends?" "One friend, perhaps," said he,
"But for the rest, I pray you let it be."

Ah! little bird (he thought), most patient bird,
Breasting thy speckled eggs the long day through,
By so much as my reason is preferred
Above thine instinct, I my work would do
Better than thou dost thine. Thou hast not stirred
This hour thy wing. Ah! russet bird, I sue
For a like patience to wear through these hours—
Bird on thy nest among the apple flowers.

I will not speak—I will not speak to thee,
My star! and soon to be my lost, lost star.
The sweetest, first, that ever shone on me,
So high above me and beyond so far;
I can forego thee, but not bear to see
My love, like rising mist, thy lustre mar:
That were a base return for thy sweet light.
Shine, though I never more shall see that thou art bright.

Never! 'Tis certain that no hope is—none!
No hope for me, and yet for thee no fear,
The hardest part of my hard task is done;
Thy calm assures me that I am not dear;
Though far and fast the rapid moments run,
Thy bosom heaveth not, thine eyes are clear;
Silent, perhaps a little sad at heart
She is. I am her friend, and I depart.

Silent she had been, but she raised her face;
"And will you end," said she, "this half-told tale?"
"Yes, it were best," he answered her. "The place
Where I left off was where he felt to fail
His courage, Madam, through the fancy base
That they who love, endure, or work, may rail
And cease—if all their love, the works they wrought,
And their endurance, men have set at nought."

"It had been better for me NOT to sing,"
My Poet said, "and for her NOT to shine;"
But him the old man answered, sorrowing,
"My son, did God who made her, the Divine
Lighter of suns, when down to that bright ring
He cast her, like some gleaming almandine,
And set her in her place, begirt with rays,
Say unto her 'Give light,' or say 'Earn praise?'"

The Poet said, "He made her to give light."
"My son," the old man answered, "blest are such;
A blessed lot is theirs; but if each night
Mankind had praised her radiance—inasmuch
As praise had never made it wax more bright,
And cannot now rekindle with its touch
Her lost effulgence, it is nought. I wot
That praise was not her blessing nor her lot."

"Ay," said the Poet, "I my words abjure,
And I repent me that I uttered them;
But by her light and by its forfeiture
She shall not pass without her requiem.
Though my name perish, yet shall hers endure;
Though I should be forgotten, she, lost gem,
Shall be remembered; though she sought not fame,
It shall be busy with her beauteous name.

"For I will raise in her bright memory,
Lost now on earth, a lasting monument,
And graven on it shall recorded be
That all her rays to light mankind were spent;
And I will sing albeit none heedeth me,
On her exemplar being still intent:
While in men's sight shall stand the record thus—
'So long as she did last she lighted us.'"

So said, he raised, according to his vow,
On the green grass, where oft his townsfolk met,

Under the shadow of a leafy bough
  That leaned toward a singing rivulet,
One pure white stone, whereon, like crown on brow,
  The image of the vanished star was set;
And this was graven on the pure white stone
In golden letters—"WHILE SHE LIVED SHE SHONE."

Madam, I cannot give this story well—
  My heart is beating to another chime;
My voice must needs a different cadence swell;
  It is yon singing bird, which all the time
Wooeth its nested mate, that doth dispel
  My thoughts. What, deem you, could a lover's rhyme
The sweetness of that passionate lay excel?
O soft, O low her voice—"I cannot tell."

[*He thinks.*]

The old man—aye he spoke, he was not hard;
  "She was his joy," he said, "his comforter,
But he would trust me. I was not debarred
  Whate'er my heart approved to say to her."
Approved! O torn and tempted and ill-starred
  And breaking heart, approve not nor demur;
It is the serpent that beguileth thee
With "God doth know" beneath this apple-tree.

Yea, God DOTH know, and only God doth know.
  Have pity, God, my spirit groans to Thee!
I bear Thy curse primeval, and I go;
  But heavier than on Adam falls on me
My tillage of the wilderness; for, lo!
  I leave behind the woman, and I see
As 'twere the gates of Eden closing o'er
To hide her from my sight for evermore.

[*He speaks.*]

I am a fool, with sudden start he cried,
  To let the song-bird work me such unrest:
If I break off again, I pray you chide,
  For morning fleeteth, with my tale at best
Half told. That white stone, Madam, gleamed beside
  The little rivulet, and all men pressed
To read the lost one's story traced thereon,
The golden legend—"While she lived she shone."

And, Madam, when the Poet heard them read,
  And children spell the letters softly through,
It may be that he felt at heart some need,
  Some craving to be thus remembered too;
It may be that he wondered if indeed
  He must die wholly when he passed from view;
It may be, wished, when death his eyes made dim,
That some kind hand would raise such stone for him.

But shortly, as there comes to most of us,
  There came to him the need to quit his home:
To tell you why were simply hazardous.
  What said I, Madam?—men were made to roam
My meaning is. It hath been always thus:
  They are athirst for mountains and sea foam;
Heirs of this world, what wonder if perchance
They long to see their grand inheritance?

He left his city, and went forth to teach
  Mankind, his peers, the hidden harmony
That underlies God's discords, and to reach
  And touch the master-string that like a sigh
Thrills in their souls, as if it would beseech
  Some hand to sound it, and to satisfy
Its yearning for expression: but no word
Till poet touch it hath to make its music heard.

[*He thinks.*]

I know that God is good, though evil dwells
  Among us, and doth all things holiest share;
That there is joy in heaven, while yet our knells
  Sound for the souls which He has summoned there;
That painful love unsatisfied hath spells
  Earned by its smart to soothe its fellow's care:
But yet this atom cannot in the whole
Forget itself—it aches a separate soul.

[*He speaks.*]

But, Madam, to my Poet I return.
  With his sweet cadences of woven words
He made their rude untutored hearts to burn
  And melt like gold refined. No brooding birds
Sing better of the love that doth sojourn
  Hid in the nest of home, which softly girds
The beating heart of life; and strait though it be,
Is straitness better than wide liberty?

He taught them, and they learned, but not the less
  Remained unconscious whence that lore they drew,
But dreamed that of their native nobleness
  Some lofty thoughts, that he had planted, grew;
His glorious maxims in a lowly dress,
  Like seed sown broadcast, sprung in all men's view.
The sower, passing onward, was not known,
And all men reaped the harvest as their own.

It may be, Madam, that those ballads sweet,
  Whose rhythmic measures yesterday we sung,
Which time and changes make not obsolete,
  But (as a river bears down blossoms flung
Upon its breast) take with them while they fleet—
  It may be from his lyre that first they sprung:

But who can tell, since work surviveth fame?—
The rhyme is left, but lost the Poet's name.

He worked, and bravely he fulfilled his trust—
So long he wandered sowing worthy seed,
Watering of wayside buds that were adust,
  And touching for the common ear his reed—
So long to wear away the cankering rust
  That dulls the gold of life—so long to plead
With sweetest music for all souls oppressed,
That he was old ere he had thought of rest.

Old and grey-headed, leaning on a staff,
  To that great city of his birth he came,
And at its gates he paused with wondering
    laugh
  To think how changed were all his thoughts
    of fame
Since first he carved the golden epitaph
  To keep in memory a worthy name,
And thought forgetfulness had been its doom
But for a few bright letters on a tomb.

The old Astronomer had long since died;
  The friends of youth were gone and far
    dispersed;
Strange were the domes that rose on every
    side;
  Strange fountains on his wondering vision
    burst;
The men of yesterday their business plied;
  No face was left that he had known at first;
And in the city gardens, lo! he sees
The saplings that he set are stately trees.

Upon the grass beneath their welcome shade,
  Behold! he marks the fair white monument,
And on its face the golden words displayed,
  For sixty years their lustre have not spent;
He sitteth by it and is not afraid,
  But in its shadow he is well content;
And envies not, though bright their gleamings
    are,
The golden letters of the vanished star.

He gazeth up: exceeding bright appears
  That golden legend to his aged eyes,
For they are dazzled till they fill with tears,
  And his lost Youth doth like a vision rise;
She saith to him, "In all these toilsome years,
  What hast thou won by work or enterprise?
What hast thou won to make amends to thee,
As thou didst swear to do for loss of me?

"O man! O white-haired man," the vision
    said,
  "Since we two sat beside this monument
Life's clearest hues are all evanishèd,
  The golden wealth thou hadst of me is spent;
The wind hath swept thy flowers, their leaves
    are shed;
  The music is played out that with thee
    went."
" Peace, peace!" he cried; "I lost thee, but,
    in truth,
There are worse losses than the loss of youth."

He said not what those losses were—but I—
  But I must leave them, for the time draws
    near.
Some lose not ONLY joy, but memory
  Of how it felt; not love that was so dear
Lose only, but the steadfast certainty
  That once they had it; doubt comes on, then
    fear,
And after that despondency. I wis
The Poet must have meant such loss as this.

But while he sat and pondered on his youth,
  He said, "It did one deed that doth remain,
For it preserved the memory and the truth
  Of her that now doth neither set nor wane,
But shine in all men's thoughts; nor sink
    forsooth,
  And be forgotten like the summer rain.
O, it is good that man should not forget
Or benefits foregone or brightness set!"

He spoke and said, "My lot contenteth me;
  I am right glad for this her worthy fame;
That which was good and great I fain would
    see
  Drawn with a halo round what rests—its
    name."
This while the Poet said, behold, there came
  A workman with his tools anear the tree,
And when he read the words he paused awhile
And pondered on them with a wondering smile.

And then he said, "I pray you, Sir, what
    mean
  The golden letters of this monument?"
In wonder quoth the Poet, "Hast thou been
  A dweller near at hand, and their intent
Hast neither heard by voice of fame, nor seen
  The marble earlier?" "Ay," said he, and
    leant
Upon his spade to hear the tale, then sigh,
And say it was a marvel, and pass by.

Then said the Poet, "This is strange to me."
  But as he mused, with trouble in his mind,
A band of maids approached him leisurely,
  Like vessels sailing with a favoring wind;
And of their rosy lips requested he,
  As one that for a doubt would solving find,
The tale, if tale there were, of that white stone,
And those fair letters—"While she lived she
    shone."

Then like a fleet that floats becalmed they stay,
  "O, Sir," saith one, "this monument is old;
But we have heard our virtuous mothers say
  That by their mothers thus the tale was told:
A Poet made it; journeying then away,
  He left us; and though some the meaning
    hold
For other than the ancient one, yet we
Receive this legend for a certainty:—

"There was a lily once, most purely white,
  Beneath the shadow of these boughs it grew;

Its starry blossom it unclosed by night,
  And a young Poet loved its shape and hue.
He watched it nightly, 'twas so fair a sight,
  Until a stormy wind arose and blew,
And when he came once more his flower to greet
  Its fallen petals drifted to his feet.

"And for his beautiful white lily's sake,
  That she might be remembered where her scent
Had been right sweet, he said that he would make
  In her dear memory a monument:
For she was purer than a driven flake
  Of snow, and in her grace most excellent;
The loveliest life that death did ever mar,
As beautiful to gaze on as a star."

"I thank you, maid," the Poet answered her,
  "And I am glad that I have heard your tale."
With that they passed; and as an inlander,
  Having heard breakers raging in a gale
And falling down in thunder, will aver
  That still, when far away in grassy vale,
He seems to hear those seething waters bound,
So in his ears the maiden's voice did sound.

He leaned his face upon his hand, and thought
  And thought, until a youth came by that way;
And once again of him the Poet sought
  The story of the star. But, well-a-day!
He said, "The meaning with much doubt is fraught,
  The sense thereof can no man surely say;
For still tradition sways the common ear,
That of a truth a star DID DISAPPEAR.

"But they who look beneath the outer shell
  That wraps the 'kernel of the people's lore,'
Hold THAT for superstition; and they tell
  That seven lovely sisters dwelt of yore
In this old city, where it so befell
  That one a Poet loved; that, furthermore,
As stars above she was pure and good,
And fairest of that beauteous sisterhood.

"So beautiful they were, those virgins seven,
  That all men called them clustered stars in song,
Forgetful that the stars abide in heaven:
  But woman bideth not beneath it long;
For O, alas! alas! one fated even,
  When stars their azure deeps began to throng,
That virgin's eyes of Poet loved waxed dim,
And all their lustrous shining waned to him.

"In summer dusk she drooped her head and sighed
  Until what time the evening star went down,
And all the other stars did shining bide
  Clear in the lustre of their old renown,

And then—the virgin laid her down and died:
  Forgot her youth, forgot her beauty's crown,
Forgot the sisters whom she loved before,
And broke her Poet's heart for evermore."

"A mournful tale, in truth," the lady saith:
  "But did he truly grieve for evermore?"
"It may be you forget," he answereth,
  That this is but a fable at the core
O' the other fable." "Though it be but breath,"
She asketh, "was it true?" Then he,
  "This lore,
Since it is fable, either way may go;
Then, if it please you, think it might be so."

"Nay, but," she saith, "if I had told your tale,
  The virgin should have lived his home to bless,
Or, must she die, I would have made to fail
  His useless love." "I tell you not the less,"
He sighs, "because it was of no avail:
  His heart the Poet would not dispossess
Thereof. But let us leave the fable now.
My Poet heard it with an aching brow."

And he made answer thus, "I thank thee, youth;
  Strange is thy story to these aged ears,
But I bethink me thou hast told a truth
  Under the guise of fable. If my tears,
Thou lost belovèd star, lost now, forsooth,
  Indeed could bring thee back among thy peers,
So new thou shouldst be deemed as newly seen,
For men forget that thou hast ever been.

"There was a morning when I longed for fame,
  There was a noontide when I passed it by,
There is an evening when I think not shame
  Its substance and its being to deny;
For if men bear in mind great deeds, the name
  Of him that wrought them shall they leave to die;
Or if his name they shall have deathless writ,
They change the deeds that first ennobled it.

"O golden letters of this monument!
  O words to celebrate a loved renown
Lost now or wrested! and to fancies lent,
  Or on a fabled forehead set for crown,
For my departed star, I am content,
  Though legends dim and years her memory drown:
For what were fame to her, compared and set
By this great truth which ye make lustrous yet?"

"Adieu!" the Poet said, "my vanished star,
  Thy duty and thy happiness were one.
Work is heaven's hest; its fame is sublunar:
  The fame thou dost not need—the work is done.

For thee I am content that these things are ;
  More than content were I, my race being run,
Might it be true of me, though none thereon
Should muse regretful—'While he lived he
    shone.'"

So said, the Poet rose and went his way,
  And that same lot he proved whereof he
    spake.
Madam, my story is told out ; the day
  Draws out her shadows, time doth overtake
The morning. That which endeth call a lay,
  Sung after pause—a motto in the break
Between two chapters of a tale not new,
Not joyful—but a common tale. Adieu !

And that same God who made your face so fair,
  And gave your woman's heart its tenderness,
So shield the blessing he implanted there,
  That it may never turn to your distress,
And never cost you trouble or despair,
  Nor granted leave the granter comfortless ;
But like a river blest where'er it flows,
Be still receiving while it still bestows.

Adieu, he said, and paused, while she sat mute
  In the soft shadow of the apple-tree ;
The sky-lark's song rang like a joyous flute,
  The brook went prattling past her restlessly:
She let their tongues be her tongue's substitute;
  It was the wind that sighed, it was not she :
And what the lark, the brook, the wind, had said,
We cannot tell, for none interpreted.

Their counsels might be hard to reconcile,
  They might not suit the moment or the spot.
She rose, and laid her work aside the while
  Down in the sunshine of that grassy plot ;
She looked upon him with an almost smile,
  And held to him a hand that faltered not.
One moment—bird and brook went warbling on,
And the wind sighed again—and he was gone.

So quietly, as if she heard no more
  Or skylark in the azure overhead,
Or water slipping past the cressy shore,
  Or wind that rose in sighs, and sighing fled—
So quietly, until the alders hoar
    Took him beneath them ; till the downward
      spread
Of planes engulfed him in their leafy seas—
She stood beneath her rose-flushed apple-trees.

And then she stooped toward the mossy grass,
  And gathered up her work and went her way;
Straight to that ancient turret she did pass,
  And startled back some fawns that were at
    play,
She did not sigh, she never said "Alas !"
  Although he was her friend: but still that
    day,
Where elm and hornbeam spread a towering
    dome,
She crossed the dells to her ancestral home.

And did she love him ?—what if she did not ?
  Then home was still the home of happiest
    years ;
Nor thought was exiled to partake his lot,
  Nor heart lost courage through foreboding
    fears ;
Nor echo did against her secret plot,
  Nor music her betray to painful tears ;
Nor life become a dream, and sunshine dim,
And riches poverty because of him.

But did she love him ?—what and if she did ?
  Love cannot cool the burning Austral sand,
Nor show the secret waters that lie hid
  In arid valleys of that desert land.
Love has no spells can scorching winds forbid,
  Or bring the help which tarries near to hand,
Or spread a cloud for curtaining faded eyes
That gaze up dying into alien skies.

A DEAD YEAR.

I TOOK a year out of my life and
 story—
A dead year, and said, "I will hew
 thee a tomb!
'All the kings of the nations lie in
 glory;'
Cased in cedar, and shut in a sacred
 gloom;
Swathed in linen, and precious un-
 guents old;
Painted with cinnabar, and rich with gold.

"Silent they rest, in solemn salvatory,
Sealed from the moth and the owl and the
 flittermouse—
 Each with his name on his brow.
'All the kings of the nations lie in glory,
Every one in his own house:'
 Then why not thou?

"Year," I said, "thou shalt not lack
Bribes to bar thy coming back;
Doth old Egypt wear her best
In the chambers of her rest?
Doth she take to her last bed
Beaten gold and glorious red?
Envy not! for thou wilt wear
In the dark a shroud as fair;
Golden with the sunny ray
Thou withdrawest from my day;
Wrought upon with colours fine
Stolen from this life of mine:
Like the dusty Libyan kings,
Lie with two wide open wings
On thy breast, as if to say,
On these wings hope flew away;
And so housed, and thus adorned,
Not forgotten, but not scorned,
Let the dark for evermore
Close thee when I close the door;
And the dust for ages fall
In the creases of thy pall;
And no voice nor visit rude
Break thy sealèd solitude."

I took the year out of my life and story,
 The dead year, and said, "I have hewed thee
 a tomb!
'All the kings of the nations lie in glory,'
Cased in cedar, and shut in a sacred gloom;
But for the sword, and sceptre, and diadem,
 Sure thou didst reign like them."

So I laid her with those tyrants old and hoary,
 According to my vow;
For I said, "The kings of the nations lie in
 glory,
 And so shalt thou!"

"Rock," I said, "thy ribs are strong,
That I bring thee guard it long;
Hide the light from buried eyes—
Hide it lest the dead arise."
"Year," I said, and turned away,
"I am free of thee this day;
All that we two only know,
I forgive and I forego,
So thy face no more I meet
In the field or in the street."

Thus we parted, she and I;
Life hid death, and put it by;
Life hid death, and said, "Be free!
I have no more need of thee."
No more need! O mad mistake,
With repentance in its wake!
Ignorant, and rash, and blind,
Life had left the grave behind;
But had locked within its hold
With the spices and the gold,
All she had to keep her warm
In the raging of the storm.

Scarce the sunset bloom was gone,
And the little stars outshone,
Ere the dead year, stiff and stark,
Drew me to her in the dark;
Death drew life to come to her,
Beating at her sepulchre,
Crying out, "How can I part
With the best share of my heart?
Lo, it lies upon the bier,
Captive with the buried year.
O my heart!" and I fell prone,
Weeping at the sealèd stone;
"Year among the shades," I said,
"Since I live, and thou art dead,
Let my captive heart be free
Like a bird to fly to me."
And I stayed some voice to win,
None answered from within;
And I kissed the door—and night
Deepened till the stars waxed bright;
And I saw them set and wane.
And the world turn green again.

"So," I whispered, "open door,
I must tread this palace floor—
Sealèd palace, rich and dim.

A DEAD YEAR.

Let a narrow sunbeam swim
After me and on me spread
While I look upon my dead ;
Let a little warmth be free
To come after ; let me see
Through the doorway, when I sit
Looking out, the swallows flit,
Settling not till daylight goes ;
Let me smell the wild white rose,
Smell the woodbine and the May ;
Mark, upon a sunny day,
Sated from their blossoms rise
Honey-bees and butterflies.
Let me hear, O ! let me hear,
Sitting by my buried year,
Finches chirping to their young.
And the little noises flung
Out of clefts where rabbits play,
Or from falling water-spray ;
And the gracious echoes woke
By man's work : the woodman's stroke,
Shout of shepherd, whistlings blithe,
And the whetting of the scythe ;
Let this be, lest shut and furled
From the well-belovèd world,
I forget her yearnings old,
And her troubles manifold,
Strivings sore, submissions meet,
And my pulse no longer beat,
Keeping time and bearing part
With the pulse of her great heart.

"So ! swing open door and shade
Take me : I am not afraid,
For the time will not be long ;
Soon I shall have waxen strong—
Strong enough my own to win
From the grave it lies within."

And I entered. On her bier
Quiet lay the buried year ;
I sat down where I could see
Life without and sunshine free,
Death within. And I between,
Waited my own heart to wean
From the shroud that shaded her
In the rock-hewn sepulchre—
Waited till the dead should say,
"Heart, be free of me this day"—
Waited with a patient will—
AND I WAIT BETWEEN THEM STILL.

I take the year back to my life and story,
The dead year, and say, "I will share in thy tomb.
 'All the kings of the nations lie in glory;'
Cased in cedar, and shut in a sacred gloom !
They reigned in their lifetime with sceptre and
   diadem,
      But thou excellest them ;
For life doth make thy grave her oratory,
      And the crown is still on thy brow
 'All the kings of the nations lie in glory,'
      And so dost thou."

REFLECTIONS.

Written for THE PORTFOLIO SOCIETY, July, 1862.

Looking over a Gate at a Pool in a Field.

WHAT change has made the pastures sweet
    And reached the daisies at my feet,
    And cloud that wears a golden hem?
This lovely world, the hills, the sward—
    They all look fresh, as if our Lord
But yesterday had finished them.

And here's the field with light aglow ;
How fresh its boundary lime-trees show,
    And how its wet leaves trembling shine !
Between their trunks come through to me
The morning sparkles of the sea
    Below the level browsing line.

I see the pool more clear by half
Than pools where other waters laugh
    Up at the breasts of coot and rail.
There, as she passed it on her way,
I saw reflected yesterday
    A maiden with a milking-pail.

There, neither slowly nor in haste,
One hand upon her slender waist,
    The other lifted to her pail,
She rosy in the morning light,
Among the water-daisies white,
    Like some fair sloop appeared to sail.

Against her ankles as she trod,
The lucky buttercups did nod.
    I leaned upon the gate to see :
The sweet thing looked, but did not speak ;
A dimple came in either cheek,
    And all my heart was gone from me.

Then, as I lingered on the gate,
And she came up like coming fate,
    I saw my picture in her eyes—
Clear dancing eyes, more black than sloes,
Cheeks like the mountain pink, that grows
    Among white-headed majesties,

I said, "A tale was made of old
That I would fain to thee unfold ;
    Ah ! let me—let me tell the tale."
But high she held her comely head ;
"I cannot heed it now," she said,
    "For carrying of the milking-pail."

She laughed. What good to make ado ?
I held the gate, and she came through,
    And took her homeward path anon.
From the clear pool her face had fled ;
It rested on my heart instead,
    Reflected when the maid was gone.

With happy youth, and work content,
So sweet and stately on she went,
    Right careless of the untold tale.
Each step she took I loved her more,
And followed to her dairy door
    The maiden with the milking-pail.

II.

For hearts where wakened love doth lurk,
How fine, how blest a thing is work !
    For work does good when reasons fail—
Good ; yet the axe at every stroke
The echo of a name awoke—
    Her name is Mary Martindale.

I'm glad that echo was not heard
Aright by other men : a bird
    Knows doubtless what his own notes tell ;
And I know not; but I can say
I felt as shame-faced all that day
    As if folks heard her name right well.

And when the west began to glow
I went—I could not choose but go—
    To that same dairy on the hill ;
And while sweet Mary moved about
Within, I came to her without,
    And leaned upon the window-sill.

The garden border where I stood
Was sweet with pinks and southernwood.
    I spoke—her answer seemed to fail :
I smelt the pinks I could not see ;
The dusk came down and sheltered me,
    And in the dusk she heard my tale.

And what is left that I should tell?
I begged a kiss, I pleaded well:
   The rosebud lips did long decline;
But yet I think, I think 'tis true,
That, leaned at last into the dew,
   One little instant they were mine.

O life! how dear thou hast become:
She laughed at dawn, and I was dumb,
   But evening counsels best prevail.
Fair shines the blue that o'er her spreads,
Green be the pastures where she treads,
   The maiden with the milking-pail!

THE LETTER L.

ABSENT.

E sat on grassy slopes that meet
   With sudden dip the level
      strand ;
   The trees hung overhead—
      our feet
         Were on the sand.

   Two silent girls, a thoughtful
      man,
We sunned ourselves in open light,
And felt such April airs as fan
      The Isle of Wight ;

And smelt the wall-flower in the crag
   Whereon that dainty waft had fed,
Which made the bell-hung cowslip wag
      Her delicate head ;

And let alighting jackdaws fleet
   Adown it open-winged, and pass
Till they could touch with outspread feet
      The warmèd grass.

The happy wave ran up and rang
   Like service bells a long way off,
And down a little freshet sprang
      From mossy trough,

And splashed into a rain of spray,
   And fretted on with daylight's loss,
Because so many blue-bells lay
      Leaning across.

Blue martins gossiped in the sun,
   And pairs of chattering daws flew by,
And sailing brigs rocked softly on
      In company.

Wild cherry boughs above us spread
   The whitest shade was ever seen,
And flicker, flicker, came and fled
      Sun spots between.

Bees murmured in the milk-white bloom
   As babes will sigh for deep content
When their sweet hearts for peace make room,
      As given, not lent.

And we saw on ; we said no word,
   And one was lost in musings rare,
One buoyant as the waft that stirred
      Her shining hair.

His eyes were bent upon the sand,
   Unfathomed deeps within them lay,
A slender rod was in his hand—
      A hazel spray.

Her eyes were resting on his face,
   As shyly glad by stealth to glean
Impressions of his manly grace
      And guarded mien ;

The mouth with steady sweetness set,
   And eyes conveying unaware
The distant hint of some regret
      That harbored there.

She gazed, and in the tender flush
   That made her face like roses blown,
And in the radiance and the hush,
      Her thought was shown.

It was a happy thing to sit
   So near nor mar his reverie ;
She looked not for a part in it,
      So meek was she.

But it was solace for her eyes,
   And for her heart, that yearned to him,
To watch apart in loving wise
      Those musings dim.

Lost—lost, and gone ! The Pelham woods
   Were full of doves that cooed at ease ;
The orchis filled her purple hoods
      For dainty bees.

He heard not ; all the delicate air
   Was fresh with falling water-spray :
It mattered not—he was not there,
      But far away.

Till with the hazel in his hand,
   Still drowned in thought, it thus befell :
He drew a letter on the sand—
      The letter L.

And looking on it straight there wrought
   A ruddy flush about his brow ;
His letter woke him : absent thought
      Rushed homeward now.

And half-abashed, his hasty touch
   Effaced it with a tell-tale care,
As if his action had been much,
      And not his air.

And she? she watched his open palm
   Smooth out the letter from the sand,
And rose, with aspect almost calm,
     And filled her hand

With cherry bloom, and moved away
   To gather wild forget-me-not,
And let her errant footsteps stray
     To one sweet spot,

As if she coveted the fair
   White linen of the silver-weed,
And cuckoo-pint that shaded there
     Empurpled seed.

She had not feared, as I divine,
   Because she had not hoped.   Alas!
The sorrow of it! for that sign
     Came but to pass;

And yet it robbed her of the right
   To give, who looked not to receive,
And made her blush in love's despite
     That she should grieve.

A shape in white, she turned to gaze;
   Her eyes were shaded with her hand,
And half-way up the winding ways
     We saw her stand.

Green hollows of the fringèd cliff,
   Red rocks that under waters show,
Blue reaches, and a sailing skiff,
     Were spread below.

She stood to gaze, perhaps to sigh,
   Perhaps to think; but who can tell,
How heavy on her heart must lie
     The letter L!

She came anon with quiet grace;
   And "What," she murmured, "silent yet!"
He answered, "'Tis a haunted place,
     And spell-beset.

"O speak to us, and break the spell!"
   "The spell is broken," she replied.
"I crossed the running brook, it fell,
     It could not bide.

"And I have brought a budding world,
   Of orchis spires and daisies rank,
And ferny plumes but half uncurled,
     From yonder bank;

"And I shall weave of them a crown,
   And at the well-head launch it free,
That so the brook may float it down,
     And out to sea.

"There may it to some English hands
   From fairy meadow seem to come;
The fairyest of fairy lands—
     The land of home."

"Weave on," he said, and as she wove
   We told how currents in the deep,
With branches from a lemon grove,
     Blue bergs will sweep.

And messages from shipwrecked folk
   Will navigate the moon-led main,
And painted boards of splintered oak
     Their port regain.

Then floated out by vagrant thought,
   My soul beheld on torrid sand
The wasteful water set at nought
     Man's skilful hand,

And suck out gold-dust from the box,
   And wash it down in weedy whirls,
And split the wine-keg on the rocks,
     And lose the pearls.

"Ah! why to that which needs it not,"
   Methought, "should costly things be given?
How much is wasted, wrecked, forgot,
     On this side heaven!"

So musing, did mine ears awake
   To maiden tones of sweet reserve,
And manly speech that seemed to make
     The steady curve

Of lips that uttered it defer
   Their guard, and soften for the thought:
She listened, and his talk with her
     Was fancy fraught.

"There is not much in liberty"—
   With doubtful pauses he began;
And said to her and said to me,
     "There was a man—

"There was a man who dreamed one night
   That his dead father came to him;
And said, when fire was low, and light
     Was burning dim—

"'Why vagrant thus, my sometime pride,
   Unloved, unloving, wilt thou roam?
Sure home is best!' The son replied,
     'I have no home.'

"'Shall not I speak?' his father said,
   'Who early chose a youthful wife,
And worked for her, and with her led
     My happy life.

"'Ay, I will speak, for I was young
   As thou art now, when I did hold
The prattling sweetness of thy tongue
     Dearer than gold;

"'And rosy from thy noonday sleep
   Would bear thee to admiring kin,
And all thy pretty looks would keep
     My heart within.

"'Then after, 'mid thy young allies—
  For thee ambition flushed my brow—
I coveted the schoolboy prize
    Far more than thou.

"'I thought for thee, I thought for all
  My gamesome imps that round me grew;
The dews of blessing heaviest fall
    Where care falls too.

"'And I that sent my boys away,
  In youthful strength to earn their bread,
And died before the hair was grey
    Upon my head—

"'I say to thee, though free from care,
  A lonely lot, an aimless life,
The crowning comfort is not there—
    Son, take a wife.'

"'Father beloved,' the son replied,
  And failed to gather to his breast,
With arms in darkness searching wide,
    The formless guest.

"'I am but free, as sorrow is,
  To dry her tears, to laugh, to talk;
And free, as sick men are, I wis
    To rise and walk.

"'And free, as poor men are, to buy
  If they have nought wherewith to pay;
Nor hope, the debt before they die,
    To wipe away.

"'What 'vails it there are wives to win,
  And faithful hearts for those to yearn,
Who find not aught thereto akin
    To make return?

"'Shall he take much who little gives,
  And dwells in spirit far away,
When she that in his presence lives,
    Doth never stray,

"'But waking, guideth as beseems
  The happy house in order trim,
And tends her babes; and sleeping, dreams
    Of them, and him?

"O base, O cold,'"—while thus he spake
  The dream broke off, the vision fled;
He carried on his speech awake
    And sighing said—

"'I had—ah happy man!—I had
  A precious jewel in my breast,
And while I kept it I was glad
    At work, at rest!

"'Call it a heart, and call it strong
  As upward stroke of eagle's wing;
Then call it weak, you shall not wrong
    The beating thing.

"'In tangles of the jungle reed,
  Whose heats are lit with tiger eyes,
In shipwreck drifting with the weed
    'Neath rainy skies,

"'Still youthful manhood, fresh and keen,
  At danger gazed with awed delight,
As if sea would not drown, I ween,
    Nor serpent bite.

"'I had—ah happy! but 'tis gone,
  The priceless jewel; one came by,
And saw and stood awhile to con
    With curious eye,

"'And wished for it, and faintly smiled
  From under lashes black as doom,
With subtle sweetness, tender, mild,
    That did illume

"'The perfect face, and shed on it
  A charm, half feeling, half surprise,
And brim with dreams the exquisite
    Brown blessèd eyes.

"'Was it for this, no more but this,
  I took and laid it in her hand,
By dimples ruled, to hint submiss,
    By frown unmanned?

"'It was for this—and O farewell
  The fearless foot, the present mind,
And steady will to breast the swell
    And face the wind!

"'I gave the jewel from my breast,
  She played with it a little while
As I sailed down into the west,
    Fed by her smile;

"'Then weary of it—far from land,
  With sigh as deep as destiny,
She let it drop from her fair hand
    Into the sea,

"'And watched it sink; and I—and I,—
  What shall I do, for all in vain?
No wave will bring, no gold will buy,
    No toil attain;

"'Nor any diver reach to raise
  My jewel from the blue abyss;
Or could they, still I should but praise
    Their work amiss.

"'Thrown, thrown away! But I love yet
  The fair, fair hand which did the deed:
That wayward sweetness to forget
    Were bitter meed.

"'No, let it lie, and let the wave
  Roll over it for evermore;
Whelmed where the sailor hath his grave—
    The sea her store.

"'My heart, my sometime happy heart!
  And O for once let me complain,
I must forego life's better part—
  Man's dearer gain.

"'I worked afar that I might rear
  A peaceful home on English soil;
I labored for the gold and gear—
  I loved my toil.

"'For ever in my spirit spake
  The natural whisper, "Well 'twill be
When loving wife and children break
  Their bread with thee!"

"'The gathered gold is turned to dross,
  The wife hath faded into air,
My heart is thrown away, my loss
  I cannot spare.

"'Not spare unsated thought her food—
  No, not one rustle of the fold,
Nor scent of eastern sandalwood,
  Nor gleam of gold;

"'Nor quaint devices of the shawl,
  Far less the drooping lashes meek;
The gracious figure, lithe and tall,
  The dimpled cheek;

"''And all the wonders of her eyes,
  And sweet caprices of her air,
Albeit, indignant reason cries,
  Fool! have a care.

"'Fool! join not madness to mistake;
  Thou knowest she loved thee not a whit;
Only that she thy heart might break—
  She wanted it,

"'Only the conquered thing to chain
  So fast that none might set it free,
Nor other woman there might reign
  And comfort thee.

"'Robbed, robbed of life's illusions sweet;
  Love dead outside her closèd door,
And passion fainting at her feet
  To wake no more;

"'What canst thou give that unknown bride
  Whom thou didst work for in the waste,
Ere fated love was born, and cried—
  Was dead, ungraced?

"'No more but this, the partial care,
  The natural kindness for its own,
The trust that waxeth unaware,
  As worth is known:

"'Observance, and complacent thought
  Indulgent, and the honor due
That many another man has brought
  Who brought love too.

"'Nay, then, forbid it Heaven!' he said,
  'The saintly vision fades from me;
O bands and chains! I cannot wed—
  I am not free.'"

With that he raised his face to view;
  "What think you," asking, "of my tale?
And was he right to let the dew
  Of morn exhale,

"And burdened in the noontide sun,
  The grateful shade of home forego—
Could he be right—I ask as one
  Who fain would know?"

He spoke to her and spoke to me;
  The rebel rose-hue dyed her cheek;
The woven crown lay on her knee;
  She would not speak.

And I with doubtful pause—averse
  To let occasion drift away—
I answered—"If his case were worse
  Than word can say,

"Time is a healer of sick hearts,
  And women have been known to choose,
With purpose to allay their smarts,
  And tend their bruise,

"These for themselves. Content to give,
  In their own lavish love complete,
Taking for sole prerogative
  Their tendance sweet.

"Such meeting in their diadem
  Of crowning love's ethereal fire,
Himself he robs who robbeth them
  Of their desire.

"Therefore the man who, dreaming, cried
  Against his lot that evensong,
I judge him honest, and decide
  That he was wrong."

"When I am judged, ah may my fate,"
  He whispered, "in thy code be read!
Be thou both judge and advocate."
  Then turned, he said—

"Fair weaver!" touching, while he spoke,
  The woven crown, the weaving hand,
"And do you this decree revoke,
  Or may it stand?

"This friend, you ever think her right—
  She is not wrong, then?" Soft and low
The little trembling word took flight:
  She answered, "No."

PRESENT.

A meadow where the grass was deep,
  Rich, square, and golden to the view,
A belt of elms with level sweep
  About it grew.

The sun beat down on it, the line
Of shade was clear beneath the trees;
There, by a clustering eglantine,
  We sat at ease.

And O the buttercups! that field
  O' the cloth of gold, where pennons swam—
Where France set up his lilied shield,
  His oriflamb,

And Henry's lion-standard rolled:
What was it to their matchless sheen,
Their million million drops of gold
  Among the green!

We sat at ease in peaceful trust,
  For he had written, "Let us meet;
My wife grew tired of smoke and dust,
  And London heat,

"And I have found a quiet grange,
  Set back in meadows sloping west,
And there our little ones can range
  And she can rest.

"Come down, that we may show the view,
  And she may hear your voice again,
And talk her woman's talk with you
  Along the lane."

Since he had drawn with listless hand
  The letter, six long years had fled,
And winds had blown about the sand,
  And they were wed.

Two rosy urchins near him played,
  Or watched, entranced, the shapely ships
That with his knife for them he made
  Of elder slips.

And where the flowers were thickest shed,
  Each blossom like a burnished gem,
A creeping baby reared its head,
  And cooed at them.

And calm was on the father's face,
  And love was in the mother's eyes;
She looked and listened from her place,
  In tender wise.

She did not need to raise her voice
  That they might hear, she sat so nigh;
Yet we could speak when 'twas our choice,
  And soft reply.

Holding our quiet talk apart
  Of household things; till, all unsealed,
The guarded outworks of the heart
  Began to yield;

And much that prudence will not dip
  The pen to fix and send away,
Passed safely over from the lip
  That summer day.

"I should be happy," with a look
  Towards her husband where he lay,
Lost in the pages of his book,
  Soft did she say.

"I am, and yet no lot below
  For one whole day eludeth care;
To marriage all the stories flow,
  And finish there:

"As if with marriage came the end,
  The entrance into settled rest,
The calm to which love's tossings tend,
  The quiet breast.

"For me love played the low preludes,
  Yet life began but with the ring,
Such infinite solicitudes
  Around it cling.

"I did not for my heart divine
  Her destiny so meek to grow;
The higher nature matched with mine
  Will have it so.

"Still I consider it, and still
  Acknowledge it my master made,
Above me by the steadier will
  Of nought afraid.

"Above me by the candid speech;
  The temperate judgment of its own;
The keener thoughts that grasp and reach
  At things unknown.

"But I look up and he looks down,
  And thus our married eyes can meet;
Unclouded his, and clear of frown,
  And gravely sweet.

"And yet, O good, O wise and true!
  I would for all my fealty,
That I could be as much to you
  As you to me;

"And knew the deep secure content
  Of wives who have been hardly won,
And, long petitioned, gave assent,
  Jealous of none.

"But proudly sure in all the earth
  No other in that homage shares,
Nor other woman's face or worth
  Is prized as theirs."

I said: "*And yet no lot below
For one whole day eludeth care.*
Your thought." She answered, "Even so,
  I would beware

"Regretful questionings; be sure
   That very seldom do they rise,
Nor for myself do I endure—
      I sympathize.

"For once"—she turned away her head,
   Across the grass she swept her hand—
"There was a letter once," she said,
      "Upon the sand."

"There was, in truth, a letter writ
   On sand," I said, "and swept from view;
But that same hand which fashioned it
      Is given to you.

"Efface the letter; wherefore keep
   An image which the sands forego?"
"Albeit that fear had seemed to sleep,"
      She answered low,

"I could not choose but wake it now;
   For do but turn aside your face,
A house on yonder hilly brow
      Your eyes may trace.

"The chestnut shelters it; ah me,
   That I should have so faint a heart!
But yestereve, as by the sea
      I sat apart,

"I heard a name, I saw a hand
   Of passing stranger point that way—
And will he meet her on the strand,
      When late we stray?

"For she is come, for she is there,
   I heard it in the dusk, and heard
Admiring words, that named her fair,
      But little stirred

"By beauty of the wood and wave,
   And weary of an old man's sway;
For it was sweeter to enslave
      Than to obey."

—The voice of one that near us stood,
   The rustle of a silken fold,
A scent of eastern sandalwood,
      A gleam of gold!

A lady! in the narrow space
   Between the husband and the wife,
But nearest him,—she showed a face
      With dangers rife;

A subtle smile that dimpling fled,
   As night-black lashes rose and fell:
I looked, and to myself I said,
      "The letter L."

He, too, looked up, and with arrest
   Of breath and motion held his gaze,
Nor cared to hide within his breast
      His deep amaze:

Nor spoke till on her near advance
   His dark cheek flushed a ruddier hue;
And with his change of countenance
      Hers altered too.

"Lenore!" his voice was like the cry
   Of one entreating; and he said
But that—then paused with such a sigh
      As mourns the dead.

And seated near, with no demur
   Of bashful doubt she silence broke,
Though I alone could answer her
      When first she spoke.

She looked: her eyes were beauty's own;
   She shed their sweetness into his;
Nor spared the married wife one moan
      That bitterest is.

She spoke, and lo, her loveliness
   Methought she damaged with her tongue;
And every sentence made it less,
      So false they rung.

The rallying voice, the light demand,
   Half flippant, half unsatisfied;
The vanity sincere and bland—
      The answers wide.

And now her talk was of the East,
   And next her talk was of the sea;
"And has the love for it increased
      You shared with me?"

He answered not, but grave and still
   With earnest eyes her face perused,
And locked his lips with steady will,
      As one that mused—

That mused and wondered. Why his gaze
   Should dwell on her, methought, was plain;
But reason that should wonder raise
      I sought in vain.

And near and near the children drew,
   Attracted by her rich array,
And gems that trembling into view
      Like raindrops lay.

He spoke: the wife her baby took
   And pressed the little face to hers;
What pain soe'er her bosom shook,
      What jealous stirs

Might stab her heart, she hid them so,
   The cooing babe a veil supplied;
And if she listened none might know,
      Or if she sighed;

Or if forecasting grief and care
   Unconscious solace thence she drew,
And lulled her babe, and unaware
      Lulled sorrow too.

The lady, she interpreter
 For looks or language wanted none,
If yet dominion stayed with her—
   So lightly won ;

If yet the heart she wounded sore
 Could yearn to her, and let her see
The homage that was evermore
   Disloyalty ;

If sign would yield that it had bled,
 Or rallied from the faithless blow,
Or sick or sullen stooped to wed,
   She craved to know.

Now dreamy deep, now sweetly keen,
 Her asking eyes would round him shine ;
But guarded lips and settled mien
   Refused the sign.

And unbeguiled and unbetrayed,
 The wonder yet within his breast,
It seemed a watchful part he played
   Against her quest.

Until with accent of regret
 She touched upon the past once more,
As if she dared him to forget
   His dream of yore.

And words of little weight let fall
 The fancy of the lower mind ;
How waxing life must needs leave all
   Its best behind ;

How he had said that "he would fain
 (One morning on the halcyon sea)
That life would at a stand remain
   Eternally ;

"And sails be mirrored in the deep,
 As then they were for evermore,
And happy spirits wake and sleep
   Afar from shore :

"The well-contented heart be fed
 Ever as then, and all the world
(It were not small) unshadowèd
   When sails were furled.

"Your words"—a pause, and quietly
 With touch of calm self ridicule :
"It may be so—for then," said he,
   "I was a fool."

With that he took his book, and left
 An awkward silence to my care,
That soon I filled with questions deft
   And debonair ;

And slid into an easy vein,
 The favorite picture of the year ;
The grouse upon her lord's domain—
   The salmon weir ;

Till she could feign a sudden thought
 Upon neglected guests and rise,
And make us her adieux, with nought
   In her dark eyes

Acknowledging or shame or pain ;
 But just unveiling for our view
A little smile of still disdain
   As she withdrew.

Then nearer did the sunshine creep,
 And warmer came the wafting breeze ;
The little babe was fast asleep
   On mother's knees.

Fair was the face that o'er it leant,
 The cheeks with beauteous blushes dyed ;
The downcast lashes, shyly bent,
   That failed to hide

Some tender shame. She did not see ;
 She felt his eyes that would not stir,
She looked upon her babe, and he
   So looked at her.

So grave, so wondering, so content,
 As one new waked to conscious life,
Whose sudden joy with fear is blent,
   He said, "My wife."

"My wife, how beautiful you are !"
 Then closer at her side reclined,
"The bold brown woman from afar
   Comes, to me blind.

" And by comparison, I see
 The majesty of matron grace,
And learn how pure, how fair can be
   My own wife's face :

" Pure with all faithful passion, fair
 With tender smiles that come and go ;
And comforting as April air
   After the snow.

" Fool that I was ! my spirit frets
 And marvels at the humbling truth,
That I have deigned to spend regrets
   On my bruised youth.

"Its idol mocked thee, seated nigh,
 And shamed me for the mad mistake ;
I thank my God He could deny,
   And she forsake.

"Ah, who am I, that God hath saved
  Me from the doom I did desire,
And crossed the lot myself had craved,
  To set me higher?

"What have I done that He should bow
  From heaven to choose a wife for me?
And what deserved, He should endow
  My home with THEE?

"My wife!" With that she turned her face
  To kiss the hand about her neck;
And I went down and sought the place
  Where leaped the beck—

The busy beck, that still would run
  And fall, and falter its refrain;
And pause and shimmer in the sun,
  And fall again.

It led me to the sandy shore,
  We sang together, it and I—
"The daylight comes, the dark is o'er,
  The shadows fly."

I lost it on the sandy shore,
  "O wife!" its latest murmurs fell,
"O wife, be glad, and fear no more,
  The letter L."

THE HIGH TIDE ON THE COAST OF LINCOLNSHIRE.

(1571.)

THE old mayor climbed the belfry
    tower,
  The ringers ran by two, by three;
  "Pull, if ye never pulled before;
  Good ringers, pull your best,"
    quoth he.
  "Play uppe, play uppe, O Boston
    bells!
  Ply all your changes, all your swells!
Play uppe 'The Brides of Enderby.'"

Men say it was a stolen tyde—
  The Lord that sent it, He knows all;
But in myne ears doth still abide
  The message that the bells let fall:
And there was nought of strange, beside
The flights of mews and peewits pied
  By millions crouched on the old sea wall.

I sat and spun within the doore,
  My thread brake off, I raised myne eyes;
The level sun, like ruddy ore,
  Lay sinking in the barren skies;
And dark against day's golden death
She moved where Lindis wandereth,
My sonne's faire wife, Elizabeth.

"Cusha! Cusha! Cusha!" calling,
  Ere the early dews were falling,
Farre away I heard her song.
  "Cusha! Cusha!" all along;
Where the reedy Lindis floweth,
  Floweth, floweth,
From the meads where melick groweth
Faintly came her milking song—

"Cusha! Cusha! Cusha!" calling,
  "For the dews will soone be falling;
Leave your meadow grasses mellow,
  Mellow, mellow;
Quit your cowslips, cowslips yellow;
Come uppe Whitefoot, come uppe Lightfoot;
Quit the stalks of parsley hollow,
  Hollow, hollow;
Come uppe Jetty, rise and follow,
From the clovers lift your head;
Come uppe Whitefoot, come uppe Lightfoot,
Come uppe Jetty, rise and follow,
Jetty, to the milking shed."

If it be long, ay, long ago,
  When I beginne to think howe long,
Againe I hear the Lindis flow,
  Swift as an arrowe, sharpe and strong;
And all the aire, it seemeth mee,
Bin full of floating bells (sayth shee),
That ring the tune of Enderby.

Alle fresh the level pasture lay,
  And not a shadowe mote be seene,
Save where full fyve good miles away
  The steeple towered from out the greene;
And lo! the great bell farre and wide
Was heard in all the country side
That Saturday at eventide.

The swanherds where their sedges are
  Moved on in sunset's golden breath,
The shepherde lads I heard afarre,
  And my sonne's wife, Elizabeth;
Till floating o'er the grassy sea
Came down that kindly message free,
The "Brides of Mavis Enderby."

Then some looked uppe into the sky,
  And all along where Lindis flows
To where the goodly vessels lie,
  And where the lordly steeple shows.
They sayde, "And why should this thing be?
What danger lowers by land or sea?
They ring the tune of Enderby!

"For evil news from Mablethorpe,
  Of pyrate galleys warping down;
For shippes ashore beyond the scorpe,
  They have not spared to wake the towne:
But while the west bin red to see,
And storms be none, and pyrates flee,
Why ring 'The Brides of Enderby?'"

I looked without, and lo! my sonne
  Came riding downe with might and main:
He raised a shout as he drew on,
  Till all the welkin rang again,
"Elizabeth! Elizabeth!"
(A sweeter woman ne'er drew breath
Than my sonne's wife, Elizabeth.)

"The olde sea wall (he cried) is downe,
  The rising tide comes on apace,
And boats adrift in yonder towne
  Go sailing uppe the market place."
He shook as one that looks on death:
"God save you, mother!" straight he saith;
"Where is my wife, Elizabeth?"

"Good sonne, where Lindis winds her way,
  With her two bairns I marked her long;
And ere yon bells beganne to play
  Afar I heard her milking song."

He looked across the grassy lea,
To right, to left, " Ho Enderby !"
They rang " The Brides of Enderby !"

With that he cried and beat his breast;
　For lo ! along the river's bed
A mighty eygre reared his crest,
　And uppe the Lindis raging sped.
It swept with thunderous noises loud ;
Shaped like a curling snow-white cloud,
Or like a demon in a shroud.

And rearing Lindis backward pressed
　Shook all her trembling bankes amaine ;
Then madly at the eygre's breast
　Flung uppe her weltering walls again.
Then bankes came downe with ruin and rout—
Then beaten foam flew round about—
Then all the mighty floods were out.

So farre, so fast the eygre drave,
　The heart had hardly time to beat,
Before a shallow seething wave
　Sobbed in the grasses at oure feet :
The feet had hardly time to flee
Before it break against the knee,
And all the world was in the sea.

Upon the roofe we sate that night,
　The noise of bells went sweeping by ;
I marked the lofty beacon light
　Stream from the church tower, red and high—
A lurid mark and dread to see ;
And awsome bells they were to mee,
That in the dark rang " Enderby."

They rang the sailor lads to guide
　From roofe to roofe who fearless rowed ;
And I—my sonne was at my side,
　And yet the ruddy beacon glowed ;
And yet he moaned beneath his breath,
" O come in life, or come in death !
O lost ! my love, Elizabeth."

And didst thou visit him no more?
　Thou didst, thou didst, my daughter deare ;
The waters laid thee at his doore,
　Ere yet the early dawn was clear.
Thy pretty bairns in fast embrace,
The lifted sun shone on thy face,
Down drifted to thy dwelling-place.

That flow strewed wrecks about the grass,
　That ebbe swept out the flocks to sea ;
A fatal ebbe and flow, alas !
　To manye more than myne and mee :
But each will mourn his own (she saith),
And sweeter woman ne'er drew breath
Than my sonne's wife, Elizabeth.

I shall never hear her more
By the reedy Lindis shore,
　" Cusha ! Cusha ! Cusha !" calling,
Ere the early dews be falling ;
I shall never hear her song,
　" Cusha ! Cusha !" all along
Where the sunny Lindis floweth,
　　Goeth, floweth ;
From the meads where melick groweth,
When the water winding down,
Onward floweth to the town.

I shall never see her more
Where the reeds and rushes quiver,
　Shiver, quiver ;
Stand beside the sobbing river,
Sobbing, throbbing, in its falling
To the sandy lonesome shore ;
I shall never hear her calling,
" Leave your meadow-grasses mellow,
　Mellow, mellow ;
Quit your cowslips, cowslips yellow ;
Come uppe Whitefoot, come uppe Light-
　　foot ;
Quit your pipes of parsley hollow,
　Hollow, hollow ;
Come uppe Lightfoot, rise and follow ;
　Lightfoot, Whitefoot,
From your clovers lift the head ;
Come uppe Jetty, follow, follow,
Jetty, to the milking shed."

AFTERNOON AT A PARSONAGE.

(THE PARSON'S BROTHER, SISTER, AND TWO CHILDREN.)

Preface.

THAT wonder man should fail
    to stay
A nursling wafted from above,
The growth celestial come astray
    That tender growth whose
    name is Love!

    It is as if high winds in heaven
    Had shaken the celestial trees,
And to this earth below had given
    Some feathered seeds from one of these.

O perfect love that 'dureth long!
    Dear growth, that shaded by the palms,
And breathed on by the angel's song,
    Blooms on in heaven's eternal calms!

How great the task to guard thee here,
    Where wind is rough, and frost is keen,
And all the ground with doubt and fear
    Is chequered birth and death between!

Space is against thee—it can part;
    Time is against thee—it can chill;
Words—they but render half the heart;
    Deeds—they are poor to our rich will.

Merton.—Though she had loved me, I had
    never bound
Her beauty to my darkness; that had been
Too hard for her. Sadder to look so near
Into a face all shadow, than to stand
Aloof, and then withdraw, and afterwards
Suffer forgetfulness to comfort her.
I think so, and I loved her; therefore I
Have no complaint; albeit she is not mine:
And yet—and yet, withdrawing I would fain
She would have pleaded duty—would have said
"My father wills it;" would have turned
    away,
As lingering, or unwillingly; for then
She would have done no damage to the past:
Now she has roughly used it—flung it down
And brushed its bloom away. If she had said,
"Sir, I have promised; therefore, lo! my
    hand"—
Would I have taken it? Ah no! by all
Most sacred, no!
        I would for my sole share
Have taken first her recollected blush
The day I won her; next her shining tears—
The tears of our long parting; and for all
The rest—her cry, her bitter heart-sick cry,
That day or night (I know not which it was,
The days being always night), that darkest
    night,
When being led to her I heard her cry,
"O blind! blind! blind!"
        Go with thy chosen mate:
The fashion of thy going nearly cured
The sorrow of it. I am yet so weak
That half my thoughts go after thee; but not
So weak that I desire to have it so.

JESSIE, seated at the piano, sings.

When the dimpled water slippeth,
    Full of laughter, on its way,
And her wing the wagtail dippeth,
    Running by the brink at play;
When the poplar leaves atremble
    Turn their edges to the light,
And the far-up clouds resemble
    Veils of gauze most clear and white;

And the sunbeams fall and flatter,
    Woodland moss and branches brown,
And the glossy finches chatter
    Up and down, up and down;
Though the heart be not attending,
    Having music of her own,
On the grass, through meadows wending,
    It is sweet to walk alone.

When the falling waters utter
    Something mournful on their way,
And departing swallows flutter,
    Taking leave of bank and brae;
When the chaffinch idly sitteth
    With her mate upon the sheaves,
And the wistful robin flitteth
    Over beds of yellow leaves;

When the clouds, like ghosts that ponder
    Evil fate, float by and frown,
And the listless wind doth wander
    Up and down, up and down:
Though the heart be not attending,
    Having sorrows of her own,
Through the fields and fallows wending,
    It is sad to walk alone.

Merton.—Blind! blind! blind!
Oh! sitting in the dark for evermore,

And doing nothing—putting out a hand
To feel what lies about me, and to say
Not "This is blue or red," but "This is cold,
And this the sun is shining on, and this
I know not till they tell its name to me."

O that I might behold once more, my God !
The shining rulers of the night and day ;
Or a star twinkling, ; or an almond tree,
Pink with her blossoms and alive with bees,
Standing against the azure ! O my sight !
Lost, and yet living in the sunlit cells
Of memory—that only lightsome place
Where lingers yet the dayspring of my youth :
The years of mourning for thy death are long.
Be kind, sweet memory ! O desert me not !
For oft thou show'st me lucent opal seas,
Fringed with their cocoa-palms, and dwarf red
 crags,
Whereon the placid moon doth "rest her chin;"
For oft by favor of thy visitings
I feel the dimness of an Indian night,
And lo ! the sun is coming. Red as rust
Between the latticed blind his presence burns,
A ruby ladder running up the wall ;
And all the dust printed with pigeons' feet,
Is reddened, and the crows that stalk anear
Begin to trail for heat their glossy wings,
And the red flowers give back at once the dew,
For night is gone, and day is born so fast,
And is so strong, that, huddled as in flight,
The fleeting darkness paleth to a shade,
And while she calls to sleep and dreams "Come
 on,"
Suddenly waked, the sleepers rub their eyes,
Which having opened, lo ! she is no more.

O misery and mourning ! I have felt—
Yes, I have felt like some deserted world
That God had done with, and had cast aside
To rock and stagger through the gulfs of space,
He never looking on it any more—
Untilled, no use, no pleasure, not desired,
Nor lighted on by angels in their flight
From heaven to happier planets, and the race
That once had dwelt on it withdrawn or dead.
Could such a world have hope that some blest
 day
God would remember her, and fashion her
Anew ?

Jessie. What dearest ? Did you speak to me ?
Child. I think he spoke to us.
M.   No, little elves,
You were so quiet that I half forgot
Your neighborhood. What are you doing there ?
J. They sit together on the window-mat
Nursing their dolls.
C.   Yes, Uncle, our new dolls—
Our best dolls, that you gave us.
M.   Did you say
The afternoon was bright ?
J.   Yes, bright indeed !
The sun is on the plane-tree, and it flames
All red and orange.

C.   I can see my father—
Look ! look ! the leaves are falling on his gown.
M. Where ?
C.   In the churchyard, Uncle—he is
 gone ;
He passed behind the tower.
M.   I heard a bell :
There is a funeral, then, behind the church.
2nd Child. Are the trees sorry when their
 leaves drop off ?
1st Child. You talk such silly words ;—no,
 not at all.
There goes another leaf.
2nd Child.   I did not see.
1st Child. Look ! on the grass, between the
 little hills,
Just where they planted Amy.
J.   Amy died—
Dear little Amy ! when you talk of her,
Say, she is gone to heaven.
2nd Child   They planted her—
Will she come up next year ?
1st Child.   No, not so soon ;
But some day God will call her to come up,
And then she will. Papa knows everything—
He said she would before he planted her.
2nd Child. It was at night she went to hea-
 ven. Last night
We saw a star before we went to bed.
1st Child. Yes, Uncle, did you know ? A
 large bright star,
And at her side she had some little ones—
Some young ones.
M.   Young ones ! no, my little maid,
Those stars are very old.
1st Child.   What ! all of them ?
M. Yes.
1st Child. Older than our father ?
M.   Older, far.
2nd Child. They must be tired of shining
 there so long.
Perhaps they wish they might come down.
J.   Perhaps !
Dear children, talk of what you understand.
Come, I must lift the trailing creepers up
That last night's wind has loosened.
1st Child.   May we help ?
Aunt, may we help to nail them ?
J.   We shall see.
Go, find and bring the hammer and some shreds.

[*Steps outside the window, lifts a branch, and
     sings.*]

 Should I change my allegiance for rancor
  If fortune changes her side ?
 Or Should I, like a vessel at anchor,
  Turn with the turn of the tide ?
 Lift ! O lift, thou lowering sky ;
  An thou wilt, thy gloom forego !
 An thou wilt not, he and I
  Need not part for drifts of snow.

M. [*within.*] Lift ! no, thou lowering sky,
 thou wilt not lift—
Thy motto readeth, "Never."

Children. Here they are!
Here are the nails! and may we help?
J. You shall,
If I should want help.
   1st Child. Will you want it, then?
Please want it—we like nailing.
   2nd Child. Yes, we do.
   J. It seems I ought to want it; hold the bough,
And each may nail in turn.

          [*Sings.*]

Like a daisy I was, near him growing :
  Must I move because favors flag,
And be like a brown wall-flower blowing
  Far out of reach in a crag?
Lift! O lift, thou lowering sky;
  An thou canst thy blue regain!
An thou canst not, he and I
  Need not part for drops of rain.

   1st Child. Now, have we nailed enough?
   J. [*trains the creepers.*] Yes, you may go;
But do not play too near the churchyard path.
   M. [*within.*] Even misfortune does not strike so near
As my dependence. O, in youth and strength
To sit a timid coward in the dark,
And feel before I set a cautious step!
It is so very dark, so far more dark
Than any night that day comes after—night
In which there would be stars, or else at least
The silvered portion of a sombre cloud
Through which the moon is plunging.
   J. [*entering.*] Merton!
   M. Yes.
   J. Dear Merton, did you know that I could hear?
   M. No: e'en my solitude is not mine now,
And if I be alone is ofttimes doubt.
Alas! far more than eyesight have I lost;
For manly courage drifteth after it—
E'en as a splintered spar would drift away
From some dismasted wreck. Hear, I complain—
Like a weak ailing woman I complain.
   J. For the first time.
   M. I cannot bear the dark.
   J. My brother! you do bear it—bear it well—
Have borne it twelve long months, and not complained.
Comfort your heart with music: all the air
Is warm with sunbeams where the organ stands.
You like to feel them on you. Come and play.
   M. My fate, my fate is lonely!
   J. So it is—
I know it is.
   M. And pity breaks my heart.
   J. Does it, dear Merton?
   M. Yes, I say it does.
What! do you think I am so dull of ear
That I can mark no changes in the tones
That reach me? Once I liked not girlish pride
And that coy quiet, chary of reply,
That held me distant: now the sweetest lips
Open to entertain me—fairest hands
Are proffered me to guide.
   J. That is not well?
   M. No; give me coldness, pride, or still disdain,
Gentle withdrawal. Give me anything
But this—a fearless, sweet, confiding ease,
Whereof I may expect, I may exact,
Considerate care, and have it—gentle speech,
And have it. Give me anything but this!
For they who give it, give it in the faith
That I will not misdeem them, and forget
My doom so far as to perceive thereby
Hope of a wife. They make this thought too plain;
They wound me—O they cut me to the heart!
When have I said to any one of them,
"I am a blind and desolate man;—come here,
I pray you—be as eyes to me?" When said,
Even to her whose pitying voice is sweet
To my dark ruined heart, as must be hands
That clasp a life-long captive's through the grate,
And who will ever lend her delicate aid
To guide me, dark incumbrance that I am!—
When have I said to her, "Comforting voice,
Belonging to a face unknown, I pray
Be my wife's voice?"
   J. Never, my brother—no,
You never have!
   M. What could she think of me
If I forgot myself so far? or what
Could she reply?
   J. You ask not as men ask
Who care for an opinion, else perhaps,
Although I am not sure—although, perhaps,
I have no right to give one—I should say
She would reply, "I will!"

       Afterthought.

Man dwells apart, though not alone,
  He walks among his peers unread;
The best of thoughts which he hath known,
  For lack of listeners are not said.

Yet dreaming on earth's clustered isles,
  He saith, "They dwell not lone like men,
Forgetful that their sunflecked smiles
  Flash far beyond each other's ken."

He looks on God's eternal suns
  That sprinkle the celestial blue,
And saith, "Ah! happy shining ones,
  I would that men were grouped like you!"

Yet this is sure: the loveliest star
  That clustered with its peers we see,
Only because from us so far
  Doth near its fellows seem to be.

SONGS OF SEVEN.

SEVEN TIMES ONE. EXULTATION.

HERE'S no dew left on the daisies and clover,
There's no rain left in heaven:
I've said my "seven times" over and over,
Seven times one are seven.

I am old, so old, I can write a letter;
My birthday lessons are done;
The lambs play always, they know no better;
They are only one times one.

O moon! in the night I have seen you sailing
And shining so round and low;
You were bright! ah bright! but your light is failing—
You are nothing now but a bow.

You moon, have you done something wrong in heaven
That God has hidden your face?
I hope if you have you will soon be forgiven,
And shine again in your place.

O velvet bee, you're a dusty fellow,
You've powdered your legs with gold!
O brave marsh marybuds, rich and yellow,
Give me your money to hold!

O columbine, open your folded wrapper,
Where two twin turtle-doves dwell!
O cuckoopint, toll me the purple clapper
That hangs in your clear green bell!

And show me your nest with the young ones in it;
I will not steal them away;
I am old! you may trust me, linnet, linnet—
I am seven times one to-day.

SEVEN TIMES TWO. ROMANCE.

You bells in the steeple, ring, ring out your changes,
How many soever they be,
And let the brown meadow-lark's note as he ranges
Come over, come over to me.

Yet bird's clearest carol by fall or by swelling
No magical sense conveys,
And bells have forgotten their old art of telling
The fortune of future days.

"Turn again, turn again," once they rang cheerily,
While a boy listened alone;
Made his heart yearn again, musing so wearily
All by himself on a stone.

Poor bells! I forgive you; your good days are over,
And mine, they are yet to be;
No listening, no longing shall aught, aught discover,
You leave the story to me.

The foxglove shoots out of the green matted heather,
Preparing her hoods of snow;
She was idle, and slept till the sunshiny weather:
O, children take long to grow.

I wish, and I wish that the spring would go faster,
Nor long summer bide so late;
And I could grow on like the foxglove and aster,
For some things are ill to wait.

I wait for the day when dear hearts shall discover,
While dear hands are laid on my head;
"The child is a woman, the book may close over,
For all the lessons are said."

I wait for my story—the birds cannot sing it,
Not one, as he sits on the tree;
The bells cannot ring it, but long years, O bring it!
Such as I wish it to be.

SEVEN TIMES THREE. LOVE.

I leaned out of window, I smelt the white clover,
Dark, dark was the garden, I saw not the gate;
"Now, if there be footsteps, he comes, my one lover—
Hush, nightingale, hush! O sweet nightingale, wait
Till I listen and hear
If a step draweth near,
For my love he is late!

"The skies in the darkness stoop nearer and nearer,
A cluster of stars hangs like fruit in the tree,

The fall of the water comes sweeter, comes
    clearer :
  To what art thou listening, and what dost
    thou see?
      Let the star-clusters grow,
      Let the sweet waters flow,
      And cross quickly to me.

"You night moths that hover where honey
    brims over
  From sycamore blossoms, or settle or sleep;
  You glow-worms, shine out, and the pathway
    discover
  To him that comes darkling along the rough
    steep.
      Ah, my sailor, make haste,
      For the time runs to waste,
      And my love lieth deep—

"Too deep for swift telling; and yet, my one
    lover,
  I've conned thee an answer, it waits thee
    to-night."
  By the sycamore passed he, and through the
    white clover,
  Then all the sweet speech I had fashioned
    took flight ;
      But I'll love him more, more
      Than e'er wife loved before,
      Be the days dark or bright.

SEVEN TIMES FOUR. MATERNITY.

Heigh ho ! daisies and buttercups,
  Fair yellow daffodils, stately and tall !
When the wind wakes how they rock in the
    grasses,
  And dance with the cuckoo-buds slender
    and small !
Here's two bonny boys, and here's mother's
    own lasses,
      Eager to gather them all.

Heigh ho ! daisies and buttercups !
  Mother shall thread them a daisy chain ;
Sing them a song of the pretty hedge-sparrow,
  That loved her brown little ones, loved them
    full fain ;
Sing, "Heart, thou art wide though the house
    be but narrow"—
      Sing once, and sing it again.

Heigh ho ! daisies and buttercups,
  Sweet wagging cowslips, they bend and they
    bow ;
A ship sails afar over warm ocean waters,
  And haply one musing doth stand at her
    prow.
O bonny brown sons, and O sweet little
    daughters,
      Maybe he thinks on you now !

Heigh ho ! daisies and buttercups,
  Fair yellow daffodils, stately and tall—
A sunshiny world full of laughter and leisure,
  And fresh hearts unconscious of sorrow and
    thrall !
Send down on their pleasure smiles passing its
    measure,
      God that is over all !

SEVEN TIMES FIVE. WIDOWHOOD.

I sleep and rest, my heart makes moan
  Before I am well awake ;
"Let me bleed ! O let me alone,
  Since I must not break !"

For children wake, though fathers sleep
  With a stone at foot and at head :
O sleepless God, for ever keep,
  Keep both living and dead !

I lift mine eyes, and what to see,
  But a world happy and fair !
I have not wished it to mourn with me—
  Comfort is not there.

O what anear but golden brooms,
  And a waste of reedy rills·!
O what afar but the fine glooms
  On the rare blue hills !

I shall not die, but live for lore—
  How bitter it is to part !
O to meet thee, my love, once more !
  O my heart, my heart !

No more to hear, no more to see !
  O that an echo might wake
And waft one note of thy psalm to me
  Ere my heart-strings break !

I should know it how faint soe'er,
  And with angel voices blent ;
O once to feel thy spirit anear ;
  I could be content !

Or once between the gates of gold,
  While an entering angel trod,
But once—thee sitting to behold
  On the hills of God !

SEVEN TIMES SIX. GIVING IN MARRIAGE.

To bear, to nurse, to rear,
  To watch, and then to lose :
To see my bright ones disappear,
  Drawn up like morning dews—
To bear, to nurse, to rear,
  To watch, and then to lose :
This have I done when God drew near
  Among his own to choose.

To hear, to heed, to wed.
  And with thy lord depart
In tears that he, as soon as shed,
  Will let no longer smart.
To hear, to heed, to wed,
  This while thou didst I smiled,

For now it was not God who said,
  "Mother, give ME thy child."

O fond, O fool, and blind,
  To God I gave with tears ;
But when a man like grace would find,
  My soul put by her fears—
O fond, O fool, and blind,
  God guards in happier spheres ;
That man will guard where he did bind
  Is hope for unknown years.

To hear, to heed, to wed,
  Fair lot that maidens choose,
Thy mother's tenderest words are said,
  Thy face no more she views ;
Thy mother's lot, my dear,
  She doth in nought accuse ;
Her lot to bear, to nurse, to rear,
  To love—and then to lose.

SEVEN TIMES SEVEN. LONGING FOR HOME.

I.

A song of a boat :—
  There was once a boat on a billow ;
Lightly she rocked to her port remote,
And the foam was white in her wake like snow,
And her frail mast bowed when the breeze
    would blow,
    And bent like a wand of willow.

II.

I shaded mine eyes one day when a boat
  Went curtseying over the billow,
I marked her course till a dancing mote
  She faded out on the moonlit foam,
And I stayed behind in the dear loved home ;
And my thoughts all day were about the boat
  And my dreams upon the pillow.

III.

I pray you hear my song of a boat,
  For it is but short :—
My boat, you shall find none fairer afloat,
  In river or port.
Long I looked out for the lad she bore,
  On the open desolate sea,
And I think he sailed to the heavenly shore,
  For he came not back to me—
    Ah me !

IV.

A song of a nest :—
  There was once a nest in a hollow :
Down in the mosses and knot-grass pressed,
  Soft and warm, and full to the brim—
Vetches leaned over it purple and dim,
  With buttercup buds to follow.

V.

I pray you hear my song of a nest,
  For it is not long :—
You shall never light, in a summer quest
  The bushes among—
Shall never light on a prouder sitter,
  A fairer nestful, nor ever know
A softer sound than their tender twitter,
  That wind-like did come and go.

VI.

I had a nestful once of my own,
  Ah happy, happy I !
Right dearly I loved them : but when they
    were grown
  They spread out their wings to fly—
O, one after one they flew away
  Far up to the heavenly blue,
To the better country, the upper day,
  And—I wish I was going too.

VII.

I pray you, what is the nest to me,
  My empty nest ?
And what is the shore where I stood to see
  My boat sail down to the west ?
Can I call that home where I anchor yet,
  Though my good man has sailed ?
Can I call that home where my nest was set,
  Now all its hope hath failed ?
Nay, but the port where my sailor went,
  And the land where my nestlings be :
There is the home where my thoughts are sent,
  The only home for me—
    Ah me !

A COTTAGE IN A CHINE.

E reached the place by night,
   And heard the waves break-
     ing;
   They came to meet us with
     candles alight
    To show the path we were
     taking.
   A myrtle trained on the gate,
     was white
With tufted flowers down shaking.

With head beneath her wing,
   The little wren was sleeping—
So near, I had found it an easy thing
   To steal her for my keeping
From the myrtle bough that with easy swing
   Across the path was sweeping.

Down rocky steps rough-hewed,
   Where cup-mosses flowered,
And under the trees, all twisted and rude,
   Wherewith the dell was dowered,
They led us, where deep in its solitude
   Lay the cottage, leaf-embowered.

The thatch was all bespread
   With climbing passion flowers;
They were wet, and glistened with raindrops,
    shed
   That day in genial showers.
"Was never a sweeter nest," we said,
   "Than this little nest of ours."

We laid us down to sleep:
   But as for me—waking,
I marked the plunge of the muffled deep
   On its sandy reaches breaking;
For heart-joyance doth sometimes keep
   From slumber, like heart-aching.

And I was glad that night,
   With no reason ready,
To give my own heart for its deep delight,
   That flowed like some tidal eddy,
Or shone like a star that was rising bright
   With comforting radiance steady.

But on a sudden—hark!
   Music struck asunder
Those meshes of bliss, and I wept in the dark,
   So sweet was the unseen wonder;
So swiftly it touched, as if struck at a mark,
   The trouble that joy kept under.

I rose—the moon outshone:
   I saw the sea heaving,
And a little vessel sailing alone,
   The small crisp wavelet cleaving;
'Twas she as she sailed to her port unknown—
   Was the track of sweetness leaving.

We know they music made
   In heaven, ere man's creation;
But when God threw it down to us that strayed,
   It dropt with lamentation,
And ever since doth its sweetness shade
   With sighs for its first station.

Its joy suggests regret—
   Its most for more is yearning;
And it brings to the soul that its voice hath met
   No rest that cadence learning,
But a conscious part in the sighs that fret
   Its nature for returning.

O Eve, sweet Eve! methought
   When sometimes comfort winning;
As she watched the first children's tender sport,
   Sole joy born since her sinning,
If a bird anear them sang, it brought
   The pang as at beginning.

While swam the unshed tear,
   Her prattlers little heeding,
Would murmur, "This bird, with its carol clear,
   When the red clay was kneaden,
And God made Adam our father dear,
   Sang to him thus in Eden."

The moon went in—the sky
   And earth and sea hiding,
I laid me down, with the yearning sigh
   Of that strain in my heart abiding;
I slept, and the barque that had sailed so nigh
   In my dream was ever gliding.

I slept, but waked amazed
   With sudden noise frighted,
And voices without, and a flash that dazed
   My eyes from candles lighted.
"Ah! surely," methought, "by these shouts
    upraised,
   Some travellers are benighted."

A voice was at my side—
   "Waken, madam, waken!
The long prayed-for ship at her anchor doth ride.
   Let the child from its rest be taken,
For the captain doth weary both for babe and
    for bride—
   Waken, madam, waken!

"The home you left but late,
  He speeds to it light-hearted;
By the wires he sent this news, and straight
  To you with it they started."
O joy for a yearning heart too great,
  O union for the parted!

We rose up in the night,
  The morning star was shining;
We carried the child in its slumber light
  Out by the myrtles twining;
Orion over the sea hung bright,
  And glorious in declining.

Mother, to meet her son,
  Smiled first, then wept the rather;
And wife, to bind up those links undone,
  And cherished words to gather,
And to show the face of her little one,
  That had never seen its father.

That cottage in a chine,
  We were not to behold it;
But there may the purest of sunbeams shine,
  May freshest flowers enfold it,
For sake of the news which our hearts must twine
  With the bower where we were told it!

Now oft, left lone again,
  Sit mother and sit daughter,
And bless the good ship that sailed over the main,
  And the favoring winds that brought her;
While still some new beauty they fable and feign
  For the cottage by the water.

PERSEPHONE.

Written for THE PORTFOLIO SOCIETY, January, 1862.

Subject given—"Light and Shade."

HE stepped upon Sicilian grass,
    Demeter's daughter fresh and
        fair,
A child of light, a radiant lass,
    And gamesome as the morning
        air,
The daffodils were fair to see,
They nodded lightly on the lea,
Persephone—Persephone !

Lo ! one she marked of rarer growth
    Than orchis or anemone ;
For it the maiden left them both,
    And parted from her company.
Drawn nigh she deemed it fairer still,
And stooped to gather by the rill
The daffodil, the daffodil.

What ailed the meadow that it shook ?
    What ailed the air of Sicily ?
She wondered by the brattling brook,
    And trembled with the trembling lea.
"The coal-black horses rise—they rise :
O mother, mother !" low she cries—
Persephone—Persephone !

"O light, light, light !" she cries, "farewell ;
    The coal-black horses wait for me.
O shade of shades, where I must dwell,
    Demeter, mother, far from thee !
Ah, fated doom that I fulfil !
Ah, fateful flower beside the rill !
The daffodil, the daffodil !"

What ails her that she comes not home ?
    Demeter seeks her far and wide,
And gloomy-browed doth ceaseless roam
    From many a morn till eventide.
"My life, immortal though it be,
Is nought," she cries, "for want of thee,
Persephone, Persephone !

"Meadows of Enna, let the rain
    No longer drop to feed your rills,
Nor dew refresh the fields again,
    With all their nodding daffodils !
Fade, fade and droop, O lilied lea,
Where thou, dear heart, were reft from me—
Persephone—Persephone !"

She reigns upon her dusky throne,
    'Mid shades of heroes dread to see ;
Among the dead she breathes alone,
    Persephone—Persephone !
Or seated on the Elysian hill
She dreams of earthly daylight still,
And murmurs of the daffodil.

A voice in Hades soundeth clear,
    The shadows mourn and flit below ;
It cries—"Thou Lord of Hades, hear,
    And let Demeter's daughter go.
The tender corn upon the lea
Droops in her goddess gloom when she
Cries for her lost Persephone.

"From land to land she raging flies,
    The green fruit falleth in her wake,
And harvest fields beneath her eyes
    To earth the grain unripened shake.
Arise, and set the maiden free ;
Why should the world such sorrow dree
By reason of Persephone ?"

He takes the cleft pomegranate seeds :
    "Love, eat with me this parting day ;
Then bids them fetch the coal-black steeds—
    Demeter's daughter, wouldst away ?"
The gates of Hades set her free ;
"She will return full soon," saith he—
"My wife, my wife Persephone."

Low laughs the dark king on his throne—
    "I gave her of pomegranate seeds."
Demeter's daughter stands alone
    Upon the fair Eleusian meads.
Her mother meets her. "Hail !" saith she ;
"And doth our daylight dazzle thee,
My love, my child Persephone ?

"What moved thee, daughter, to forsake
    Thy fellow-maids that fatal morn,
And give thy dark lord power to take
    Thee living to his realm forlorn ?"
Her lips reply without her will,
As one addressed who slumbereth still—
"The daffodil, the daffodil !"

Her eyelids droop with light oppressed,
  And sunny wafts that round her stir,
Her cheek upon her mother's breast—
  Demeter's kisses comfort her.
Calm Queen of Hades, art thou she
Who stepped so lightly on the lea—
Persephone, Persephone?

When in her destined course, the moon
  Meets the deep shadow of this world,
And laboring on doth seem to swoon
  Through awful wastes of dimness whirled—
Emerged at length, no trace hath she
Of that dark hour of destiny,
Still silvery sweet—Persephone.

The greater world may near the less,
  And draw it through her weltering shade,
But not one biding trace impress
  Of all the darkness that she made;
The greater soul that draweth thee
Hath left his shadow plain to see
On thy fair face, Persephone!

Demeter sighs, but sure 'tis well
  The wife should love her destiny:
They part, and yet, as legends tell,
  She mourns her lost Persephone;
While chant the maids of Enna still—
"O fateful flower beside the rill—
The daffodil, the daffodil!"

A SEA SONG.

OLD Albion sat on a crag of late,
   And sung out—"Ahoy! ahoy!
Long life to the captain, good luck to the mate,
   And this to my sailor boy!
     Come over, come home,
     Through the salt sea foam,
   My sailor, my sailor boy!

"Here's a crown to be given away, I ween,
   A crown for my sailor's head,
And all for the worth of a widowed queen,
   And the love of the noble dead,
     And the fear and fame
     Of the island's name
   Where my boy was born and bred.

"Content thee, content thee, let it alone,
   Thou marked for a choice so rare;
Though treaties be treaties, never a throne
   Was proffered for cause as fair,
     Yet come to me home,
     Through the salt sea foam,
   For the Greek must ask elsewhere.

"'Tis pity, my sailor, but who can tell?
   Many lands they look to me;
One of these might be wanting a Prince as well,
   But that's as hereafter may be."
     She raised her white head
     And laughed; and she said
   "That's as hereafter may be."

BROTHERS, AND A SERMON.

'T was a village built in a green rent,
Between two cliffs that skirt the dangerous bay,
A reef of level rock runs out to sea,
And you may lie on it and look sheer down,
Just where the "Grace of Sunderland" was lost,
And see the elastic banners of the dulse
Rock softly, and the orange star-fish creep
Across the laver, and the mackerel shoot
Over and under it, like silver boats
Turning at will and plying under water.

There on that reef we lay upon our breasts,
My brother and I, and half the village lads,
For an old fisherman had called to us
With "Sirs, the syle be come." "And what are they?"
My brother said. "Good lack!" the old man cried,
And shook his head; "to think you gentlefolk
Should ask what syle be! Look you; I can't say
What syle be called in your fine dictionaries,
Nor what name God Almighty calls them by
When their food's ready and He sends them south;
But our folk call them syle, and nought but syle,
And when they're grown, why then we call them herring.
I tell you, Sir, the water is as full
Of them as pastures be of blades of grass;
You'll draw a score out in a landing net,
And none of them be longer than a pin.

"Syle! ay, indeed, we should be badly off,
I reckon, and so would God Almighty's gulls,"
He grumbled on in his quaint piety,
"And all his other birds, if He should say
I will not drive my syle into the south;
The fisher folk may do without my syle,
And do without the shoals of fish it draws
To follow and feed on it."

This said, we made
Our peace with him by means of two small coins,
And down we ran and lay upon the reef,
And saw the swimming infants, emerald green,
In separate shoals, the scarcely turning ebb
Bringing them in; while sleek, and not intent
On chase, but taking that which came to hand,
The full-fed mackerel and the gurnet swam
Between; and settling on the polished sea,
A thousand snow-white gulls sat lovingly
In social rings, and twittered while they fed.
The village dogs and ours, elate and brave,
Lay looking over, barking at the fish;
Fast, fast the silver creatures took the bait,
And when they heaved and floundered on the rock,
In beauteous misery, a sudden pat
Some shaggy pup would deal, then back away,
At distance eye them with sagacious doubt,
And shrink half frighted from the slippery things.

And so we lay from ebb-tide, till the flow
Rose high enough to drive us from the reef;
The fisher lads went home across the sand;
We climbed the cliff, and sat an hour or more,
Talking and looking down. It was not talk
Of much significance, except for this—
That we had more in common than of old,
For both were tired, I with overwork,
He with inaction; I was glad at heart
To rest, and he was glad to have an ear
That he could grumble to, and half in jest
Rail at entails, deplore the fate of heirs,
And the misfortune of a good estate—
Misfortune that was sure to pull him down,
Make him a dreamy, selfish, useless man:
Indeed he felt himself deteriorate
Already. Thereupon he sent down showers
Of clattering stones, to emphasize his words,
And leap the cliffs and tumble noisily
Into the seething wave. And as for me,
I railed at him and at ingratitude,
While rifling of the basket he had slung
Across his shoulders; then with right good will
We fell to work, and feasted like the gods,
Like laborers, or like eager workhouse folk
At Yuletide dinner; or, to say the whole
At once, like tired, hungry, healthy youth,
Until the meal being o'er, the tilted flask
Drained of its latest drop, the meat and bread
And ruddy cherries eaten, and the dogs
Mumbling the bones, this elder brother of mine—
This, man that never felt an ache or pain
In his broad, well-knit frame, and never knew
The trouble of an unforgiven grudge,
The sting of a regretted meanness, nor
The desperate struggle of the unendowed
For place and for possession—he began
To sing a rhyme that he himself had wrought;
Sending it out with cogitative pause,
As if the scene where he had shaped it first
Had rolled it back on him, and meeting it
Thus unaware, he was of doubtful mind
Whether his dignity it well beseemed
To sing of pretty maiden:

Goldilocks sat on the grass,
  Tying up of posies rare ;
Hardly could a sunbeam pass
  Through the cloud that was her hair.
Purple orchis lasteth long,
  Primrose flowers are pale and clear ;
O the maiden sang a song
  It would do you good to hear !

Sad before her leaned the boy,
  " Goldilocks that I love well,
Happy creature fair and coy,
  Think o' me, Sweet Amabel."
Goldilocks she shook apart,
  Looked with doubtful, doubtful eyes ;
Like a blossom on her heart
  Opened out her first surprise.

As a gloriole sign o' grace,
  Goldilocks, ah fall and flow,
On the blooming, childlike face,
  Dimple, dimple, come and go.
Give her time ; on grass and sky
  Let her gaze if she be fain :
As they looked ere he drew nigh,
  They will never look again.

Ah ! the playtime she has known,
  While her goldilocks grew long,
Is it like a nestling flown,
  Childhood over like a song ?
Yes, the boy may clear his brow,
  Though she thinks to say him nay,
When she sighs, " I cannot now—
  Come again some other day."

" Hold ! there," he cried, half angry with himself ;
" That ending goes amiss :" then turned again
To the old argument that we had held—
" Now look you !" said my brother, " you may talk
Till, weary of the talk, I answer ' Ay,
There's reason in your words ;' and you may talk
Till I go on to say, ' This should be so ;'
And you may talk till I shall further own
' It IS so ; yes, I am a lucky dog !'
Yet not the less shall I next morning wake,
And with a natural and fervent sigh,
Such as you never heaved, I shall exclaim
' What an unlucky dog I am !'" And here
He broke into a laugh. " But as for you—
You ! on all hands you have the best of me ;
Men have not robbed YOU of your birthright—work,
Nor ravaged in old days a peaceful field,
Nor wedded heiresses against their will,
Nor sinned, nor slaved, nor stooped, nor overreached,
That you might drone a useless life away
'Mid half a score of bleak and barren farms
And half a dozen bogs."
                " O rare !" I cried ;
" His wrongs go nigh to make him eloquent :
Now we behold how far bad actions reach !

Because five hundred years ago a Knight
Drove geese and beeves out from a Franklin's yard ;
Because three hundred years ago a squire—
Against her will, and for her fair estate—
Married a very ugly, red-haired maid,
The blest inheritor of all their pelf,
While in the full enjoyment of the same,
Sighs on his own confession every day.
He cracks no egg without a moral sigh,
Nor eats of beef but thinking on that wrong ;
Then, yet the more to be revenged on them,
And shame their ancient pride, if they should know,
Works hard as any horse for his degree,
And takes to writing verses."
                " Ay," he said,
Half laughing at himself. " Yet you and I,
But for those tresses which enrich us yet
With somewhat of the hue that partial fame
Calls auburn when it shines on heads of heirs,
But when it flames round brows of younger sons,
Just red—mere red ; why, but for this, I say,
And but for selfish getting of the land,
And beggarly entailing it, we two,
To-day well fed, well grown, well dressed, well read,
We might have been two horny-handed boors—
Lean, clumsy, ignorant, and ragged boors—
Planning for moonlight nights a poaching scheme,
Or soiling our dull souls and consciences
With plans for pilfering a cottage roost.

" What, chorus ! are you dumb ? you should have cried,
' So good comes out of evil ;' " and with that,
As if all pauses it was natural
To seize for songs, his voice broke out again :

Coo, dove, to thy married mate—
  She has two warm eggs in her nest :
Tell her the hours are few to wait
  Ere life shall dawn on their rest ;
And thy young shall peck at the shells, elate
  With a dream of her brooding breast.

Coo, dove, for she counts the hours,
  Her fair wings ache for flight :
By day the apple has grown in the flowers,
  And the moon has grown by night,
And the white drift settled from hawthorn bowers,
  Yet they will not seek the light.

Coo, dove ; but what of the sky ?
  And what if the storm-wind swell,
And the reeling branch come down from on high
  To the grass where daisies dwell,
And the brood belovèd should with them lie
  Or ever they break the shell ?

Coo, dove; and yet black clouds lower,
 Like fate, on the far-off sea:
Thunder and wind they bear to thy bower,
 As on wings of destiny.
Ah, what if they break in an evil hour,
 As they broke over mine and me?

What next?—we started like to girls, for lo!
The creaking voice, more harsh than rusty
 crane,
Of one who stooped behind us, cried aloud,
"Good lack! how sweet the gentleman does
 sing—
So loud and sweet, 'tis like to split his throat.
Why, Mike's a child to him, a two-years child—
A Chrisom child."
 "Who's Mike?" my brother growled
A little roughly. Quoth the fisherman—
"Mike, Sir? he's just a fisher lad, no more;
But he can sing when he takes on to sing,
So loud there's not a sparrow in the spire
But needs must hear. Sir, if I might make
 bold,
I'd ask what song that was you sung. My
 mate,
As we were shoving off the mackerel boats,
Said he, 'I'll wager that's the sort o' song
They kept their hearts up with in the Crimea.'"

"There, fisherman," quoth I, "he showed his
 wit,
Your mate; he marked the sound of savage
 war—
Gunpowder, groans, hot shot, and bursting
 shells,
And 'murderous messages' delivered by
Spent balls that break the heads of dreaming
 men."

"Ay, ay, Sir!" quoth the fisherman. "Have
 done!"
My brother. And I—"The gift belongs to few
Of sending farther than the words can reach
Their spirit and expression;" still—"Have
 done!"
He cried; and then, "I rolled the rubbish out
More loudly than the meaning warranted,
To air my lungs—I thought not on the words."

Then said the fisherman, who missed the point,
"So Mike rolls out the psalm; you'll hear him,
 Sir,
Please God you live till Sunday."
 "Even so:
And you, too, fisherman; for here, they say,
You are all church-goers."
 "Surely, Sir," quoth he,
Took off his hat, and stroked his old white
 head
And wrinkled face; then sitting by us said,
As one that utters with a quiet mind
Unchallenged truth—"'Tis lucky for the
 boats."

The boats! 'tis lucky for the boats! Our eyes
Were drawn to him as either fain would say,
What! do they send the psalm up in the spire
And pray because 'tis lucky for the boats?

But he, the brown old man, the wrinkled man,
That all his life had been a church-goer,
Familiar with celestial cadences,
Informed of all he could receive, and sure
Of all he understood—he sat content,
And we kept silence. In his reverend face
There was a simpleness we could not sound;
Much truth had passed him overhead; some
 error
He had trod under foot;—God comfort him!
He could not learn of us, for we were young
And he was old, and so we gave it up;
And the sun went into the west, and down
Upon the water stooped an orange cloud,
And the pale milky reaches flushed, as glad
To wear its colors; and the sultry air
Went out to sea, and puffed the sails of ships
With thymy wafts, the breath of trodden grass:
It took moreover music, for across
The heather belt and over pasture land
Came the sweet monotone of one slow bell,
And parted time into divisions rare,
Whereof each morsel brought its own delight.

"They ring for service," quoth the fisherman;
"Our parson preaches in the church to-night."

"And do the people go?" my brother asked.

"Ay, Sir; they count it mean to stay away,
He takes it so to heart. He's a rare man,
Our parson; half a head above us all."

"That's a great gift and notable," said I.

"Ay, Sir; and when he was a younger man
He went out in the lifeboat very oft,
Before the 'Grace of Sunderland' was wrecked.
He's never been his own man since that hour;
For there were thirty men aboard of her,
Anigh as close as you are now to me,
And ne'er a one was saved.
 They're lying now,
With two small children in a row: the church
And yard are full of seamen's graves, and few
Have any names.
 She bumped upon the reef;
Our parson, my young son, and several more
Were lashed together with a two inch rope,
And crept along to her; their mates ashore
Ready to haul them in. The gale was high,
The sea was all a boiling seething froth,
And God Almighty's guns were going off,
And the land trembled.
 "When she took the ground,
She went to pieces like a lock of hay
Tossed from a pitchfork. Ere it came to that,
The captain reeled on deck with two small
 things,

One in each arm—his little lad and lass.
Their hair was long, and blew before his face,
Or else we thought he had been saved ; he fell,
But held them fast. The crew, poor luckless
   souls !
The breakers licked them off ; and some were
   crushed,
Some swallowed in the yeast, some flung up
   dead,
The dear breath beaten out of them ? not one
Jumped from the wreck upon the reef to catch
The hands that strained to reach, but tumbled
   back
With eyes wide open. But the captain lay
And clung—the only man alive. They pray-
   ed—
'For God's sake, captain throw the children
   here !'
'Throw them !' our parson cried ; and then she
   struck ;
And he threw one, a pretty two-years child ;
But the gale dashed him on the slippery verge,
And down he went. They say they heard him
   cry.

"Then he rose up and took the other one,
And all our men reached out their hungry arms,
And cried out, 'Throw her, throw her !' and
   he did :
He threw her right against the parson's breast,
And all at once a sea broke over them,
And they that saw it from the shore have said
It struck the wreck and piecemeal scattered it,
Just as a woman might the lump of salt
That 'twixt her hands into the kneading-pan
She breaks and crumbles on her rising bread.

"We hauled our men in : two of them were
   dead—
The sea had beaten them, their heads hung
   down ;
Our parson's arms were empty, for the wave
Had torn away the pretty, pretty lamb ;
We often see him stand beside her grave :
But 'twas no fault of his, no fault of his.

"I ask your pardon, Sirs ; I prate and prate,
And never have I said what brought me here.
Sirs, if you want a boat to-morrow morn,
I'm bold to say there's ne'er a boat like mine."

"Ay, that was what we wanted," we replied ;
"A boat, his boat ;" and off he went well
   pleased.

We, too, rose up (the crimson in the sky
Flushing our faces), and went sauntering on,
And thought to reach our lodging, by the cliff.
And up and down among the heather beds,
And up and down between the sheaves, we sped.
Doubling and winding ; for a long ravine
Ran up into the land and cut us off,
Pushing out slippery ledges for the birds,
And rent with many a crevice, where the wind

Had laid up drifts of empty eggshells, swept
From the bare berths of gulls and guillemots.
So as it chanced we lighted on a path
That led into a nutwood ; and our talk
Was louder than beseemed, if we had known,
With argument and laughter ; for the path,
As we sped onward, took a sudden turn
Abrupt, and we came out on churchyard grass,
And close upon a porch, face to face
With those within, and with the thirty graves.
We heard the voice of one who preached with-
   in,
And stopped. "Come on," my brother whis-
   pered me ;
"It were more decent that we enter now ;
Come on ! we'll hear this rare old demigod :
I like strong men and large ; I like grey heads,
And grand gruff voices, hoarse though this may
   be
With shouting in the storm."
                           It was not hoarse,
The voice that preached to those few fishermen
And women, nursing mothers with the babes
Hushed on their breasts ; and yet it held them
   not :
Their drowsy eyes were drawn to look at us,
Till, having leaned our rods against the wall,
And left the dogs at watch, we entered, sat,
And were apprised that, though he saw us not,
The parson knew that he had lost the eyes
And ears of those before him, for he made
A pause—a long dead pause—and dropped his
   arms,
And stood awaiting, till I felt the red
Mount to my brow.
                  And a soft fluttering stir
Passed over all, and every mother hushed
The babe beneath her shawl, and he turned
   round
And met our eyes, unused to diffidence,
But diffident of his ; then with a sigh
Fronted the folk, lifted his grand grey head,
And said, as one that pondered now the words
He had been preaching on with new surprise,
And found fresh marvel in their sound, " Be-
   hold !
Behold !" saith He, "I stand at the door and
   knock."

Then said the parson : "What ! and shall He
   wait,
And must He wait, not only till we say,
'Good Lord, the house is clean, the hearth is
   swept,
The children sleep, the mackerel-boats are in,
And all the nets are mended ; therefore I
Will slowly to the door and open it ;'
But must He also wait where still, behold !
He stands and knocks, while we do say, 'Good
   Lord,
The gentlefolk are come to worship here,
And I will up and open to Thee soon ;
But first I pray a little longer wait,
For I am taken up with them ; my eyes

Must needs regard the fashion of their clothes,
And count the gains I think to make by them;
Forsooth, they are of much account, good
    Lord!
Therefore have patience with me—wait, dear
    Lord!
Or come again?'
            What! must He wait for THIS—
For this? Ay, He doth wait for this, and still,
Waiting for this, He, patient, raileth not;
Waiting for this, e'en this He saith, 'Behold!
I stand at the door and knock.'
                O patient hand!
Knocking and waiting—knocking in the night
When work is done! I charge you, by the sea
Whereby you fill your children's mouths, and by
The might of Him that made it—fishermen!
I charge you, mothers! by the mother's milk
He drew, and by His Father, God over all
Blessèd for ever, that ye answer Him!
Open the door with shame, if ye have sinned;
If ye be sorry, open it with sighs.
Albeit the place be bare for poverty,
And comfortless for lack of plenishing,
Be not abashed for that, but open it,
And take Him in that comes to sup with thee;
'Behold!' He saith, 'I stand at the door and
    knock.'

"Now, hear me: there be troubles in this
    world
That no man can escape, and there is one
That lieth hard and heavy on my soul,
Concerning that which is to come:—
                I say
As a man that knows what earthly trouble
    means,
I will not bear this ONE—I cannot bear
This ONE—I cannot bear the weight of you—
You—every one of you, body and soul;
You, with the care you suffer, and the loss
That you sustain: you, with the growing up
To peril, may be with the growing old
To want, unless before I stand with you
At the great white throne, I may be free of all,
And utter to the full what shall discharge
Mine obligation: nay, I will not wait
A day, for every time the black clouds rise,
And the gale freshens, still I search my soul
To find if there be ought that can persuade
To good, or aught forsooth that can beguile
From evil, that I (miserable man!
If that be so) have left unsaid, undone.

"So that when any risen from sunken wrecks,
Or rolled in by the billows to the edge
Of the everlasting strand, what time the sea
Gives up her dead, shall meet me, they may
    say
Never, 'Old man, you told us not of this;
You left us fisher-lads that had to toil
Ever in danger of the secret stab
Of rocks, far deadlier than the dagger; winds
Of breath more murderous than the cannon's;
    waves

Mighty to rock us to our death; and gulfs
Ready beneath to suck and swallow us in:
This crime be on your head; and as for us—
What shall we do? but rather—nay, not so,
I will not think it; I will leave the dead,
Appealing but to life: I am afraid
Of you, but not so much if you have sinned
As for the doubt if sin shall be forgiven.
The day was, I have been afraid of pride—
Hard man's hard pride; but now I am afraid
Of man's humility. I counsel you,
By the great God's great humbleness, and by
His pity. Be not humble over-much.
See! I will show at whose unopened doors
He stands and knocks, that you may never say,
'I am too mean, too ignorant, too lost;
He knocks at other doors, but not at mine.'

"See here! it is the night! it is the night!
And snow lies thickly, white untrodden snow,
And the wan moon upon a casement shines—
A casement crusted o'er with frosty leaves,
That make her ray less bright along the floor.
A woman sits, with hands upon her knees,
Poor tired soul! and she has nought to do,
For there is neither fire nor candle light:
The driftwood ash lies cold upon her hearth;
The rushlight flickered down an hour ago;
Her children wail a little in their sleep
For cold and hunger, and, as if that sound
Was not enough, another comes to her,
Over God's undefilèd snow—a song—
Nay, never hang your heads—I say, a song.

"And doth she curse the alehouse, and the sots
That drink the night out and their earnings
    there,
And drink their manly strength and courage
    down,
And drink away the little children's bread,
And starve her, starving by the self-same act
Her tender suckling, that with piteous eyes
Looks in her face, till scarcely she has heart
To work, and earn the scanty bit and drop
That feed the others?
            Does she curse the song?
I think not, fishermen; I have not heard
Such women curse. God's curse is curse
    enough.
To-morrow she will say a bitter thing,
Pulling her sleeve down lest the bruises show—
A bitter thing, but meant for an excuse—
'My master is not worse than many men:'
But now, ay, now, she sitteth dumb and still;
No food, no comfort, cold and poverty
Bearing her down.
            My heart is sore for her;
How long, how long? When troubles come
    of God,
When men are frozen out of work, when wives
Are sick, when working fathers fail and die,
When boats go down at sea—then nought be-
    hooves

Like patience; but for troubles wrought of men
Patience is hard—I tell you it is hard.

"O thou poor soul! it is the night—the night;
Against thy door drifts up the silent snow,
Blocking thy threshhold: 'Fall,' thou sayest,
  'fall, fall,
Cold snow, and lie and be trod underfoot,
Am not I fallen? wake up and pipe, O wind,
Dull wind! and beat and bluster at my door:
Merciful wind, sing me a hoarse rough song,
For there is other music made to-night
That I would fain not hear. Wake, thou still
  sea,
Heavily plunge. Shoot on, white waterfall.
O, I could long like thy cold icicles
Freeze, freeze, and hang upon the frosty clift
And not complain, so I might melt at last
In the warm summer sun, as thou wilt do?

"But woe is me! I think there is no sun;
My sun is sunken, and the night grows dark:
None care for me. The children cry for bread,
And I have none, and nought can comfort me;
Even if the heavens were free to such as I,
It were not much, for death is long to wait,
And heaven is far to go!'

            "And speak'st thou thus,
Despairing of the sun that sets to thee,
And of the earthly love that wanes to thee,
And of the heaven that lieth far from thee?
Peace, peace, fond fool! One draweth near
  thy door
Whose footsteps leave no print across the snow;
Thy sun has risen with comfort in his face,
The smile of heaven, to warm thy frozen heart,
And bless with saintly hand. What! is it long
To wait and far to go? Thou shalt not go;
Behold, across the snow to thee He comes,
Thy heaven descends, and is it long to wait?
Thou shalt not wait: 'This night, this night,'
  He saith,
'I stand at the door and knock.'

"It is enough—can such an one be here—
Yea, here? O God forgive you, fishermen!
One? is there only one? But do thou know,
O woman pale for want, if thou art here,
That on thy lot much thought is spent in heaven,
And, coveting the heart a hard man broke,
One standeth patient, watching in the night,
And waiting in the daytime.

                    What shall be
If thou wilt answer? He will smile on thee;
One smile of His shall be enough to heal
The wound of man's neglect; and He will sigh,
Pitying the trouble which that sigh shall cure;
And He will speak—speak in the desolate night,
In the dark night: 'For me a thorny crown
Men wove, and nails were driven in my hands
And feet: there was an earthquake, and I died;
I died, and am alive for evermore.

"'I died for thee; for thee I am alive,
And my humanity doth mourn for thee,
For thou art mine, and all thy little ones,
They, too, are mine, are mine. Behold, the
  house
Is dark, but there is brightness where the sons
Of God are singing, and, behold, the heart
Is troubled: yet the nations walk in white;
They have forgotten how to weep; and thou
Shalt also come, and I will foster thee
And satisfy thy soul; and thou shalt warm
Thy trembling life beneath the smile of God.
A little while—it is a little while—
A little while, and I will comfort thee,
I go away, but I will come again.'

"But hear me yet. There was a poor old man
Who sat and listened to the raging sea,
And heard it thunder, lunging at the cliffs
As like to tear them down. He lay at night;
And 'Lord have mercy on the lads,' said he,
'That sailed at noon, though they be none of
  mine?
For when the gale gets up, and when the wind
Flings at the window, when it beats the roof,
And lulls, and stops, and rouses up again,
And cuts the crest clean off the plunging wave,
And scatters it like feathers up the field,
Why, then I think of my two lads: my lads
That would have worked and never let me want,
And never let me take the parish pay.
No, none of mine; my lads were drowned at
  sea—
My two—before the most of these were born.
I know how sharp that cuts, since my poor wife
Walked up and down, and still walked up and
  down,
And I walked after, and one could not hear
A word the other said, for wind and sea
That raged and beat and thundered in the night—
The awfullest, the longest, lightest night
That ever parents had to spend—a moon
That shone like daylight on the breaking wave.
Ah me! and other men have lost their lads,
And other women wiped their poor dead
  mouths,
And got them home and dried them in the
  house,
And seen the driftwood lie along the coast,
That was a tidy boat but one day back,
And seen next tide the neighbors gather it
To lay it on their fires.
                Ay, I was strong
And able-bodied—loved my work;—but now
I am a useless hull: 'tis time I sunk;
I am in all men's way; I trouble them;
I am a trouble to myself: but yet
I feel for mariners of stormy nights,
And feel for wives that watch ashore. Ay, ay!
If I had learning I would pray the Lord
To bring them in: but I'm no scholar, no;
Book-learning is a world too hard for me:
But I make bold to say, 'O Lord, good Lord,
I am a broken-down poor man, a fool
To speak to Thee: but in the Book 'tis writ,

As I hear say from others that can read,
How, when Thou camest, Thou didst love the sea,
And live with fisherfolk, whereby 'tis sure
Thou knowest all the peril they go through,
And all their trouble.
                As for me, good Lord,
I have no boat ; I am too old, too old—
My lads are drowned ; I buried my poor wife;
My little lasses died so long ago
That mostly I forget what they were like.
Thou knowest, Lord ; they were such little ones
I know they went to Thee, but I forget
Their faces, though I missed them sore.
                        O Lord,
I was a strong man ; I have drawn good food
And made good money out of Thy great sea :
But yet I cried for them at nights ; and now
Although I be so old, I miss my lads,
And there be many folks this stormy night
Heavy with fears for theirs. Merciful Lord,
Comfort them ; save their honest boys, their pride,
And let them hear next ebb the blessedest,
Best sound—the boat keels grating on the sand.

" 'I cannot pray with finer words : I know
Nothing ; I have no learning, cannot learn—
Too old, too old. They say I want for nought,
I have the parish pay ; but I am dull
Of hearing, and the fire scarce warms me through.
God save me—I have been a sinful man—
And save the lives of them that still can work,
For they are good to me ; ay, good to me.
But, Lord, I am a trouble ! and I sit,
And I am lonesome, and the nights are few
That any think to come and draw a chair,
And sit in my poor place and talk awhile.
Why should they come, forsooth ? Only the wind
Knocks at my door, O long and loud it knocks,
The only thing God made that has a mind
To enter in.'
        "Yea, thus the old man spake :
These were the last words of his aged mouth—
BUT ONE DID KNOCK. One came to sup with him,
That humble, weak old man ; knocked at his door
In the rough pauses of the laboring wind.
I tell you that one knocked while it was dark,
Save where their foaming passion had made white
Those livid seething billows. What He said
In that poor place where He did talk awhile,
I cannot tell : but this I am assured,
That when the neighbors came the morrow morn,
What time the wind had bated, and the sun
Shone on the old man's floor, they saw the smile
He passed away in, and they said. ' He looks
As he had woke and seen the face of Christ,
And with that rapturous smile held out his arms
To come to Him.'

" Can such an one be here,
So old, so weak, so ignorant, so frail ?
The Lord be good to thee, thou poor old man ;
It would be hard with thee if heaven were shut
To such as have not learning ! Nay, nay, nay,
He condescends to them of low estate ;
To such as are despised He cometh down,
Stands at the door and knocks.

                    "Yet bear with me.
I have a message ; I have more to say.
Shall sorrow win His pity, and not sin—
That burden ten times heavier to be borne?
What think you ? Shall the virtuous have His care
Alone ? O virtuous women, think not scorn,
For you may lift your faces everywhere ;
And now that it grows dusk, and I can see
None though they front me straight, I fain would tell
A certain thing to you. I say to *you* ;
And if it doth concern you, as methinks
It doth, then surely it concerneth all.
I say that there was once—I say not here—
I say that there was once a castaway,
And she was weeping, weeping bitterly ;
Kneeling, and crying with a heart-sick cry·
That choked itself in sobs—' O my good name !
O my good name !' And none did hear her cry !
Nay ; and it lightened, and the storm-bolts fell,
And the rain splashed upon the roof, and still
She, storm-tost as the storming elements—
She cried with an exceeding bitter cry,
' O my good name !' And then the thunder-cloud
Stooped low and burst in darkness overhead,
And rolled, and rocked her on her knees, and shook
The frail foundations of her dwelling-place.
But she—if any neighbor had come in
(None did) : if any neighbors had come in
They might have seen her crying on her knees,
And sobbing 'Lost, lost, lost !' beating her breast—
Her breast forever pricked with cruel thorns,
The wounds whereof could neither balm assuage
Nor any patience heal—beating her brow,
Which ached, it had been bent so long to hide
From level eyes, whose meaning was contempt.

" O ye good women, it is hard to leave
The paths of virtue, and return again.
What if this sinner wept, and none of you
Comforted her ? And what if she did strive
To mend, and none of you believed her strife,
Nor looked upon her ? Mark, I do not say.
Though it was hard, you therefore were to blame
That she had aught against you, though your feet
Never drew near her door, But I beseech
Your patience. Once in old Jerusalem
A woman kneeled at consecrated feet,
Kissed them, and washed them with her tears.

                                What then?
I think that yet our Lord is pitiful:
I think I see the castaway e'en now!
And she is not alone: the heavy rain
Splashes without, and sullen thunder rolls,
But she is lying at the sacred feet
Of One transfigured.
                " And her tears flow down,
Down to her lips—her lips that kiss the print
Of nails; and love is like to break her heart!
Love and repentance—for it still doth work
Sore in her soul to think, to think that she,
Even she, did pierce the sacred, sacred feet,
And bruise the thorn-crowned head.
                        "O Lord, our Lord,
How great is Thy compassion! Come, good
    Lord,
For we will open, Come this night, good
    Lord;
Stand at the door and knock.
                        "And is this all?—
Trouble, old age and simpleness and sin—
This all? It might be all some other night:
But this night, if a voice said 'Give account
Whom hast thou with thee?' then must I reply,
'Young manhood have I, beautiful youth and
    strength,
Rich with all treasure drawn up from the crypt
Where lies the learning of the ancient world—
Brave with all thoughts that poets fling upon
The strand of life, as driftweed after storms;
Doubtless familiar with Thy mountain heads,
And the dread purity of Alpine snows,
Doubtless familiar with Thy works concealed
For ages from mankind—outlying worlds,
And many moonèd spheres—and Thy great
    store
Of stars, more thick than mealy dust which here
Powders the pale leaves of Auriculas.

This do I know, but, Lord, I know not more.

Not more concerning them—concerning Thee,
I know Thy bounty; where Thou givest much
Standing without, if any call Thee in
Thou givest more.' Speak, then, O rich and
    strong:
Open, O happy young, ere yet the hand
Of him that knocks, wearied at last, forbear;
The patient foot its thankless quest refrain,
The wounded heart for evermore withdraw."

I have heard many speak, but this one man—
So anxious not to go to heaven alone—
This one man I remember, and his look,
Till twilight overshadowed him. He ceased,
And out in darkness with the fisher folk
We passed and stumbled over mounds of moss,
And heard, but did not see, the passing beck,
Ah, graceless heart, would that it could regain
From the dim storehouse of sensations past
The impress full of tender awe, that night,
Which fell on me! It was as if the Christ
Had been drawn down from heaven to track us
    home,
And any of the footsteps following us
Might have been His.

A WEDDING SONG.

COME up the broad river, the Thames, my Dane,
My Dane with the beautiful eyes!
Thousands and thousands await thee full fain,
And talk of the wind and the skies.
Fear not from folk and from country to part,
O, I swear it is wisely done:
For (I said) I will bear me by thee, sweetheart,
As becometh my father's son.

Great London was shouting as I went down,
"She is worthy," I said, "of this;
What shall I give who have promised a crown?
O, first I will give her a kiss."
So I kissed her and brought her, my Dane, my Dane,
Through the waving wonderful crowd:
Thousands and thousands, they shouted amain,
Like mighty thunders and loud.

And they said, "He is young, the lad we love,
The heir of the Isles is young:
How we deem of his mother, and one gone above,
Can neither be said nor sung.
He brings us a pledge—he will do his part
With the best of his race and name;"
And I will, for I look to live, sweetheart,
As may suit with my mother's fame.

THE FOUR BRIDGES.

LOVE this grey old church, the
    low, long nave,
    The ivied chancel and the slen-
      der spire;
    No less its shadow on each heav-
      ing grave,
      With growing osier bound, or
        living briar;
    I love those yew-tree trunks, where
        stand arrayed
So many deep-cut names of youth and maid.

A simple custom this—I love it well—
    A carved betrothal and a pledge of truth;
    How many an eve, their linkèd names to spell,
      Beneath the yew-trees sat our village youth!
When work was over, and the new-cut hay
Sent wafts of balm from meadows where it lay.

Ah! many an eve, while I was yet a boy,
    Some village hind has beckoned me aside,
And sought mine aid, with shy and awkward
      joy,
    To carve the letters of his rustic bride,
And make them clear to read as graven stone,
Deep in the yew-tree's trunk beside his own.

For none could carve like me, and here they
    stand,
    Fathers and mothers of this present race;
And underscored by some less practised hand,
    That fain the story of its line would trace,
With children's names, and number, and the
    day
When any called to God have passed away.

I look upon them, and I turn aside,
    As oft when carving them I did erewhile;
And there I see those wooden bridges wide
    That cross the marshy hollow; there the stile
In reeds imbedded, and the swelling down,
And the white road toward the distant town.

But those old bridges claim another look,
    Our brattling river tumbles through the one;
The second spans a shallow, weedy brook;
    Beneath the others, and beneath the sun,
Like two long stilly pools, and on their breasts
Picture their wooden piles, encased in swallows'
    nests.

And round about them grows a fringe of reeds,
    And then a floating crown of lily flowers,
And yet within small silver-budded weeds;

But each clear centre evermore embowers
A deeper sky, where, stooping, you may see
The little minnows darting restlessly.

My heart is bitter, lilies, at your sweet;
    Why did the dewdrop fringe your chalices?
Why in your beauty are you thus complete,
    You silver ships—you floating palaces?
O! if need be, you must allure man's eye,
Yet wherefore blossom here? O why? O why?

O! O! the world is wide, you lily flowers,
    It hath warm forests, cleft by stilly pools,
Where every night bathe crowds of stars; and
    bowers
Of spicery hang over. Sweet air cools
And shakes the lilies among those stars that lie:
Why are ye not content to reign there? Why?

That chain of bridges, it were hard to tell
    How it is linked with all my early joy.
There was a little foot that I loved well,
    It danced across them when I was a boy;
There was a careless voice that used to sing;
There was a child, a sweet and happy thing.

Oft through that matted wood of oak and birch
    She came from yonder house upon the hill;
She crossed the wooden bridges to the church,
    And watched, with village girls, my boasted
      skill;
But loved to watch the floating lilies best,
Or linger, peering in a swallow's nest;

Linger and linger with her wistful eyes
    Drawn to the lily-buds that lay so white
And soft on crimson water; for the skies
    Would crimson, and the little cloudlets bright
Would all be flung among the flowers sheer
    down,
To flush the spaces of their clustering crown.

Till the green rushes—O, so glossy green—
    The rushes, they would whisper, rustle, shake;
And forth on floating gauze, no jewelled queen
    So rich, the green-eyed dragon-flies would
      break,
And hover on the flowers—aërial things,
With little rainbows flickering on their wings.

Ah! my heart dear! the polished pools lie still,
    Like lanes of water reddened by the west,
Till, swooping down from yon o'erhanging hill,
    The bold marsh harrier wets her tawny breast;
We scared her oft in childhood from her prey,
And the old eager thoughts rise fresh as
    yesterday.

To yonder copse by moonlight I did go,
  In luxury of mischief, half afraid,
To steal the great owl's brood, her downy snow,
  Her screaming imps to seize, the while she preyed
With yellow, cruel eyes, whose radiant glare,
Fell with their mother rage, I might not dare.

Panting I lay till her great fanning wings
  Troubled the dreams of rock-doves, slumbering nigh,
And she and her fierce mate, like evil things,
  Skimmed the dusk fields; then rising, with a cry
Of fear, joy, triumph, darted on my prey,
And tore it from the nest and fled away.

But afterward, belated in the wood,
  I saw her moping on the rifled tree,
And my heart smote me for her, while I stood
  Awakened from my careless reverie;
So white she looked, with moonlight round her shed,
So motherlike she drooped and hung her head.

O that mine eyes would cheat me! I beheld
  The godwits running by the water edge,
The mossy bridges mirrored as of old;
  The little curlews creeping from the sedge,
But not the little foot so gayly light:
O that mine eyes would cheat me, that I might!—

Would cheat me! I behold the gable ends—
  Those purple pigeons clustering on the cote;
The lane with maples overhung, that bends
  Toward her dwelling; the dry grassy moat,
Thick mullions, diamond latticed, mossed and grey,
And walls banked up with laurel and with bay.

And up behind them yellow fields of corn,
  And still ascending countless firry spires,
Dry slopes of hills uncultured, bare, forlorn,
  And green in rocky clefts with whins and briars;
Then rich cloud masses dyed the violet's hue,
With orange sunbeams dropping swiftly through.

Ay, I behold all this full easily;
  My soul is jealous of my happier eyes,
And manhood envies youth. Ah, strange to see,
  By looking merely, orange-flooded skies;
Nay, any dew-drop that may near me shine:
But never more the face of Eglantine!

She was my one companion, being herself
  The jewel and adornment of my days,
My life's completeness. O, a smiling elf,
  That I do but disparage with my praise—
My playmate; and I loved her dearly and long,
And she loved me, as the tender love the strong.

Ay, but she grew, till on a time there came
  A sudden restless yearning to my heart;
And as we went a-nesting, all for shame
  And shyness, I did hold my peace and start;
Content departed, comfort shut me out,
And there was nothing left to talk about.

She had but sixteen years, and as for me,
  Four added made my life. This pretty bird,
This fairy bird that I had cherished—she,
  Content, had sung, while I contented, heard.
The song hade eased; the bird, with nature's art,
Had brought a thorn and set it in my heart.

The restless birth of love my soul opprest,
  I longed and wrestled for a tranquil day,
And warred with that disquiet in my breast
  As one who knows there is a better way;
But, turned against myself, I still in vain
Looked for the ancient calm to come again.

My tired soul could to itself confess
  That she deserved a wiser love than mine:
To love more truly were to love her less,
  And for this truth I still awoke to pine;
I had a dim belief that it would be
A better thing for her, a blessed thing for me.

Good hast Thou made them—comforters right sweet;
  Good hast Thou made the world, to mankind lent;
Good are Thy dropping clouds that feed the wheat;
  Good are Thy stars above the firmament.
Take to Thee, take, Thy worship, Thy renown;
The good which Thou hast made doth wear Thy crown.

For, O my God, Thy creatures are so frail,
  Thy bountiful creation is so fair,
That, drawn before us like the temple veil,
  It hides the Holy Place from thought and care,
Giving man's eyes instead its sweeping fold,
Rich as with cherub wings and apples wrought of gold,

Purple and blue and scarlet—shimmering bells
  And rare pomegranates on its broidered rim,
Glorious with chain- and fret-work that the swell
  Of incense shakes to music dreamy and dim,
Till on a day comes loss, that God makes gain,
And death and darkness rend the veil in twain.

    *   *   *   *

Ah, sweetest! my beloved! each outward thing
  Recalls my youth and is instinct with thee;
Brown wood-owls in the dusk, with noiseless wing,
  Float from yon hanger to their haunted tree,
And hoot full softly. Listening, I regain
A flashing thought of thee with their remembered strain.

I will not pine—it is the careless brook,
  These amber sunbeams slanting down the vale;

It is the long tree-shadows, with their look
  Of natural peace, that make my heart to fail;
The peace of nature—No, I will not pine—
But O the contrast 'twixt her face and mine!

And still I changed—I was a boy no more;
  My heart was large enough to hold my kind,
And all the world. As hath been oft before
  With youth, I sought, but I could never find
Work hard enough to quiet my self-strife,
And use the strength of action-craving life.

She, too, was changed: her bountiful sweet
    eyes
  Looked out full lovingly on all the world,
O tender as the deeps in yonder skies
  Their beaming! but her rosebud lips were
    curled
With the soft dimple of a musing smile,
Which kept my gaze, but held me mute the
    while.

A cast of bees, a slowly moving wain,
  The scent of bean-flowers wafted up a dell,
Blue pigeons wheeling over fields of grain,
  Or bleat of folded lamb would please her
    well;
Or cooing of the early coted dove;—
  She sauntering mused of these; I, following,
    mused of love.

With her two lips that one the other pressed
  So poutingly with such a tranquil air,
With her two eyes, that on my own would rest
  So dream-like, she denied my silent prayer,
Fronted unuttered word and said them nay,
And smiled down love till it had naught to say.

The words that through mine eyes would clear-
    ly shine
  Hovered and hovered on my lips in vain;
If after pause I said but "Eglantine,"
  She raised to me her quiet eyelids twain,
And looked me this reply—look calm, yet
    bland—
"I shall not know, I will not understand."

Yet she did know my story—knew my life
  Was wrought to her with bindings many and
    strong:
That I, like Israel, served for a wife,
  And for the love I bare her thought not long,
But only a few days, full quickly told,
My seven years' service strict as his of old.

I must be brief: the twilight shadows grow,
  And steal the rose-bloom genial summer
    sheds,
And scented wafts of wind that come and go
  Have lifted dew from honied clover heads;
The seven stars shine out above the mill,
The dark delightsome woods lie veiled and still.

Hush! hush! the nightingale begins to sing,
  And stops, as ill-contented with her note;
Then breaks from out the bush with hurried
    wing,
  Restless and passionate. She tunes her
    throat,
Laments awhile in wavering trills, and then
Floods with a stream of sweetness all the glen.

The seven stars upon the nearest pool
  Lie trembling down betwixt the lily leaves,
And move like glowworms; wafting breezes
    cool
  Come down along the water, and it heaves
And bubbles in the sedge; while deep and wide
The dim night settles on the country side.

I know this scene by heart. O! once before
  I saw the seven stars float to and fro,
And stayed my hurried footsteps by the shore
  To mark the starry picture spread below:
Its silence made the tumult in my breast
More audible; its peace revealed my own un-
    rest.

I paused, then hurried on; my heart beat
    quick;
I crossed the bridges, reached the steep
    ascent,
And climbed through matted fern and hazels
    thick;
  Then darkling through the close green maples
    went
And saw—there felt love's keenest pangs
    begin—
An oriel window lighted from within—

I saw—and felt that they were scarcely cares
  Which I had known before; I drew more
    near,
And O! methought how sore it frets and wears
  The soul to part with that it holds so dear;
'Tis hard two woven tendrils to untwine,
And I was come to part with Eglantine.

For life was bitter through those words re-
    pressed,
  And youth was burdened with unspoken
    vows;
Love unrequited brooded in my breast,
  And shrank, at glance, from the belovèd
    brows:
And three long months, heart-sick, my foot
    withdrawn,
I had not sought her side by rivulet, copse, or
    lawn—

Not sought her side, yet busy thought no less
  Still followed in her wake, though far behind;
And I, being parted from her loveliness,
  Looked at the picture of her in my mind:
I lived alone, I walked with soul opprest,
And ever sighed for her, and sighed for rest.

Then I had risen to struggle with my heart,
  And said—"O heart! the world is fresh
    and fair,

And I am young; but this thy restless smart
  Changes to bitterness the morning air :
I will, I must, these weary fetters break—
I will be free, if only for her sake.

"O let me trouble her no more with sighs !
  Heart-healing comes by distance, and with time :
Then let me wander, and enrich mine eyes
  With the green forests of a softer clime,
Or list by night at sea the wind's low stave
And long monotonous rockings of the wave.

"Through open solitudes, unbounded meads,
  Where, wading on breast-high in yellow bloom,
Untamed of man, the shy white llama feeds—
  There would I journey and forget my doom;
Or far, O far as sunrise I would see
The level prairie stretch away from me.

"Or I would sail upon the tropic seas,
  Where fathom long the blood-red dulses grow,
Droop from the rock and waver in the breeze,
  Lashing the tide to foam ; while calm below
The muddy mandrakes throng those waters warm,
  And purple, gold, and green, the living blossoms swarm."

So of my father I did win consent,
  With importunities repeated long,
To make that duty which had been my bent
  To dig with strangers alien tombs among,
And bound to them through desert leagues to pace,
Or track up rivers to their starting-place.

For this I had done battle and had won,
  But not alone to tread Arabian sands,
Measure the shadows of a southern sun,
  Or dig out gods in the old Egyptian lands ;
But for the dream wherewith I thought to cope—
The grief of love unmated with love's hope.

And now I would set reason in array,
  Methought, and fight for freedom manfully,
Till by long absence there would come a day
  When this my love would not be pain to me;
But if I knew my rosebud fair and blest
I should not pine to wear it on my breast.

The days fled on: another week should fling
  A foreign shadow on my lengthening way ;
Another week, yet nearness did not bring
  A braver heart that hard farewell to say.
I let the last day wane, the dusk begin,
Ere I had sought that window lighted from within.

Sinking and sinking, O my heart ! my heart !
  Will absence heal thee whom its shade doth rend ?

I reached the little gate, and soft within
  The oriel fell her shadow. She did lend
Her loveliness to me, and let me share
The listless sweetness of those features fair.

Among thick laurels in the gathering gloom,
  Heavy for this our parting, I did stand ;
Beside her mother in the lighted room,
  She sitting leaned her cheek upon her hand;
And as she read, her sweet voice floating through
The open casement seemed to mourn me an adieu.

Youth ! youth ! how buoyant are thy hopes ! they turn,
  Like marigolds, toward the sunny side.
My hopes were buried in a funeral urn,
  And they sprung up like plants and spread them wide ;
Though I had schooled and reasoned them away,
They gathered smiling near and prayed a holiday.

Ah, sweetest voice ! how pensive were its tones,
  And how regretful its unconscious pause !
"Is it for me her heart this sadness owns,
  And is our parting of to-night the cause ?
Ah, would it might be so !" I thought, and stood
Listening entranced among the underwood.

I thought it would be something worth the pain
  Of parting, to look once in those deep eyes,
And take from them an answering look again :
  "When eastern palms," I thought, "about me rise,
If I might carve our names upon the rind,
Betrothed, I would not mourn, though leaving thee behind."

I can be patient, faithful, and most fond
  To unacknowledged love; I can be true
To this sweet thraldom, this unequal bond,
  This yoke of mine that reaches not to you :
O, how much more could costly parting buy—
If not a pledge, one kiss, or failing that, a sigh !

I listened, and she ceased to read ; she turned
  Her face toward the laurels where I stood :
Her mother spoke—O wonder ! hardly learned ;
  She said, "There is a rustling in the wood ;
Ah, child ! if one draw near to bid farewell,
Let not thine eyes an unsought secret tell.

"My daughter, there is nothing held so dear
  As love, if only it be hard to win.
The roses that in yonder hedge appear
  Outdo our garden-buds which bloom within ;
But since the hand may pluck them every day,
Unmarked they bud, bloom, drop, and drift away.

"My daughter, my belovèd, be not you
  Like those same roses." O bewildering
    word!
My heart stood still, a mist obscured my view:
  It cleared; still silence. No denial stirred
The lips beloved; but straight, as one opprest,
  She, kneeling, dropped her face upon her
    mother's breast.

This said, "My daughter, sorrow comes to all;
  Our life is checked with shadows manifold:
But woman has this more—she may not call
  Her sorrow by its name. Yet love not told,
And only born of absence and by thought,
With thought and absence may return to
    nought."

And my belovèd lifted up her face,
  And moved her lips as if about to speak;
She dropped her lashes with a girlish grace,
  And the rich damask mantled in her cheek:
I stood awaiting till she should deny
Her love, or with sweet laughter put it by.

But, closer nestling to her mother's heart,
  She, blushing, said no word to break my
    trance,
For I was breathless; and, with lips apart,
  Felt my breast pant and all my pulses dance,
And strove to move, but could not for the
    weight
Of unbelieving joy, so sudden and so great,

Because she loved me. With a mighty sigh
  Breaking away, I left her on her knees,
And blest the laurel bower, the darkened sky,
  The sultry night of August. Through the
    trees,
Giddy with gladness, to the porch I went,
And hardly found the way for joyful wonder-
    ment.

Yet, when I entered, saw her mother sit
  With both hands cherishing the graceful
    head,
Smoothing the clustered hair, and parting it
  From the fair brow; she, rising, only said,
In the accustomed tone, the accustomed word,
The careless greeting that I always heard;

And she resumed her merry, mocking smile,
  Though tear-drops on the glistening lashes
    hung.
O woman! thou wert fashioned to beguile:
  So have all sages said, all poets sung.
She spoke of favoring winds and waiting ships,
With smiles of gratulation on her lips.

And then she looked and faltered: I had grown
  So suddenly in life and soul a man:
She moved her lips, but could not find a tone
  To set her mocking music to; began
One struggle for dominion, raised her eyes,
And straight withdrew them, bashful through
    surprise.

The color over cheek and bosom flushed;
  I might have heard the beating of her heart,
But that mine own beat louder; when she
    blushed,
  The hand within mine own I felt to start,
But would not change my pitiless decree
To strive with her for might and mastery.

She looked again, as one that, half afraid,
  Would fain be certain of a doubtful thing;
Or one beseeching "Do not me upbraid!"
  And then she trembled like the fluttering
Of timid little birds, and silent stood,
No smile wherewith to mock my hardihood.

She turned, and to an open casement moved
  With girlish shyness, mute beneath my gaze,
And I on downcast lashes unreproved
    Could look as long as pleased me; while,
      the rays
Of moonlight round her, she her fair head bent,
In modest silence to my words attent.

How fast the giddy whirling moments flew!
  The moon had set; I heard the midnight
    chime;
Hope is more brave than fear, and joy than
    dread,
  And I could wait unmoved the parting time.
It came; for by a sudden impulse drawn,
She, risen, stepped out upon the dusky lawn.

A little waxen taper in her hand,
  Her feet upon the dry and dewless grass,
She looked like one of the celestial band,
  Only that on her cheeks did dawn and pass
Most human blushes; while, the soft light
    thrown
On vesture pure and white, she seemed yet
    fairer grown.

Her mother, looking out toward her, sighed,
  Then gave her hand in token of farewell,
And with her warning eyes, that seemed to
    chide,
  Scarce suffered that I sought her child to tell
The story of my life, whose every line
No other burden bore than—Eglantine.

Black thunder-clouds were rising up behind,
  The waxen taper burned full steadily;
It seemed as if dark midnight had a mind
  To hear what lovers say, and her decree
Had passed for silence, while she, dropped to
    ground
With raiment floating wide, drank in the sound.

O happiness! thou dost not leave a trace
  So well defined as sorrow. Amber light,
Shed like a glory on her angel face,
  I can remember fully, and the sight
Of her fair forehead and her shining eyes,
And lips that smiled in sweet and girlish wise.

I can remember how the taper played
  Over her small hands and her vesture white;
How it struck up into the trees, and laid
  Upon their under leaves unwonted light;
And when she held it low, how far it spread
O'er velvet pansies slumbering on their bed.

I can remember that we spoke full low,
  That neither doubted of the other's truth;
And that with footsteps slower and more slow,
  Hands folded close for love, eyes wet for ruth:
Beneath the trees, by that clear taper's flame,
We wander till the gate of parting came.

But I forget the parting words she said,
  So much they thrilled the all-attentive soul;
For one short moment human heart and head
  May bear such bliss—its present is the whole:
I had that present, till in whispers fell
With parting gesture her subdued farewell.

Farewell! she said, in act to turn away,
  But stood a moment still to dry her tears,
And suffered my enfolding arm to stay
  The time of her departure. O ye years
That intervene betwixt that day and this!
You all received your hue from that keen pain and bliss.

O mingled pain and bliss! O pain to break
  At once from happiness so lately found,
And four long years to feel for her sweet sake
  The incompleteness of all sight and sound.
But bliss to cross once more the foaming brine—
O bliss to come again and make her mine!

I cannot—O, I cannot more recall!
  But I will soothe my troubled thoughts to rest
With musing over journeyings wide, and all
  Observance of this active-humored west,
And swarming cities steeped in eastern day,
With swarthy tribes in gold and striped array.

I turn from these, and straight there will succeed
  (Shifting and changing at the restless will),
Imbedded in some deep Circassian mead,
  White wagon-tilts, and flocks that eat their fill
Unseen above, while comely shepherds pass,
And scarcely show their heads above the grass.

—The red Sahara in an angry glow,
  With amber fogs, across its hollows trailed
Long strings of camels, gloomy-eyed and slow,
  And women on their necks, from gazers veiled,
And sun-swart guides who toil across the sand
To groves of date-trees on the watered land.

Again—the brown sails of an Arab boat,
  Flapping by night upon a glassy sea,
Whereon the moon and planets seem to float,
  More bright of hue than they were wont to be,

While shooting-stars rain down with crackling sound,
And, thick as swarming locusts, drop to ground.

Or far into the heat among the sands
  The gembok nations, snuffing up the wind,
Drawn by the scent of water—and the bands
  Of tawny-bearded lions pacing, blind
With the sun-dazzle in their midst, opprest
With prey, and spiritless for lack of rest!

What more? Old Lebanon, the frosty-browed,
  Setting his feet among oil-olive trees,
Heaving his bare brown shoulder through a cloud;
  And after, grassy Carmel, purple seas,
Flattering his dreams and echoing in his rocks,
Soft as the bleating of his thousand flocks.

Enough: how vain this thinking to beguile,
  With recollected scenes, an aching breast!
Did not I, journeying, muse on her the while?
  Ah, yes! for every landscape comes impressed—
Ay, written on, as by an iron pen—
With the same thought I nursed about her then.

Therefore let memory turn again to home;
  Feel, as of old, the joy of drawing near;
Watch the green breakers and the wind-tossed foam,
  And see the land-fog break, dissolve, and clear;
Then think a skylark's voice far sweeter sound
Than ever thrilled but over English ground;

And walk, glad, even to tears, among the wheat,
  Not doubting this to be the first of lands;
And, while in foreign words this murmuring, meet
  Some little village schoolgirls (with their hands
Full of forget-me-nots), who greeting me,
I count their English talk delightsome melody;

And seat me on a bank, and draw them near,
  That I may feast myself with hearing it,
Till shortly they forget their bashful fear,
  Push back their flaxen curls, and round me sit—
Tell me their names, their daily tasks, and show
Where wild wood strawberries in the copses grow.

So passed the day in this delightsome land:
  My heart was thankful for the English tongue—
For English sky with feathery cloudlets spanned—
  For English hedge with glistening dewdrops hung,
I journeyed, and at glowing eventide
Stopped at a rustic inn by the wayside.

That night I slumbered sweetly, being right glad
  To miss the flapping of the shrouds; but lo!
A quiet dream of beings twain I had,
  Behind the curtain talking soft and low :
Methought I did not heed their utterance fine,
Till one of them said softly, "Eglantine."

I started up awake, 'twas silence all :
  My own fond heart had shaped that utterance clear ;
And "Ah !" methought, "how sweetly did it fall,
  Though but in a dream, upon the listening ear !
How sweet from other lips the name well known—
That name, so many a year heard only from mine own !

I thought awhile, then slumber came to me,
  And tangled all my fancy in her maze,
And I was drifting on a raft at sea,
  The near all ocean, and the far all haze ;
Through the white polished water sharks did glide,
And up in heaven I saw stars to guide.

"Have mercy, God !" but lo ! my raft uprose ;
  Drip, drip, I heard the water splash from it ;
My raft had wings, and as the petrel goes,
  It skimmed the sea, then brooding seemed to sit
The milk-white mirror, till, with sudden spring,
It flew straight upward like a living thing.

But strange !—I went not also in that flight,
  For I was entering at a cavern's mouth ;
Trees grew within, and screaming birds of night
  Sat on them, hiding from the torrid south.
On, on I went, while gleaming in the dark
Those trees with blanchèd leaves stood pale and stark.

The trees had flower-buds, nourished in deep night,
  And suddenly, as I went farther in,
They opened, and they shot out lambent light ;
  Then all at once arose a railing din
That frighted me : "It is the ghosts," I said,
"And they are railing for their darkness fled.

"I hope they will not look me in the face ;
  It frighteth me to hear their laughter loud ;"
I saw them troop before with jaunty pace,
  And one would shake off dust that soiled her shroud ;
But now, O joy unhoped ! to calm my dread,
Some moonlight filtered through a cleft o'erhead.

I climbed the lofty trees—the blanchèd trees—
  The cleft was wide enough to let me through ;
I clambered out and felt the balmy breeze,
  And stepped on churchyard grasses wet with dew.
O happy chance ! O fortune to admire !
I stood beside my own loved village spire.

And as I gazed upon the yew-tree's trunk,
  Lo, far off music—music in the night !
So sweet and tender as it swelled and sunk ;
  It charmed me till I wept with keen delight,
And in my dream, methought as it drew near
The very clouds in heaven stooped low to hear.

Beat high, beat low, wild heart so deeply stirred,
  For high as heaven runs up the piercing strain ;
The restless music fluttering like a bird
  Bemoaned herself, and dropped to earth again,
Heaping up sweetness till I was afraid
That I should die of grief when it did fade.

And it DID fade ; but while with eager ear
  I drank its last long echo dying away,
I was aware of footsteps that drew near,
  And round the ivied chancel seemed to stray :
O soft above the hallowed place they trod—
Soft as the fall of foot that is not shod !

I turned—'twas even so—yes, Eglantine !
  For at the first I had divined the same ;
I saw the moon on her shut eyelids shine,
  And said "She is asleep ;" still on she came;
Then, on her dimpled feet, I saw it gleam,
And thought—" I know that this is but a dream."

My darling ! O my darling ! not the less
  My dream went on because I knew it such ;
She came towards me in her loveliness—
  A thing too pure, methought, for mortal touch ;
The rippling gold did on her bosom meet,
The long white robe descended to her feet.

The fringèd lids drooped low, as sleep-oppressed ;
  Her dreamy smile was very fair to see,
And her two hands were folded to her breast,
  With somewhat held between them heedfully.
O fast asleep ! and yet methought she knew
And felt my nearness those shut eyelids through.

She sighed ; my tears ran down for tenderness—
  "And have I drawn thee to me in my sleep ?
Is it for me thou wanderest shelterless,
  Wetting thy steps in dewy grasses deep ?
O if this be !" I said—"yet speak to me ;
I blame my very dream for cruelty."

Then from her stainless bosom she did take
  Two beauteous lily flowers that lay therein,
And with slow-moving lips a gesture make,
  As one that some forgotten words doth win :

"They floated on the pool," methought she said,
And water trickled from each lily's head.

It dropped upon her feet—I saw it gleam
 Along the ripples of her yellow hair,
And stood apart, for only in a dream
 She would have come, methought, to meet me there.
She spoke again—"Ah fair! ah fresh they shine!
And there are many left, and these are mine."

I answered her with flattering accents meet—
 "Love, they are whitest lilies e'er were blown,"
"And sayest thou so?" she sighed in murmurs sweet;
 "I have nought else to give thee now, mine own!
For it is night. Then take them, love!" said she:
"They have been costly flowers to thee—and me."

While thus she said I took them from her hand,
 And, overcome with love and nearness woke;
And overcome with ruth that she should stand
 Barefooted on the grass that; when she spoke,
Her mystic words should take so sweet a tone,
And of all names her lips should choose "My own."

I rose, I journeyed, neared my home, and soon
 Beheld the spire peer out above the hill:
It was a sunny harvest afternoon,
 When by the churchyard wicket, standing still,
I cast my eager eyes abroad to know
If change had touched the scenes of long ago.

I looked across the hollow; sunbeams shone
 Upon the old house with the gable ends:
"Save that the laurel-trees are taller grown,
 No change," methought, "to its grey wall extends.
What clear bright beams on yonder lattice shine!
There did I sometime talk with Eglantine."

There standing with my very goal in sight,
 Over my haste did sudden quiet steal;
I thought to dally with my own delight,
 Nor rush on headlong to my garnered weal,
But taste the sweetness of a short delay,
And for a little moment hold the bliss at bay.

The church was open; it perchance might be
 That there to offer thanks I might essay,
Or rather, as I think, that I might see
 The place where Eglantine was wont to pray.
But so it was; I crossed that portal wide,
And felt my riot joy to calm subside.

The low depending curtains, gently swayed,
 Cast over arch and roof a crimson glow;
But, ne'ertheless, all silence and all shade
 It seemed, save only for the rippling flow
Of their long foldings, when the sunset air
Sighed through the casements of the house of prayer.

I found her place, the ancient oaken stall,
 Where in her childhood I had seen her sit,
Most saint-like and most tranquil there of all,
 Folding her hands, as if a dreaming fit—
A heavenly vision had before her strayed
Of the Eternal Child in lowly manger laid.

I saw her prayer-book laid upon the seat,
 And took it in my hand, and felt more near
In fancy to her, finding it most sweet
 To think how very oft, low kneeling there,
In her devout thoughts she had let me share,
And set my graceless name in her pure prayer.

My eyes were dazzled with delightful tears—
 In sooth they were the last I ever shed;
For with them fell the cherished dream of years.
 I looked, and on the wall above my head,
Over her seat, there was a tablet placed,
With one word only on the marble traced.—

Ah, well! I would not overstate that woe,
 For I have had some blessings, little care;
But since the falling of that heavy blow,
 God's earth has never seemed to me so fair;
Nor any of His creatures so divine,
Nor sleep so sweet;—the word was—EGLANTINE.

A MOTHER SHOWING THE PORTRAIT OF HER CHILD.

(F. M. L.)

IVING CHILD or pictured cherub
Ne'er o'er matched its baby grace;
And the mother, moving nearer,
Looked it calmly in the face;
Then with slight and quiet gesture,
And with lips that scarcely smiled,
Said—"A Portrait of my daughter
When she was a child."

Easy thought was hers to fathom,
Nothing hard her glance to read,
For it seemed to say, "No praises
For this little child I need :
If you see, I see far better,
And I will not feign to care
For a stranger's prompt assurance
That the face is fair."

Softly clasped and half extended,
She her dimpled hands doth lay :
So they doubtless placed them, saying—
"Little one, you must not play."
And while yet his work was growing,
This the painter's hand hath shown,
That the little heart was making
Pictures of its own.

Is it warm in that green valley,
Vale of childhood, where you dwell?
Is it calm in that green valley,
Round whose bournes such great hills swell?
Are there giants in the valley—
Giants leaving footprints yet?
Are there angels in the valley?
Tell me—I forget.

Answer, answer, for the lilies,
Little one, o'ertop you much,
And the mealy gold within them
You can scarcely reach to touch;
O how far their aspect differs,
Looking up and looking down !
You look up in that green valley—
Valley of renown.

Are there voices in the valley,
Lying near the heavenly gate?
When it opens, do the harp-strings,
Touched within, reverberate?
When, like shooting-stars, the angels
To your couch at nightfall go,
Are their swift wings heard to rustle?
Tell me ! for you know.

Yes, you know; and you are silent,
Not a word shall asking win ;
Little mouth more sweet than rosebud
Fast it locks the secret in.
Not a glimpse upon your present
You unfold to glad my view ;
Ah, what secrets of your future
I could tell to you !

Sunny present! thus I read it,
By remembrance of my past :—
Its to-day and its to-morrow
Are as lifetimes vague and vast ;
And each face in that green valley
Takes for you an aspect mild,
And each voice grows soft in saying—
"Kiss me, little child !"

As a boon the kiss is granted :
Baby mouth, your touch is sweet,
Takes the love without the trouble
From those lips that with it meet ;
Gives the love, O pure ! O tender !
Of the valley where it grows,
But the baby heart receiveth
MORE THAN IT BESTOWS.

Comes the future to the present—
"Ah !" she saith, " too blithe of mood ;
Why that smile which seems to whisper—
'I am happy, God is good ?'
God IS good : that truth eternal
Sown for you in happier years,
I must tend it in my shadow,
Water it with tears.

"Ah, sweet present ! I must lead thee
By a daylight more subdued ;
There must teach thee low to whisper—
'I am mournful, God is good !'"
Peace, thou future ! clouds are coming,
Stooping from the mountain crest,
But that sunshine floods the valley
Let her—let her rest.

Comes the future to the present—
"Child," she saith, "and wilt thou rest ?
How long, child, before thy footsteps
Fret to reach yon cloudy crest ?
Ah, the valley !—angels guard it,
But the heights are brave to see ;
Looking down were long contentment :
Come up, child, to me."

So she speaks, but do not heed her,
Little maid with wondrous eyes,
Not afraid, but clear and tender,

Blue, and filled with prophecies ;
Thou for whom life's veil unlifted
  Hangs, whom warmest valleys fold,
Lift the veil, the charm dissolveth—
    Climb, but heights are cold.

There are buds that fold within them,
  Closed and covered from our sight,
Many a richly-tinted petal,
  Never looked on by the light :
Fain to see their shrouded faces,
  Sun and dew are long at strife,
Till at length the sweet buds open—
    Such a bud is life.

When the rose of thine own being
  Shall reveal its central fold,
Thou shalt look within and marvel,
  Fearing what thine eyes behold ;
What it shows and what it teaches
  Are not things wherewith to part ;
Thorny rose ! that always costeth
    Beatings at the heart.

Look in fear, for there is dimness ;
  Ills unshapen float anigh.
Look in awe : for this same nature
  Once the Godhead deigned to die.
Look in love, for He doth love it,
  And its tale is best of lore :
Still humanity grows dearer,
    Being learned the more.

Learn, but not the less bethink thee
  How that all can mingle tears ;
But his joy can none discover,
  Save to them that are his peers ;
And that they whose lips do utter
  Language such as bards have sung—
Lo ! their speech shall be to many
    As an unknown tongue.

Learn, that if to thee the meaning
  Of all other eyes be shown,
Fewer eyes can ever front thee,
  That are skilled to read thine own ;
And that if thy love's deep current
  Many another's far outflows
Then thy heart must take for ever
    LESS THAN IT BESTOWS.

STRIFE AND PEACE.

Written for THE PORTFOLIO SOCIETY, October, 1861.

THE yellow poplar leaves came down,
    And like a carpet lay,
No waftings were in the sunny air
    To flutter them away;
And he stepped on blithe and debonair
    That warm October day.

"The boy," saith he, "hath got his own,
    But sore has been the fight,
For ere his life began the strife
    That ceased but yesternight;
For the will," he said, "the kinsfolk read,
    And read it not aright.

"His cause was argued in the court
    Before his christening day,
And counsel was heard, and judge demurred,
    And bitter waxed the fray;
Brother with brother spake no word
    When they met in the way.

"Against each one did each contend,
    And all against the heir.
I would not bend, for I knew the end—
    I have it for my share,
And nought repent, though my first friend
    From henceforth I must spare.

"Manor and moor and farm and wold
    Their greed begrudged him sore,
And parchments old with passionate hold
    They guarded heretofore;
And they carped at signature and seal,
    But they may carp no more.

"An old affront will stir the heart
    Through years of rankling pain,
And I feel the fret that urged me yet
    That warfare to maintain;
For an enemy's loss may well be set
    Above an infant's gain.

"An enemy's loss I go to prove;
    Laugh out thou little heir!
Laugh in his face who vowed to chase
    Thee from thy birthright fair;
For I come to set thee in thy place:
    Laugh out, and do not spare."

A man of strife, in wrathful mood
    He neared the nurse's door;
With poplar leaves the roof and eaves
    Were thickly scattered o'er,
And yellow as they a sunbeam lay
    Along the cottage floor.

"Sleep on, thou pretty, pretty lamb,"
    He hears the fond nurse say;
"And if angels stand at thy right hand,
    As now belike they may,
And if angels meet at thy bed's feet,
    I fear them not this day.

"Come wealth, come want to thee, dear heart,
    It was all one to me,
For thy pretty tongue far sweeter rung
    Than coinèd gold and fee;
And ever the while thy waking smile
    It was right fair to see.

"Sleep, pretty bairn, and never know
    Who grudged and who transgressed;
Thee to retain I was full fain,
    But God, He knoweth best!
And His peace upon thy brow lies plain
    As the sunshine on thy breast!"

The man of strife, he enters in,
    Looks, and his pride doth cease;
Anger and sorrow shall be to-morrow
    Trouble, and no release;
But the babe whose life awoke the strife
    Hath entered into peace.

A STORY OF DOOM

AND OTHER POEMS..

Poems.

THE DREAMS THAT CAME TRUE.

I SAW in a vision once, our mother-sphere
    The world, her fixed foredoomèd
        oval tracing,
    Rolling and rolling on and resting
        never,
    While like a phantom fell, be-
        hind her pacing
    The unfurled flag of night, her
        shadow drear
Fled as she fled and hung to her forever.

Great heaven! methought, how strange a doom
    to share,
    Would I may never bear
    Inevitable darkness after me
(Darkness endowed with drawings strong,
    And shadowy hands that cling unendingly),
    Nor feel that phantom-wings behind me
        sweep,
As she feels night pursuing through the long
    Illimitable reaches of "the vasty deep."

God save you gentlefolks. There was a man
    Who lay awake at midnight on his bed,
    Watching the spiral flame that feeding ran
    Among the logs upon his hearth, and shed
A comfortable glow, both warm and dim,
On crimson curtains that encompassed him.

Right stately was his chamber, soft and white
    The pillow, and his quilt was eider-down.
What mattered it to him through all that night
    The desolate driving cloud might lower and
        frown,
And winds were up the eddying sleet to chase,
That drave and drave and found no settling-
        place?

What mattered it that leafless trees might rock,
    Or snow might drift athwart his window-
        pane?
He bare a charmèd life against their shock,
    Secure from cold, hunger and weather stain;
Fixed in his right, and born to good estate,
From common ills set by and separate.

From work and want and fear of want apart,
    This man (men called him Justice Wilver-
        more)—
This man had comforted his cheerful heart
    With all that it desired from every shore,
He had a right,—the right of gold is strong,—
He stood upon his right his whole life long.

Custom makes all things easy, and content
    Is careless, therefore on the storm and cold,
As he lay waking, never a thought he spent,
    Albeit across the vale beneath the wold,
Along a reedy mere that frozen lay,
A range of sordid hovels stretched away.

What cause had he to think on them forsooth?
    What cause that night beyond another night?
He was familiar even from his youth
    With their long ruin and their evil plight.
The wintry wind would search them like a
        scout,
The water froze within as freely as without.

He think upon them? No! They were for-
    lorn,
    So were the cowering inmates whom they
        held;
A thriftless tribe, to shifts and leanness born,
    Ever complaining: infancy or eld
Alike. But there was rent, or long ago
Those cottage roofs had met with overthrow.

For this they stood; and what his thoughts
    might be
    This winter night, I know not; but I know
That, while the creeping flame fed silently
    And cast upon his bed a crimson glow,
The Justice slept, and shortly in his sleep
He fell to dreaming, and his dream was deep.

He dreamed that over him a shadow came;
    And when he looked to find the cause, behold
Some person knelt between him and the flame:
    A cowering figure of one frail and old,—
A woman; and she prayed as he descried,
And spread her feeble hands, and shook and
        sighed.

"Good heaven!" the Justice cried, and being
    distraught,
He called not to her, but he looked again:
She wore a tattered cloak, but she had naught
    Upon her head; and she did quake amain,
And spread her wasted hands and poor attire
To gather in the brightness of his fire.

"I know you, woman!" then the Justice cried;
    "I know that woman well," he cried aloud;
"The shepherd Aveland's widow: God me
    guide!
A pauper kneeling on my hearth": and
    bowed,
The hag, like one at home, its warmth to share!
"How dares she to intrude? What does she
    here?

"Ho, woman, ho!"—but yet she did not stir,
    Though from her lips a fitful plaining broke;
"I'll ring my people up to deal with her;
    I'll rouse the house," he cried; but while he
    spoke
He turned, and saw, but distant from his bed,
Another form,—a Darkness with a head,

Then, in a rage, he shouted "Who are you?"
    For little in the gloom he might discern.
"Speak out; speak now; or I will make you
    rue
The hour!" but there was silence, and a stern,
Dark face from out the dusk appeared to lean,
And then again drew back, and was not seen.

"God!" cried the dreaming man, right im-
    piously,
    "What have I done, that these my sleep
    affray!"
"God!" said the Phantom, "I appeal to Thee,
    Appoint Thou me this man to be my prey."
"God!" sighed the kneeling woman, frail and
    old,
"I pray Thee take me, for the world is cold."

Then said the trembling Justice, in affright,
    "Fiend, I adjure thee, speak thine errand
    here!"
And lo! it pointed in the falling light
    Toward the woman, answering, cold and
    clear,
"Thou art ordained an answer to thy prayer;
But first to tell *her* tale that kneeleth there."

"*Her* tale!" the Justice cried. "A pauper's
    tale!"
And he took heart at this so low behest,
And let the stoutness of his will prevail,
    Demanding, "Is 't for *her* you break my rest?
She went to jail of late for stealing wood,
She will again for this night's hardihood.

"I sent her; and to morrow, as I live,
    I will commit her for this trespass here."
"Thou wilt not!" quoth the Shadow, "thou
    wilt give

Her story words"; and then it stalked anear
And showed a lowering face, and, dread to see,
A countenance of angered majesty.

Then said the Justice, all his thoughts astray,
    With that material Darkness chiding him,
"If this must be, then speak to her, I pray,
    And bid her move, for all the room is dim
By reason of the place she holds to-night:
She kneels between me and the warmth and
    light."

"With adjurations deep and drawings strong,
    And with the power," it said, "unto me
    given,
I call upon thee, man, to tell thy wrong,
    Or look no more upon the face of Heaven.
Speak! though she kneel throughout the live-
    long night,
And yet shall kneel between thee and the light."

This when the Justice heard, he raised his hands,
    And held them as the dead in effigy
Hold theirs when carved upon a tomb. The
    bands
Of fate had bound him fast: no remedy
Was left: his voice unto himself was strange,
And that unearthly vision did not change.

He said, "That woman dwells anear my door,
    Her life and mine began the selfsame day,
And I am hale and hearty: from my store
    I never spared her aught: she takes her way
Of me unheeded; pining, pinching care
Is all the portion that she has to share.

"She is a broken-down, poor, friendless wight,
    Through labor and through sorrow early old;
And I have known of this her evil plight,
    Her scanty earnings, and her lodgment cold;
A patienter poor soul shall ne'er be found:
She labored on my land the long year round.

"What wouldst thou have me say, thou fiend
    abhorred?
Show me no more thine awful visage grim.
If thou obey'st a greater, tell thy lord
    That I have paid her wages. Cry to him!
He has not *much* against me. None can say
I have not paid her wages day by day.

"The spell! It draws me. I must speak
    again;
And speak against myself; and speak aloud.
The woman once approached me to complain—
    'My wages are so low.' I may be proud;
It is a fault." "Ay," quoth the phantom fell,
"Sinner! it is a fault: thou sayest well."

"She made her moan, 'My wages are so
    low.'"
    "Tell on!" "She said," he answered,
    "'My best days
Are ended, and the summer is but slow

To come : and my good strength for work
  decays
By reason that I live so hard, and lie
On winter nights so bare for poverty.'"

"And you replied," began the lowering shade,
  "And I replied," the Justice followed on,
"That wages like to mine my neighbor paid ;
  And if I raised the wages of the one
Straight should the others murmur ; further-
  more,
The winter was as winters gone before,

"No colder and not longer." "Afterward?"
  The Phantom questioned. "Afterward," he
  groaned,
"She said my neighbor was a right good lord,
  Never a roof was broken that he owned ;
He gave much coal and clothing, 'Doth he
  so ?
Work for my neighbor, then,' I answered.
  'Go !'

"'You are full welcome.' Then she mumbled
  out
She hoped I was not angry ; hoped, forsooth,
I would forgive her : and I turned about,
  And said I should be angry in good truth
If this should be again, or ever more
  She dared to stop me thus at the church door."

"Then?" quoth the Shade ; and he, con-
  strained, said on,
"Then she, reproved, curtseyed herself
  away."
"Hast met her since?" it made demand anon ;
  And after pause, the Justice answered, "Ay ;
Some wood was stolen ; my people made a
  stir ;
She was accused, and I did sentence her."

But yet and yet, the dreaded questions came :
  "And didst thou weigh the matter,—taking
  thought
Upon her sober life and honest fame ?"
  "I gave it," he replied, with gaze distraught ;
"I gave it, Fiend, the usual care ; I took
  The usual pains ; I could not nearer look,

"Because—because their pilfering had got head.
  What wouldst thou more ? The neighbors
  pleaded hard,
'Tis true, and many tears the creature shed ;
  But I had vowed their prayers to disregard,
Heavily strike the first that robbed my land,
  And put down thieving with a steady hand.

"She said she was not guilty. Ay, 'tis true
  She said so, but the poor are liars all.
O thou fell Fiend, what wilt thou ? Must I
  view
Thy darkness yet, and must thy shadow fall
  Upon me miserable ? I have done
No worse, no more than many a scathless one."

"Yet," quoth the Shade, "if ever to thine ears
  The knowledge of her blamelessness was
  brought,
Or others have confessed with dying tears
  The crime she suffered for, and thou hast
  wrought
All reparation in thy power, and told
  Into her empty hand thy brightest gold :—

"If thou hast honored her, and hast proclaimed
  Her innocence and thy deplorèd wrong,
Still thou art naught ; for thou shalt yet be
  blamed
In that she, feeble, came before thee, strong,
  And thou, in cruel haste to deal a blow,
Because thou hadst been angered, worked her
  woe.

"But didst thou right her ? Speak !" The
  Justice sighed,
And beaded drops stood out upon his brow ;
"How could I humble me," forlorn he cried,
  "To a base beggar ? Nay, I will avow
That I did ill. I will reveal the whole ;
I kept that knowledge in my secret soul."

"Hear him !" the Phantom muttered ; "hear
  this man,
O changeless God upon the judgment
  throne."
With that, cold tremors through his pulses ran,
  And lamentably he did make his moan ;
While, with its arms upraised above his head,
The dim dread visitor approached his bed.

"Into these doors," it said, "which thou hast
  closed,
Daily this woman shall from henceforth come ;
Her kneeling form shall yet be interposed,
  Till all thy wretched hours have told their
  sum,—
Shall yet be interposed by day, by night,
  Between thee, sinner, and the warmth and
  light.

"Remembrance of her want shall make thy
  meal
Like ashes, and thy wrong thou shalt not
  right.
But what ! nay, verily, nor wealth nor weal
  From henceforth shall afford thy soul delight.
Till men shall lay thy head beneath the sod,
There shall be no deliverance, saith my God."

"Tell me thy name," the dreaming Justice
  cried ;
"By what appointment dost thou doom me
  thus ?"
"'Tis well thou shouldst know me," it replied,
  "For mine thou art, and naught shall sever
  us ;
From thine own lips and life I draw my force ;
The name thy nation give me is REMORSE."

This when he heard, the dreaming man cried
  out,
And woke affrighted; and a crimson glow
The dying ember shed. Within; without,
In eddying rings the silence seemed to flow;
The wind had lulled, and on his forehead shone
The last low gleam; he was indeed alone.

"O, I have had a fearful dream," said he;
"I will take warning, and for mercy trust;
The fiend Remorse shall never dwell with me;
I will repair that wrong, I will be just,
I will be kind, I will my ways amend."
Now the first dream is told unto its end.

Anigh the frozen mere a cottage stood,
  A piercing wind swept round and shook the
    door,
The shrunken door, and easy way made good,
  And drave long drifts of snow along the floor.
It sparkled there like diamonds, for the moon
Was shining in, and night was at the noon.

Before her dying embers, bent and pale,
  A woman sat because her bed was cold;
She heard the wind, the driving sleet and hail,
  And she was hunger-bitten, weak, and old;
Yet while she cowered, and while the casement
    shook,
Upon her trembling knees she held a book—

A comfortable book for them that mourn,
  And good to raise the courage of the poor;
It lifts the veil and shows, beyond the bourne,
  Their Elder Brother, from His home secure,
That for them desolate He died to win,
Repeating, "Come, ye blessed, enter in."

What thought she on, this woman? on her days
  Of toil, or on the supperless night forlorn?
I think not so; the heart but seldom weighs
  With conscious care a burden always borne;
And she was used to these things, had grown
    old
In fellowship with toil, hunger, and cold.

Then did she think how sad it was to live
  Of all the good this world can yield bereft?
No, her untutored thoughts she did not give
  To such a theme; but in their warp and weft
She wove a prayer; then in the midnight deep
Faintly and slow she fell away to sleep.

A strange, a marvellous sleep, which brought
    a dream,
  And it was this: that all at once she heard
The pleasant babbling of a little stream
  That ran beside her door, and then a bird
Broke out in songs. She looked, and lo!
    the rime
And snow had melted; it was summer time!

And all the cold was over, and the mere
  Full sweetly swayed the flags and rushes
    green;
The mellow sunlight poured right warm and
    clear
  Into her casement, and thereby were seen
Fair honeysuckle flowers, and wandering bees
Were hovering round the blossom-laden trees.

She said, "I will betake me to my door,
  And will look out and see this wondrous
    sight,
How summer is come back, and frost is o'er,
  And all the air warm waxen in a night."
With that she opened, but for fear she cried,
For lo! two Angels,—one on either side.

And while she looked, with marvelling mea-
    sureless,
  The Angels stood conversing face to face,
But neither spoke to her. "The wilderness,"
  One Angel said, "the solitary place,
Shall yet be glad for Him." And then full
    fain
The other Angel answered, "He shall reign."

And when the woman heard, in wondering
    wise,
  She whispered, "They are speaking of my
    Lord."
And straightway swept across the open skies
  Multitudes like to these. They took the
    word,
That flock of Angels, "He shall come again,
My Lord, my Lord!" they sang, "and He
    shall reign!"

Then, they, drawn up into the blue o'erhead,
  Right happy, shining ones, made haste to
    flee;
And those before her one to other said,
  "Behold he stands aneath yon almond-tree."
This when the woman heard, she fain had
    gazed,
But paused for reverence, and bowed down
    amazed.

After she looked, for this her dream was deep;
  She looked, and there was naught beneath
    the tree;
Yet did her love and longing overleap
  The fear of Angels, awful though they be,
And she passed out between the blessed things,
And brushed her mortal weeds against their
    wings.

O, all the happy world was in its best,
  The trees were covered thick with buds and
    flowers,
And these were dropping honey; for the rest,
  Sweetly the birds were piping in their
    bowers;
Across the grass did groups of Angels go,
And Saints in pairs were walking to and fro.

Then did she pass toward the almond-tree,
  And none she saw beneath it; yet each Saint
Upon His coming meekly bent the knee,

And all their glory as they gazed waxed
    faint.
And then a lighting Angel neared the place,
And folded his fair wings before his face.

She also knelt, and spread her aged hands
    As feeling for the sacred human feet ;
She said, "Mine eyes are held, but if He
    stands
Anear, I will not let Him hence retreat
Except He bless me." Then, O sweet ! O
    fair !
Some words were spoken but she knew not
    where.

She knew not if beneath the boughs they woke,
    Or dropt upon her from the realms above ;
"What wilt thou, woman?" in the dream He
    spoke ;
"Thy sorrow moveth Me, thyself I love ;
Long have I counted up thy mournful years,
Once I did weep to wipe away thy tears."

She said : "My one Redeemer, only blest,
    I know Thy voice, and from my yearning
    heart
Draw out my deep desire, my great request,
    My prayer, that I might enter where Thou
    art.
Call me, O call from this world troublesome,
And let me see Thy face." He answered,
    "Come."

Here is the ending of the second dream.
It is a frosty morning, keen and cold,
Fast locked are silent mere and frozen stream.
    And snow lies sparkling on the desert wold ;
With savory morning meats they spread the
    board,
But Justice Wilvermore will walk abroad.

"Bring me my cloak," quoth he, as one in
    haste.
"Before you breakfast, sir ?" his man
    replies.
"Ay," quoth he, quickly, and he will not taste
Of aught before him, but in urgent wise,
As he would fain some carking care allay,
Across the frozen field he takes his way.

"A dream ! how strange that it should move
    me so,
    'Twas but a dream," quoth Justice Wilver-
    more :
"And yet I cannot peace nor pleasure know,
    For wrongs I have not heeded heretofore ;
Silver and gear the crone shall have of me,
And dwell for life in yonder cottage free.

" For visions of the night are fearful things,
    Remorse is dread, though merely in a dream ;
I will not subject me to visitings
    Of such a sort again.   I will esteem
My peace above my pride.   From natures rude
A little gold will buy me gratitude.

" The woman shall have leave to gather wood,
    As much as she may need the long year
    round ;
She shall, I say ; moreover, it were good
    Yon other cottage roofs to render sound.
Thus to my soul the ancient peace restore,
And sleep at ease," quoth Justice Wilvermore.

With that he nears the door : a frosty rime
    Is branching over it, and drifts are deep
Against the wall.   He knocks, and there is
    time—
(For none doth open),—time to list the
    sweep
And whistle of the wind along the mere,
Through beds of stiffened reeds and rushes
    sear.

"If she be out, I have my pains for naught,"
    He saith, and knocks again, and yet once
    more,
But to his ear nor step nor stir is brought ;
    And after pause he doth unlatch the door
And enter.   No ; she is not out, for see,
She sits asleep 'mid frost-work winterly.

Asleep, asleep before her empty grate,
    Asleep, asleep, albeit the landlord call.
"What, dame," he saith, aud comes toward
    her straight,
"Asleep so early !"   But whate'er befall
She sleepeth ; then he nears her, and behold
He lays a hand on hers, and it is cold.

Then doth the Justice to his home return ;
    From that day forth he wears a sadder brow;
His hands are opened, and his heart doth learn
    The patience of the poor.   He made a vow
And keeps it, for the old and sick have shared
His gifts, their sordid homes he hath repaired.

And some he hath made happy, but for him
    Is happiness no more.   He doth repent,
And now the light of joy is waxen dim,
    Are all his hopes towards the Highest sent ;
He looks for mercy, and he waits release
Above, for this world doth not yield him peace.

Night after night, night after desolate night,
    Day after day, day after tedious day,
Stands by his fire, and dulls its gleamy light,
    Paceth behind or meets him in the way ;
Or shares the path by hedge-row, mere, or
    stream,
The visitor that doomed him in his dream.

Thy kingdom come.
I heard a Seer cry : "The wilderness,
    The solitary place,
Shall yet be glad for Him, and He shall bless

(Thy kingdom come) with His revealéd face
The forests; they shall drop their precious gum,
And shed for Him their balm; and He shall yield
The grandeur of His speech to charm the field.

"Then all the soothéd winds shall drop to listen,
(Thy kingdom come,)
Comforted waters waxen calm shall glisten
With bashful tremblement beneath His smile;
And Echo ever the while
Shall take, and in her awful joy repeat,
The laughter of His lips—(Thy kingdom come):
And hills that sit apart shall be no longer dumb;
  No, they shall shout and shout,
Raining their lovely loyalty along the dewy plain:
  And valleys round about,

"And all the well-contented land, made sweet
  With flowers she opened at His feet,
Shall answer; shout and make the welkin ring,
And tell it to the stars, shout, shout, and sing;
  Her cup being full to the brim,
  Her poverty made rich with Him,
Her yearning satisfied to its utmost sum—
Lift up thy voice, O Earth, prepare thy song,
  It shall not yet be long,
Lift up, O Earth, for He shall come again,
Thy Lord; and He shall reign, and He SHALL reign—
  Thy kingdom come."

SONGS ON THE VOICES OF BIRDS.

INTRODUCTION.

CHILD AND BOATMAN.

"MARTIN, I wonder who makes all the songs."
"You do, sir."
"Yes, I wonder how they come."
"Well, boy, I wonder what you'll wonder next!"
"But somebody must make them?"
"Sure enough."
"Does your wife know?"
"She never said she did."
"You told me that she knew so many things."
"I said she was a London woman, sir,
And a fine scholar, but I never said
She knew about the songs."
"I wish she did."
"And I wish no such thing; she knows enough,
She knows too much already. Look you now,
This vessel's off the stocks, a tidy craft."
"A schooner, Martin?"
"No, boy, no; a brig,
Only she's schooner rigged,—a lovely craft."
"Is she for me? O thank you, Martin dear,
What shall I call her?"
"Well, sir, what you please."
"Then write on her 'The Eagle.'"
"Bless the child!
Eagle! why, you know naught of eagles, you.
When we lay off the coast, up Canada way,
And chanced to be ashore when twilight fell,
That was the place for eagles; bald they were,
With eyes as yellow as gold."
"O, Martin, dear,
Tell me about them."
"Tell! there's naught to tell,
Only they snored o' nights and frighted us."
"Snored?"
"Ay, I tell you, snored; they slept upright
In the great oaks by scores; as true as time,
If I'd had aught upon my mind just then,
I wouldn't have walked that wood for unknown gold;
It was most awful. When the moon was full,
I've seen them fish at night, in the middle watch,
When she got low. I've seen them plunge like stones,
And come up fighting with a fish as long,
Ay, longer than my arm; and they would sail—
When they had struck its life out—they would sail

Over the deck, and show their fell, fierce eyes,
And croon for pleasure, hug the prey, and speed
Grand as a frigate on the wind."
"My ship,
She must be called 'The Eagle' after these,
And, Martin, ask your wife about the songs
When you go in at dinner time."
"Not I."

THE NIGHTINGALE HEARD BY THE UNSATISFIED HEART.

WHEN in a May-day hush
Chanteth the Missel-thrush,
The harp o' the heart makes answer with murmurous stirs;
When Robin-redbreast sings,
We think on building springs,
And Culvers when they coo are love's remembrancers.

But thou in the trance of light
Stayest the feeding night,
And Echo makes sweet her lips with the utterance wise,
And casts at our glad feet,
In a wisp of fancies fleet,
Life's fair, life's unfulfilled, impassioned prophecies.

Her central thought full well
Thou hast the wit to tell,
To take the sense o' the dark and to yield it so;
The moral of moonlight
To set in a cadence bright,
And sing our loftiest dream that we thought none did know.

I have no nest as thou,
Bird on the blossoming bough,
Yet over thy tongue outfloweth the song o' my soul,
Chanting, "Forego thy strife,
The spirit out-acts the life,
But MUCH is seldom theirs who can perceive THE WHOLE.

"Thou drawest a perfect lot
All thine, but holden not,
Lie low, at the feet of beauty that ever shall bide;

There might be sorer smart
Than thine, far-seeing heart,
Whose fate is still to yearn and not be satisfied."

SAND MARTINS.

I PASSED an inland-cliff precipitate;
From tiny caves peeped many a sooty poll;
In each a mother martin sat elate,
And of the news delivered her small soul.

Fantastic chatter! hasty, glad, and gay,
Whereof the meaning was not ill to tell:
"Gossip, how wags the world with you to-day?"
"Gossip, the world wags well, the world wags well."

And heark'ning, I was sure their little ones
Were in the bird-talk, and discourse was made
Concerning hot sea-bights and tropic suns,
For a clear sultriness the tune conveyed;—

And visions of the sky as of a cup
Hailing down light on pagan Pharaoh's sand,
And quivering air-waves trembling up and up,
And blank stone faces marvellously bland.

"When should the young be fledged and with them hie
Where costly day drops down in crimson light?
(Fortunate countries of the fire-fly
Swarm with blue diamonds all the sultry night,

"And the immortal moon takes turn with them.)
When should they pass again by that red land
Where lovely mirage works a broidered hem
To fringe with phantom-palms a robe of sand?

"When should they dip their breasts again and play
In slumberous azure pools, clear as the air,
Where rosy-winged flamingoes fish all day,
Stalking amid the lotos-blossom fair?

"Then, over-podded tamarinds bear their flight,
While cassias blossom in the zone of calms,
And so betake them to a south sea-bight,
To gossip in the crowns of cocoa-palms

"Whose roots are in the spray. O haply, there
Some dawn, white-wingèd they might chance to find
A frigate, standing in to make more fair
The loneliness unaltered of mankind.

"A frigate come to water; nuts would fall,
And nimble feet would climb the flower-flushed strand,
While northern talk would ring, and therewithal
The martins would desire the cool north land.

"And all would be as it had been before;
Again, at eve, there would be news to tell;
Who passed should hear them chant it o'er and o'er,
'Gossip, how wags the world?' 'Well, gossip, well.'"

A POET IN HIS YOUTH, AND THE CUCKOO BIRD.

ONCE upon a time, I lay
Fast asleep at dawn of day;
Windows open to the south,
Fancy pouting her sweet mouth
To my ear.

She turned a globe
In her slender hand, her robe
Was all spangled; and she said
As she sat at my bed's head,
"Poet, poet, what! asleep?
Look! the ray runs up the steep
To your roof." Then in the golden
Essence of romances olden,
Bathed she my entrancèd heart.
And she gave a hand to me,
Drew me onward; "Come!" said she;
And she moved with me apart,
Down the lovely vale of Leisure.

Such its name was, I heard say,
For some Fairies trooped that way;
Common people of the place,
Taking their accustomed pleasure,
(All the clocks being stopped,) to race
Down the slope on paltreys fleet.
Bridle bells made tinkling sweet;
And they said, "What signified
Faring home till eventide:
There were pies on every shelf,
And the bread would bake itself."
But for that I cared not, fed,
As it were, with angels' bread,
Sweet as honey; yet next day
All foredoomed to melt away;
Gone before the sun waxed hot,
Melted manna that *was not.*

Rock-dove's poetry of plaint,
Or the starling's courtship quaint;
Heart made much of, 'twas a boon
Won from silence, and too soon
Wasted in the ample air:
Building rooks far distant were.

Scarce at all would speak the rills,
And I saw the idle hills,
In their amber hazes deep,
Fold themselves and go to sleep,
Though it was not yet high noon.

Silence? Rather music brought
From the spheres! As if a thought,
Having taken wings, did fly
Through the reaches of the sky.
Silence? No, a sumptuous sigh
That had found embodiment,
That had come across the deep
After months of wintry sleep,
And with tender heavings went
Floating up the firmament.

"O," I mourned, half slumbering yet,
"'Tis the voice of *my* regret,—
Mine!" and I awoke. Full sweet
Saffron sunbeams did me greet;
And the voice it spake again,
Dropped from yon blue cup of light
Or some cloudlet swan's-down white
On my soul, that drank full fain
The sharp joy—the sweet pain—
Of its clear, right innocent,
Unreprovèd discontent.
How it came—where it went—
Who can tell? The open blue
Quivered with it, and I, too,
Trembled. I remembered me
Of the springs that used to be,
When a dimpled white-haired child,
Shy and tender and half wild,
In the meadows I had heard
Some way off the talking bird,
And had felt it marvellous sweet,
For it laughed: it did me greet,
Calling me: yet hid away
In the woods, it would not play.
No.

And all the world about,
While a man will work or sing,
Or a child pluck flowers of spring,
Thou wilt scatter music out,
Rouse him with thy wandering note,
Changeful fancies set afloat,
Almost tell with thy clear throat,
But not quite, the wonder-rife,
Most sweet riddle, dark and dim,
That he searcheth all his life,
Searcheth yet, and ne'er expoundeth;
And so, winnowing of thy wings,
Touch and trouble his heart's strings,
That a certain music soundeth
In that wondrous instrument,
With a trembling upward sent,
That is reckoned sweet above
By the Greatness surnamed Love.

"O, I hear thee in the blue;
Would that I might wing it too!
O to have what hope hath seen!
O to be what might have been!

"O to set my life, sweet bird,
To a tune that oft I heard
When I used to stand alone
Listening to the lovely moan
Of the swaying pines o'erhead,
While, a-gathering of bee-bread
For their living, murmured round,
As the pollen dropped to ground,
All the nations from the hives;
And the little brooding wives
On each nest, brown dusty things,
Sat with gold-dust on their wings.
Then beyond (more sweet than all)
Talked the tumbling waterfall;
And there were, and there were not
(As might fall and form anew
Bell-hung drops of honey-dew)
Echoes of—I know not what;
As if some right-joyous elf,
While about his own affairs,
Whistled softly otherwheres.
Nay, as if our mother dear,
Wrapped in sun-warm atmosphere,
Laughed a little to herself,
Laughed a little as she rolled,
Thinking on the days of old.

"Ah! there be some hearts, I wis,
To which nothing comes amiss.
Mine was one. Much secret wealth
I was heir to: and by stealth,
When the moon was fully grown,
And she thought herself alone,
I have heard her, ay, right well,
Shoot a silver message down
To the unseen sentinel
Of a still, snow-thatchèd town.

"Once, awhile ago, I peered
In the nest where Spring was reared.
There she, quivering her fair wings,
Flattered March with chirrupings;
And they fed her; nights and days,
Fed her mouth with much sweet food,
And her heart with love and praise,
Till the wild thing rose and flew
Over woods and water-springs,
Shaking off the morning dew
In a rainbow from her wings.

"Once (I will to you confide
More),—O, once in forest wide,
I, benighted, overheard
Marvellous mild echoes stirred,
And a calling half defined,
And an answering from afar;
Somewhat talkèd with a star,
And the talk was of mankind.

"'Cuckoo, cuckoo!'
Float anear in upper blue:
Art thou yet a prophet true?
Wilt thou say, 'And having seen
Things that be, and have not been,
Thou art free o' the world, for naught
Can despoil thee of thy thought?'

Nay, but make me music yet,
Bird, as deep as my regret;
For a certain hope hath set,
Like a star, and left me heir
To a crying for its light,
An aspiring infinite,
And a beautiful despair!

"Ah! no more, no more, no more,
I shall lie at thy shut door,
Mine ideal, my desired,
Dreaming thou wilt open it,
And step out, thou most admired,
By my side to fare, or sit,
Quenching hunger and all drouth
With the wit of thy fair mouth,
Showing me the wishéd prize
In the calm of thy dove's eyes,
Teaching me the wonder-rife
Majesties of human life,
All its fairest possible sum,
And the grace of its to come.
"What a difference! Why of late
All sweet music used to say,
'She will come, and with thee stay
To-morrow, man, if not to-day.'
Now it murmurs, 'Wait, wait, wait!'"

A RAVEN IN A WHITE CHINE.

I saw, when I looked up, on either hand,
A pale high chalk-cliff, reared aloft in white;
A narrowing rent soon closed toward the land—
Toward the sea an open yawning bight.

The polished tide, with scarce a hint of blue,
  Washed in the bight; above with angry moan
A raven that was robbed, sat up in view,
  Croaking and crying on a ledge alone.

"Stand on thy nest, spread out thy fateful wings,
  With sullen hungry love bemoan thy brood,
For boys have wrung their necks, those imp-like things,
  Whose beaks dripped crimson daily at their food.

"Cry, thou black prophetess! cry and despair;
  None love thee, none! Their father was thy foe,
Whose father in his youth did know thy lair,
  And steal thy little demons long ago.

"Thou madest many childless for their sake,
  And picked out many eyes that loved the light.
Cry, thou black prophetess! sit up, awake,
  Forebode; and ban them through the desolate night."

Lo! while I spake it, with a crimson hue
  The dipping sun endowed that silver flood,
And all the cliffs flushed red, and up she flew,
  The bird, as mad to bathe in airy blood.

"Nay, thou mayst cry, the omen is not thine,
  Thou aged priestess of fell doom, and fate.
It is not blood: thy gods are making wine,
  They spilt the must outside their city gate,

"And stained their azure pavement with the lees:
  They will not listen though thou cry aloud.
Old Chance, thy dame, sits mumbling at her ease,
  Nor hears; the fair hag, Luck, is in her shroud.

"They heed not, they withdraw the sky-hung sign;
  Thou hast no charm against the favorite race;
Thy gods pour out for it, not blood but wine:
  There is no justice in their dwelling-place!

"Safe in their father's house the boys shall rest,
  Though thy fell brood doth stark and silent lie;
Their unborn sons may yet despoil thy nest:
  Cry, thou black prophetess! lift up! cry, cry!"

THE WARBLING OF BLACKBIRDS.

When I hear the waters fretting,
  When I see the chestnut letting
All her lovely blossom falter down, I think,
  "Alas the day!"
Once, with magical sweet singing,
  Blackbirds set the woodland ringing,
That awakes no more while April hours wear themselves away.

In our hearts fair hope lay smiling,
  Sweet as air, and all beguiling;
And there hung a mist of bluebells on the slope and down the dell;
  And we talked of joy and splendor
  That the years unborn would render,
And the blackbirds helped us with the story, for they knew it well.

Piping, fluting, "Bees are humming,
  April's here, and summer's coming;
Don't forget us when you walk, a man with men, in pride and joy;
  Think on us in alleys shady,
  When you step a graceful lady;
For no fairer day have we to hope for, little girl and boy.

"Laugh and play, O lisping waters,
  Lull our downy sons and daughters;

Come, O wind, and rock their leafy cradle in
    thy wanderings coy;
When they wake, we'll end the measure
    With a wild sweet cry of pleasure,
And a 'Hey down derry, let's be merry! little
    girl and boy!'"

SEA-MEWS IN WINTER TIME.

I WALKED beside a dark gray sea,
    And said, "O world, how cold thou art!
Thou poor white world, I pity thee,
    For joy and warmth from thee depart.

"Yon rising wave licks off the snow,
    Winds on the crag each other chase,
In little powdery whirls they blow
    The misty fragments down its face.

"The sea is cold, and dark its rim,
    Winter sits cowering on the wold,
And I, beside this watery brim,
    Am also lonely, also cold."

I spoke, and drew toward a rock,
    Where many mews made twittering sweet;
Their wings upreared, the clustering flock
    Did pat the sea-grass with their feet.

A rock but half submerged, the sea
    Ran up and washed it while they fed;
Their fond and foolish ecstacy
    A wondering in my fancy bred.

Joy companied with every cry,
    Joy in their food, in that keen wind,
That heaving sea, that shaded sky,
    And in themselves, and in their kind.

The phantoms of the deep at play!
    What idless graced the twittering things;
Luxurious paddlings in the spray,
    And delicate lifting up of wings.

Then all at once a flight, and fast
    The lovely crowd flew out to sea;
If mine own life had been recast,
    Earth had not been more changed to me.

"Where is the cold? Yon clouded skies
    Have only dropped their curtains low
To shade the old mother where she lies,
    Sleeping a little, 'neath the snow.

"The cold is not in crag, nor scar,
    Not in the snows that lap the lea,
Not in yon wings that beat afar,
    Delighting, on the crested sea;

"No, nor in yon exultant wind
    That shakes the oak and bends the pine.
Look near, look in, and thou shalt find
    No sense of cold, fond fool, but thine!"

With that I felt the gloom depart,
And thoughts within me did unfold,
Whose sunshine warmed me to the heart:
    I walked in joy, and was not cold.

LAURANCE.

I.

He knew she did not love him; but so long
As rivals were unknown to him, he dwelt
At ease, and did not find his love a pain.

He had much deference in his nature, need
To honor,—it became him: he was frank,
Fresh, hardy, of a joyous mind, and strong,—
Looked all things straight in the face. So when she came
Before him first, he looked at her, and looked
No more, but colored to his healthful brow,
And wished himself a better man, and thought
On certain things, and wished they were undone,
Because her girlish innocence, the grace
Of her unblemished pureness, wrought in him
A longing and aspiring, and a shame
To think how wicked was the world,—that world
Which he must walk in,—while from her (and such
As she was) it was hidden; there was made
A clean path, and the girl moved on like one
In some enchanted ring.

In his young heart
She reigned, with all the beauties that she had,
And all the virtues that he rightly took
For granted; there he set her with her crown,
And at her first enthronement he turned out
Much that was best away, for unaware
His thoughts grew noble. She was always there
And knew it not, and he grew like to her,
And like to what he thought her.

Now he dwelt
With kin that loved him well,—two fine old folk,
A rich, right honest yeoman, and his dame,—
Their only grandson he, their pride, their heir.

To these one daughter had been born, one child,
And as she grew to woman, "Look," they said,
"She must not leave us; let us build a wing,
With cheerful rooms and wide, to our old grange;
There may she dwell, with her good man, and all God sends them." Then the girl in her first youth
Married a curate,—handsome, poor in purse,
Of gentle blood and manners, and he lived
Under her father's roof as they had planned.

Full soon, for happy years are short, they filled
The house with children; four were born to them.
Then came a sickly season; fever spread
Among the poor. The curate, never slack
In duty, praying by the sick, or, worse,
Burying the dead, when all the air was clogged
With poisonous mist, was stricken; long he lay
Sick, almost to the death, and when his head
He lifted from the pillow, there was left
One only of that pretty flock: his girls,
His three, were cold beneath the sod; his boy,
Their eldest born, remained.

The drooping wife
Bore her great sorrow in such quiet wise,
That first they marvelled at her, then they tried
To rouse her, showing her their bitter grief,
Lamenting, and not sparing; but she sighed,
"Let me alone; it will not be for long."
Then did her mother tremble, murmuring out,
"Dear child, the best of comfort will be soon,
O, when you see this other little face,
You will, please God, be comforted."
She said,
"I shall not live to see it;" but she did,—
A little sickly face, a wan, thin face.
Then she grew eager, and her eyes were bright
When she would plead with them, "Take me away,
Let me go south; it is the bitter blast
That chills my tender babe; she cannot thrive
Under the desolate, dull, mournful cloud."
Then all they journeyed south together, mute
With past and coming sorrow, till the sun,
In gardens edging the blue tideless main,
Warmed them and calmed the aching at their hearts,
And all went better for a while; but not
For long. They sitting by the orange trees
Once rested, and the wife was very still:
A woman with narcissus flowers heaped up
Let down her basket from her head, but paused
With pitying gesture, and drew near and stooped,
Taking a white wild face upon her breast.
The little babe on its poor mother's knees,
None marking it, none knowing else, had died.
The fading mother could not stay behind,
Her heart was broken; but it awed them most
To feel they must not, dared not, pray for life,
Seeing she longed to go, and went so gladly.

After, these three, who loved each other well,
Brought their one child away, and they were best
Together in the wide old grange. Full oft
The father talked with the mother talked of her,
Their daughter, but the husband nevermore ;
He looked for solace in his work, and gave
His mind to teach his boy. And time went on,
Until the grandsire prayed those other two,
"Now part with him ; it must be ; for his good :
He rules and knows it ; choose for him a school,
Let him have all the advantages, and all
Good training that should make a gentleman."

With that they parted from their boy, and lived
Longing between his holidays, and time
Sped ; he grew on till he had eighteen years.
His father loved him, wished to make of him
Another parson ; but the farmer's wife
Murmured at that—"No, no, they learned bad ways,
They ran in debt at college ; she had heard
That many rued the day they sent their boys
To college" : and between the two broke in
His grandsire, "Find a sober, honest man,
A scholar, for our lad should see the world
While he is young, that he may marry young.
He will not settle and be satisfied
Till he has run about the world awhile.
Good lack, I longed to travel in my youth,
And had no chance to do it. Send him off,
A sober man being found to trust him with,—
One with the fear of God before his eyes."
And he prevailed ; the careful father chose
A tutor, young, the worthy matron thought,—
In truth, not ten years older than her boy,
And glad as he to range, and keen for snows,
Desert, and ocean. And they made strange choice
Of where to go, left the sweet day behind,
And pushed up north in whaling ships, to feel
What cold was, see the blowing whale come up,
And Arctic creatures, while a scarlet sun
Went round and round, crowd on the clear blue berg.

Then did the trappers have them ; and they heard
Nightly the whistling calls of forest-men
That mocked the forest wonners ; and they saw
Over the open, raging up like doom,
The dangerous dust-cloud that was full of eyes—
The bisons. So were three years gone like one ;
And the old cities drew them for a while,
Great mothers, by the Tiber and the Seine ;
They have hid many sons hard by their seats,
But all the air is stirring with them still,
The waters murmur of them, skies at eve
Are stained with their rich blood, and every sound
Means men.

At last, the fourth year running out,
The youth came home. And all the cheerful house
Was decked in fresher colors, and the dame
Was full of joy. But in the father's heart
Abode a painful doubt. "It is not well ;
He cannot spend his life with dog and gun.
I do not care that my one son should sleep
Merely for keeping him in breath, and wake
Only to ride to cover."

Not the less
The grandsire pondered. "Ay, the boy must WORK
Or SPEND ; and I must let him spend ; just stay
Awhile with us, and then from time to time
Have leave to be away with those fine folk
With whom, these many years, at school, and now,
During his sojourn in the foreign towns,
He has been made familiar." Thus a month
Went by. They liked the stirring ways of youth,
The quick elastic step, and joyous mind,
Ever expectant of it knew not what,
But something higher than has e'er been born
Of easy slumber and sweet competence.
And as for him, the while they thought and thought,
A comfortable instinct let him know
How they had waited for him to complete
And give a meaning to their lives ; and still
At home, but with a sense of newness there,
And frank and fresh as in the school-boy days,
He oft—invading of his father's haunts,
The study where he passed the silent morn—
Would sit, devouring with a greedy joy
The piled-up books, uncut as yet ; or wake
To guide with him by night the tube, and search,
Ay, think to find new stars ; then, risen betimes,
Would ride about the farm, and list the talk
Of his hale grandsire.

But a day came round,
When, after peering in his mother's room,
Shaded and shuttered from the light, he oped
A door, and found the rosy grandmother
Ensconced and happy in her special pride,
Her store-room. She was corking syrups rare,
And fruits all sparkling in a crystal coat.
Here, after choice of certain cakes well known,
He, sitting on her bacon chest at ease,
Sang as he watched her, till right suddenly,
As if a new thought came, "Goody," quoth he,
"What, think you, do they want to do with me ?
What have they planned for me that I should do ?"

"Do, laddie !" quoth she, faltering, half in tears ;
"Are you not happy with us ? not content ?
Why would ye go away ? There is no need

That ye should DO at all. O, bide at home.
Have we not plenty?"

"Even so," he said;
"I did not wish to go."

"Nay, then," quoth she,
"Be idle; let me see your blessed face.
What, is the horse your father chose for you
Not to your mind? He is? Well, well, re-
   main;
Do as you will, so you but do it here.
You shall not want for money."

But his arms
Folding, he sat and twisted up his mouth
With comical discomfiture.

"What then,"
She sighed, "what is it, child, that you would
   like?"
"Why," said he, "farming."

And she looked at him,
Fond, foolish woman that she was, to find
Some fitness in the worker for the work,
And she found none. A certain grace there
   was
Of movement, and a beauty in the face,
Sunbrowned and healthful beauty, that had
   come
From his grave father; and she thought,
" Good lack,
A farmer! he is fitter for a duke.
He walks—why, how he walks! if I should
   meet
One like him, whom I knew not, I should ask,
And who may that be?" So the foolish thought
Found words. Quoth she, half laughing, half
   ashamed,
"We planned to make of you—a gentleman."
And, with engaging sweet audacity,—
She thought it nothing less,—he, looking up,
With a smile in his blue eyes, replied to her,
"And haven't you done it?" Quoth she,
   lovingly,
"I think we have, laddie; I think we have."

"Then," quoth he, "I may do what best I
   like;
It makes no matter. Goody, you were wise
To help me in it, and to let me farm;
I think of getting into mischief else!"
"No! do ye laddie?" quoth the dame, and
   laughed.
"But ask my grandfather," the youth went on,
"To let me have the farm he bought last year,
The little one, to manage. I like land;
I want some." And she, womanlike, gave
   way,
Convinced; and promised, and made good her
   word,
And that same night upon the matter spoke,
In presence of the father and the son.

"Roger," quoth she, "our Laurance wants to
   farm;
"I think he might do worse." The father sat
Mute, but right glad. The grandson, breaking
   in,
Set all his wish and his ambition forth;
But cunningly the old man hid his joy,
And made conditions with a faint demur.
Then, pausing, "Let your father speak," quoth
   he;
"I am content if he is." At his word
The parson took him; ay, and, parson like,
Put a religious meaning in the work,
Man's earliest work, and wished his son God
   speed.

II.

Thus all were satisfied, and, day by day,
For two sweet years a happy course was theirs;
Happy, but yet the fortunate, the young
Loved, and much cared-for, entered on his
   strife,—
A stirring of the heart, a quickening keen
Of sight and hearing to the delicate
Beauty and music of an altered world,—
Began to walk in that mysterious light
Which doth reveal and yet transform; which
   gives
Destiny, sorrow, youth, and death, and life,
Intenser meaning; in disquieting
Lifts up; a shining light: men call it Love.

Fair, modest eyes had she, the girl he loved;
A silent creature, thoughtful, grave, sincere.
She never turned from him with sweet caprice,
Nor changing moved his soul to troublous
   hope,
Nor dropped for him her heavy lashes low,
But excellent in youthful grace came up;
And, ere his words were ready, passing on,
Had left him all a-tremble; yet made sure
That by her own true will, and fixed intent,
She held him thus remote. Therefore, albeit
He knew she did not love him, yet so long
As of a rival unaware, he dwelt
All in the present, without fear, or hope,
Enthralled and whelmed in the deep sea of
   love,
And could not get his head above its wave
To search the far horizon, or to mark
Whereto it drifted him.

So long, so long;
Then, on a sudden, came the ruthless fate,
Showed him a bitter truth, and brought him
   bale
All in the tolling out of noon.

'Twas thus:
Snow-time was come; it had been snowing
   hard;
Across the churchyard path he walked; the
   clock

Began to strike, and, as he passed the porch,
Half turning, through a sense that came to him
As of some presence in it, he beheld
His love, and she had come for shelter there ;
And all her face was fair with rosy bloom,
The blush of happiness ; and one held up
Her ungloved hand in both his own, and stooped
Toward it, sitting by her. O, her eyes
Were full of peace and tender light : they looked
One moment in the ungraced lover's face
While he was passing in the snow ; and he
Received the story, while he raised his hat
Retiring. Then the clock left off to strike,
And that was all. It snowed, and he walked on ;
And in a certain way he marked the snow,
And walked, and came upon the open heath ;
And in a certain way he marked the cold,
And walked as one that had no starting-place
Might walk, but not to any certain goal.

And he strode on toward a hollow part,
Where from the hillside gravel had been dug,
And he was conscious of a cry, and went,
Dulled in his sense, as though he heard it not ;
Till a small farm-house drudge, a half-grown girl,
Rose from the shelter of a drift that lay
Against the bushes, crying, "God ! O God,
O my good God, he sends us help at last."
Then, looking hard upon her came, to him
The power to feel and to perceive. Her teeth
Chattered, and all her limbs with shuddering failed,
And in her threadbare shawl was wrapped a child
That looked on him with wondering, wistful eyes.

"I thought to freeze," the girl broke out with tears ;
"Kind sir, kind sir," and she held out the child,
As praying him to take it ; and he did ;
And gave to her the shawl, and swathed his charge
In the foldings of his plaid ; and when it thrust
Its small round face against his breast, and felt
With small red hands for warmth, unbearable
Pains of great pity rent his straitened heart,
For the poor upland dwellers had been out
Since morning dawn, at early milking time,
Wandering and stumbling in the drift. And now,
Lamed with a fall, half crippled by the cold,
Hardly prevailed his arm to drag her on,
That ill-clad child, who yet the younger child
Had motherly cared to shield. So toiling through
The great white storm coming, and coming yet,
And coming till the world confounded sat
With all her fair familiar features gone,
The mountains muffled in an eddying swirl,

He led or bore them, and the little one
Peered from her shelter, pleased ; but oft would
mourn
The elder, "They will beat me : O my can,
I left my can of milk upon the moor."
And he compared her trouble with his own,
And had no heart to speak. And yet 'twas keen ;
It filled her to the putting down of pain
And hunger,—what could his do more ?

He brought
The children to their home, and suddenly
Regained himself, and, wondering at himself,
That he had borne, and yet been dumb so long,
The weary wailing of the girl, he paid
Money to buy her pardon ; heard them say,
"Peace, we have feared for you ; forget the milk,
It is no matter !" and went forth again
And waded in the snow, and quietly
Considered in his patience what to do
With all the dull remainder of his days.

With dusk he was at home, and felt it good
To hear his kindred talking, for it broke
A mocking endless echo in his soul,
"It is no matter !" and he could not choose
But mutter though the weariness o'ercame
His spirit, "Peace, it is no matter ; peace,
It is no matter !" For he felt that all
Was as it had been, and his father's heart
Was easy, knowing not how that same day
Hope with her tender colors and delight
(He should not care to have him know) were dead ;
Yea, to all these, his nearest and most dear,
It was no matter. And he heard them talk
Of timber felled, of certain fruitful fields,
And profitable markets.

All for him
Their plans, and yet the echoes swarmed and swam
About his head, whenever there was pause ;
"It is no matter !" And his greater self
Arose in him and fought. "It matters much,
It matters all to these, that not to-day
Nor ever they should know it. I will hide
The wound ; ay, hide it with a sleepless care.
What ! shall I make these three to drink of rue,
Because my cup is bitter ?" And he thrust
Himself in thought away, and made his ears
Hearken, and caused his voice, that yet did seem
Another, to make answer, when they spoke,
As there had been no snow-storm, and no porch,
And no despair.

So this went on awhile
Until the snow had melted from the wold,
And he, one noonday, wandering up a lane,
Met on a turn the woman whom he loved.

Then, even to trembling he was moved; his
  speech
Faltered; but when the common kindly words
Of greeting were all said, and she passed on,
He could not bear her sweetness and his pain.
"Muriel!" he cried; and when she heard her
  name,
She turned. "You know I love you," he
  broke out.
She answered, "Yes," and sighed.

                               "O, pardon me,
Pardon me," quoth the lover; "let me rest
In certainty, and hear it from your mouth:
Is he with whom I saw you once of late
To call you wife?" "I hope so," she replied;
And over all her face the rose-bloom came,
As, thinking on that other, unaware
Her eyes waxed tender. When he looked on
  her,
Standing to answer him with lovely shame,
Submiss, and yet not his, a passionate,
A quickened sense of his great impotence
To drive away the doom got hold on him;
He set his teeth to force the unbearable
Misery back; his wide-awakened eyes
Flashed as with flame.

                          And she, all overawed
And mastered by his manhood, waited yet,
And trembled at the deep she could not sound,—
A passionate nature in a storm,—a heart
Wild with a mortal pain, and in the grasp
Of an immortal love.

                           "Farewell," he said,
Recovering words; and, when she gave her
  hand,
"My thanks for your good candor; for I feel
That it has cost you something." Then, the
  blush
Yet on her face, she said: "It was your due:
But keep this matter from your friends and kin,
We would not have it known." Then, cold
  and proud,
Because there leaped from under his straight
  lids,
And instantly was veiled a keen surprise,—
"He wills it, and I therefore think it well."
Thereon they parted; but from that time forth,
Whether they met on festal eve, in field
Or at the church, she ever bore herself
Proudly, for she had felt a certain pain;
The disapproval hastily betrayed
And quickly hidden hurt her. "'T'was a
  grace,"
She thought, "to tell this man the thing he
  asked,
And he rewards me with surprise. I like
No one's surprise, and least of all bestowed
Where he bestowed it."

                         But the spring came on.
Looking to wed in April, all her thoughts
Grew loving; she would fain the world had
  waxed
More happy with her happiness, and oft
Walking among the flowery woods she felt
Their loveliness reach down into her heart,
And knew with them the ecstasies of growth,
The rapture that was satisfied with light,
The pleasure of the leaf in exquisite
Expansion, through the lovely, longed-for
  spring.

And as for him—(Some narrow hearts there are
That suffer blight when that they fed upon,
As something to complete their being, fails,
And they retire into their holds and pine,
And long restrained grow stern. But some
  there are
That in a sacred want and hunger rise,
And draw the misery home and live with it,
And excellent in honor wait, and will
That somewhat good should yet be found in it,
Else wherefore were they born?)—and as for
  him,
He loved her, but his peace and welfare made
The sunshine of three lives. The cheerful
  grange
Threw open wide its hospitable doors,
And drew in guests for him. The garden
  flowers,
Sweet budding wonders, all were set for him.
In him the eyes at home were satisfied,
And if he did but laugh the ear approved.
What then? He dwelt among them as of old,
And taught his mouth to smile.

                            And time went on,
Till on a morning, when the perfect Spring
Rested among her leaves, he, journeying home
After short sojourn in a neighboring town,
Stopped at the little station on the line
That ran between his woods; a lonely place
And quiet, and a woman and a child
Got out. He noted them, but, walking on
Quickly, went back into the wood, impelled
By hope, for, passing, he had seen his love,
And she was sitting on a rustic seat
That overlooked the line, and he desired
With longing indescribable, to look
Upon her face again. And he drew near.
She was right happy; she was waiting there.
He felt that she was waiting for her Lord.
She cared no whit if Laurance went or stayed,
But answered when he spoke, and dropped her
  cheek
In her fair hand.

                         And he, not able yet
To force himself away, and nevermore
Behold her, gathered blossom, primrose flowers,
And wild anemone, for many a clump
Grew all about him, and the hazel rods
Were nodding with their catkins. But he
  heard
The stopping train, and felt that he must go;
His time was come. There was naught else to
  do

Or hope for. With the blossom he drew near,
And would have had her take it from his hand;
But she, half lost in thought, held out her own,
And then remembering him and his long love,
She said, "I thank you; pray you now forget,
Forget me, Laurance," and her lovely eyes
Softened; but he was dumb, till through the trees
Suddenly broke upon their quietude
The woman and her child. And Muriel said,
"What will you?" She made answer quick and keen,
"Your name, my lady; 'tis your name I want,
Tell me your name." Not startled, not displeased,
But with a musing sweetness on her mouth,
As if considering in how short a while
It would be changed, she lifted up her face
And gave it, and the little child drew near
And pulled her gown, and prayed her for the flowers.
Then Laurance, not content to leave them so,
Nor yet to wait the coming lover, spoke:
"Your errand with this lady?" "And your right
To ask it?" she broke out with sudden heat
And passion: "What is that to you? Poor child!
Madam!" And Muriel lifted up her face
And looked,—they looked into each other's eyes.
"That man who comes," the clear-voiced woman cried,—
"That man with whom you think to wed so soon,—
You must not heed him. What! the world is full
Of men, and some are good, and most, God knows,
Better than he,—that I should say it!— far
Better." And down her face the large tears ran,
And Muriel's wild dilated eyes looked up,
Taking a terrible meaning from her words;
And Laurance stared about him, half in doubt
If this were real, for all things were so blithe,
And soft air tossed the little flowers about;
The child was singing, and the blackbirds piped,
Glad in fair sunshine. And the women both
Were quiet, gazing in each other's eyes.

He found his voice, and spoke: "This is not well,
Though whom you speak of should have done you wrong;
A man that could desert and plan to wed
Will not his purpose yield to God and right,
Only to law. You, whom I pity so much,
If you be come this day to urge a claim,
You will not tell me that your claim will hold;
'Tis only, if I read aright, the old,
Sorrowful, hateful story."

     Muriel sighed
With a dull patience that he marvelled at:
"Be plain with me. I know not what to think,
Unless you are his wife. Are you his wife?
Be plain with me." And all too quietly,
With running down of tears, the answer came,
"Ay, madam, ay! the worse for him and me."
Then Muriel heard her lover's foot anear.
And cried upon him with a bitter cry,
Sharp and despairing. And those two stood back,
With such affright and violent anger stirred,
He broke from out the thicket to her side,
Not knowing. But, her hands before her face,
She sat; and, stepping close, that woman came
And faced him. Then said Muriel, "O my heart,
Herbert!"—and he was dumb and ground his teeth,
And lifted up his hand and looked at it,
And at the woman; but a man was there
Who whirled her from her place and thrust himself
Between them; he was strong,—a stalwart man:
And Herbert, thinking on it, knew his name.
"What good," quoth he, "though you and I shoud strive
And wrestle on this April day? A word,
And not a blow, is what these women want:
Master yourself, and say it." But he, weak
With passion and great anguish, flung himself
Upon the seat and cried, "O lost, my love!
O Muriel, Muriel!" And the woman spoke,
"Sir, 'twas an evil day you wed with me:
And you were young; I know it, sir, right well.
Sir, I have worked; I have not troubled you,
Not for myself, nor for your child. I know
We are not equal." "Hold!" he cried' "have done;
Your still, tame words are worse than hate or scorn.
Get from me! Ay, my wife, my wife, indeed!
All's done. You hear it, Muriel; if you can,
O sweet, forgive me."

     Then the woman moved
Slowly away; her little singing child
Went in her wake; and Muriel dropped her hands,
And sat before these two that loved her so,
Mute and unheeding. There were angry words,
She knew, but yet she could not hear the words;
And afterwards the man she loved stooped down
And kissed her forehead once, and then withdrew
To look at her, and with a gesture pray
Her pardon. And she tried to speak, but failed,
And presently, and soon, O,—he was gone.

She heard him go, and Laurance, still as stone,
Remained beside her; and she put her hand
Before her face again, and afterward

She heard a voice, as if, a long way off,
Some one entreated, but she could not heed.
Thereon he drew her hand away, and raised
Her passive from her seat. So then she knew
That he would have her go with him, go
 home,—
It was not far to go,—a dreary home.
A crippled aunt, of birth and lineage high,
Had, in her youth, and for a place and home,
Married the stern old rector ; and the girl
Dwelt with them : she was orphaned,—had no
 kin
Nearer than they. And Laurance brought her in,
And spared to her the telling of this woe.
He sought her kindred where they sat apart,
And laid before them all the cruel thing,
As he had seen it. After, he retired ;
And restless, and not master of himself,
He day and night haunted the rectory lanes ;
And all things, even to the spreading out
Of leaves, their flickering shadows on the
 ground,
Or sailing of the slow, white cloud, or peace
And glory and great light on mountain heads,—
All things were leagued against him, ministered
By likeness or by contrast to his love.
But what was that to Muriel, though her peace
He would have purchased for her with all
 prayers,
And costly passionate, despairing tears ?
O, what to her that he should find it worse
To bear her life's undoing than his own.

She let him see her, and she made no moan,
But talked full calmly of indifferent things,
Which when he heard, and marked the faded
 eyes
And lovely wasted cheek, he started up
With "This I cannot bear !" and shamed to
 feel
His manhood giving way, and utterly
Subdued by her sweet patience and his pain,
Made haste and from the window sprang, and
 paced,
Battling and chiding with himself, the maze.

She suffered, and he could not make her well
For all his loving ; he was naught to her.
And now his passionate nature, set astir,
Fought with the pain that could not be en-
 dured ;
And like a wild thing, suddenly aware
That it is caged, which flings and bruises all
Its body at the bars, he rose, and raged
Against the misery : then he made all worse
With tears. But when he came to her again,
Willing to talk as they had talked before,
She sighed, and said, with that strange quiet-
 ness,
"I know you have been crying :" and she
 bent
Her own fair head and wept.

       She felt the cold--
The freezing cold that deadened all her life—
Give way a little ; for this passionate
Sorrow, and all for her relieved her heart,
And brought some natural warmth, some na-
 tural tears.

III.

And after that, though oft he sought her door,
He might not see her. First they said to him,
"She is not well ;" and afterwards, "Her
 wish
Is ever to be quiet." Then in haste
They took her from the place, because so fast
She faded. As for him,—though youth and
 strength
Can bear the weight as of a world, at last
The burden of it tells,—he heard it said,
When autumn came, "The poor sweet thing
 will die :
That shock was mortal." And he cared no
 more
To hide, if yet he could have hidden, the blight
That was laying waste his heart. He journeyed
 south
To Devon, where she dwelt with other kin,
Good, kindly women ; and he wrote to them,
Praying that he might see her ere she died.

So in her patience she permitted him
To be about her, for it eased his heart ;
And as for her that was to die soon,
What did it signify ? She let him weep
Some passionate tears beside her couch, she
 spoke
Pitying words, and then they made him go.
It was enough, they said ; her time was short,
And he had seen her. He HAD seen, and felt
The bitterness of death ; but he went home,
Being satisfied in that great longing now,
And able to endure what might befall.

And Muriel lay, and faded with the year ;
She lay at the door of death, that opened not
To take her in ; for when the days once more
Began a little to increase, she felt,—
And it was sweet to her, she was so young,—
She felt a longing for the time of flowers,
And dreamed that she was walking in that
 wood
With her two feet among the primroses.
Then when the violet opened, she rose up
And walked. The tender leaf and tender light
Did solace her ; but she was white and wan,
The shadow of that Muriel in the wood
Who listened to those deadly words.

         And now
Empurpled seas began to blush and bloom,
Doves made sweet moaning, and the guelder-
 rose
In a great stillness dropped, and ever dropped,
Her wealth about her feet, and there it lay,
And drifted not at all. The lilac spread
Odorous essence round her ; and full oft,
When Muriel felt the warmth her pulses cheer,

She, faded, sat among the May-tide bloom,
And with a reverent quiet in her soul,
Took back—it was His will—her time, and sat
Learning again to live.

    Thus as she sat
Upon a day, she was aware of one
Who at a distance marked her. This again
Another day, and she was vexed, for yet
She longed for quiet; but she heard a foot
Pass once again, and beckoned through the
 trees.
"Laurance!" And all impatient of unrest
And strife, ay, even of the sight of them,
When he drew near, with tired, tired lips,
As if her soul upbraided him, she said,
"Why have you done this thing?" He an-
 swered her,
"I am not always master in the fight:
I could not help it."

   "What!" she sighed, "not yet!
O, I am sorry"; and she talked to him
As one who looked to live, imploring him,—
"Try to forget me. Let your fancy dwell
Elsewhere, nor me enrich with it so long;
It wearies me to think of this your love.
Forget me!"

   He made answer, "I will try:
The task will take me all my life to learn,
Or, were it learned, I know not how to live;
This pain is part of life and being now,—
It is myself; but yet—but I will try."
Then she spoke friendly to him,—of his home,
His father, and the old, brave, loving folk;
She bade him think of them. And not her
 words,
But having seen her, satisfied his heart.
He left her, and went home to live his life,
And all the summer heard it said of her,
"Yet, she grows stronger;" but when the
 autumn came
Again she drooped.

   A bitter thing it is
To lose at once the lover and the love;
For who receiveth not may yet keep life
In the spirit with bestowal. But for her,
This Muriel, all was gone. The man she loved,
Not only from her present had withdrawn,
But from her past, and there was no such man,
There never had been.

   He was not as one
Who takes love in, like some sweet bird, and
 holds
The wingèd fluttering stranger to his breast,
Till, after transient stay, all unaware
It leaves him: it has flown. No; this may live
In memory,—loved till death. He was not
 vile:
For who by choice would part with that pure
 bird,
And loose the exultation of its song?

He had not strength of will to keep it fast,
Nor warmth of heart to keep it warm, nor life
Of thought to make the echo sound for him
After the song was done. Pity that man:
His music is all flown, and he forgets
The sweetness of it, till at last he thinks
'T was no great matter. But he was not vile,
Only a thing to pity most in man,
Weak,—only poor, and, if he knew it, undone.
But Herbert! When she mused on it, her soul
Would fain have hidden him forevermore,
Even from herself,—so pure of speech, so frank,
So full of household kindness. Ah, so good
And true! A little, she had sometimes
 thought,
Despondent for himself, but strong of faith
In God, and faith in her, this man had seemed.

Ay, he was gone! and she whom he had wed,
As Muriel learned, was sick, was poor, was sad,
And Muriel wrote to comfort her, and send,
From her small store, money to help her need,
With, "pray you keep it secret." Then the
 whole
Of the cruel tale was told.

   What more? She died.
Her kin, profuse of thanks, not bitterly,
Wrote of the end. "Our sister fain had seen
Her husband; prayed him sore to come. But
 no.
And then she prayed him that he would forgive,
Madam, her breaking of the truth to you.
Dear madam, he was angry, yet we think
He might have let her see, before she died,
The words she wanted, but he did not write
Till she was gone,—'I neither can forgive,
Nor would I if I could,'"

   "Patience, my heart!
And this, then, is the man I loved!"

     But yet
He sought a lower level, for he wrote,
Telling the story with a different hue,—
Telling of freedom. He desired to come,
"For now," said he, "O love, may all be
 well."
And she rose up against it in her soul,
For she despised him. And with passionate
 tears
Of shame, she wrote, and wrote only these
 words,—
"Herbert, I will not see you."

   Then she drooped
Again; it is so bitter to despise;
And all her strength, when autumn leaves down
 dropped,
Fell from her. "Ah!" she thought, "I rose
 up once,
I cannot rise up now; here is the end."
And all her kinsfolk thought, "It is the end."

But when that other heard, "It is the end,"
His heart was sick, and he, as by a power

Far stronger than himself, was driven to her.
Reason rebelled against it, but his will
Required it of him with a craving strong
As life, and passionate though hopeless pain.

She, when she saw his face, considered him
Full quietly, let all excuses pass
Not answered, and considered yet again.

"He had heard that she was sick; what could he do
But come, and ask her pardon that he came?"
What could he do, indeed?—a weak white girl
Held all his heartstrings in her small white hand;
His youth, and power, and majesty were hers,
And not his own.

          She looked, and pitied him,
Then spoke: "He loves me with a love that lasts.
Ah me! that I might get away from it,
Or, better, hear it said that love is NOT,
And then I could have rest. My time is short,
I think,—so short." And roused against himself
In stormy wrath, that it should be his doom
Her to disquiet whom he loved, ay, her
For whom he would have given all his rest,
If there were any left to give,—he took
Her words up bravely, promising once more
Absence, and praying pardon; but some tears
Dropped quietly upon her cheek.

          "Remain,"
She said, "for there is something to be told,
Some words that you must hear.

          "And first, hear this:
God has been good to me; you must not think
That I despair. There is a quiet time
Like evening in my soul. I have no heart,
For cruel Herbert killed it long ago,
And death strides on. Sit, then, and give your mind
To listen, and your eyes to look at me.
Look at my face, Laurance, how white it is;
Look at my hand,—my beauty is all gone."
And Laurance lifted up his eyes; he looked,
But answered, from their deeps that held no doubt,
Far otherwise than she had willed: they said,
"Lovelier than ever."

          Yet her words went on,
Cold, and so quiet, "I have suffered much,
And I would fain that none who care for me
Should suffer a like pang that I can spare.
Therefore," said she, and not at all could blush,
"I have brought my mind of late to think of this:
That since your life is spoilt (not willingly,
My God, not willingly, by me), 'twere well
To give you choice of griefs.

          "Were it not best
To weep for a dead love, and afterwards
Be comforted the sooner, that she died
Remote, and left not in your house and life
Aught to remind you? That indeed, were best.
But were it best to weep for a dead wife,
And let the sorrow spend and satisfy
Itself with all expression, and so end?
I think not so; but if for you 'tis best,
Then,—do not answer with too sudden words:
It matters much to you; not much, not much
To me,—then truly I will die your wife;
I will marry you."

          What was he like to say,
But, overcome with love and tears, to choose
The keener sorrow,—take it to his heart,
Cherish it, make it part of him, and watch
Those eyes, that were his light, till they should close?

He answered her with eager, faltering words,
"I choose,—my heart is yours,—die in my arms."

But was it well? Truly, at first, for him
It was not well: he saw her fade, and cried,
"When may this be?" She answered, "When you will,"
And cared not much, for very faint she grew,
Tired and cold. Oft in her soul she thought,
"If I could slip away before the ring
Is on my hand, it were a blessed lot
For both,—a blessed thing for him, and me."

But it was not so; for the day had come,—
Was over; days and months had come, and Death,—
Within whose shadow she had lain, which made
Earth and its loves, and even its bitterness,
Indifferent,—Death withdrew himself, and life
Woke up, and found that it was folded fast,
Drawn to another life for evermore.
O, what a waking! After it there came
Great silence. She got up once more, in spring,
And walked, but not alone, among the flowers.
She thought within herself, "What have I done?
How shall I do the rest?" And he, who felt
Her inmost thought, was silent even as she.
"What have we done?" she thought. But as for him,
When she began to look him in the face,
Considering, "Thus and thus his features are,"
For she had never thought on them before,
She read their grave repose aright. She knew
That in the stronghold of his heart, held back,
Hidden reserves of measureless content
Kept house with happy thought, for her sake mute.

Most patient Muriel! when he brought her home,

She took the place they gave her,—strove to please
His kin, and did not fail, but yet thought on,
"What have I done? how shall I do the rest?
Ah! so contented, Laurance, with this wife
That loves you not, for all the stateliness
And grandeur of your manhood, and the deeps
In your blue eyes." And after that awhile
She rested from such thinking, put it by
And waited. She had thought on death before;
But no, this Muriel was not yet to die;
And when she saw her little tender babe,
She felt how much the happy days of life
Outweigh the sorrowful. A tiny thing,
Whom when it slept the lovely mother nursed
With reverent love, whom when it woke she fed
And wondered at, and lost herself in long
Rapture of watching, and contentment deep.

Once while she sat, this babe upon her knee,
Her husband and his father standing nigh,
About to ride; the grandmother, all pride
And consequence, so deep in learned talk
Of infants, and their little ways and wiles,
Broke off to say, "I never saw a babe
So like its father." And the thought was new
To Muriel; she looked up, and when she looked,
Her husband smiled. And she, the lovely bloom
Flushing her face, would fain he had not known,
Nor noticed her surprise. But he did know;
Yet there was pleasure in his smile, and love
Tender and strong. He kissed her, kissed his babe,
With "Goody, you are left in charge, take care."

"As if I needed telling," quoth the dame;
And they were gone.

Then Muriel, lost in thought,
Gazed; and the grandmother, with open pride,
Tended the lovely pair; till Muriel said,
"Is she so like? Dear granny, get me now
The picture that his father has;" and soon
The old woman put it in her hand.
The wife,
Considering it with deep and strange delight,
Forgot for once her babe, and looked and learned.

A mouth for mastery and manful work,
A certain brooding sweetness in the eyes,
A brow, the harbor of grave thought, and hair
Saxon of hue. She conned; then blushed again,
Remembering now, when she had looked on him,
The sudden radiance of her husband's smile.

But Muriel did not send the picture back;
She kept it; while her beauty and her babe
Flourished together, and in health and peace
She lived.

Her husband never said to her,
"Love, are you happy?" never said to her,
"Sweet, do you love me?" and at first, whene'er
They rode together in the lanes, and paused,
Stopping their horses, when the day was hot,
In the shadow of a tree, to watch the clouds,
Ruffled in drifting on the jagged rocks
That topped the mountains,—when she sat by him,
Withdrawn at even while the summer stars
Came starting out of nothing, as new made,
She felt a little trouble, and a wish
That he would yet keep silence, and he did.
That one reserve he would not touch, but still
Respected.

Muriel grew more brave in time,
And talked at ease, and felt disquietude
Fade. And another child was given to her.

"Now we shall do," the old great-grandsire cried,
"For this is the right sort, a boy." "Fie, fie,"
Quoth the good dame; "but never heed you, love,
He thinks them both as right as right can be."

But Laurance went from home, ere yet the boy
Was three weeks old. It fretted him to go,
But yet he said, "I must:" and she was left
Much with the kindly dame, whose gentle care
Was like a mother's; and the two could talk
Sweetly, for all the difference in their years.

But unaware, the wife betrayed a wish
That she had known why Laurance left her thus.
"Ay, love," the dame made answer; "for he said,
'Goody,' before he left, 'if Muriel ask
No question, tell her naught; but if she let
Any disquietude appear to you,
Say what you know.'" "What?" Muriel said, and laughed,
"I ask, then."

"Child, it is that your old love,
Some two months past, was here. Nay, never start:
He's gone. He came, our Laurance met him near;
He said that he was going over seas,
'And might I see your wife this only once,
And get her pardon?'"

"Mercy!" Muriel cried,
"But Laurance does not wish it?"

"Nay, now, nay,"
Quoth the good dame.

"I cannot," Muriel cried;
"He does not, surely, think I should."

"Not he,"
The kind old woman said, right soothingly.
"Does not he ever know, love, ever do
What you like best?"

And Muriel, trembling yet,
Agreed. "I heard him say," the dame went on,
"For I was with him when they met that day,
'It would not be agreeable to my wife.'"

Then Muriel, pondering—"And he said no more?
You think he did not add, 'nor to myself?'"
And with her soft, calm, inward voice, the dame
Unruffled answered, "No, sweet heart, not he:
What need he care?" "And why not?"
Muriel cried,
Longing to hear the answer. "O, he knows,
He knows, love, very well:"—with that she smiled.
"Bless your fair face, you have not really thought
He did not know you loved him?"

Muriel said
"He never told me, Goody, that he knew."
"Well," quoth the dame, "but it may chance, my dear,
That he thinks best to let old troubles sleep:
Why need he rouse them? You are happy, sure?
But if one asks, 'Art happy?' why, it sets
The thoughts a-working. No, say I, let love,
Let peace and happy folk alone."

"He said,
'It would not be agreeable to my wife.'
And he went on to add; in course of time
That he would ask you, when it suited you,
To write a few kind words."

"Yes," Muriel said,
"I can do that."

"So Laurance went, you see,"
The soft voice added, "to take down that child.
Laurance had written oft about the child,
And now, at last, the father made it known
He could not take him. He has lost, they say,
His money, with much gambling; now he wants
To lead a good, true, working life. He wrote,
And let this so be seen, that Laurance went
And took the child, and took the money down
To pay."

And Muriel found her talking sweet,
And asked once more, the rather that she longed
To speak again of Laurance, "And you think
He knows I love him?"

"Ay, good sooth, he knows
No fear; but he is like his father, love.
His father never asked my pretty child
One prying question; took her as she was;
Trusted her; she has told me so: he knew
A woman's nature. Laurance is the same.
He knows you love him; but he will not speak
No, never. Some men are such gentlemen!";

SONGS OF THE NIGHT WATCHES,

WITH AN INTRODUCTORY SONG OF EVENING, AND A CONCLUDING SONG OF THE EARLY DAY.

INTRODUCTORY.

(Old English Manner.)

APPRENTICED.

"COME out and hear the waters shoot, the owlet hoot, the owlet hoot ;
Yon crescent moon, a golden boat, hangs dim behind the tree, O !
The dropping thorn makes white the grass, O sweetest lass, and sweetest lass ;
Come out and smell the ricks of hay adown the croft with me, O !"

" My granny nods before her wheel, and drops her reel, and drops her reel ;
My father with his crony talks as gay as gay can be, O !
But all the milk is yet to skim, ere light wax dim, ere light wax dim ;
How can I step adown the croft, my 'prentice lad with thee, O?"

"And must ye bide, yet waiting's long, and love is strong, and love is strong ;
And O ! had I but served the time, that takes so long to flee, O !
And thou, my lass, by morning's light wast all in white, wast all in white,
And parson stood within the rails, a-marrying me and thee, O."

THE FIRST WATCH.

TIRED.

I.

O, I would tell you more, but I am tired ;
For I have longed, and I have had my will ;
I pleaded in my spirit, I desired :
"Ah ! let me only see him, and be still All my days after."

           Rock, and rock, and rock,
Over the falling, rising watery world,
   Sail, beautiful ship, along the leaping main ;
The chirping land-birds follow flock on flock
   To light on a warmer plain.
White as weaned lambs the little wavelets curled,
     Fall over in harmless play,
     As these do far away ;
Sail, bird of doom, along the shimmering sea,
All under thy broad wings that overshadow thee.

II.

           I am so tired,
If I would comfort me, I know not how,
For I have seen thee, lad, as I desired,
And I have nothing left to long for now.

Nothing at all. And did I wait for thee,
   Often and often, while the light grew dim,
And through the lilac-branches I could see,
   Under a saffron sky, the purple rim
O' the heaving moorland ! Ay. And then would float
Up from behind—as it were a golden boat,

Freighted with fancies, all o' the wonder of life,
   Love—such a slender moon, going up and up,
Waxing so fast from night to night,
And swelling like an orange flower-bud, bright,
   Fated, methought, to round as to a golden cup,
And hold to my two lips life's best of wine.
   Most beautiful crescent moon,
     Ship of the sky !
Across the unfurrowed reaches sailing high.
   Methought that it would come my way full soon,
Laden with blessings that were all, all mine,—
   A golden ship, with balm and spiceries rife,
   That ere its day was done should hear thee call me wife.

III.

All over ! the celestial sign hath failed ;
The orange flower-bud shuts ; the ship hath sailed,
And sunk behind the long low-lying hills.

The love that fed on daily kisses dieth;
The love kept warm by nearness lieth,
   Wounded and wan;
The love hope nourished bitter tears distil,
  And faints with naught to feed upon.
Only there stirreth very deep below
The hidden beating slow,
And the blind yearning, and the long-drawn breath
Of the love that conquers death.

IV.

Had we not loved full long, and lost all fear,
  My ever, my only dear?
Yes; and I saw thee start upon thy way,
   So sure that we should meet
    Upon our trysting day.
And even absence then to me was sweet,
  Because it brought me time to brood
  Upon thy dearness in the solitude.
   But ah! to stay, and stay,
And let that moon of April wane itself away,
  And let the lovely May
Make ready all her buds for June;
And let the glossy finch forego her tune
That she brought with her in the spring,
And nevermore, I think, to me can sing;
And then to lead thee home another bride,
  In the sultry summer-tide,
And all forget me save for shame full sore,
That made thee pray me, absent, "See my
    face no more."

V.

O, hard, most hard! But while my fretted
   heart
  Shut out, shut down, and full of pain,
   Sobbed to itself apart,
   Ached to itself in vain,
  One came who loveth me
    As I love thee, ...
And let my God remember him for this,
As I do hope He will forget thy kiss,
  Nor visit on thy stately head
Aught that thy mouth hath sworn, or thy two
    eyes have said. . . .
He came, and it was dark. He came, and
   sighed,
Because he knew the sorrow,—whispering low,
And fast, and thick, as one that speaks by rote;
!"The vessel lieth in the river reach,
  A mile above the beach,
And she will sail at the turning o' the tide."
  He said, "I have a boat,
   And were it good to go,
And unbeholden in the vessel's wake
Look on the man thou lovedst, and forgive,
  As he embarks, a shameful fugitive.
    Come then, with me."

VI.

O, how he sighed! The little stars did wink,
And it was very dark. I gave my hand,—
He led me out across the pasture land,
  And through the narrow croft,
  Down to the river's brink.
When thou wast full in spring, thou little sleepy
   thing,
The yellow flags that broidered thee would stand
Up to their chins in water, and full oft
WE pulled them and the other shining flowers,
  That all are gone to-day:
WE two, that had so many things to say,
  So many hopes to render clear:
And they are all gone after thee, my dear,—
  Gone after those sweet hours,
  That tender light, that balmy rain;
  Gone "as a wind that passeth away,
   And cometh not again."

VII.

I only saw the stars,—I could not see
  The river,—and they seemed to lie
As far below as the other stars were high.
I trembled like a thing about to die:
It was so awful 'neath the majesty
Of that great crystal height that overhung
  The blackness at our feet,
  Unseen to fleet and fleet
  The flocking stars among,
And only hear the dipping of the oar,
And the small wave's caressing of the darksome
   shore.

VIII.

  Less real it was than any dream.
Ah me! to hear the bending willows shiver,
As he shot quickly from the silent river,
  And felt the swaying and the flow
That bore us down the deeper, wider stream,
  Whereto its nameless waters go:
O! I shall always, when I shut mine eyes,
  See that weird sight again;
The lights from anchored vessels hung;
The phantom moon that sprung
Suddenly up in dim and angry wise,
  From the rim o' the moaning main,
  And touched with elfin light
The two long oars whereby we made our
   flight,
  Along the reaches of the night;
  Then furrowed up a lowering cloud,
Went in, and left us darker than before,
To feel our way as the midnight watches wore,
And lie in HER lee, with mournful faces bowed,
That should receive and bear with her away
The brightest portion of my sunniest day,—
The laughter of the land, the sweetness of the
   shore.

IX.

And I beheld thee: saw the lantern flash
Down on thy face, when thou didst climb the
   side.
And thou wert pale, pale as the patient bride
  That followed: both a little sad,

Leaving of home and kin. Thy courage glad,
    That once did bear thee on,
That brow of thine had lost ; the fervor rash
Of unforeboding youth thou hadst foregone.
O, what a little moment, what a crumb
Of comfort for a heart to feed upon !
        And that was all its sum :
        A glimpse and not a meeting,—
        A drawing near by night,
    To sigh to thee an unacknowledged greeting,
And all between the flashing of a light
    And its retreating.

X.

Then after, ere she spread her wafting wings,
The ship,—and weighed her anchor to depart,
We stole from her dark lee, like guilty things ;
    And there was silence in my heart,
And silence in the upper and the nether deep.
    O sleep ! O sleep !
Do not forget me. Sometimes come and sweep,
Now I have nothing left, thy healing hand
Over the lids that crave thy visits bland,
        Thou kind, thou comforting one :
    For I have seen his face, as I desired,
    And all my story is done.
    O, I am tired !

THE MIDDLE WATCH.

I.

I WOKE in the night, and the darkness was
    heavy and deep ;
    I had known it was dark in my sleep,
    And I rose and looked out,
And the fathomless vault was all sparkling,
    set thick round about
With the ancient inhabiters silent, and wheeling too far
For man's heart, like a voyaging frigate, to sail,
    where remote
    In the sheen of their glory they float,
Or man's soul, like a bird, to fly near, of their
    beams to partake,
    And dazed in their wake,
    Drink day that is born of a star.
I murmured, "Remoteness and greatness, how
    deep you are set,
    How afar in the rim of the whole ;
You know nothing of me, nor of man, nor of
    earth, O. nor yet
Of our light-bearer,—drawing the marvellous
    moons as they roll,
    Of our regent, the sun.
I look on you trembling, and think, in the
    dark with my soul,
'How small is our place 'mid the kingdoms
    and nations of our God :
    These are greater than we, every one.'"

And there falls a great fear, and a dread cometh
    over, that cries,
    "O my hope ! Is there any mistake?
Did He speak ? Did I hear? Did I listen
    aright, if He spake?
Did I answer Him duly? for surely I now am
    awake,
    If never I woke until now."
And a light, baffling wind, that leads nowhither,
    plays on my brow.
As a sleep, I must think on my day, of my
    path as untrod,
Or trodden in dreams, in a dreamland whose
    coasts are a doubt ;
Whose countries recede from my thoughts, as
    they grope round about,
    And vanish, and tell me not how.
Be kind to our darkness, O Fashioner, dwelling in light,
    And feeding the lamps of the sky ;
Look down upon this one, and let it be sweet
    in Thy sight,
    I pray Thee, to-night.
O watch whom Thou madest to dwell on its
    soil, Thou Most High !
For this is a world full of sorrow (there may be
    but one) ;
Keep watch o'er its dust, else Thy children for
    aye are undone,
    For this is a world where we die.

II.

With that, a still voice in my spirit that moved
    and that yearned,
    (There fell a great calm while it spake,)
I had heard it erewhile, but the noises of life are
    so loud,
That sometimes it dies in the cry of the street
    and the crowd :
To the simple it cometh,—the child, or asleep,
    or awake,
And they know not from whence ; of its nature
    the wise never learned
By his wisdom ; its secret the worker ne'er
    earned
By his toil ; and the rich among men never
    bought with his gold ;
    Nor the times of its visiting monarchs
        controlled,
    Nor the jester put down with his jeers
(For it moves where it will), nor its season
    the aged discerned
    By thought in the ripeness of years.
O elder than reason, and stronger than will !
    A voice when the dark world is still :
Whence cometh it? Father Immortal, Thou
    knowest ! and we,—
We are sure of that witness, that sense which
    is sent us of Thee ;
For it moves, and it yearns in its fellowship
    mighty and dread,
And let down to our hearts it is touched by the
    tears that we shed ;

It is more than all meanings, and over all strife;
  On its tongue are the laws of our life,
  And it counts up the times of the dead.

III.

I will fear you, O stars, never more.
I have felt it! Go on, while the world is
    asleep,
Golden islands, fast moored in God's infinite
    deep.
Hark, hark to the words of sweet fashion, the
    harpings of yore!
How they sang to Him, seer and saint, in the
    far away lands!
  "The heavens are the work of Thy hands;
  They shall perish, but Thou shalt endure;
  Yea, they all shall wax old,—
But Thy throne is established, O God, and
    Thy years are made sure ;
  They shall perish, but Thou shalt endure;
  They shall pass like a tale that is told."

  Doth He answer, the Ancient of Days?
  Will He speak in the tongue and the
    fashion of men?
(Hist! hist! while the heaven-hung multitudes
    shine in His praise,
His language of old.) Nay, He spoke with
    them first; it was then
  They lifted their eyes to His throne :
"They shall call on Me, 'Thou art our
    Father, our God, Thou alone!'
For I made them, I led them in deserts and
    desolate ways ;
  I have found them a Ransom Divine ;
I have loved them with love everlasting, the
    children of men ;
  I swear by Myself, they are Mine."

THE MORNING WATCH.

THE COMING IN OF THE "MER-MAIDEN."

The moon is bleached as white as wool,
  And just dropping under ;
Every star is gone but three,
  And they hang far asunder,—
There's a sea-ghost all in gray,
  A tall shape of wonder !

I am not satisfied with sleep,—
  The night is not ended.
But look how the sea-ghost comes,
  With wan skirts extended,
Stealing up in this weird hour,
  When light and dark are blended.

A vessel ! To the old pier end
  Her happy course she's keeping ;
I heard them name her yesterday :
  Some were pale with weeping ;
Some with their heart-hunger sighed ;
  She's in,—and they are sleeping.

O ! now with fancied greetings blest,
  They comfort their long aching :
The sea of sleep hath borne to them
  What would not come with waking,
And the dreams shall most be true
  In their blissful breaking.

The stars are gone, the rose-bloom comes,—
  No blush of maid is sweeter ;
The red sun, half way out of bed,
  Shall be the first to greet her.
None tell the news, yet sleepers wake,
  And rise, and run to meet her.

Their lost they have, they hold ; from pain
  A keener bliss they borrow.
How natural is joy, my heart !
  How easy after sorrow !
For once, the best is come that hope
  Promised them "to-morrow."

CONCLUDING SONG OF DAWN.

(Old English Manner.)

A MORN OF MAY.

All the clouds about the sun lay up in golden
    creases,
(Merry rings the maiden's voice that sings at
    dawn of day;)
Lambkins woke and skipped around to dry
    their dewy fleeces,
So sweetly as she carolled, all on a morn of
    May.

Quoth the Serjeant, "Here I'll halt ; here's
    wine of joy for drinking ;
To my heart she sets her hand, and in the strings
    doth play ;
All among the daffodils, and fairer to my think-
    ing,
And fresh as milk and roses, she sits this morn
    of May."

Quoth the Sergeant, "Work is work, but any
    ye might make me,
If I worked for you, dear lass, I'd count my
    holiday.
I'm your slave for good and all, an' if ye will
    but take me,
So sweetly as ye carol upon this morn of May."

"Medals count for worth," quoth she, "and
    scars are worn for honor ;
But a slave an' if ye be, kind wooer, go your
    way."

All the nodding daffodils woke up and laughed
    upon her.
O! sweetly did she carol, all on that morn of
    May.

Gladsome leaves upon the bough, they fluttered
    fast and faster,
Fretting brook, till he would speak, did chide
    the dull delay :
Beauty! when I said a slave, I think I meant
    a master ;
So sweetly as ye carol all on this morn of May.

"Lass, I love you! Love is strong, and some
    men's hearts are tender."

Far she sought o'er wood and wold, but found
    not aught to say ;
Mounting lark nor mantling cloud would any
    counsel render,
Though sweetly she had carolled upon that
    morn of May.

Shy, she sought the wooer's face, and deemed
    the wooing mended ;
Proper man he was, good sooth, and one would
    have his way :
So the lass was made a wife, and so the song
    was ended.
O! sweetly she did carol all on that morn of
    May.

A STORY OF DOOM.

BOOK I.

NILOIYA said to Noah, "What aileth thee,
My master, unto whom is my desire,
The father of my sons?" He answered her,
"Mother of many children, I have heard
The Voice again." "Ah, me!" she saith, "ah, me!
What spake it!" and with that Niloiya sighed.

This when the Master-builder heard, his heart
Was sad in him, the while he sat at home
And rested after toil. The steady rap
O' the shipwright's hammer sounding up the vale
Did seem to mock him; but her distaff down
Niloiya laid, and to the doorplace went,
Parted the purple covering seemly hung
Before it, and let in the crimson light
Of the descending sun. Then looked he forth,—
Looked, and beheld the hollow where the ark
Was a-preparing; where the dew distilled
All night from the leaves of old lign-aloe-trees,
Upon the gliding river; where the palm,
The almug, and the gophir shot their heads
Into the crimson brede that dyed the world:
And lo! he marked—unwieldy, dark and huge—
The ship, his glory and his grief,—too vast
For that still river's floating,—building far
From mightier streams, amid the pastoral dells
Of shepherd kings.

Niloiya spake again:
"What said the Voice, thou well-beloved man?"
He laboring with his thought that troubled him,
Spoke on behalf of God "Behold," said he,
"A little handful of unlovely dust
He fashioned to a lordly grace, and when
He laughed upon its beauty, it waxed warm,
And with His breath awoke a living soul.

"Shall not the Fashioner command His work?
And who am I, that, if He whisper, 'Rise,
Go forth upon Mine errand,' should reply,
'Lord, God, I love the woman and her sons,—
I love not scorning; I beseech Thee, God,
Have me excused.'"

She answered him, "Tell on."
And he, continuing, reasoned with his soul:

"What though I—like some goodly lama sunk
In meadow grass, eating her way at ease,
Unseen of them that pass, and asking not
A wider prospect than of yellow flowers
That nod above her head—should lay me down,
And willingly forget this high behest,
There should be yet no tarrying. Furthermore,
Though I went forth to cry against the doom,
Earth crieth louder, and she draws it down:
It hangeth balanced over us; she crieth,
And it shall fall. O! as for me, my life
Is bitter, looking onward, for I know
That in the fulness of the time shall dawn
That day: my preaching shall not bring forth fruit,
Though for its sake I leave thee. I shall float
Upon the abhorrèd sea, that mankind hate,
With thee and thine."

She answered: "God forbid!
For, sir, though men be evil, yet the deep
They dread, and at the last will surely turn
to Him, and He long-suffering will forgive,
And chide the waters back to their abyss,
To cover the pits where doleful creatures feed.
Sir, I am much afraid; I would not hear
Of riding on the waters: look you, sir,
Better it were to die with you by hand
Of them that hate us, than to live, ah me!
Rolling among the furrows of the unquiet,
Unconsecrate, unfriendly, dreadful sea."

He saith again: "I pray thee, woman, peace,
For thou wilt enter, when that day appears,
The fateful ship."

"My Lord," quoth she, "I will.
But O, good sir, be sure of this, be sure
The Master calleth; for the time is long
That thou hast warned the world: thou art but here
Three days; the song of welcoming but now
Is ended. I behold thee, I am glad;
And wilt thou go again? Husband, I say,
Be sure who 't is that calleth; O, be sure,
Be sure. My mother's ghost came up last night,
Whilst I thy beard, held in my hands, did kiss,
Leaning anear thee, wakeful through my love,
And watchful of thee till the moon went down.

"She never loved me since I went with thee
To sacrifice among the hills: she smelt
The holy smoke, and could no more divine
Till the new moon. I saw her ghost come up;
It had a snake with a red comb of fire
Twisted about its waist,—the doggish head

Lolled on its shoulder, and so leered at me.
'This woman might be wiser,' quoth the ghost;
'Shall there be husbands for her found below,
When she comes down to us? O, fool! O, fool!
She must not let her man go forth, to leave
Her desolate, and reap the whole world's scorn,
A harvest for himself.' With that they passed."

He said: " My crystal drop of perfectness,
I pity thee; it was an evil ghost:
Thou wilt not heed the counsel?" "I will not,"
Quoth she; "I am loyal to the Highest. Him
I hold by even as thou, and deem Him best.
Sir, am I fairer than when last we met?"

"God add," said he, "unto thy much yet more,
As I do think thou art." "And think you, sir,"
Niloiya saith, "that I have reached the prime?"
He answering, "Nay, not yet." "I would 't were so,"
She plaineth, "for the daughters mock at me:
Her locks forbear to grow, they say, so sore
She pineth for the master, Look you, sir,
They reach but to the knee. But thou art come,
And all goes merrier. Eat, my lord, of all
My supper that I set, and afterward
Tell me, I pray thee, somewhat of thy way;
Else shall I be despised as Adam was,
Who compassed not the learning of his sons,
But, grave and silent, oft would lower his head
And ponder, following of great Isha's feet,
When she would walk with her fair brow upraised,
Scorning the children that she bare to him."

"Ay," quoth the master; "but they did amiss
When they despised their father: knowest thou that?"

"Sure he was foolisher," Niloiya saith,
"Than any that came after. Furthermore,
He had not heart nor courage for to rule:
He let the mastery fall from his slack hand.
Had not our glorious mother still borne up
His weakness, chid with him, and sat apart,
And listened, when the fit came over him
To talk on his lost garden, he had sunk
Into the slave of slaves."

"Nay, thou must think
How he had dwelt long, God's loved husbandman,
And looked in hope among the tribes for one
To be his fellow, ere great Isha, once
Waking, he found at his left side, and knew
The deep delight of speech." So Noah, and thus
Added, "And therefore was his loss the more;
For though the creatures he had singled out
His favorites, dared for him the fiery sword
And followed after him,—shall bleat of lamb
Console one for the foregone talk of God?
Or in the afternoon, his faithful dog,
Fawning upon him, make his heart forget
At such a time, and such a time, to have heard
What he shall hear no more?

"O, as for him,
It was for this that he full oft would stop,
And, lost in thought, stand and revolve that deed,
Sad muttering, "Woman! we reproach thee not;
Though thou didst eat mine immortality;
Earth, be not sorry; I was free to choose.'
Wonder not, therefore, if he walked forlorn.
Was not the helpmeet given to raise him up
From his contentment with the lower things?
Was she not somewhat that he could not rule
Beyond the action, that he could not have
By the mere holding, and that still aspired
And drew him after her? So, when deceived
She fell by great desire to rise, he fell
By loss of upward drawing, when she took
An evil tongue to be her counsellor:
'Death is not as the death of lower things,
Rather a glorious change begrudged of Heaven,
A change to being as gods,'—he from her hand,
Upon reflection, took of death that hour,
And ate it (not the death that she had dared);
He ate it knowing. Then divisions came.
She, like a spirit strayed who lost the way,
Too venturesome, among the farther stars,
And hardly cares, because it hardly hopes
To find the path to heaven; in bitter wise
Did bear to him degenerate seed, and he,
Once having felt her upward drawing, longed,
And yet aspired, and yearned to be restored,
Albeit she drew no more."

"Sir, ye speak well,"
Niloiya saith, "but yet the mother sits
Higher than Adam. He did understand
Discourse of birds and all four-footed things,
But she had knowledge of the many tribes
Of angels and their tongues; their playful ways
And greetings when they met. Was she not wise?
They say she knew much that she never told,
And had a voice that called to her as thou."

"Nay," quoth the Master-shipwright, "who am I
That I should answer? As for me, poor man,
Here is my trouble: 'if there be a Voice,'
At first I cried, 'let me behold the mouth
That uttereth it.' Thereon it held its peace.
But afterward, I, journeying up the hill,
Did hear it hollower than an echo fallen
Across some clear abyss; and I did stop,
And ask of all my company, 'What cheer?
If there be spirits abroad that call to us,
Sirs, hold your peace and hear.' So they gave heed,
And one man said, 'It is the small grounddoves

That peck upon the stony hillocks;' one,
'It is the mammoth in yon cedar swamp
That cheweth in his dream;' and one, 'My
    lord,
It is the ghost of him that yesternight
We slew, because he grudged to yield his wife
To thy great father, when he peaceably
Did send to take her.' Then I answered;
'Pass,'
And they went on; and I did lay mine ear
Close to the earth; but there came up there-
    from
No sound, nor any speech; I waited long,
And in the saying, 'I will mount my beast
And on,' I was as one that in a trance
Beholdeth what is coming, and I saw
Great waters and a ship; and somewhat spake,
'Lo, this shall be; let him that heareth it,
And seeth it, go forth to warn his kind,
For I will drown the world."

                    "Niloiya saith,
"Sir, was that all that ye went forth upon?"
The master, he replieth, "Ay, at first,
That same was all: but many days went by,
While I did reason with my heart and hope
For more, and struggle to remain, and think,
'Let me be certain;' and so think again,
'The counsel is but dark; would I had more!
When I have more to guide me, I will go.'
And afterward, when reasoned on too much,
It seemed remoter, then I only said,
'O, would I had the same again;' and still
I had it not.

                    "Then at the last I cried,
'If the unseen be silent, I will speak
And certify my meaning to myself.
Say that He spoke, then He will make that
    good
Which He hath spoken. Therefore it were
    best
To go, and do His bidding. All the earth
Shall hear the judgment so, and none may cry
When the doom falls, "Thou God art hard on
    us;
We knew not Thou wert angry. O! we are
    lost,
Only for lack of being warned."

            "'But say
That He spoke not, and merely it befell
That I being weary had a dream. Why, so
He could not suffer damage; when the time
Was past, and that I threatened had not come,
Men would cry out on me, haply me kill,
For troubling their content. They would not
    swear,
"God, that did send this man, is proved un-
    true,"
But rather, "Let him die; he lied to us;
God never sent him." Only Thou, great King,
Knowest if Thou didst speak or no. I leave
The matter here. If Thou wilt speak again,
I go in gladness. If Thou wilt not speak,

Nay, if Thou never didst, I not the less
Shall go, because I have believed, what time
I seemed to hear Thee, and the going stands
With memory of believing.' Then I washed,
And did array me in the sacred gown,
And take a lamb."

            "Ay, sir" Niloiya sighed,
"I following, and I knew not anything
Till, the young lamb asleep in thy two arms,
We, moving up among the silent hills,
Paused in a grove to rest; and many slaves
Came near to make obeisance, and to bring
Wood for the sacrifice, and turf and fire.
Then in their hearing thou didst say to me,
'Behold, I know thy good fidelity,
And theirs that are about us; they would
    guard
The mountain passes, if it were my will
Awhile to leave thee;' and the pygmies laughed
For joy, that thou wouldst trust inferior things;
And put their heads down, as their manner is,
To touch our feet. They laughed, but sore I
    wept;
Sir, I could weep now; ye did ill to go
If that was all your bidding; I had thought
God drave thee, and thou couldst not choose
    but go."

Then said the son of Lamech, "Afterward,
When I had left thee, He whom I had served
Met with me in the visions of the night,
To comfort me for that I had withdrawn
From thy dear company. He sware to me
That no man should molest thee, no, nor touch
The bordering of mine utmost field. I say,
When I obeyed, He made His matters plain.
With whom could I have left thee, but with
    them;
Born in thy mother's house, and bound thy
    slaves?"

She said, "I love not pygmies; they are
    naught."
And he, "Who made them pygmies?" Then
    she pushed
Her veiling hair back from her round, soft eyes,
And answered, wondering, "Sir, my mothers
    did;
Ye know it." And he drew her near to sit
Beside him on the settle, answering, "Ay."
And they went on to talk as writ below,
If any one shall read:

                "Thy mother did,
And they that went before her. Thinkest thou
That they did well?"

                "They had been overcome,
And when the angered conquerors drave them
    out,
Behove them find some other way to rule,
They did but use their wits. Hath not man
    aye
Been cunning in dominion, among beasts

To breed for size or swiftness, or for sake
Of the white wool he loveth, at his choice?
What harm if coveting a race of men
That could but serve, they sought among their
   thralls,
Such as were low of stature, men and maids;
Ay, and of feeble will and quiet mind?
Did they not spend much gear to gather out
Such as I tell of, and for matching them
One with another for a thousand years?
What harm, then, if there came of it a race,
Inferior in their wits, and in their size,
And well content to serve?"

                  "What harm?" thou sayest.
My wife doth ask, 'What harm?'"

                      "Your pardon, sir.
I do remember that there came one day,
Two of the grave old angels that God made,
When first He invented life (right old they
   were,
And plain, and venerable); and they said,
Rebuking of my mother as with hers
She sat, 'Ye do not well, ye wives of men,
To match your wit against the Maker's will,
And for your benefit to lower the stamp
Of His fair image, which He set at first
Upon man's goodly frame; ye do not well
To treat His likeness even as ye treat
The bird and beast that perish.'"

                     "Said they aught
To appease the ancients, or to speak them
   fair?"

"How know I? 'Twas a slave that told it
   me.
My mother was full old when I was born,
And that was in her youth. What think you,
   sir?
Did not the giants likewise ill?"

                        "To that
I have no answer ready. If a man,
When each one is against his fellow, rule,
Or unmolested dwell, or unreproved,
Because, for size and strength, he standeth first,
He will thereof be glad; and if he say,
'I will to wife choose me a stately maid,
And leave a goodly offspring;' 'sooth, I think,
He sinneth not: for good to him and his
He would be strong and great. Thy people's
   fault
Was, that for ill to others, they did plot
To make them weak and small."

                    "But yet they steal
Or take in war the strongest maids, and such
As are of highest stature; ay, and oft
They fight among themselves for that same
   cause.
And they are proud against the King of heaven:
They hope in course of ages they shall come
To be as strong as He."

                      The Master said,
"I will not hear thee talk thereof; my heart
Is sick for all this wicked world. Fair wife,
I am right weary. Call thy slaves to thee,
And bid that they prepare the sleeping place.
O would that I might rest! I fain would rest,
And, no more wandering, tell a thankless
   world
My never-heeded tale!"

                      With that she called.
The moon was up and some few stars were out,
While heavy at the heart he walked abroad
To meditate before his sleep. And yet
Niloiya pondered, "Shall my master go?
And will my master go? What 'vaileth it,
That he doth spend himself, over the waste
A-wandering, till he reach outlandish folk,
That mock his warning? O, what 'vaileth it,
That he doth lavish wealth to build yon ark,
Whereat the daughters, when they eat with me,
Laugh? O my heart! I would the Voice were
   stilled.
Is not he happy? Who, of all the earth,
Obeyeth like to me? Have not I learned
From his dear mouth to utter seemly words,
And lay the powers my mother gave me by?
Have I made offerings to the dragon? Nay.
And I am faithful when he leaveth me
Lonely betwixt the peakéd mountain tops
In this long valley, where no stranger foot
Can come without my will. He shall not go.
Not yet, not yet! But three days—only
   three—
Beside me, and a-muttering on the third,
'I have heard the Voice again.' Be dull, O
   dull,
Mind and remembrance! Mother, ye did ill;
'T is hard unlawful knowledge not to use.
Why, O dark mother, opened ye the way?"
Yet when he entered, and did lay aside
His costly robe of sacrifice,—the robe
Wherein he had been offering, ere the sun
Went down,—forgetful of her mother's craft,
She lovely and submiss did mourn to him:
"Thou wilt not go,—I pray thee do not go,
Till thou hast seen thy children." And he
   said,
"I will not. I have cried, and have prevailed:
To-morrow it is given me by the Voice
Upon a four-days' journey to proceed,
And follow down the river, till its waves
Are swallowed in the sand, where no flesh
   dwells.

"'There,' quoth the Unrevealéd, 'we shall
   meet,
And I will counsel thee; and thou shalt turn
And rest thee with the mother, and with them
She bare.' Now, therefore, when the morn
   appears,
Thou fairest among women, call thy slaves,
And bid them yoke the steers, and spread thy
   car

With robes, the choicest work of cunning hands;
Array thee in thy rich apparel, deck
Thy locks with gold; and while the hollow vale
I thread beside yon river, go thou forth
Atween the mountains to my father's house,
And let thy slaves make all obeisance due,
And take and lay an offering at his feet.
Then light, and cry to him, 'Great King, the son
Of old Methuselah, thy son hath sent
To fetch the growing maids, his children, home."

"Sir," quoth the woman, "I will do this thing,
So thou keep faith with me, and yet return.
But will the Voice, think you, forget to chide,
Nor that Unseen, who calleth, buffet thee,
And drive thee on?"

    He saith, "It will keep faith.
Fear not. I have prevailed, for I besought,
And lovingly it answered. I shall rest,
And dwell with thee till after my three sons
Come from the chase." She said, "I let them forth
In fear, for they are young. Their slaves are few.
The giant elephants be cunning folk;
They lie in ambush, and will draw men on
To follow,—then will turn and tread them down."
"Thy father's house unwisely planned," said he,
"To drive them down upon the growing corn
Of them that were their foes; for now, behold,
They suffer while the unwieldy beasts delay
Retirement to their lands, and, meanwhile, pound
The damp, deep meadows to a pulpy mash;
Or wallowing in the waters, foul them; nay,
Tread down the banks, and let them forth to flood
Their cities; or assailed and falling, shake
The walls, and taint the wind, ere thirty men,
Over the hairy terror piling stones
Or earth, prevail to cover it."

    She said,
"Husband, I have been sorry, thinking oft
I would my sons were home; but now so well
Methinks it is with me, that I am fain
To wish they might delay, for thou wilt dwell
With me till after they return, and thou
Hast set thine eyes upon them. Then, ah me!
I must sit joyless in my place; bereft
As trees that suddenly have dropped their leaves,
And dark as nights that have no moon."

    She spake:
The hope o' the world did hearken, but reply
Made none. He left his hand on her fair locks
As she lay sobbing; and the quietness
Of night began to comfort her, the fall
Of far-off waters, and the wingèd wind
That went among the trees. The patient hand,
Moreover, that was steady, wrought with her,
Until she said, "What wilt thou? Nay, I know.
I therefore answer what thou utterest not.
*Thou lovest me well, and not for thine own will
Consentest to depart.* What more? Ay, this:
*I do avow that He which calleth thee
Hath right to call; and I do swear the Voice
Shall have no let of me to do Its will.*"

BOOK II.

Now ere the sunrise, while the morning star
Hung yet behind the pine-bough, woke and prayed
The world's great shipwright, and his soul was glad
Because the Voice was favorable. Now
Began the tap o' the hammer, now ran forth
The slaves preparing food. They therefore ate
In peace together; then Niloiya forth
Behind the milk-white steers went on her way;
And the great Master-builder, down the course
Of the long river, on his errand sped,
And as he went, he thought:

    [They do not well
Who, walking up a trodden path, all smooth
With footsteps of their fellows, and made straight
From town to town, will scorn at them that wonn
Under the covert of God's eldest trees
(Such as He planted with His hand, and fed
With dew before rain fell, till they stood close
And awful; drank the light up as it dropt,
And kept the dusk of ages at their roots),—
They do not well who mock at such, and cry,
"We peaceably, without or fault or fear,
Proceed, and miss not of our end; but these
Are slow and fearful; with uncertain pace,
And ever reasoning of the way, they oft,
After all reasoning, choose the worser course,
And, plunged in swamp, or in the matted growth
Nigh smothered, struggle, all to reach a goal
Not worth their pains." Nor do they well whose work
Is still to feed and shelter them and theirs,
Get gain, and gathered store it, to think scorn
Of those who work for a world (no wages paid
By a Master hid in light), and sent alone
To face a laughing multitude, whose eyes
Are full of damaging pity, that forbears
To tell the harmless laborer, ''Thou art mad.'']

And as he went he thought: "They counsel me,
Ay, with a kind of reason in their talk,

'Consider; call thy soberer thought to aid:
Why to but one man should a message come?
And why, if but to one, to thee? Art thou
Above us, greater, wiser? Had He sent,
He had willed that we should heed. Then since He knoweth
That such as thou a wise man cannot heed,
He did not send.' My answer, 'Great and wise,
If He had sent with thunder, and a voice
Leaping from Heaven, ye must have heard; but so
Ye had been robbed of choice, and, like the beasts,
Yoked to obedience. God makes no men slaves.'
They tell me, 'God is great above thy thought:
He meddles not; and this small world is ours,
These many hundred years we govern it;
Old Adam, after Eden, saw Him not.'
Then I, 'It may be He is gone to knead
More clay. But look, my masters; one of you,
Going to warfare, layeth up his gown,
His sickle, or his gold, and thinks no more
Upon it, till young trees have waxen great;
At last, when he returneth, he will seek
His own. And God, shall He not do the like?
And, having set new worlds a-rolling, come
And say, "I will betake me to the earth
That I did make;" and, having found it vile,
Be sorry. Why should man be free, you wise,
And not the Master?' Then they answer, 'Fool!
A man shall cast a stone into the air
For pastime, or for lack of heed,—but He!
Will He come fingering of His ended work,
Fright it with His approaching face, or snatch
One day the rolling wonder from its ring,
And hold it quivering, as a wanton child
Might take a nestling from its downy bed,
And having satisfied a careless wish,
Go thrust it back into its place again?'
To such I answer, and, that doubt once mine,
I am assured that I do speak aright:
'Sirs, the significance of this your doubt
Lies in the reason of it; ye do grudge
That these your lands should have another Lord;
Ye are not loyal, therefore ye would fain
Your King would bide afar. But if ye looked
For countenance and favor when He came,
Knowing yourselves right worthy, would ye care,
With cautious reasoning, deep and dark, to prove
That He would never come, and would your wrath
Be hot against a prophet? Nay, I wot
That as a flatterer you would look on him,—
"Full of sweet words thy mouth is: if He come,—
We think not that He will,—but if He come,
Would it might be to-morrow, or to-night,
Because we look for praise." ' "

Now, as he went,
The noontide heats came on, and he grew faint;
But while he sat below an almug-tree,
A slave approached with greeting. "Master, hail!"
He answered, "Hail! what wilt thou?" Then she said,
"The palace of thy fathers standeth nigh."
"I know it," quoth he; and she said again,
"The Elder, learning thou wouldst pass, hath sent
To fetch thee." Then he rose and followed her.
So first they walked beneath a lofty roof
Of living bough and tendril, woven on high
To let no drop of sunshine through, and hung
With gold and purple fruitage, and the white
Thick cups of scented blossom. Underneath,
Soft grew the sward and delicate, and flocks
Of egrets, ay, and many cranes, stood up,
Fanning their wings, to agitate and cool
The noonday air, as men with heed and pains
Had taught them, marshalling and taming them
To bear the wind in on their moving wings.

So long time as a nimble slave would spend
In milking of her cow, they walked at ease;
Then reached the palace, all of forest trunks,
Brought whole and set together, made. Therein
Had dwelt old Adam, when his mighty sons
Had finished it, and up to Eden gate
Had journeyed for to fetch him. "Here," they said
"Mother and father, ye may dwell, and here
Forget the garden wholly."
So he came
Under the doorplace, and the women sat,
Each with her finger on her lips; but he,
Having been called, went on, until he reached
The jewelled settle, wrought with cunning work
Of gold and ivory, whereon they wont
To set the Elder. All with sleekest skins,
That striped and spotted creatures of the wood
Had worn, the seat was covered, but thereon
The Elder was not: by the steps thereof,
Upon the floor, whereto his silver beard
Did reach, he sat, and he was in his trance.
Upon the settle many doves were perched,
That set the air a-going with their wings;
These opposite, the world's great Shipwright stood
To wait the burden; and the Elder spake:
"Will He forget me? Would He might forget!
Old, old! The hope of old Methuselah
Is all in His forgetfulness." With that,
A slave-girl took a cup of wine, and crept
Anear him saying, "Taste;" and when his lips
Had touched it, lo, he trembled, and he cried,
"Behold, I prophesy."

Then straight they fled
That were about him, and did stand apart
And stop their ears. For he from time to time,
Was plagued with that same fate to prophesy,
And spake against himself, against his day
And time, in words that all men did abhor.
Therefore, he, warning them what time the fit
Came on him, saved them, that they heard it
    not.
So while they fled, he cried: "I saw the God
Reach out of Heaven His wonderful right
    hand.
Lo, lo! He dipt it in the unquiet sea,
And in its curvéd palm beheld the ark,
As in a vast calm lake, came floating on.
Ay, then His other hand—the cursing hand—
He took and spread between us and the sun,
And all was black; the day was blotted out,
And horrible staggering took the frighted earth.
I heard the water hiss, and then methinks
The crack as of her splitting. Did she take
The palaces that are my brothers dear,
And huddle them with all their ancientry
Under into her breast? If it was black,
How could this old man see? There was a
    noise
I' the dark, and He drew back His hand
    again.
I looked——It was a dream,—let no man say
It was aught else. There, so—the fit goes by.
Sir, and my daughters, is it eventide?—
Sooner than that, saith old Methuselah
Let the vulture lay his beak to my green limbs.
What! art Thou envious?—are the sons of
    men
Too wise to please Thee, and to do Thy will?
Methuselah, he sitteth on the ground,
Clad in his gown of age, the pale white gown,
And goeth not forth to war; his wrinkled
    hands
He claspeth round his knees; old, very old.
Would he could steal from Thee one secret
    more—
The secret of Thy youth! O envious God!
We die. The words of old Methuselah
And his prophecy are ended."

                    Then the wives,
Beholding how he trembled, and the maids
And children, came anear, saying, "Who art
    Thou
That standest gazing on the Elder? Lo,
Thou dost not well: withdraw: for it was thou
Whose stranger presence troubled him, and
    brought
The fit of prophecy." And he did turn
To look upon them, and their majesty
And glorious beauty took away his words;
And, being pure among the vile, he cast
In his thought a veil of snow-white purity
Over the beauteous throng. "Thou dost not
    well,"
They said. He answered: "Blossoms o' the
    world,
Fruitful as fair, never in watered glade,

Where in the youngest grass blue cups push
    forth,
And the white lily reareth up her head,
And purples cluster, and the saffron flower
Clear as a flame of sacrifice breaks out,
And every cedar-bough, made delicate
With climbing roses, drops in white and red,—
Saw I (good angels keep you in their care)
So beautiful a crowd."

                    With that they stamped,
Gnashed their white teeth, and, turning, fled
    and spat
Upon the floor. The Elder spake to him,
Yet shaking with the burden, "Who art
    thou?"
He answered, "I, the man whom thou didst
    send
To fetch through this thy woodland, do forbear
To tell my name; thou lovest it not, great
    sire,—
No, nor mine errand. To thy house I spake,
Touching their beauty." "Wherefore didst
    thou spite,"
Quoth he, "the daughters?" and it seemed
    he lost
Count of that prophecy, for very age,
And from his thin lips dropt a trembling
    laugh.
"Wicked old man," quoth he, "this wise
    old man
I see as 'twere not I. Thou bad old man,
What shall be done to thee? for thou didst
    burn
Their babes, and strew the ashes all about,
To rid the world of His white soldiers. Ay,
Scenting of human sacrifice, they fled.
Cowards! I heard them winnow their great
    wings:
They went to tell Him; but they came no
    more.
The women hate to hear of them, so sore
They grudged their little ones; and yet no way
There was but that. I took it; I did well."

With that he fell to weeping. "Son," said
    he,
"Long have I hid mine eyes from stalwart
    men,
For it is hard to lose the majesty
And pride and power of manhood: but to-day,
Stand forth into the light, that I may look
Upon thy strength, and think, EVEN THUS
    DID I,
IN THE GLORY OF MY YOUTH, MORE LIKE TO
    GOD
THAN LIKE HIS SOLDIERS, FACE THE VASSAL
    WORLD."

Then Noah stood forward in his majesty,
Shouldering the golden billhook, wherewithal
He wont to cut his way, when tangled in
The matted hayes. And down the opened roof
Fell slanting beams upon his stately head,

And streamed along his gown, and made to
    shine
The jewelled sandals on his feet.

                            And lo,
The Elder cried aloud: "I prophesy.
Behold, my son is as a fruitful field
When all the lands are waste. The archers
    drew—
They drew the bow against him; they were
    fain
To slay: but he shall live—my son shall live,
And I shall live by him in the other days.
Behold the prophet of the Most High God:
Hear him. Behold the hope o' the world,
    what time
She lieth under. Hear him; he shall save
A seed alive, and sow the earth with man.
O earth! earth! earth! a floating shell of wood
Shall hold the remnant of thy mighty lords.
Will this old man be in it? Sir, and you
My daughters, hear him! Lo, this white old
    man
He sitteth on the ground. (Let be, let be:
Why dost Thou trouble us to make our tongue
Ring with abhorréd words?) The prophecy
Of the Elder, and the vision that he saw
They both are ended."

                Then said Noah: "the life
Of this my lord is low for very age:
Why then, with bitter words upon thy tongue,
Father of Lamech, dost thou anger Him?
Thou canst not strive against Him now." He
    said:
"Thy feet are toward the valley, where lie
    bones
Bleaching upon the desert. Did I love
The lithe strong lizards that I yoked and set
To draw my car? and were they not possessed?
Yea, all of them were liars. I loved them well.
What did the Enemy, but on a day
When I behind my talking team went forth,
They sweetly lying, so that all men praised
Their flattering tongues, and mild persuasive
    eyes,—
What did the Enemy but send His slaves,
Angels, to cast down stones upon their heads
And break them? Nay, I could not stir
    abroad
But havoc came; they never crept or flew,
Beyond the shelter that I builded here,
But straight the crowns I had set upon their
    heads
Were marks for myrmidons that in the clouds
Kept watch to crush them. Can a man forgive
That hath been warred on thus? I will not.
    Nay,
I swear it—I, the man Methuselah."
The Master-shipwright, he replied, "'Tis true,
Great loss was that; but they that stood thy
    friends,
The wicked spirits, spoke upon their tongues,
And cursed the God of heaven. What marvel,
    sir,
If He was angered?" But the Elder cried,
"They all are dead,—the toward beasts I
    loved;
My goodly team, my joy, they all are dead;
Their bones lie bleaching in the wilderness:
And I will keep my wrath for evermore
Against the Enemy that slew them. Go,
Thou coward servant of a tyrant King,
Go down the desert of the bones, and ask,
'My King, what bones are these? Methuselah,
The white old man that sitteth on the ground,
Sendeth a message, "Bid them that they live,
And let my lizards run up every path
They wont to take when out of silver pipes,
The pipes that Jubal wrought into my roof,
I blew a sweeter cry than song-bird's throat
Hath ever formed; and while they laid their
    heads
Submiss upon my threshold, poured away
Music that welled by heartsful out, and made
The throats of men that heard to swell, their
    breasts
To heave with the joy of grief; yea, caused
    the lips
To laugh of men asleep.

                        Return to me
The great wise lizards; ay, and them that flew
My pursuivants before me. Let me yoke
Again that multitude; and here I swear
That they shall draw my car and me thereon
Straight to the ship of doom. So men shall
    know
My loyalty, that I submit, and Thou
Shalt yet have honor, O mine Enemy,
By me. The speech of old Methuselah."'"

Then Noah made answer, "By the living God,
That is no enemy to men, great sire,
I will not take thy message; hear thou Him.
'Behold (He saith that suffereth thee), behold,
The earth that I made green cries out to Me,
Red with the costly blood of beauteous man.
I am robbed, I am robbed (He saith); they
    sacrifice
To evil demons of My blameless flocks,
That I did fashion with My hand. Behold,
How goodly was the world! I gave it thee
Fresh from its finishing. What hast thou done?
I will cry out to the waters, *Cover it,
And hide it from its Father. Lo, Mine eyes
Turn from it shamed.*'"

                    With that the old man laughed
Full softly. "Ay," quoth he, "a goodly
    world,
And we have done with it as we did list.
Why did he give it us? Nay, look you, son:
Five score they were that died in yonder waste;
And if He crieth, 'Repent, be reconciled,'
I answer, 'Nay, my lizards;' and again,
If He will trouble me in this mine age,
'Why hast Thou slain my lizards?' Now my
    speech
Is cut away from all my other words,

Standing alone. The Elder sweareth it,
The man of many days, Methuselah."

Then answered Noah, "My Master, hear it not;
But yet have patience;" and he turned himself,
And down betwixt the ordered trees went forth,
And in the light of evening made his way
Into the waste to meet the Voice of God.

BOOK III.

ABOVE the head of great Methuselah
There lay two demons in the opened roof,
Invisible, and gathered up his words;
For when the Elder prophesied, it came
About, that hidden things were shown to them,
And burdens that he spake against his time.

(But never heard them such as dwelt with him;
Their ears they stopped, and willed to live at ease
In all delight; and perfect in their youth,
And strong, disport them in the perfect world.)

Now these were fettered that they could not fly,
For a certain disobedience they had wrought
Against the ruler of their host; but not
The less they loved their cause; and when the feet
O' the Master-builder were no longer heard,
They, slipping to the sward, right painfully,
Did follow, for the one to the other said,
"Behooves our master know of this; and us,
Should he be favourable, he may loose
From these our bonds."

And thus it came to pass,
That while at dead of night the old dragon lay
Coiled in the cavern where he dwelt, the watch
Pacing before it saw in middle air
A boat, that gleamed like fire, and on it came,
And rocked as it drew near, and then it burst
And went to pieces, and there fell therefrom,
Close at the cavern's mouth, two glowing balls.

Now there was drawn a curtain nigh the mouth
Of that deep cave, to testify of wrath.
The dragon had been wroth with some that served,
And chased them from him; and his oracles,
That wont to drop from him, were stopped, and men
Might only pray to him through that fell web
That hung before him. Then did whisper low
Some of the little spirits that bat-like clung
And cluster'd round the opening. "Lo," they said,
While gazed the watch upon those glowing balls,
"These are like moons eclipsed; but let them

Red on the moss, and sear its dewy spires,
Until our lord give leave to draw the web,
And quicken reverence by his presence dread,
For he will know and call to them by name,
And they will change. At present he is sick,
And wills that none disturb him." So they lay,
And there was silence, for the forest tribes
Came never near that cave. Wiser than men,
They fled the serpent hiss that oft by night
Came forth of it, and feared the wan dusk forms
That stalked among the trees, and in the dark
Those whiffs of flame that wandered up the sky
And made the moonlight sickly.

Now the cave
Was marvellous for beauty, wrought with tools
Into the living rock, for there had worked
All cunning men, to cut on it with signs
And shows, yea, all the manner of mankind.
The fateful apple-tree was there, a bough
Bent with the weight of him that us beguiled;
And lilies of the field did seem to blow
And bud in the storied stone. There Tubal sat,
Who from his harp delivered music, sweet
As any in the spheres. Yea, more;
Earth's latest wonder on the walls appeared,
Unfinished, workmen clustering on its ribs;
And farther back, within the rock hewn out,
Angelic figures stood, that impious hands
Had fashioned; many golden lamps they held
By golden chains depending, and their eyes
All tended in a reverent quietude
Toward the couch whereon the dragon lay.
The floor was beaten gold; the curly lengths
Of his last coils lay on it, hid from sight
With a coverlet made stiff with crusting gems,
Fire-opals shooting, rubies, fierce bright eyes
Of diamonds, or the pale green emerald,
That changed their lustre when he breathed.

His head
Feathered with crimson combs, and all his neck,
And half-shut fans of his admired wings,
That in their scaly splendor put to shame
Or gold or stone, lay on his ivory couch
And shivered; for the dragon suffered pain:
He suffered and he feared. It was his doom,
The tempter, that he never should depart
From the bright creature that in Paradise
He for his evil purpose erst possessed,
Until it died. Thus only, spirit of might
And chiefest spirit of ill, could he be free.

But with its nature wed, as souls of men
Are wedded to their clay, he took the dread
Of death and dying, and the coward heart
Of the beast, and craven terrors of the end
Sank him that habited within it to dread
Disunion. He, a dark dominion erst
Rebellious, lay and trembled, for the flesh
Daunted his immaterial. He was sick
And sorry. Great ones of the earth had sent

Their chief musicians for to comfort him,
Chanting his praise, the friend of man, the god
That gave them knowledge, at so great a price
And co tly. Yea, the riches of the mine,
And glorious broidered work, and woven gold,
And all things wisely made, they at his feet
Laid daily ; for they said, " This mighty one,
All the world wonders after him. He lieth
Sick in his dwelling ; he hath long foregone
(To do us good) dominion, and a throne,
And his brave warfare with the Enemy,
So much he pitieth us that were denied
The gain and gladness of this knowledge. Now
Shall he be certified of gratitude,
And smell the sacrifice that most he loves."
The night was dark, but every lamp gave forth
A tender, lustrous beam. His beauteous wings
The dragon fluttered, cursed awhile, then turned
And moaned with lamentable voice, " I thirst,
Give me to drink." Thereon stepped out in haste,
From inner chambers, lovely ministrants,
Young boys with radiant locks and peaceful eyes,
And poured out liquor from their cups to cool
His parchéd tongue, and kneeling held it nigh
In jewelled basins sparkling ; and he lapped,
And was appeased, and said, " I will not hide
Longer my much-desired face from men.
Draw back the web of separation." Then
With cries of gratulation ran they forth,
And flung it wide, and all the watch fell low,
Each on his face, as drunk with sudden joy.
Thus marked he, glowing on the branchéd moss,
Those red rare moons, and let his serpent eyes
Consider them full subtly, " What be these?"
Inquiring : and the little spirits said,
" As we for thy protection (having heard
That wrathful sons of darkness walk to-night,
Such as do oft ill-use us) clustered here,
We marked a boat afire, that sailed the skies,
And furrowed up like spray a billowy cloud,
And, lo, it went to pieces, scattering down
A rain of sparks and these two angry moons."
Then said the dragon, " Let my guard and you,
Attendant hosts, recede ;" and they went back,
And formed about the cave a widening ring,
Then, halting, stood afar ; and from the cave
The snaky wonder spoke, with hissing tongue,
" If ye were Tartis and Deleisonon,
Be Tartis and Deleisonon once more."

Then egg-like cracked the glowing balls, and forth
Started black angels, trampling hard to free
Their fettered feet from out the smoking shell.

And he said, " Tartis and Deleisonon,
Your lord I am : draw nigh." " Thou art our lord,"
They answered, and with fettered limbs full low

They bent and made obeisance. Furthermore,
" O fiery flying serpent, after whom
The nations go, let thy dominion last,"
They said, " forever." And the serpent said,
" It shall : unfold your errand." They replied,
One speaking for a space, and afterward
His fellow taking up the word with fear,
And panting, " We were set to watch the mouth
Of great Methuselah. There came to him
The son of Lamech two days since." " My lord,
They prophesied, the Elder prophesied,
Unwitting, of the flood of waters,—ay,
A vision was before him, and the lands
Lay under water drowned. He saw the ark—
It floated in the Enemy's right hand."
" Lord of the lost, the son of Lamech fled
Into the wilderness to meet His voice
That reigneth, and we, diligent to hear
Aught that might serve thee, followed, but, forbid
To enter, lay upon its boundary cliff,
And wished for morning."

" When the dawn was red
We sought the man, we marked him ; and he prayed,—
Kneeling, he prayed in the valley, and he said—"
" Nay," quoth the serpent, " spare me, what devout
He fawning grovelled to the All-powerful ;
But if of what shall hap he aught let fall,
Speak that." They answered, " He did pray as one
That looketh to outlive mankind,—and more,
We are certified by all his scattered words,
That HE will take from men their length of days,
And cut them off like grass in its first flower :
From henceforth this shall be."

That when he heard,
The dragon made to the night his moan.

" And more,"
They said, " that He above would have men know
That He doth love them, whoso will repent,
To that man He is favorable, yea,
Will be his loving Lord."

The dragon cried,
" The last is worse than all. O man, thy heart
Is stout against His wrath. But will He love?
I heard it rumored in the heavens of old,
(And doth He love ?). Thou wilt not, canst not, stand
Against the love of God. Dominion fails ;
I see it float from me, that long have worn
Fetters of flesh to win it. Love of God !
I cry against thee ; thou art worse than all."
They answered, " Be not moved, admiréd chief

And trusted of mankind;" and they went on
And fed him with the prophecies that fell
From the Master-shipwright in his prayer.

       But prone
He lay, for he was sick; at every word
Prophetic cowering. As a bruising blow,
It fell upon his head and daunted him,
Until they ended, saying, "Prince, behold,
Thy servants have revealed the whole."

       Thereon
He out of snaky lips did hiss forth thanks.
Then said he, "Tartis and Deleisonon,
Receive your wages." So their fetters fell;
And they, retiring, lauded him, and cried,
"King, reign forever." Then he mourned,
 "Amen."

And he—being left alone—he said: "A light!
I see a light,—a star among the trees,—
An angel." And it drew toward the cave,
But with its sacred feet touched not the grass,
Nor lifted up the lids of its pure eyes,
But hung a span's length from that ground pollute,
At the opening of the cave.

      And when he looked,
The dragon cried, "Thou newly-fashioned thing,
Of name unknown, thy scorn becomes thee not.
Doth not thy Master suffer what thine eyes
Thou countest all too clean to open on?"
But still it hovered, and the quietness
Of holy heaven was on the drooping lids;
And not as one that answereth, it let fall
The music from its mouth, but like to one
That doth not hear, or, hearing, doth not heed.

"A message: 'I have heard thee, while remote
I went My rounds among the unfinished stars.'
A message: 'I have left thee to thy ways,
And mastered all thy vileness, for thy hate
I have made to serve the ends of My great love.
Hereafter will I chain thee down. To-day
One thing thou art forbidden; now thou knowest
The name thereof: I told it thee in heaven,
When thou wert sitting at My feet. Forbear
To let that hidden thing be whispered forth:
For man, ungrateful (and thy hope it was,
That so ungrateful he might prove), would scorn,
And not believe it, adding so fresh weight
Of condemnation to the doomèd world.
Concerning that, thou art forbid to speak;
Know thou didst count it, falling from My tongue,
A lovely song, whose meaning was unknown,
Unknowable, unbearable to thought,
But sweeter in the hearing than all harps
Toned in My holy hollow. Now thine ears
Are opened, know it, and discern and fear,
Forbearing speech of it for evermore."

So said, it turned, and with a cry of joy,
As one released, went up: and it was dawn,
And all boughs dropped with dew, and out of mist
Came the red sun and looked into the cave.

But the dragon, left a-tremble, called to him,
From the nether kingdom, certain of his friends,—
Three whom he trusted, councillors accursed.
A thunder-cloud stooped low and swathed the place
In its black swirls, and out of it they rushed,
And hid them in recesses of the cave,
Because they could not look upon the sun,
Sith light is pure. And Satan called to them,—
All in the dark, in his great rage he spake:
"Up," quoth the dragon; "it is time to work,
Or we are all undone." And he did hiss,
And there came shudderings over land and trees,
A dimness after dawn. The earth threw out
A blinding fog, that crept toward the cave,
And rolled up blank before it like a veil—
A curtain to conceal its habiters.
Then did those spirits move upon the floor,
Like pillars of darkness, and with eyes aglow.
One had a helm for covering of the scars
That seamed what rested of a goodly face;
He wore his visor up, and all his words
Were hollower than an echo from the hills:
He was hight Make. And lo, his fellow-fiend
Came after, holding down his dastard head,
Like one ashamed: now this for craft was great;
The dragon honored him. A third sat down
Among them, covering with his wasted hand
Somewhat that pained his breast.

      And when the fit
Of thunder, and the sobbings of the wind,
Were lulled, the dragon spoke with wrath and rage,
And told them of his matters: "Look to this,
If ye be loyal;" adding, "Give your thoughts,
And let me have your counsel in this need."

One spirit rose and spake, and all the cave
Was full of sighs, "The words of Make the Prince,
Of him once delegate in Betelgeux:
Whereas of late the manner is to change,
We know not where 't will end; and now my words
Go thus: give way, be peaceable, lie still
And strive not, else the world that we have won
He may, to drive us out, reduce to naught.

"For while I stood in mine obedience yet,
Steering of Betelgeux my sun, behold,
A moon, that evil ones did fill, rolled up
Astray, and suddenly the Master came,
And while, a million strong, like rooks they rose,
He took and broke it, flung it here and there,

And called a blast to drive the powder forth;
And it was fine as dust, and blurred the skies,
Farther than 'tis from hence to this young sun.
Spirits that passed upon their work that day,
Cried out, "How dusty 't is." Behooves us, then,
That we depart, as leaving unto Him
This goodly world and goodly race of man.
Not all are doomed: hereafter it may be
That we find place on it again.   But if,
Too zealous to preserve it, and the men
Our servants, we oppose Him, He may come,
And, choosing rather to undo His work
Than strive with it for aye, make so an end."

He sighing paused. Lo, then the serpent hissed
In impotent rage, "Depart! and how depart!
Can flesh be carried down where spirits wonn?
Or I, most miserable, hold my life
Over the airless, bottomless gulf, and bide
The buffetings of yonder shoreless sea?
O death, thou terrible doom: O death, thou dread
Of all that breathe."

               A spirit rose and spake:
"Whereas in Heaven is power, is much to fear;
For this admired country we have marred.
Whereas in Heaven is love (and there are days
When yet I can recall what love was like),
Is naught to fear. A threatening makes the whole,
And clogged with strong conditions: 'O, repent,
Man, and I turn.' He, therefore, powerful now,
And more so, master, that ye bide in clay,
Threateneth that He may save. They shall not die."

The dragon said, "I tremble, I am sick."
He said with pain of heart, "How am I fallen!
For I keep silence; yea, I have withdrawn
From haunting of His gates, and shouting up
Defiance. Wherefore doth He hunt me out
From this small world, this little one, that I
Have been content to take unto myself,
I here being loved and worshippéd?   He knoweth
How much I have foregone; and must He stoop
To whelm the world, and heave the floors o' the deep,
Of purpose to pursue me from my place?
And since I gave men knowledge, must He take
Their length of days whereby they perfect it?
So shall He scatter all that I have stored,
And get them by degrading them. I know
That in the end it is appointed me
To fade. I will not fade before the time."

A spirit rose, the third, a spirit ashamed
And subtle, and his face he turned aside :
"Whereas," said he, "we strive against both power
And love, behooves us that we strive aright.
Now some of old my comrades yesterday
I met, as they did journey to appear
In the Presence; and I said, 'My master lieth
Sick yonder, otherwise (for no decree
There stands against it) he would also come
And make obeisance with the sons of God.'
They answered, naught denying. Therefore, lord,
'Tis certain that ye have admittance yet ;
And what doth hinder? Nothing but this breath.
Were it not well to make an end and die,
And gain admittance to the King of kings?
What if thy slaves by thy consent should take
And bear thee on their wings above the earth,
And suddenly let fall,—how soon 'twere o'er!
We should have fear and sinking at the heart ;
But in a little moment we should see,
Rising majestic from a ruined heap,
The stately spirit that we served of yore."

The serpent turned his subtle deadly eyes
Upon the spirit and hissed; and, sick with shame,
It bowed itself together, and went back
With hidden face.   "This counsel is not good,"
The other twain made answer; "look, my lord,
Whereas 'tis evil in thine eyes, in ours
'Tis evil also ; speak, for we perceive
That on thy tongue the words of counsel sit,
Ready to fly to our right greedy ears,
That long for them."   And Satan, flattered thus
(For ever may the serpent kind be charmed
With soft, sweet words, and music deftly played),
Replied, "Whereas I surely rule the world,
Behooves that ye prepare for me a path,
And that I, putting of my pains aside,
Go stir rebellion in the mighty hearts
O' the giants ; for He loveth them, and looks
Full oft complacent on their glorious strength.
He willeth that they yield, that He may spare;
But, by the blackness of my loathéd den,
I say they shall not, no, they shall not yield ;
Go, therefore, take to you some harmless guise,
And spread a rumor that I come. I, sick,
Sorry, and aged, hasten. I have heard
Whispers that out of heaven dropped unaware.
I caught them up, and sith they bode men harm,
I am ready for to comfort them ; yea, more,
To counsel, and I will that they drive forth
The women, the abhorréd of my soul ;
Let not a woman breathe where I shall pass,
Lest the curse falleth, and she bruise my head.
Friends, if it be their mind to send for me
An army, and triumphant draw me on

In the golden car you wot of, and with shouts,
I would not that ye hinder them. Ah, then
Will I make hard their hearts, and grieve Him sore
That loves them, O, by much too well to wet
Their stately heads, and soil those locks of strength
Under the fateful brine. Then afterward,
While He doth reason vainly with them, I
Will offer Him a pact : 'Great King, a pact,
And men shall worship Thee, I say they shall,
For I will bid them do it, yea, and leave
To sacrifice their kind, so Thou my name
Wilt suffer to be worshipped after Thine."

"Yea, my lord Satan," quoth they, "do this thing,
And let us hear thy words, for they are sweet."

Then he made answer, "By a messenger
Have I this day been warned. There is a deed
I may not tell of, lest the people add
Scorn of a Coming Greatness to their faults.
Why this? Who careth, when about to slay,
And slay indeed, how well they have deserved
Death whom he slayeth? Therefore yet is hid
A meaning of some mercy that will rob
The nether world. Now look to it,—'Twere vain,
Albeit this deluge He would send indeed,
That we expect the harvest ; He would yet
Be the Master-reaper ; for I heard it said,
Them that be young and know Him not, and them
That are bound and may not build, yea, more, their wives,
Whom suffering not to hear the doom, they keep
Joyous behind the curtains, every one
With maidens nourished in the house, and babes
And children at her knees—(then what remain!)
He claimeth and will gather for His own.
Now, therefore, it were good by guile to work,
Princes, and suffer not the doom to fall.
There is no evil like to love. I heard
Him whisper it. Have I put on this flesh
To ruin his two children beautiful,
And shall my deed confound me in the end,
Through awful imitation? Love of God,
I cry against thee ; thou art worst of all."

BOOK IV.

Now while these evil ones took counsel strange,
The son of Lamech journeyed home ; and, lo !
A company came down, and struck the track
As he did enter it. There rode in front
Two horsemen, young and noble, and behind
Were following slaves with tent gear ; others led
Strong horses, others bare the instruments
O' the chase, and in the rear dull camels lagged,
Sighing, for they were burdened, and they loved
The desert sands above that grassy vale.

And as they met, those horsemen drew the rein,
And fixed on him their grave untroubled eyes ;
He in his regal grandeur walked alone,
And had nor steed nor follower, and his mien
Was grave and like to theirs. He said to them,
"Fair sirs, whose are ye?" They made answer cold,
"The beautiful woman, sir, our mother dear,
Niloiya, bare us to great Lamech's son."
And he, replying, " I am he." They said,
" We know it, sir. We have remembered you
Through many seasons. Pray you let us not ;
We fain would greet our mother." And they made
Obeisance and passed on ; then all their train,
Which while they spoke had halted, moved apace,
And, while the silent father stood, went by,
He gazing after, as a man that dreams ;
For he was sick with their cold, quiet scorn,
That seemed to say, "Father, we own you not,
We love you not, for you have left us long,—
So long, we care not that you come again."

And while the sullen camels moved, he spake
To him that led the last, " There are but two
Of these my sons; but where doth Japhet ride?
For I would see him." And the leader said,
"Sir, ye shall find him, if ye follow up
Along the track. Afore the noonday meal
The young men, even our masters, bathed ;
(there grows
A clump of cedars by the bend of yon
Clear river)—There did Japhet, after meat,
Being right weary, lay him down and sleep.
There, with a company of slaves and some
Few camels, ye shall find him."

                            And the man,
The father of these three, did let him pass,
And struggle and give battle to his heart,
Standing as motionless as pillar set
To guide a wanderer in a pathless waste
But all his strength went from him, and he strove
Vainly to trample out and trample down
The misery of his love unsatisfied,—
Unutterable love flung in his face.

Then he broke out in passionate words, that cried
Against his lot : "I have lost my own, and won
None other ; no, not one ! Alas, my sons !
That I have looked to for my solacing,
In the bitterness to come. My children dear !"

And when from his own lips he heard those
    words,
With passionate stirring of the heart, he wept.

And none came near to comfort him. His face
Was on the ground; but having wept, he rose
Full hastily, and urged his way to find
The river; and in hollow of his hand
Raised up the water to his brow: "This son,
This other son of mine," he said, "shall see
No tears upon my face." And he looked on,
Beheld the camels, and a group of slaves
Sitting apart from some one fast asleep,
Where they had spread out webs of broidery
    work
Under a cedar tree; and he came on,
And when they made obeisance he declared
His name, and said, "I will beside my son
Sit till he wakeneth." So Japhet lay
A-dreaming, and his father drew to him.
He said, "This cannot scorn me yet;" and
    paused,
Right angry with himself, because the youth,
Albeit of stately growth, so languidly
Lay with a listless smile upon his mouth,
That was full sweet and pure; and as he
    looked,
He half forgot his trouble in his pride.
"And is this mine?" said he, "my son! mine
    own!
(God, thou art good!) O, if this turn away,
That pang shall be past bearing. I must think
That all the sweetness of his goodly face
Is copied from his soul. How beautiful
Are children to their fathers! Son, my heart
Is greatly glad because of thee; my life
Shall lack of no completeness in the days
To come. If I forget the joy of youth,
In thee shall I be comforted; ay, see
My youth, a dearer than my own again."

And when he ceased, the youth, with sleep
    content,
Murmured a little, turned himself, and woke.

He woke, and opened on his father's face
The darkness of his eyes; but not a word
The Master-shipwright said,—his lips were
    sealed;
He was not ready, for he feared to see
This mouth curl up with scorn. And Japhet
    spoke,
Full of the calm that cometh after sleep:
"Sir, I have dreamed of you. I pray you, sir,
What is your name?" And even with his
    words
His countenance changed. The son of Lamech
    said,
"Why art thou sad? What have I done to
    thee?"
And Japhet answered, "O, methought I fled
In the wilderness before a maddened beast,
And you came up and slew it; and I thought
You were my father; but I fear me, sir,
My thoughts were vain." With that his fa-
    ther said,
"Whate'er of blessing Thou reserv'st for me,
God! if Thou wilt not give to both, give here:
Bless him with both Thy hands;" and laid his
    own
On Japhet's head.

                    Then Japhet looked on him,
Made quiet by content, and answered low,
With faltering laughter, glad and reverent:
    "Sir,
You are my father?" "Ay," quoth he, "I
    am!
Kiss me, my son; and let me hear my name,
My much desiréd name, from your dear lips."

Then after, rested, they betook them home:
And Japhet, walking by the Master, thought,
"I did not will to love this sire of mine;
But now I feel as if I had always known
And loved him well; truly, I see not why,
But I would rather serve him than go free
With my two brethren." And he said to him,
"Father!"—who answered, "I am here, my
    son."
And Japhet said, "I pray you, sir, attend
To this my answer: let me go with you,
For, now I think on it, I do not love
The chase, nor managing the steed, nor yet
The arrows and the bow; but rather you,
For all you do and say, and you yourself,
Are goodly and delightsome in mine eyes.
I pray you, sir, when you go forth again,
That I may also go." And he replied,
"I will tell thy speech unto the Highest; He
Shall answer it. But I would speak to thee
Now of the days to come. Know thou, most
    dear
To this thy father, that the drenchéd world,
When risen clean washed from water, shall
    receive
From thee her lordliest governors, from thee
Daughters of noblest soul."

                    So Japhet said,
"Sir, I am young, but of my mother straight
I will go ask a wife, that this may be.
I pray you, therefore, as the manner is
Of fathers, give me land that I may reap
Corn for sustaining of my wife, and bruise
The fruit of the vine to cheer her." But he
    said,
"Dost thou forget? or dost thou not believe,
My son?" He answered, "I did ne'er be-
    lieve,
My father, ere to-day; but now, methinks,
Whatever thou believest I believe,
For thy belovéd sake, If this then be
As thou (I hear) hast said, and earth doth bear
The last of her wheat harvests, and make ripe
The latest of her grapes; yet hear me, sir,
None of the daughters shall be given to me
If I be landless." Then his father said,

"Lift up thine eyes toward the north, my
   son!"
And so he did. "Behold thy heritage!"
Quoth the world's prince and master, "far
   away
Upon the side o' the north, where green the
   field
Lies every season through, and where the dews
Of heaven are wholesome, shall thy children
   reign;
I part it to them, for the earth is mine;
The Highest gave it me: I make it theirs.
Moreover, for thy marriage gift, behold
The cedars where thou sleepedst! There are
   vines;
And up the rise is growing wheat. I give
(For all, alas! is mine)—I give thee both
For dowry, and my blessing."

      And he said,
"Sir you are good, and therefore the Most High
Shall bless me also. Sir, I love you well."

BOOK V.

AND when two days were over, Japhet said,
"Mother, so please you, get a wife for me."
The mother answered, "Dost thou mock me,
   son?
'Tis not the manner of our kin to wed
So young. Thou knowest it; art thou not
   ashamed?
Thou carest not for a wife?" And the youth
   blushed,
And made for answer; "This, my father,
   saith
The doom is nigh; now therefore find a maid,
Or else shall I be wifeless all my days.
And as for me, I care not; but the lands
Are parted, and the goodliest share is mine.
And lo! my brethren are betrothed; their
   maids
Are with thee in the house. Then why not
   mine?
Didst thou not diligently search for these
   Among the noblest born of all the earth,
And bring them up? My sisters, dwell they
   not
With women that bespake them for their sons?
Now therefore, let a wife be found for me,
Fair as the day, and gentle to my will
As thou art to my father's." When she heard,
Niloiya sighed, and answered, "It is well."
And Japhet went out from her presence.

        Then
Quoth the great Master: "Wherefore sought
   ye not,
Woman, these many days, nor tired at all,
Till ye had found, a maiden for my son?
In this ye have done ill." Niloiya said:
"Let not my lord be angry. All my soul
Is sad: my lord hath walked afar so long,
That some despise thee; yea, our servants fail
Lately to bring their stint of corn and wood.
And, sir, thy household slaves do steal away
To thy great father, and our lands lie waste,—
None till them: therefore think the women
   scorn
To give me—whatsoever gems I send,
And goodly raiment (yea, I seek afar,
And sue with all desire and humbleness
Through every master's house, but no one
   gives)—
A daughter for my son." With that she
   ceased.

Then said the Master: "Some thou hast with
   thee,
Brought up among thy children, dutiful
And fair; thy father gave them for my slaves,—
Children of them whom he brought captive
   forth
From their own heritage." And she replied,
Right scornfully: "Shall Japhet wed a slave?"
Then said the Master: "He shall wed: look
   thou
To that. I say not he shall wed a slave:
But, by the might of One that made him mine,
I will not quit thee for my doomèd way
Until thou wilt betroth him. Therefore, haste,
Beautiful woman, loved of me and mine,
To bring a maiden, and to say, 'Behold
A wife for Japhet.'" Then she answered,
"Sir,
It shall be done."

      And forth Niloiya sped.
She gathered all her jewels,—all she held
Of costly or of rich,—and went out again
With some few slaves that yet abode with her,
For daily they were fewer; and went forth,
With fair and flattering words, among her
   feres,
And fain had wrought with them: and she had
   hope
That made her sick, it was so faint; and then
She had fear, and after she had certainty,
For all did scorn her. "Nay," they cried,
"O fool!
If this be so, and on a watery world
Ye think to rock, what matters if a wife
Be free or bond? There shall be none to rule,
If she have freedom: if she have it not,
None shall there be to serve."

        And she alit,
The time being done, desponding at her door,
And went behind a screen, where should have
   wrought
The daughters of the captives; but there
   wrought
One only, and this rose from off the floor,
Where she the river rush full deftly wove,
And made obeisance. Then Niloiya said,
"Where are thy fellows?" And the maid
   replied,
"Let not Niloiya, this my lady loved,

Be angry; they are fled since yesternight."
Then said Niloiya, "Amarant, my slave,
When have I called thee by thy name before?"
She answered, "Lady, never;" and she took
And spread her broidered robe before her face.
Niloiya spoke thus: "I am come to woe,
And thou to honor." Saying this, she wept
Passionate tears; and all the damsel's soul
Was full of yearning wonder, and her robe
Slipped from her hand, and her right innocent face
Was seen betwixt her locks of tawny hair
That dropped about her knees, and her two eyes
Blue as the much-loved flower that rims the beck,
Looked sweetly on Niloiya; but she knew
No meaning in her words: and she drew nigh,
And kneeled and said, "Will this my lady speak?
Her damsel is desirous of her words."
Then said Niloiya, "I, thy mistress, sought
A wife for Japhet, and no wife is found."
And yet again she wept with grief of heart,
Saying, "Ah me, miserable! I must give—
A wife,—the Master willeth it,—a wife,
Ah me! unto the high-born. He will scorn
His mother and reproach me. I must give—
None else have I to give—a slave—even thee."
This further spake Niloiya: "I was good,—
Had rue on thee, a tender sucking child,
When they did tear thee from thy mother's breast;
I fed thee, gave thee shelter, and I taught
Thy hands all cunning arts that women prize.
But out on me! my good is turned to ill.
O Japhet, well beloved!" And she rose up,
And did restrain herself, saying, "Dost thou heed?
Behold, this thing shall be." The damsel sighed,
"Lady, I do." Then went Niloiya forth.

And Amarant murmured in her deep amaze,
"Shall Japhet's little children kiss my mouth?
And will he sometimes take them from my arms,
And almost care for me for their sweet sake?
I have not dared to think I loved him,—now
I know it well: but O, the bitterness
For him!" And ending thus, the damsel rose,
For Japhet entered. And she bowed herself
Meekly and made obeisance, but her blood
Ran cold about her heart, for all his face
Was colored with his passion.

                          Japhet spoke:
He said, "My father's slave;" and she replied,
Low drooping her fair head, "My master's son."
And after that a silence fell on them,
With trembling at her heart, and rage at his.
And Japhet, mastered of his passion, sat
And could not speak. O, cruel seemed his fate,—
So cruel her that told it, so unkind.
His breast was full of wounded love and wrath
Wrestling together; and his eyes flashed out
Indignant lights, as all amazed he took
The insult home that she had offered him,
Who should have held his honor dear.

                          And, lo,
The misery choked him, and he cried in pain,
"Go, get thee forth;" but, she all white and still,
Parted her lips to speak, and yet spake not,
Nor moved. And Japhet rose up passionate,
With lifted arm as one about to strike;
But she cried out and met him, and she held
With desperate might his hand, and prayed to him,
"Strike not, or else shall men from henceforth say,
Japhet is like to us." And he shook off
The damsel, and he said, "I thank thee, slave;
For never have I stricken yet or child
Or woman. Not for thy sake am I glad,
Nay, but for mine. Get hence. Obey my words,"
Then Japhet lifted up his voice, and wept.

And no more he restrained himself, but cried,
With heavings of the heart, "O hateful day!
O day that shuts the door upon delight!
A slave! to wed a slave! O loathed wife,
Hated of Japhet's soul." And after, long,
With face between his hands, he sat, his thoughts
Sullen and sore; then scorned himself, and saying,
"I will not take her, I will die unwed,
It is but that;" lift up his eyes and saw
The slave, and she was sitting at his feet;
And he, so greatly wondering that she dared
The disobedience, looked her in the face
Less angry than afraid, for pale she was
As lily yet unsmiled on by the sun;
And he, his passion being spent, sighed out,
"Low am I fallen indeed. Hast thou no fear,
That thou dost flout me?" but she gave to him
The sighing echo of his sigh, and mourned,
"No."

            And he wondered, and he looked again,
For in her heart there was a new-born pang,
That cried; but she, as mothers with their young,
Suffered, yet loved it; and there shone a strange
Grave sweetness in her blue unsullied eyes.
And Japhet, leaning from the settle, thought,
"What is it? I will call her by her name,
To comfort her, for also she is naught
To blame; and since I will not her to wife,
She falls back from the freedom she had hoped."

Then he said, "Amarant;" and the damsel drew
Her eyes down slowly from the shaded sky
Of even, and she said, "My master's son,
Japhet;" and Japhet said, "I am not wroth
With thee, but wretched for my mother's deed,
Because she shamed me."

And the maiden said,
"Doth not thy father love thee well, sweet sir?"
"Ay," quoth he, "well." She answered, "Let the heart
Of Japhet, then, be merry. Go to him
And say, 'The damsel whom my mother chose
Sits by her in the house; but as for me,
Sir, ere I take her, let me go with you
To that same outland country. Also, sir,
My damsel hath not worked as yet the robe
Of her betrothal;' now, then, sith he loves,
He will not say thee nay. Herein for a while
Is respite, and thy mother far and near
Will seek again: It may be she will find
A fair, free maiden."

Japhet said, "O maid,
Sweet are thy words; but what if I return,
And all again be as it is to-day?"
Then Amarant answered, "Some have died in youth;
But yet, I think not, sir, that I shall die.
Though ye shall find it even as I had died,—
Silent, for any words I might have said;
Empty for any space I might have filled.
Sir, I will steal away, and hide afar;
But if a wife be found, then will I bide
And serve." He answered, "O, thy speech is good;
Now, therefore (since my mother gave me thee),
I will reward it; I will find for thee
A goodly husband, and will make him free,
Thee also."

Then she started from his feet,
And, red with shame and anger, flashed on him
The passion of her eyes; and put her hands
With catching of the breath to her fair throat,
And stood in her defiance lost to fear,
Like some fair hind in desperate danger turned
And brought to bay, and wild in her despair.
But shortly, "I remember," quoth she, low,
With raining down of tears and broken sighs,
"That I am Japhet's slave;" beseech you, sir,
As ye were ever gentle, ay, and sweet
Of language to me, be not harder now.
Sir, I was yours to take; I knew not, sir,
That also ye might give me. Pray you, sir,
Be pitiful,—be merciful to me,
A slave." He said, "I thought to do thee good,
For good hath been thy counsel;" but she cried,

"Good master, be you therefore pitiful
To me a slave." And Japhet wondered much
At her, and at her beauty, for he thought,
None of the daughters are so fair as this,
Nor stand with such a grace majestical;
She in her locks is like the travelling sun,
Setting, all clad in coifing clouds of gold.
And would she die unmatched?" He said to her,
"What! wilt thou sail alone in yonder ship,
And dwell alone hereafter?" "Ay," she said,
"And serve my mistress."

"It is well," quoth he,
And held his hand to her, as is the way
Of masters. Then she kissed it, and she said,
"Thanks for benevolence," and turned herself,
Adding, "I rest, sir, on your gracious words;"
Then stepped into the twilight and was gone.

And Japhet having found his father, said,
"Sir, let me also journey when ye go."
Who answered, "Hath thy mother done her part?"
He said, "Yea, truly, and my damsel sits
Before her in the house; and also, sir,
She said to me, 'I have not worked, as yet,
The garment of betrothal.'" And he said,
"'Tis not the manner of our kin to speak
Concerning matters that a woman rules;
But hath thy mother brought a damsel home,
And let her see thy face, then all is one
As ye were wed." He answered, "Even so,
It matters nothing; therefore, hear me, sir;
The damsel being mine, I am content
To let her do according to her will;
And when we shall return, so surely, sir,
As I shall find her by my mother's side,
Then will I take her;" and he left to speak;
His father answering, "Son, thy words are good."

BOOK VI.

NIGHT. Now a tent was pitched, and Japhet sat
In the door and watched, for on a litter lay
The father of his love. And he was sick
To death; but daily he would rouse him up,
And stare upon the light, and ever say,
"On, let us journey;" but it came to pass
That night, across their path a river ran,
And they who served the father and the son
Had pitched the tents beside it, and had made
A fire, to scare away the savagery
That roamed in that great forest, for their way
Had led among the trees of God.

The moon
Shone on the river, like a silver road
To lead them over; but when Japhet looked,
He said, "We shall not cross it. I shall lay

This well-belovèd head low in the leaves,—
Not on the farther side. From time to time,
The water-snakes would stir its glassy flow
With curling undulations, and would lay
Their heads along the banks, and, subtle-eyed,
Consider those long spirting flames, that danced,
When some red log would break and crumble down,
And show his dark despondent eyes, that watched,
Wearily, even Japhet's. But he cared
Little; and in the dark, that was not dark,
But dimness of confused incertitude,
Would move a-near all silently, and gaze
And breathe, and shape itself, a manèd thing
With eyes; and still he cared not, and the form
Would falter, then recede, and melt again
Into the farther shade. And Japhet said:
"How long? The moon hath grown again in heaven,
After her caving twice, since we did leave
The threshold of our home; and now what 'vails
That far on tumbled mountain snow we toiled,
Hungry, and weary, all the day; by night
Waked with a dreadful trembling underneath,
To look, while every cone smoked, and there ran
Red brooks adown, that licked the forest up,
While in the pale white ashes wading on
We saw no stars?—what 'vails, if afterward,
Astonished with great silence, we did move
Over the measureless, unknown desert mead;
While all the day, in rents and crevices,
Would lie the lizard and the serpent kind,
Drowsy; and in the night take fearsome shapes,
And oft-times woman-faced and woman-haired
Would trail their snaky length, and curse and mourn;
Or there would wander up, when we were tired,
Dark troops of evil ones, with eyes morose,
Withstanding us, and staring;—O, what 'vails
That in the dread deep forest we have fought
With following packs of wolves? These men of might,
Even the giants shall not hear the doom
My father came to tell them of. Ah me!
If God indeed had sent him, would he lie
(For he is stricken with a sore disease)
Helpless outside their city?"

                Then he rose,
And put aside the curtains of the tent,
To look upon his father's face; and lo!
The tent being dark, he thought that somewhat sat
Beside the litter; and he set his eyes
To see it, and saw not; but only marked
Where, fallen away from manhood and from power,
His father lay. Then he came forth again,
Trembling, and crouched beside the dull red fire,
And murmured, "Now it is the second time:
An old man, as I think (but scarcely saw),
Dreadful of might. Its hair was white as wool:
I dared not look; perhaps I saw not aught,
But only knew that it was there: the same
Which walked beside us once when he did pray."
And Japhet hid his face between his hands
For fear, and grief of heart, and weariness
Of watching; and he slumbered not, but mourned
To himself, a little moment, as it seemed,
For sake of his loved father; then he lift
His eyes, and day had dawned. Right suddenly
The moon withheld her silver, and she hung
Frail as a cloud. The ruddy flame that played
By night on dim, dusk trees, and on the flood,
Crept red amongst the logs, and all the world
And all the water blushed and bloomed. The stars
Were gone and golden shafts came up, and touched
The feathered heads of palms, and green was born
Under the rosy cloud, and purples flew
Like veils across the mountains; and he saw,
Winding athwart them, bathed in blissful peace,
And the sacredness of morn, the battlements
And out-posts of the giants; and there ran
On the other side the river, as it were,
White mounds of marble, tabernacles fair,
And towers below a line of inland cliff;
These were their fastnesses, and here their homes.

In valleys and the forest, all that night,
There had been woe; in every hollow place,
And under walls, like drifted flowers, or snow,
Women lay mourning; for the serpent lodged
That night within the gates, and had decreed,
"I will (or ever I come) that ye drive out
The women, the abhorrèd of my soul."

Therefore, more beauteous than all climbing bloom,
Purple and scarlet, cumbering of the boughs,
Or flights of azure doves that lit to drink
The water of the river; or, new born,
The quivering butterflies in companies,
That slowly crept adown the sandy marge,
Like living crocus beds, and also drank,
And rose an orange cloud: their hollowed hands
They dipped between the lilies, or with robes
Full of ripe fruitage, sat and peeled and ate,
Weeping; or comforting their little ones,
And lulling them with sorrowful long hymns
Among the palms.

                So went the earlier morn.
Then came a messenger, while Japhet sat
Mournfully, and he said, "The men of might
Are willing; let thy master, youth, appear."

And Japhet said, "So be it"; and he thought,
"Now will I trust in God"; and he went in
And stood before his father, and he said,
"My father"; but the Master answered not,
But gazed upon the curtains of his tent,
Nor knew that one had called him. He was
    clad
As ready for the journey, and his feet
Were sandalled, and his staff was at his side;
And Japhet took the gown of sacrifice
And spread it on him, and he laid his crown
Upon his knees, and he went forth, and lift
His hand to heaven, and cried, "My father's
    God!"
But neither whisper came nor echo fell
When he did listen. Therefore he went on:
"Behold, I have a thing to say to thee.
My father charged thy servant, 'Let not ruth
Prevail with thee to turn and bear me hence,
For God appointed me my task, to preach
Before the mighty.' I must do my part
(O let jt not displease thee), for he said
But yesternight, 'When they shall send for me,
Take me before them.' And I sware to him.
I pray thee, therefore, count his life and mine
Precious; for I that sware, I will perform."

Then cried he to his people, "Let us hence:
Take up the litter." And they set their feet
Toward the raft whereby men crossed that flood.

And while they journeyed, lo, the giants sat
Within the fairest hall where all were fair,
Each on his carven throne, o'er-canopied
With work of women. And the dragon lay
In a place of honor; and with subtlety
He counselled them, for they did speak by
    turns;
And they, being proud, might nothing master
    them,
But guile alone; and he did fawn on them;
And when the younger taunted him, submiss
He testified great humbleness, and cried,
"A cruel God, forsooth! but nay, O nay,
I will not think it of Him, that He meant
To threaten these. O, when I look on them,
How doth my soul admire."

                        And one stood forth,
The youngest; of his brethren named "the
    Rock."
"Speak out," quoth he, "thou toothless,
    slavering thing,
What is it? thinkest thou that such as we
Should be afraid? What is this goodly doom?"
And Satan laughed upon him. "Lo," said he,
"Thou art not fully grown, and every one
I look on standeth higher by the head,
Yea, and the shoulders, than do other men;
Forsooth, thy servant thought not thou wouldst
    fear,
Thou and thy fellows." Then with one accord,
"Speak," cried they; and with mild persuasive
    eyes,
And flattering tongue, he spoke.

                        "Ye mighty ones,
It hath been known to you these many days
How that for piety I am much famed.
I am exceeding pious: if I lie,
As hath been whispered, it is but for sake
Of God, and that ye should not think Him
    hard,
For I am all for God. Now some have thought
That He hath also (and it may be so
Or yet may not be so) on me been hard;
Be not ye therefore wroth, for my poor sake;
I am contented to have earned your weal,
Though I must therefore suffer.

                        Now to-day
One cometh, yea, an harmless man, a fool,
Who boasts he hath a message from our God,
And lest that you, for bravery of heart
And stoutness being angered with his prate,
Should lift a hand, and kill him, I am here."

Then spoke the Leader, "How now, snake?
    Thy words
Ring false. Why ever liest thou, snake, to us?
Thou coward! none of us will see thee harmed.
I say thou liest. The land is strewed with
    slain;
Myself have hewn down companies, and blood
Makes fertile all the field. Thou knowest it
    well;
And hast thou, driveller, panting sore for age,
Come with a force to bid us spare one fool?"

And Satan answered, "Nay you! be not wroth;
Yet true it is, and yet not all the truth.
Your servant would have told the rest, if now
(For fulness of your life being fretted sore
At mine infirmities, which God in vain
I supplicate to heal) ye had not caused
My speech to stop." And he they called "the
    Oak"
Made answer, "'T is a good snake, let him be.
Why would ye fright the poor old craven beast?
Look how his lolling tongue doth foam for fear.
Ye should have mercy, brethren, on the weak.
Speak, dragon, thou hast leave; make stout
    thy heart.
What! hast thou lied to this great company?
It was, we know it was, for humbleness;
Thou wert not willing to offend with truth."

"Yea, majesties," quoth Satan, "thus it was,"
And lifted up appealing eyes, and groaned;
"O, can it be, compassionate as brave,
And housed in cunning works themselves have
    reared,
And served in gold, and warmed with minivere,
And ruling nobly, that He, not content
Unless alone He reigneth, looks to bend
Or break them in, like slaves to cry to Him,
'What is Thy will with us, O Master dear?'
Or else to eat of death?

                        For my part, lords,
I cannot think it: for my piety

And reason, which I also share with you,
Are my best lights, and ever counsel me,
'Believe not aught against thy God; believe,
Since thou canst never reach to do Him wrong,
That He will never stoop to do thee wrong.
Is He not just and equal, yea, and kind?
Therefore, O majesties, it is my mind,
Concerning him ye wot of, thus to think
The message is not like what I have learned,
By reason and experience, of the God.
Therefore no message 'tis. The man is mad."
Thereat the Leader laughed for scorn. "Hold, snake;
If God be just, there SHALL be reckoning days.
We rather would he were a partial God,
And, being strong, He sided with the strong.
Turn now thy reason to the other side,
And speak for that; for as to justice, snake,
We would have none of it."

     And Satan fawned:
"My lord is pleased to mock at my poor wit:
Yet in my pious fashion I must talk:
For say that God was wroth with man, and came
And slew him that should make an empty world,
But not a better nation."

     This replied,
"Truth, dragon, yet He is not bound to mean
A better nation; maybe, He designs,
If none will turn again, a punishment
Upon an evil one."

     And Satan cried
"Alas! my heart being full of love for men,
I cannot choose but think of God as like
To me; and yet my piety concludes,
Since He will have your fear, that love alone
Sufficeth not, and I admire, and say,
'Give me, O friends, your love, and give to God
Your fear.'" But they cried out in wrath and rage,
"We are not strong that any we will fear,
Nor specially a foe that means us ill."

BOOK VII.

AND while he spoke there was a noise without;
The curtains of the door were flung aside,
And some with heavy feet bare in, and set
A litter on the floor.

     The Master lay
Upon it, but his eyes were dimmed and set;
And Japhet, in despairing weariness,
Leaned it beside. He marked the mighty ones,
Silent for pride of heart, and in his place
The jewelled dragon; and the dragon laughed,
And subtly peered at him, till Japhet shook
With rage and fear. The snaky wonder cried,
Hissing, "Thou brown-haired youth, come up to me;
I fain would have thee for my shrine afar,
To serve among an host as beautiful
As thou: draw near." It hissed, and Japhet felt
Horrible drawings, and cried out in fear,
"Father, O help, the serpent draweth me!"
And struggled and grew faint, as in the toils
A netted bird. But still his father lay
Unconscious, and the mighty did not speak,
But half in fear and half for wonderment
Beheld. And yet again the dragon laughed,
And leered at him and hissed; and Japhet strove
Vainly to take away his spell-set eyes,
And moved to go to him, till piercingly
Crying out, "God! forbid it, God in heaven!"
The dragon lowered his head, and shut his eyes
As feigning sleep; and, suddenly released,
He fell back staggering; and at noise of it,
And clash of Japhet's weapons on the floor,
And Japhet's voice crying out, "I loathe thee, snake!
I hate thee! O, I hate thee!" came again,
The senses of the shipwright; and he, moved,
And looking, as one 'mazed, distressfully
Upon the mighty, said, "One called on God:
Where is my God? If God have need of me,
Let Him come down and touch my lips with strength,
Or dying I shall die."

     It came to pass,
While he was speaking, that the curtains swayed:
A rushing wind did move throughout the place,
And all the pillars shook, and on the head
Of Noah the hair was lifted, and there played
A somewhat, as it were a light, upon
His breast; then fell a darkness, and men heard
A whisper, as of one that spake. With that,
The daunted mighty ones kept silent watch
Until the wind had ceased and darkness fled.
When it grew light, there curled a cloud of smoke
From many censers where the dragon lay.
It hid him. He had called his ministrants,
And bid them veil him thus, that none might look;
Also the folk who came with Noah had fled.

But Noah was seen, for he stood up erect,
And leaned on Japhet's hand. Then, after pause,
The Leader said, "My brethren, it were well
(For naught we fear) to let this sorcerer speak."
And they did reach toward the man their staves,
And cry with loud accord, "Hail, sorcerer, hail!"

And he made answer, "Hail! I am a man
That is a shipwright. I was born afar

To Lamech, him that reigns a king, to wit,
Over the land of Jalal. Majesties,
I bring a message,—lay you it to heart ;
For there is wrath in heaven : my God is wroth.
'Prepare your houses, or I come,' saith He,
'A Judge.' Now, therefore, say not in your hearts,
'What have we done?' Your dogs may answer that,
To make whom fiercer for the chase ye feed
With captives whom ye slew not in the war,
But saved alive, and living throw to them
Daily. Your wives may answer that, whose babes
Their firstborn ye do take and offer up
To this abhorrèd snake, while yet the milk
Is in their innocent mouths,—your maiden babes
Tender. Your slaves may answer that,—the gangs
Whose eyes ye did put out to make them work
By night unwitting (yea, by multitudes
They work upon the wheel in chains). Your friends
May answer that,—(their bleachèd bones cry out,)
For ye did, wickedly, to eat their lands,
Turn on their valleys, in a time of peace,
The rivers, and they, choking in the night,
Died unavenged. But rather, (for I leave
To tell of more, the time would be so long
To do it, and your time, O mighty ones,
Is short),—but rather say, 'We sinners know
Why the Judge standeth at the door,' and turn
While yet there may be respite, and repent.
'Or else,' saith he that formèd you, 'I swear,
By all the silence of the time to come,
By the solemnities of death,—yea, more,
By Mine own power and love which ye have scorned,
That I will come. I will command the clouds,
And raining they shall rain ; yea, I will stir
With all my storms the ocean for your sake,
And break for you the boundary of the deep.

"'Then shall the mighty mourn.
                         Should I forbear,
That have been patient? I will not forbear !
For yet,' saith He, 'the weak cry out ; for yet
The little ones do languish ; and the slave
Lifts up to Me his chain. I, therefore, I
Will hear them. I by death will scatter you ;
Yea, and by death will draw them to My breast,
And gather them to peace.

                         But yet,' saith He,
'Repent, and turn you. Wherefore will ye die?'

"Turn then, O turn, while yet the enemy
Untamed of man fatefully moans afar ;
For if ye will not turn, the doom is near.
Then shall the crested wave make sport, and beat
You mighty at your doors. Will ye be wroth?
Will ye forbid it ? Monsters of the deep
Shall suckle in your palaces their young,
And swim atween your hangings, all of them
Costly with broidered work, and rare with gold
And white and scarlet (there did ye oppress,—
There did ye make you vile) ; but ye shall lie
Meekly, and storm and wind shall rage above,
And urge the weltering wave.

                         'Yet,' saith thy God.
'Son,' ay, to each of you He saith, 'O son,
Made in My image, beautiful and strong,
Why wilt thou die? Thy father loves thee well.
Repent and turn thee from thine evil ways,
O son ! and no more dare the wrath of love.
Live for thy Father's sake that formèd thee.
Why wilt thou die?' Here will I make an end."

Now ever on his daïs the dragon lay,
Feigning to sleep ; and all the mighty ones
Were wroth, and chided, some against the woe,
And some at whom the sorcerer they had named,—
Some at their fellows, for the younger sort—
As men the less acquaint with deeds of blood,
And given to learning and the arts of peace
(Their fathers having crushed rebellion out
Before their time)—lent favorable ears.
They said, "A man, or false or fanatic,
May claim good audience if he fill our ears
With what is strange : and we would hear again."

The Leader said, "An audience hath been given.
The man hath spoken, and his words are naught ;
A feeble threatener, with a foolish threat,
And it is not our manner that we sit
Beyond the noonday ; " then they grandly rose,
A stalwart crowd, and with their Leader moved
To the tones of harping, and the beat of shawns,
And the noise of pipes, away. But some were left
About the Master ; and the feigning snake
Couched on his daïs.

                         Then one to Japhet said,—
One called "the Cedar Tree,"—"Dost thou, too, think
To reign upon our lands when we lie drowned?"
And Japhet said, "I think not, nor desire,
Nor in my heart consent, but that ye swear
Allegiance to the God, and live." He cried,
To one surnamed "the Pine,"—"Brother, behooves
That deep we cut our names in yonder crag,

Else when this youth returns, his sons may ask
Our names, and he may answer, 'Matters not,
For my part I forget them."
                            Japhet said,
"They might do worse than that, they might deny
That such as you have ever been." With that
They answered, "No, thou dost not think it, no!"
And Japhet, being chafed, replied in heat,
"And wherefore? if ye say of what is sworn,
'He will not do it,' shall it be more hard
For future men, if any talk on it,
To say, 'He did not do it?'" They replied,
With laughter, "Lo you! he is stout with us.
And yet he cowered before the poor old snake.
Sirrah! when you are saved, we pray you now
To bear our might in mind,—do, sirrah, do;
And likewise tell your sons, '"The Cedar Tree"
Was a good giant, for he struck me not,
Though he was young and full of sport, and though
I taunted him.'"

            With that they also passed.
But there remained who with the shipwright spoke :
"How wilt thou certify to us thy truth?"
And he related to them all his ways
From the beginning : of the Voice that called ;
Moreover, how the ship of doom was built.

And one made answer, "Shall the mighty God
Talk with a man of wooden beams and bars?
No, thou mad preacher, no. If He, Eterne,
Be ordering of His far infinitudes,
And darkness cloud a world, it is but chance,
As if the shadow of His hand had fallen
On one that He forgot, and troubled it."

Then said the Master, "Yet—who told thee so?"

And from his dais the feigning serpent hissed :
"Preacher, the light within, it was that shined,
And told him so. The pious will have dread
Him to declare such as ye rashly told.
The course of God is one. It likes not us
To think of Him as being acquaint with change:
It were beneath Him. Nay, the finished earth
Is left to her great masters. They must rule ;
They do ; and I have set myself between,—
A visible thing for worship, sith His face
(For He is hard) He showeth not to men.
Yea, I have set myself 'twixt God and man,
To be interpreter, and teach mankind
A pious lesson by my piety.
He loveth not, nor hateth, nor desires,—
It were beneath Him."

                And the Master said,
"Thou liest. Thou wouldst lie away the world,
If He whom thou hast dared to speak against
Would suffer it." "I may not chide with thee,"
It answered, "NOW ; but if there come such time
As thou hast prophesied, as I now reign
In all men's sight, shall my dominion then
Reach to be mighty in their souls. Thou, too,
Shalt feel it, prophet." And he lowered his head.

Then quoth the Leader of the young men :
"Sir,
We scorn you not ; speak further ; yet our thought
First answer. Not but by a miracle
Can this thing be. The fashion of the world
We heretofore have never known to change ;
And will God change it now?"

                He then replied :
"What is thy thought? THERE IS NO MIRACLE?
There is a great one, which thou hast not read
And never shalt escape. Thyself, O man,
Thou art the miracle. Lo, if thou sayest,
'I am one, and fashioned like the gracious world,
Red clay is all my make, myself, my whole,
And not my habitation,' then thy sleep
Shall give thee wings to play among the rays
O' the morning. If thy thought be, 'I am one—
A spirit among spirits—and the world
A dream my spirit dreameth of, my dream
Being all,' the dominating mountains strong
Shall not for that forbear to take thy breath,
And rage with all their winds, and beat thee back,
And beat thee down when thou wouldst set thy feet
Upon their awful crests. Ay, thou thyself,
Being in the world and of the world, thyself
Hast breathed in breath from Him that made the world.
Thou dost inherit, as thy Maker's son,
That which He is, and that which He hath made :
Thou art thy Father's copy of Himself,—
THOU art thy FATHER'S MIRACLE.

                "Behold,
He buildeth up the stars in companies ;
He made for them a law. To man He said,
'Freely I give thee freedom.' What remains?
O, it remains, if thou, the image of God,
Wilt reason well, that thou shalt know His ways ;
But first thou must be loyal,—love, O man,
Thy Father,—hearken when He pleads with thee,
For there is something left of Him e'en now—
A witness for thy Father in thy soul,
Albeit thy better state thou hast foregone.

"Now, then, be still, and think not in thy
  soul,
'The rivers in their course forever run,
And turn not from it. He is like to them
Who made them.' Think the rather, 'With
  my foot
I have turned the rivers from their ancient way,
To water grasses that were fading. What!
Is God my Father as the river wave,
That yet descendeth,—like the lesser thing
He made, and not like me, a living son,
That changed the watercourse to suit his will?'

"Man is the miracle in nature. God
Is the ONE MIRACLE to man. Behold,
'There is a God,' thou sayest. Thou sayest
  well:
In that thou sayest all. To Be is more
Of wonderful than, being, to have wrought,
Or reigned, or rested.

               Hold then there, content
Learn that to love is the one way to know
Or God or man: it is not love received
That maketh man to know the inner life
Of them that love him; his own love bestowed
Shall do it. Love thy Father, and no more
His doings shall be strange. Thou shalt not
  fret
At any counsel, then, that He will send,—
No, nor rebel, albeit He have with thee
Great reservations. Know, to Be is more
Than to have acted; yea, or, after rest
And patience, to have risen and been wroth,
Broken the sequence of an ordered earth,
And troubled nations."

            Then the dragon sighed.
"Poor fanatic," quoth he, "thou speakest well.
Would I were like thee, for thy faith is strong,
Albeit thy senses wander. Yea, good sooth,
My masters, let us not despise, but learn
Fresh loyalty from this poor loyal soul.
Let us go forth—(myself will also go
To head you)—and do sacrifice; for that,
We know, is pleasing to the mighty God:
But as for building many arks of wood,
O majesties! when he shall counsel you
HIMSELF, then build. What say you, shall it
  be
An hundred oxen,—fat, well liking, white?
An hundred? why, a thousand were not much
To such as you." Then Noah lift up his arms
To heaven, and cried, "Thou aged shape of
  sin,
The Lord rebuke thee."

BOOK VIII.

THEN one ran, crying, while Niloiya wrought,
"The Master cometh!" and she went within
To adorn herself for meeting him. And Shem
Went forth and talked with Japhet in the field,
And said, "It is well, my brother?" He re-
  plied,
"Well! and, I pray you, is it well at home?"

But Shem made answer, "Can a house be well,
If he that should command it bides afar?
Yet well is thee, because a fair free maid
Is found to wed thee; and they bring her in
This day at sundown. Therefore is much haste
To cover thick with costly webs the floor,
And pluck and cover thick the same with leaves
Of all sweet herbs,—I warrant, ye shall hear
No footfall where she treadeth; and the seats
Are ready, spread with robes; the tables set
With golden baskets, red pomegranates shred
To fill them; and the rubied censors smoke,
Heaped up with ambergris and cinnamon,
And frankincense and cedar."

                   Japhet said,
"I will betroth her to me straight"; and went
(Yet labored he with sore disquietude)
To gather grapes and reap and bind the sheaf
For his betrothal. And his brother spake,
"Where is our father? doth he preach to-day?"
And Japhet answered, "Yea. He said to me,
'Go forward; I will follow when the folk
By yonder mountain-hold, I shall have warn-
  ed.'"

And Shem replied, "How thinkest thou?—
  thine ears
Have heard him oft." He answered, "I do
  think
These be the last days of this old fair world."
Then he did tell him of the giant folk;
How they than he were taller by the head;
How one must stride that will ascend the steps
That lead to their wide halls; and how they
  drave,
With manful shouts, the mammoth to the north;
And how the talking dragon lied and fawned,
They seated proudly on their ivory thrones,
And scorning him; and of their peakéd hoods,
And garments wrought upon, each with the
  tale
Of him that wore it,—all his manful deeds
(Yea, and about their skirts were effigies
Of kings that they had slain; and some, whose
  swords
Many had pierced, wore vestures all of red,
To signify much blood): and of their pride
He told, but of the vision in the tent
He told him not.

               And when they reached the house,
Niloiya met them, and to Japhet cried
"All hail, right fortunate! Lo, I have found
A maid. And now thou hast done well to
  reap
The late ripe corn." So he went in with her,
And she did talk with him right motherly:
"It hath been fully told me how ye loathed
To wed thy father's slave; yea, she herself,
Did she not all declare to me?"

He said,
"Yet is thy damsel fair, and wise of heart."
"Yea," quoth his mother; "she made clear to me
How ye did weep, my son, and ye did vow,
'I will not take her?' Now it was not I
That wrought to have it so." And he replied,
"I know it." Quoth the mother, "It is well;
For that same cause is laughter in my heart,"
"But she is sweet of language," Japhet said.
"Ay," quoth Niloiya, "and thy wife no less
Whom thou shalt wed anon—forsooth, anon—
It is a lucky hour. Thou wilt?" He said,
"I will." And Japhet laid the slender sheaf
From off his shoulder, and he said, "Behold,
My father! Then Niloiya turned herself,
And lo! the shipwright stood. "All hail!" quoth she,
And bowed herself, and kissed him on the mouth;
But while she spake with him, sorely he sighed;
And she did hang about his neck the robe
Of feasting, and she poured upon his hands
Clear water, and anointed him, and set
Before him bread.

And Japhet said to him,
"My father, my belovéd, wilt thou yet
Be sad because of scorning? Eat, this day;
For as an angel in their eyes thou art
Who stand before thee." But he answered, "Peace!
Thy words are wide."

And when Niloiya heard,
She said, "Is this a time for mirth of heart
And wine? Behold I thought to wed my son,
Even this Japhet; but is this a time,
When sad is he to whom is my desire,
And lying under sorrow as from God?"

He answered, "Yea, it is a time of times;
Bring in the maid." Niloiya said, "The maid
That first I spoke on shall not Japhet wed:
It likes not her, nor yet it likes not me.
But I have found another; yea, good sooth,
The damsel will not tarry, she will come
With all her slaves by sundown."

And she said,
"Comfort thy heart, and eat; moreover, know
How that thy great work even to-day is done.
Sir thy great ship is finished, and the folk
(For I, according to thy will, have paid
All that was left us to them for their wage)
Have brought, as to a storehouse, flour of wheat,
Honey and oil,—much victual; yea, and fruits,
Curtains and household gear, And, sir, they say
It is thy will to take it for thy hold,
Our fastness and abode." He answered, "Yea,
Else wherefore was it built?" She said, "Good sir,

I pray you make us not the whole earth's scorn.
And now, to-morrow in thy father's house
Is a great feast, and weddings are toward;
Let be the ship, till after, for thy words
Have ever been, 'If God shall send a flood,
There will I dwell;" I pray you, therefore, wait
At least till He DOTH send it."

And he turned,
And answered nothing. Now the sun was low
While yet she spake; and Japhet came to them
In goodly raiment, and upon his arm
The garment of betrothal. And with that
A noise, and then brake in a woman-slave
And Amarant. This, with folding of her hands,
Did say full meekly, "If I do offend,
Yet have not I been willing to offend;
For now this woman will not be denied
Herself to tell her errand."

And they sat.
Then spoke the woman, "If I do offend,
Pray you forgive the bondslave, for her tongue
Is for her mistress. 'Lo,' my mistress saith,
'Put off thy bravery, bridegroom; fold away,
Mother, thy webs of pride, thy costly robes
Woven of many colors. We have heard
Thy master. Lo, to-day right evil things
He prophesied to us that were his friends;
Therefore, my answer:—God do so to me;
Yea, God do so to me, more also, more
Than he did threaten, if my damsel's foot
Ever draw nigh thy door.'"

And when she heard,
Niloiya sat amazed, in grief of soul.
But Japhet came unto the slave, where low
She bowed herself for fear. He said, "Depart;
Say to thy mistress, 'It is well.'" With that
She turned herself, and she made haste to flee,
Lest any, for those evil words she brought,
Would smite her. But the bondmaid of the house
Lift up her hand and said, "If I offend,
It was not of my heart: thy damsel knew
Naught of this matter." And he held to her
His hand and touched her, and said, "Amarant!"
And when she looked upon him, she did take
And spread before her face her radiant locks,
Trembling. And Japhet said, "Lift up thy face,
O fairest of the daughters, thy fair face;
For, lo! the bridegroom standeth with the robe
Of thy betrothal!"—and he took her locks
In his two hands to part them from her brow,
And laid them on her shoulders; and he said,
"Sweet are the blushes of thy face," and put
The robe upon her, having said, "Behold,
I have repented me; and oft by night,
In the waste wilderness, while all things slept,

I thought upon thy words, for they were sweet.

"For this I make thee free. And now thy-
self
Art loveliest in mine eyes; I look, and lo!
Thou art of beauty more than any thought
I had concerning thee. Let, then, this robe,
Wrought on with imagery of fruitful bough,
And graceful leaf, and birds with tender eyes,
Cover the ripples of thy tawny hair."
So, when she held her peace, he brought her
nigh
To hear the speech of wedlock; ay, he took
The golden cup of wine to drink with her,
And laid the sheaf upon her arms. He said,
Like as my fathers in the older days
Led home the daughters whom they chose,
do I;
Like as they said, 'Mine honor have I set
Upon thy head!' do I. Eat of my bread,
Rule in my house, be mistress of my slaves,
And mother of my children."

And he brought
The damsel to his father, saying, "Behold
My wife! I have betrothed her to myself;
I pray you, kiss her." And the Master did:
He said, "Be mother of a multitude,
And let them to their father even so
Be found as he is found to me."

With that
She answered, "Let this woman, sir, find
grace
And favor in your sight."

And Japhet said,
"Sweet mother, I have wed the maid ye chose
And brought me first. I leave her in thy
hand;
Have care on her till I shall come again
And ask her of thee." So they went apart,
He and his father, to the marriage feast.

BOOK IX.

THE prayer of Noah. The man went forth by
night
And listened; and the earth was dark and
still,
And he was driven of his great distress
Into the forest; but the birds of night
Sang sweetly; and he fell upon his face,
And cried, "God, God! Thy billows and
Thy waves
Have swallowed up my soul.

Where is my God?
For I have somewhat yet to plead with Thee;
For I have walked the strands of Thy great
deep,
Heard the dull thunder of its rage afar,
And its dread moaning. O, the field is sweet—
Spare it. The delicate woods make white
their trees
With blossom,—spare them. Life is sweet;
behold
There is much cattle, and the wild and tame,
Father, do feed in quiet,—spare them.

God!
Where is my God? The long wave doth not
rear
Her ghostly crest to lick the forest up,
And like a chief in battle fall,—not yet.
The lightnings pour not down, from ragged
holes
In heaven, the torment of their forkèd tongues,
And, like fell serpents, dart and sting,—not
yet.
The winds awake not, with their awful wings
To winnow, even as chaff, from out their track,
All that withstandeth, and bring down the pride
Of all things strong and all things high— .

Not yet.
O, let it not be yet. Where is my God?
How am I saved, if I and mine be saved
Alone? I am not saved, for I have loved
My country and my kin. Must I, Thy thrall,
Over their lands be lord when they are gone?
I would not: spare them, Mighty. Spare
Thyself,
For Thou dost love them greatly,—and if
not . . ."

Another praying unremote, a Voice
Calm as the solitude between wide stars.

"Where is my God, who loveth this lost world,
Lost from its place and name, but won for
Thee?
Where is my multitude, my multitude,
That I shall gather?" And white smoke went
up
From incense that was burning, but there
gleamed
No light of fire, save dimly to reveal
The whiteness rising, as the prayer of him
That mourned. "My God, appear for me,
appear;
Give me my multitude, for it is mine.
The bitterness of death I have not feared,
To-morrow shall Thy courts, O God, be full.
Then shall the captive from his bonds go free,
Then shall the thrall find rest, that knew not
rest
From labor and from blows. The sorrowful—
That said of joy, 'What is it?' and of songs,
'We have not heard them'—shall be glad and
sing;
Then shall the little ones that knew not Thee,
And such as heard not of Thee, see Thy face,
And, seeing, dwell content."

The prayer of Noah.
He cried out in the darkness, "Hear, O God,

Hear HIM: hear this one; through the gates of death.
If life be all past praying for, O give
To Thy great multitude a way to peace;
Give them to HIM.

But yet," said he, "O yet,
If there be respite for the terrible,
The proud, yea, such as scorn Thee—and if not . . .
Let not mine eyes behold their fall."

He cried,
"Forgive. I have not done Thy work, Great Judge,
With a perfect heart; I have but half believed,
While in accustomed language I have warned;
And now there is no more to do, no place
For my repentance, yea, no hour remains
For doing of that work again. O lost,
Lost world!" And while he prayed, the daylight dawned.

And Noah went up into the ship, and sat
Before the Lord. And all was still; and now
In that great quietness the sun came up,
And there were marks across it as it were,
The shadow of a Hand upon the sun,—
Three fingers dark and dread, and afterward
There rose a white thick mist, that peacefully
Folded the fair earth in her funeral shroud,—
The earth that gave no token, save that now
There fell a little trembling under foot.

And Noah went down, and took and hid his face
Behind his mantle, saying, "I have made
Great preparation, and it may be yet,
Beside my house, whom I did charge to come
This day to meet me, there may enter in
Many that yesternight thought scorn of all
My bidding." And because the fog was thick,
He said, "Forbid it, heaven, if such there be,
That they should miss the way." And even then
There was a noise of weeping and lament;
The words of them that were affrighted, yea,
And cried for grief of heart. There came to him
The mother and her children, and they cried,
"Speak, father, what is this? What hast thou done?"

And when he lifted up his face, he saw
Japhet, his well-belovéd, where he stood
Apart; and Amarant leaned upon his breast,
And hid her face, for she was sore afraid;
And lo! the robes of her betrothal gleamed
White in the deadly gloom.

And at his feet
The wives of his two other sons did kneel,
And wring their hands.

One cried, "O, speak to us;
We are affrighted; we have dreamed a dream,
Each to herself. For me, I saw in mine
The grave old angels, like to shepherds, walk,
Much cattle following them. Thy daughter looked,
And they did enter here."

The other lay
And moaned, "Alas! O father, for my dream
Was evil: lo, I heard when it was dark,
I heard two wicked ones contend for me.
One said, 'And wherefore should this woman live,
When only for her children, and for her,
Is woe and degradation?' Then he laughed,
The other crying, 'Let alone, O Prince;
Hinder her not to live and bear much seed,
Because I hate her.'"

But he said, "Rise up,
Daughters of Noah, for I have learned no words
To comfort you." Then spake her lord to her,
"Peace! or I swear that for thy dream myself
Will hate thee also."

And Niloiya said,
" My sons, if one of you will hear my words,
Go now, look out, and tell me of the day,
How fares it?"

And the fateful darkness grew.
But Shem went up to do his mother's will;
And all was one as though the frighted earth
Quivered and fell a-trembling; then they hid
Their faces every one, till he returned,
And spake not. "Nay," they cried, "what hast thou seen?
O, is it come to this?" He answered them,
"The door is shut."

CONTRASTED SONGS.

SAILING BEYOND SEAS.

(Old Style.)

METHOUGHT the stars were blinking bright,
And the old brig's sails unfurled;
I said, "I will sail to my love this night
At the other side of the world."
I stepped aboard—we sailed so fast—
The sun shot up from the bourne;
But a dove that perched upon the mast
Did mourn, and mourn, and mourn.
O fair dove! O fond dove!
And dove with the white breast,
Let me alone, the dream is my own,
And my heart is full of rest.

My true love fares on this great hill,
Feeding his sheep for aye;
I looked in his hut, but all was still,
My love was gone away.
I went to gaze in the forest creek,
And the dove mourned on apace;
No flame did flash, nor fair blue reek
Rose up to show me his place.
O last love! O first love!
My love with the true heart,
To think I have come to this your home,
And yet—we are apart!

My love! He stood at my right hand,
His eyes were grave and sweet.
Methought he said, "In this far land,
O, is it thus we meet?
Ah, maid most dear, I am not here;
I have no place—no part—
No dwelling more by sea or shore,
But only in thy heart."
O fair dove! O fond dove!
Till night rose over the bourne,
The dove on the mast, as we sailed fast,
Did mourn, and mourn, and mourn.

REMONSTRANCE.

DAUGHTERS of Eve! your mother did not well:
She laid the apple in your father's hand,
And we have read, O wonder! what befell,—
The man was not deceived, nor yet could stand;
He chose to lose, for love of her, his throne,—
With her could die, but could not live alone.

Daughters of Eve! he did not fall so low,
Nor fall so far, as that sweet woman fell;
For something better, than as gods to know,
That husband in that home left off to dwell:
For this, till love be reckoned, less than lore,
Shall man be first and best forevermore.

Daughters of Eve! it was for your dear sake
The world's first hero died an uncrown'd king;
But God's great pity touched the grand mistake,
And made his married love a sacred thing:
For yet his nobler sons, if aught be true,
Find the lost Eden in their love to you.

SONG FOR THE NIGHT OF CHRIST'S RESURRECTION.

(A Humble Imitation.)

"And birds of calm sit brooding on the charmèd wave.

IT is the noon of night,
And the world's Great Light
Gone out, she widow-like doth carry her:
The moon hath veiled her face,
Nor looks on that dread place
Where He lieth dead in sealèd sepulchre;
And heaven and hades, emptied, lend
Their flocking multitudes to watch and wait the end.
Tier above tier they rise,
Their wings new line the skies,
And shed out comforting light among the stars;
But they of the other place
The heavenly signs deface,
The gloomy brand of hell their brightness mars;
Yet high they sit in thronèd state,—
It is the hour of darkness to them dedicate.

And first and highest set,
Where the black shades are met,
The lord of night and hades leans him down;
His gleaming eye-balls show
More awful than the glow
Which hangeth by the points of his dread crown;
And at his feet, where lightnings play,
The fatal sisters sit and weep, and curse their day.

Lo! one, with eyes all wide,
 As she were sight denied,
Sits blindly feeling at her distaff old;
 One as distraught with woe,
 Letting the spindle go,
Her starry-sprinkled gown doth shivering
  fold;
 And one right mournful hangs her
  head,
Complaining, "Woe is me! I may not cut
  the thread.

 "All men of every birth,
 Yea, great ones of the earth,
Kings and their councillors, have I drawn
  down;
 But I am held of Thee,—
 Why dost Thou trouble me,
To bring me up, dead King, that keep'st
  Thy crown?
 Yet for all courtiers hast but ten
Lowly, unlettered, Galilean fishermen.

 "Olympian heights are bare
 Of whom men worshipped there,
Immortal feet their snows may print no
  more;
 Their stately powers below
 Lie desolate, nor know
This thirty years Thessalian grove or shore;
 But I am elder far than they;—
Where is the sentence writ that I must pass
  away?

 "Art thou come up for this,
 Dark Regent, awful Dis?
And hast thou moved the deep to mark
  our ending?
 And stirred the dens beneath
 To see us eat of death,
With all the scoffing heavens toward us
  bending?
 Help! powers of ill, see not us die!"
But neither demon dares, nor angel deigns,
  reply.

 Her sisters, fallen on sleep,
 Fade in the upper deep,
And their grim lord sits on, in doleful
  trance;
 Till her black veil she rends,
 And with her death-shriek bends
Downward the terrors of her countenance;
 Then, whelmed in night, and no more
  seen,
They leave the world a doubt if ever such have
  been.

 And the winged armies twain
 Their awful watch maintain;
They mark the earth at rest with her Great
  Dead.
 Behold, from Antres wide,
 Green Atlas heave his side;

 His moving woods their scarlet clusters
  shed,
 The swathing coif his front that cools,
And tawny lions lapping at his palm-edged
  pools.

 Then like a heap of snow,
 Lying where grasses grow,
See glimmering, while the moony lustres
  creep,
 Mild-mannered Athens, dight
 In dewy marbles white,
Among her goddesses and gods asleep;
 And, swaying on a purple sea,
The many moorèd galleys clustering at her
  quay.

 Also, 'neath palm-trees' shade,
 Amid their camels laid,
The pastoral tribes with all their flocks at
  rest;
 Like to those old-world folk
 With whom two angels broke
The bread of men at Abram's courteous
  'quest,
 When, listening as they prophesied,
His desert princess, being reproved, her laugh
  denied.

 Or from the Morians' land
 See worshipped Nilus bland,
Taking the silver road he gave the world,
 To wet his ancient shrine
 With waters held divine,
And touch his temple steps with wavelets
  curled,
 And list, ere darkness change to gray,
Old minstrel-throated Memnon chanting in the
  day.

 Moreover, Indian glades,
 Where kneel the sun-swart maids,
On Gunga's flood their votive flowers to
  throw,
 And launch i' the sultry night
 Their burning cressets bright,
Most like a fleet of stars that southing go,
 Till on her bosom prosperously
She floats them shining forth to sail the lullèd
  sea.

 Nor bend they not their eyn
 Where the watch-fires shine,
By shepherds fed, on hills of Bethlehem:
 They mark, in goodly wise,
 The city of David rise,
The gates and towers of rare Jerusalem;
 And hear the 'scapèd Kedron fret,
And night dews dropping from the leaves of
  Olivet.

 But now the setting moon
 To curtained lands must soon,
In her obedient fashion, minister;

She first, as loath to go,
    Lets her last silver flow
Upon her Master's sealéd sepulchre;
    And trees that in the garden spread,
She kisseth all for sake of His low-lying head.

    Then 'neath the rim goes down;
    And night with darker frown
Sinks on the fateful garden watchéd long;
    When some despairing eyes,
    Far in the murky skies,
The unwished waking by their gloom foretell;
    And blackness up the welkin swings,
And drinks the mild effulgence from celestial wings.

    Last, with amazéd cry,
    The hosts asunder fly,
Leaving an empty gulf of blackest hue;
    Whence straightway shooteth down,
    By the Great Father thrown,
A mighty angel, strong and dread to view;
    And at his fall the rocks are rent,
The waking world doth quake with mortal tremblement;

    The regions far and near
    Quail with a pause of fear,
More terrible than aught since time began;
    The winds that dare not fleet,
    Drop at his awful feet,
And in its bed wails the wide ocean;
    The flower of dawn forbears to blow,
And the oldest running river cannot skill to flow.

    At stand, by that dread place,
    He lifts his radiant face,
And looks to heaven with reverent love and fear;
    Then, while the welkin quakes,
    And muttering thunder breaks,
And lightnings shoot and ominous meteors drear,
    And all the daunted earth doth moan,
He from the doors of death rolls back the sealéd stone.—

    —In regal quiet deep,
    Lo, One new waked from sleep!
Behold, He standeth in the rock-hewn door!
    Thy children shall not die—
    Peace, peace, thy Lord is by!
He liveth!—they shall live forevermore.
    Peace! lo, He lifts a priestly hand,
And blesseth all the sons of men in every land.

    Then, with great dread and wail,
    Fall down like storms of hail,
The legions of the lost in fearful wise;
    And they whose blissful race
    Peoples the better place

Lift up their wings to cover their fair eyes,
    And through the waxing saffron brede,
Till they are lost in light, recede, and yet recede.

    So while the fields are dim,
    And the red sun his rim
First heaves, in token of his reign benign,
    All stars the most admired,
    Into their blue retired,
Lie hid,—the faded moon forgets to shine,—
    And, hurrying down the sphery way,
Night flies, and sweeps her shadow from the path of day.

    But look! the Saviour blest,
    Calm after solemn rest,
Stands in the garden 'neath His olive-boughs;
    The earliest smile of day
    Doth on His vesture play,
And light the majesty of His still brows;
    While angels hang with wings outspread,
Holding the new-won crown above His saintly head.

SONG OF MARGARET.

Ay, I saw her, we have met,—
    Married eyes how sweet they be,—
Are you happier, Margaret,
    Than you might have been with me?
Silence! make no more ado!
    Did she think I should forget?
Matters nothing, though I knew,
    Margaret, Margaret.

Once those eyes, full sweet, full shy,
    Told a certain thing to mine;
What they told me I put by,
    O, so careless of the sign.
Such an easy thing to take,
    And I did not want it then;
Fool! I wish my heart would break,
    Scorn is hard on hearts of men.

Scorn of self is bitter work,—
    Each of us has felt it now:
Bluest skies she counted mirk,
    Self-betrayed of eyes and brow;
As for me, I went my way,
    And a better man drew nigh,
Fain to earn with long essay,
    What the winner's hand threw by.

Matters not in deserts old,
    What was born, and waxed, and yearned,
Year to year its meaning told,
    I am come,—its deeps are learned,—

Come, but there is naught to say,—
  Married eyes with mine have met.
Silence! O, I had my day,
  Margaret, Margaret.

SONG OF THE GOING AWAY.

"OLD man, upon the green hillside,
  With yellow flowers besprinkled o'er,
How long in silence wilt thou bide
  At this low stone door?

"I stoop: within 'tis dark and still;
  But shadowy paths methinks there be,
And lead they far into the hill?"
  "Traveller, come and see."

"'Tis dark, 'tis cold, and hung with gloom;
  I care not now within to stay;
For thee and me is scarcely room,
  I will hence away."

"Not so, not so, thou youthful guest,
  Thy foot shall issue forth no more:
Behold the chamber of thy rest,
  And the closing door!"

"O, have I 'scaped the whistling ball,
  And striven on smoky fields of fight,
And scaled the 'leaguered city's wall
  In the dangerous night;

"And borne my life unharmèd still
  Through foaming gulfs of yeasty spray,
To yield it on a grassy hill
  At the noon of day?"

"Peace! say thy prayers, and go to sleep,
  Till *some time*, ONE my seal shall break,
And deep shall answer unto deep,
  When He crieth, 'AWAKE!'"

A LILY AND A LUTE.

(Song of the uncommunicated Ideal.)

I.

I OPENED the eyes of my soul.
                        And behold,
A white river-lily: a lily awake, and aware—
For she set her face upward—aware how in
    scarlet and gold
A long wrinkled cloud, left behind of the wan-
    dering air,
  Lay over with fold upon fold,
  With fold upon fold.

And the blushing sweet shame of the cloud
    made her also ashamed,
The white river-lily, that suddenly knew she
    was fair;
And over the far-away mountains that no man
    hath named,
  And that no foot hath trod,
Flung down out of heavenly places, there fell,
    as it were,
A rose-bloom, a token of love, that should
    make them endure,
Withdrawn in snow silence for ever, who keep
    themselves pure,
  And look up to God.

Then I said, "In rosy air,
Cradled on thy reaches fair,
While the blushing early ray
Whitens into perfect day,
River-lily, sweetest known,
Art thou set for me alone?
Nay, but I will bear thee far,
Where yon clustering steeples are,
And the bells ring out o'erhead,
And the stated prayers are said;
And the busy farmers pace,
Trading in the market-place;
And the country lasses sit
By their butter, praising it;
And the latest news is told,
While the fruit and cream are sold,
And the friendly gossips greet,
Up and down the sunny street.
For," I said, "I have not met,
White one, any folk as yet
Who would send no blessing up,
Looking on a face like thine;
For thou art as Joseph's cup,
And by thee might they divine.

"Nay! but thou a spirit art;
Men shall take thee in the mart
For the ghost of their best thought,
Raised at noon, and near them brought
Or the prayer they made last night,
Set before them all in white."

And I put out my rash hand,
For I thought to draw to land
The white lily. Was it fit
Such a blossom should expand,
Fair enough for a world's wonder,
And no mortal gather it?
No. I strove, and it went under,
And I drew, but it went down;
And the water-weeds' long tresses,
And the overlapping cresses,
Sullied its admired crown.
Then along the river strand,
Trailing, wrecked, it came to land,
Of its beauty half despoiled,
And its snowy pureness soiled:
O! I took it in my hand,—
You will never see it now,
White and golden as it grew:
No, I cannot show it you,

Nor the cheerful town endow
With the freshness of its brow.

If a royal painter, great
With the colors dedicate
To a dove's neck, a sea-bight,
And the flickerings over white
Mountain summits far away,—
One content to give his mind
To the enrichment of mankind,
And the laying up of light
In men's houses,—on that day,
Could have passed in kingly mood,
Would he ever have endued
Canvass with the peerless thing,
In the grace that it did bring,
And the light that o'er it flowed,
With the pureness that it showed,
And the pureness that it meant?
Could he skill to make it seen
As he saw? For this, I ween,
He were likewise impotent.

II.
I opened the doors of my heart.

                And behold,
There was music within and a song,
And echoes did feed on the sweetness, repeat-
    ing it long.
I opened the doors of my heart. And behold,
There was music that played itself out in æo-
    lian notes;
Then was heard, as a far away bell at long
    intervals tolled,
    That murmurs and floats,
And presently dieth, forgotten of forest and
    wold,
And comes in all passion again and a tremble-
    ment soft,
That maketh the listener full oft
To whisper, "Ah! would I might hear it for-
    ever and aye,
    When I toil in the heat of the day,
    When I walk in the cold."

I opened the door of my heart. And
    behold,
There was music within and a song.
But while I was hearkening, lo, blackness with-
    out, thick and strong,
Came up and came over, and all that sweet
    fluting was drowned,
    I could hear it no more;
For the welkin was moaning, the waters were
    stirred on the shore,
    And trees in the dark all around
Were shaken. It thundered. "Hark, hark!
    there is thunder to-night!
The sullen long wave rears her head, and
    comes down with a will;
The awful white tongues are let loose, and the
    stars are all dead;
There is thunder! it thunders! and ladders of
    light
Run up. there is thunder!" I said,
"Loud thunder? it thunders! and up in the
    dark overhead,
A down-pouring cloud, (there is thunder!) a
    down-pouring cloud
Hails out her fierce message, and quivers the
    deep in its bed,
And cowers the earth held at bay; and they
    mutter aloud,
And pause with an ominous tremble, till, great
    in their rage,
The heavens and earth come together, and
    meet with a crash;
And the fight is so fell as if Time had come
    down with the flash.
    And the story of life was all read,
    And the Giver had turned the last page.

Now their bar the pent water-floods lash,
And the forest trees give out their language
    austere with great age;
And there flieth o'er moor and o'er hill,
And there heaveth at intervals wide,
The long sob of nature's great passion, as loath
    to subside,
Until quiet drop down on the tide,
And mad Echo hath moaned herself still.

Lo! or ever I was 'ware,
In the silence of the air,
Through my heart's wide open door,
Music floated forth once more,
Floated to the world's dark rim,
And looked over with a hymn;
Then came home with flutings fine,
And discoursed in tones divine
Of a certain grief of mine;
And went downward and went in,
Glimpses of my soul to win,
And discovered such a deep
That I could not choose but weep,
For it lay, a land-locked sea,
Fathomless and dim to me.

O the song! it came and went,
Went and came.

                I have not learned
Half the lore whereto it yearned,
Half the magic that it meant.
Water booming in a cave;
Or the swell of some long wave,
Setting in from unrevealed
Countries; or a foreign tongue,
Sweetly talked and deftly sung,
While the meaning is half sealed;
May be like it. You have heard
Also;—can you find a word
For the naming of such song?
No; a name would do it wrong.
You have heard it in the night,
In the dropping rain's despite,
In the midnight darkness deep,
When the children were asleep,
And the wife—no, let that be;

SHE asleep! She knows right well
What the song to you and me,
While we breathe, can never tell;
She hath heard its faultless flow,
Where the roots of music grow.

While I listened, like young birds,
Hints were fluttering; almost words—
Leaned and leaned, and nearer came;—
Everything had changed its name.

Sorrow was a ship, I found,
Wrecked with them that in her are,
On an island richer far
Than the port where they were bound.
Fear was but the awful boom
Of the old great bell of doom,
Tolling, far from earthly air,
For all worlds to go to prayer.
Pain, that to us mortals clings,
But the pushing of our wings,
That we have no use for yet,
And the uprooting of our feet
From the soil where they are set,
And the land we reckon sweet.
Love in growth, the grand deceit
Whereby men the perfect greet;
Love in wane, the blessing sent
To be (howsoe'er it went)
Nevermore with earth content.

O, full sweet, and O, full high,
Ran that music up the sky;
But I cannot sing it you,
More than I can make you view
With my paintings labial,
Sitting up in awful row,
White old men majestical,
Mountains in their gowns of snow,
Ghosts of kings; as my two eyes,
Looking over speckled skies,
See them now. About their knees,
Half in haze, there stands at ease
A great army of green hills,
Some bareheaded; and, behold,
Small green mosses creep on some.
Those be mighty forests old;
And white avalanches come
Through yon rents, where now distils
Sheeny silver, pouring down
To a tune of old renown,
Cutting narrow pathways through
Gentian belts of airy blue,
To a zone where starwort blows,
And long reaches of the rose.

So, that haze all left behind,
Down the chestnut forests wind,
Past yon jagged spires, where yet
Foot of man was never set;
Past a castle yawning wide,
With a great breach in its side,
To a nest-like valley, where,
Like a sparrow's egg in hue,
Lie two lakes, and teach the true
Color of the sea-maid's hair.

What beside? The world beside!
Drawing down and down to greet
Cottage clusters at our feet,—
Every scent of summer tide,—
Flowery pastures all aglow;
(Men and women mowing go
Up and down them;) also soft
Floating of the film aloft,
Fluttering of the leaves alow.
Is this told? It is not told.
Where's the danger? where's the cold
Slippery danger up the steep?
Where yon shadow fallen asleep?
Chirping bird and tumbling spray,
Light, work, laughter, scent of hay,
Peace, and echo, where are they?

Ah, they sleep, sleep all untold;
Memory must their grace enfold
Silently; and that high song
Of the heart, it doth belong
To the hearers. Not a whit,
Though a chief musician heard.
Could he make a tune for it.

Though a lute fell deftly strung,
And the sweetest bird e'er sung,
Could have tried it,—O, the lute
For that wondrous song were mute,
And the bird would do her part,
Falter, fail, and break her heart,—
Break her heart, and furl her wings,
On the unexpressive strings.

GLADYS AND HER ISLAND.

(On the Advantages of the Poetical Temperament.)

AN IMPERFECT FABLE WITH A
DOUBTFUL MORAL.

HAPPY Gladys! I rejoice with her,
For Gladys saw the island.

     It was thus:
They gave a day for pleasure in the school
Where Gladys taught; and all the other girls
Were taken out to picnic in a wood.
But it was said, "We think it were not well
That little Gladys should acquire a taste
For pleasure, going about, and needless change.
It would not suit her station: discontent
Might come of it; and all her duties now
She does so pleasantly, that we were best
To keep her humble." So they said to her,
"Gladys, we shall not want you, all to-day.
Look, you are free; you need not sit at work:
No, you may take a long and pleasant walk
Over the sea-cliff, or upon the beach
Among the visitors."

     Then Gladys blushed
For joy, and thanked them. What! a holiday,
A whole one, for herself! How good! how kind!
With that the marshalled carriages drove off;
And Gladys, sobered with her weight of joy,
Stole out beyond the groups upon the beach—
The children with their wooden spades, the band
That played for lovers, and the sunny stir
Of cheerful life and leisure—to the rocks,
For these she wanted most, and there was time
To mark them; how like ruined organs prone
They lay, or leaned their giant fluted pipes,
And let the great white-crested reckless wave
Beat out their booming melody.

     The sea
Was filled with light; in clear blue caverns curled
The breakers, and they ran, and seemed to romp,
As playing at some rough and dangerous game,
While all the nearer waves rushed in to help,
And all the farther heaved their heads to peep,
And tossed the fishing-boats. Then Gladys laughed,

And said, "O happy tide, to be so lost
In sunshine, that one dare not look at it;
And lucky cliffs, to be so brown and warm;
And yet how lucky are the shadows, too,
That lurk beneath their ledges. It is strange,
That in remembrance though I lay them up,
They are forever, when I come to them,
Better than I had thought. O, something yet
I had forgotten. Oft I say, 'At least
This picture is imprinted; thus and thus,
The sharpened serried jags run up, run out,
Layer on layer.' And I look—up—up—
High, higher up again, till far aloft
They cut into their ether—brown, and clear,
And perfect. And I, saying, 'This is mine,
To keep,' retire; but shortly come again,
And they confound me with a glorious change.
The low sun out of rain-clouds stares at them;
They redden, and their edges drip with—what?
I know not, but 'tis red. It leaves no stain,
For the next morning they stand up like ghosts
In a sea-shroud, and fifty thousand mews
Sit there, in long white files, and chatter on,
Like silly school-girls in their silliest mood.

"There is the boulder where we always turn.
O, I have longed to pass it; now I will.
What would THEY say? for one must slip and spring;
'Young ladies! Gladys! I am shocked. My dears,
Decorum, if you please; turn back at once.
Gladys, we blame you most; you should have looked
Before you.' Then they sigh—how kind they are!
'What will become of you, if all your life
You look a long way off?—look anywhere,
And everywhere, instead of at your feet,
And where they carry you!' Ah, well, I know
It is a pity," Gladys said; "but then
We cannot all be wise: happy for me
That other people are.

     And yet I wish—
For sometimes very right and serious thoughts
Come to me—I do wish that they would come
When they are wanted!—when I teach the sums
On rainy days, and when the practising
I count to, and the din goes on and on,
Still the same tune and still the same mistake,
Then I am wise enough: sometimes I feel

GLADYS AND HER ISLAND.

Quite old. I think that it will last, and say,
'Now my reflections do me credit! now
I am a woman!' and I wish they knew
How serious all my duties look to me.
And how my heart hushed down and shaded lies,
Just like the sea when low, convenient clouds
Come over, and drink all its sparkles up.
But does it last? Perhaps, that very day,
The front door opens: out we walk in pairs;
And I am so delighted with this world,
That suddenly has grown, being new washed,
To such a smiling, clean, and thankful world,
And with a tender face shining through tears,
Looks up into the sometime lowering sky,
That has been angry, but is reconciled,
And just forgiving her that I,—that I—
O, I forget myself: what matters how!
And then I hear (but always kindly said)
Some words that pain me so—but just, but true:
'For if your place in this establishment
Be but subordinate, and if your birth
Be lowly, it the more behooves— Well, well,
No more. We see that you are sorry.' Yes!
I am always sorry THEN; but now—O, now,
Here is a bight more beautiful than all."

"And did they scold her, then, my pretty one?
And did she want to be as wise as they,—
To bear a bucklered heart and priggish mind?
Ay, you may crow; she did! but no, no, no,
The night-time will not let her; all the stars
Say nay to that; the old sea laughs at her.
Why! Gladys is a child; she has not skill
To shut herself within her own small cell,
And build the door up, and to say, 'Poor me!
I am a prisoner;' then, to take hewn stones,
And, having built the windows up, to say,
'O, it is dark! there is no sunshine here;
There never has been.'"

Strange! how very strange!
A woman passing Gladys with a babe,
To whom she spoke these words, and only looked
Upon the babe, who crowed and pulled her curls,
And never looked at Gladys, never once.
"A simple child," she added, and went by,
"To want to change her greater for their less;
But Gladys shall not do it, no, not she;
We love her—dont we?—far too well for that."

Then Gladys, flushed with shame and keen surprise,
"How could she be so near, and I not know?
And have I spoken out my thought aloud?
I must have done, forgetting. It is well
She walks so fast, for I am hungry now,
And here is water cantering down the cliff,
And here a shell to catch it with, and here
The round plump buns they gave me, and the fruit.

Now she is gone behind the rock. O, rare
To be alone!" So Gladys sat her down,
Unpacked her little basket, ate and drank,
Then pushed her hands into the warm dry sand,
And thought the earth was happy, and she too
Was going round with it in happiness,
That holiday. "What was it that she said?"
Quoth Gladys, cogitating; "they were kind,
The words that woman spoke. She does not know!
'Her greater for their less,'—it makes me laugh,—
But yet," sighed Gladys, "though it must be good
To look and to admire, one should not wish
To steal THEIR virtues, and to put them on,
Like feathers from another wing; beside,
That calm, and that grave consciousness of worth,
When all is said, would little suit with me,
Who am not worthy. When our thoughts are born.
Though they be good and humble, one should mind
How they are reared, or some will go astray
And shame their mother. Cain and Abel both
Were only once removed from innocence.
Why did I envy them? That was not good;
Yet it began with my humility."

But as she spake, lo, Gladys raised her eyes,
And right before her on the horizon's edge,
Behold, an island. First, she looked away
Along the solid rocks and steadfast shore,
For she was all amazed, believing not,
And then she looked again, and there again
Behold, an island! And the tide had turned,
The milky sea had got a purple rim,
And from the rim that mountain island rose,
Purple, with two high peaks; the northern peak
The higher, and with fell and precipice,
It ran down steeply to the water's brink;
But all the southern line was long and soft,
Broken with tender curves, and, as she thought,
Covered with forest or with sward. But, look!
The sun was on the island; and he showed
On either peak a dazzling cap of snow.
Then Gladys held her breath; she said, "Indeed,
Indeed it is an island: how is this,
I never saw it till this fortunate
Rare holiday?" And while she strained her eyes,
She thought that it began to fade; but not
To change as clouds do, only to withdraw
And melt into its azure; and at last,
Little by little, from her hungry heart,
That longed to draw things marvellous to itself,
And yearned towards the riches and the great
Abundance of the beauty God hath made,
It passed away. Tears started in her eyes,
And when they dropt, the mountain isle was gone;

The careless sea had quite forgotten it,
And all was even as it had been before.

And Gladys wept, but there was luxury
In her self-pity, while she softly sobbed,
"O, what a little while! I am afraid
I shall forget that purple mountain isle,
The lovely hollows atween her snow-clad
 peaks,
The grace of her upheaval where she lay
Well up against the open. O my heart,
Now I remember how this holiday
Will soon be done, and now my life goes on
Not fed; and only in the noonday walk
Let to look silently at what it wants,
Without the power to wait or pause awhile,
And understand and draw within itself
The richness of the earth. A holiday!
How few I have! I spend the silent time
At work, while all THEIR pupils are gone
 home,
And feel myself remote. They shine apart;
They are great planets, I a little orb;
My little orbit far within their own
Turns, and approaches not. But yet, the
 more
I am alone when those I teach return:
For they, as planets of some other sun,
Not mine, have paths that can but meet my
 ring
Once in a cycle. O, how poor I am!
I have not got laid up in this blank heart
Any indulgent kisses given me
Because I had been good, or, yet more sweet,
Because my childhood was itself a good
Attractive thing for kisses, tender praise,
And comforting. An orphan-school at best
Is a cold mother in the winter time,
('Twas mostly winter when new orphans came,)
An unregardful mother in the spring.

"Yet once a year (I did mine wrong) we went
To gather cowslips. How we thought on it
Beforehand, pacing, pacing the dull street,
To that one tree, the only one we saw
From April,—if the cowslips were in bloom
So early; or, if not, from opening May
Even to September. Then there came the
 feast
At Epping. If it rained that day, it rained
For a whole year to us; we could not think
Of fields and hawthorn hedges, and the leaves
Fluttering, but still it rained, and ever rained.

"Ah, well, but I am here; but I have seen
The gay gorse bushes in their flowering time;
I know the scent of bean-fields; I have heard
The satisfying murmur of the main."

The woman! she came round the rock again
With her fair baby, and she sat her down
By Gladys, murmuring, "Who forbade the
 grass
To grow by visitations of the dew?
Who said in ancient time to the desert pool,

'Thou shalt not wait for angel visitors
To trouble thy still water?' Must we bide
At home? The lore, beloved, shall fly to us
On a pair of sumptuous wings. Or, may we
 breathe
Without? O, we shall draw to us the air
That times and mystery feed on. This shall
 lay
Unchidden hands upon the heart o' the world,
And feel it beating. Rivers shall run on,
Full of sweet language as a lover's mouth,
Delivering of a tune to make her youth
More beautiful than wheat when it is green.

"What else?—(O, none shall envy her!) The
 rain
And the wild weather will be most her own,
And talk with her o' nights; and if the winds
Have seen aught wondrous, they will tell it her
In a mouthful of strange moans,—will bring
 from far,
Her ears being keen, the lowing and the mad,
Masterful trampling of the bison herds,
Tearing down headlong with their bloodshot
 eyes,
In savage rifts of hair; the crack and creak
Of ice-floes in the frozen sea, the cry
Of the white bears, all in a dim blue world
Mumbling their meals by twilight; or the rock
And majesty of motion, when their heads
Primeval trees toss in a sunny storm,
And hail their nuts down on unweeded fields,
No holidays," quoth she; "drop, drop, O,
 drop,
Thou tired skylark, and go up no more;
You lime-trees, cover not your head with bees,
Nor give out your good smell. She will not
 look;
No, Gladys cannot draw your sweetness in,
For lack of holidays." So Gladys thought,
"A most strange woman, and she talks of me."
With that a girl ran up: "Mother," she said,
"Come out of this brown bight, I pray you
 now,
It smells of fairies." Gladys thereon thought,
"The mother will not speak to me, perhaps
The daughter may," and asked her courteously,
"What do the fairies smell of?" But the girl
With peevish pout replied, "You know, you
 know."
"Not I," said Gladys; then she answered her,
"Something like buttercups. But, mother,
 come,
And whisper up a porpoise from the foam,
Because I want to ride."

          Full slowly, then,
The mother rose, and ever kept her eyes
Upon her little child. "You freakish maid,"
Said she, "now mark me, if I call you one,
You shall not scold nor make him take you far."
"I only want—you know I only want,"
The girl replied—"to go and play awhile
Upon the sand by Lagos." Then she turned
And muttered low, "Mother, is this the girl

GLADYS AND HER ISLAND.

Who saw the island?" But the mother frowned.
"When may she go to it?" the daughter asked.
And Gladys, following them, gave all her mind
To hear the answer. "When she wills to go;
For yonder comes to shore the ferry-boat."
Then Gladys turned to look, and even so
It was; a ferry-boat, and far away
Reared in the offing, lo, the purple peaks
Of her loved island.

    Then she raised her arms,
And ran toward the boat, crying out, "O rare,
The island! fair befall the island; let
Me reach the island." And she sprang on board,
And after her stepped in the freakish maid
And the fair mother, brooding o'er her child;
And this one took the helm, and that let go
The sail, and off they flew, and furrowed up
A flaky hill before, and left behind
A sobbing snake-like tail of creamy foam;
And dancing hither, thither, sometimes shot
Toward the island; then, when Gladys looked,
Were leaving it to leeward. And the maid
Whistled a wind to come and rock the craft,
And would be leaning down her head to mew
At cat-fish, then lift out into her lap
And dandle baby-seals, which, having kissed,
She flung to their sleek mothers, till her own
Rebuked her in good English, after cried,
"Luff, luff, we shall be swamped." "I will not luff,"
Sobbed the fair mischief; "you are cross to me."
"For shame!" the mother shrieked; "luff, luff, my dear;
Kiss and be friends, and thou shalt have the fish
With the curly tail to ride on." So she did,
And presently, a dolphin bouncing up,
She sprang upon his slippery back,—"Farewell,"
She laughed, was off, and all the sea grew calm.

Then Gladys was much happier, and was 'ware
In the smooth weather that this woman talked
Like one in sleep, and murmured certain thoughts
Which seemed to be like echoes of her own.
She nodded, "Yes, the girl is going now
To her own island. Gladys poor? Not she!
Who thinks so? Once I met a man in white,
Who said to me, 'The thing that might have been,'
Is called, and questioned why it hath not been;
And can it give good reason, it is set
Beside the actual, and is reckoned in
To fill the empty gaps of life.' Ah, so
The possible stands by us ever fresh,
Fairer than aught which any life hath owned,
And makes divine amends. Now this was set
Apart from kin, and not ordained a home;
An equal;—and not suffered to fence in
A little plot of earthly good, and say,

'Tis mine; but in bereavement of the part,
O, yet to taste the whole,—to understand
The grandeur of the story, not to feel
Satiate with good possessed, but evermore
A healthful hunger for the great idea,
The beauty and the blessedness of life."

"Lo, now the shadow!" quoth she, breaking off,
"We are in the shadow." Then did Gladys turn,
And, O, the mountain with the purple peaks
Was close at hand. It cast a shadow out,
And they were in it: and she saw the snow,
And under that the rocks, and under that
The pines, and then the pasturage; and saw
Numerous dips, and undulations rare,
Running down seaward, all astir with lithe
Long canes, and lofty feathers; for the palms
And spice-trees of the south, nay, every growth,
Meets in that island.

    So that woman ran
The boat ashore, and Gladys set her foot
Thereon. Then all at once much laughter rose;
Invisible folk set up exultant shouts,
"It all belongs to Gladys"; and she ran
And hid herself among the nearest trees
And panted, shedding tears.

    So she looked round
And saw that she was in a banyan grove,
Full of wild peacocks,—pecking on the grass,
A flickering mass of eyes, blue, green and gold,
Or reaching out their jewelled necks, where high
They sat in rows along the boughs. No tree
Cumbered with creepers let the sunshine through,
But it was caught in scarlet cups, and poured
From these on amber tufts of bloom, and dropped
Lower on azure stars. The air was still,
As if awaiting somewhat, or asleep,
And Gladys was the only thing that moved,
Excepting—no, they were not birds—what then?
Glorified rainbows with a living soul?
While they passed through a sunbeam they were seen,
Not otherwhere, but they were present yet
In shade. They were at work, pomegranate fruit
That lay about removing,—purple grapes,
That clustered in the path, clearing aside.
Through a small spot of light would pass and go
The glorious happy mouth and two fair eyes
Of somewhat that made rustlings where it went;
But when a beam would strike the ground sheer down.
Behold them! they had wings, and they would pass
One after other with the sheeny fans,
Bearing them slowly, that their hues were seen,
Tender as russet crimson dropt on snows,

Or where they turned flashing with gold and dashed
With purple glooms. And they had feet, but these
Did barely touch the ground. And they took heed
Not to disturb the waiting quietness;
Nor rouse up fawns, that slept beside their dams;
Nor the fair leopard, with her sleek paws laid
Across her little drowsy cubs; nor swans,
That, floating, slept upon a grassy pool;
Nor rosy cranes, all slumbering in the reeds,
With heads beneath their wings. For this, you know,
Was Eden. She was passing through the trees
That made a ring about it, and she caught
A glimpse of glades beyond. All she had seen
Was nothing to them; but words are not made
To tell that tale. No wind was let to blow,
And all the doves were bidden to hold their peace.
Why? One was working in a valley near,
And none might look that way. It was understood
That He had nearly ended that His work;
For two shapes met, and one to other spake,
Accosting him with, "Prince, what worketh He?"
Who whispered, "Lo! He fashioneth red clay."
And all at once a little trembling stir
Was felt in the earth, and every creature woke,
And laid its head down, listening. It was known
Then that the work was done; the new-made king
Had risen and set his feet upon his realm,
And it acknowledged him.

     But in her path
Came some one that withstood her, and he said,
"What doest thou here?" Then she did turn and flee,
Among those colored spirits, through the grove,
Trembling for haste; it was not well with her
Till she came forth of those thick banyan trees,
And set her feet upon the common grass,
And felt the common wind.

     Yet once beyond,
She could not choose but cast a backward glance.
The lovely matted growth stood like a wall,
And means of entering were not evident,—
The gap had closed. But Gladys laughed for joy;
She said, "Remoteness and a multitude
Of years are counted nothing here. Behold,
To-day I have been in Eden. O, it blooms
In my own island."

     And she wandered on,
Thinking, until she reached a place of palms,
And all the earth was sandy where she walked,—
Sandy and dry,—strewed with papyrus-leaves,
Old idols, rings and pottery, painted lids
Of mummies (for perhaps it was the way
That leads to dead old Egypt), and withal
Excellent sunshine cut out sharp and clear
The hot prone pillars, and the carven plinths,—
Stone lotos cups, with petals dipped in sand,
And wicked gods, and sphinxes bland, who sat
And smiled upon the ruin. O, how still!
Hot, blank, illuminated with the clear
Stare of an unveiled sky. The dry stiff leaves
Of palm-trees never rustled, and the soul
Of that dead ancientry was itself dead.
She was above her ankles in the sand,
When she beheld a rocky road, and, lo!
It bare in it the ruts of chariot wheels,
Which erst had carried to their pagan prayers
The brown old Pharaohs; for the ruts led on
To a great cliff, that either was a cliff
Or some dread shrine in ruins,—partly reared
In front of that same cliff, and partly hewn
Or excavate within its heart. Great heaps
Of sand and stones on either side there lay;
And, as the girl drew on, rose out from each,
As from a ghostly kennel, gods unblest,
Dog-headed, and behind them wingéd things
Like angels; and this carven multitude
Hedged in, to right and left, the rocky road.

  At last, the cliff,—and in the cliff a door
Yawning; and she looked in, as down the throat
Of some stupendous giant, and beheld
No floor, but wide, worn flights of steps, that led
Into a dimness. When the eyes could bear
That change to gloom, she saw, flight after flight,
Flight after flight, the worn, long stair go down,
Smooth with the feet of nations dead and gone.
So she did enter; also she went down
Till it was dark, and yet again went down,
Till, gazing upward at that yawning door,
It seemed no larger, in its height remote,
Than a pin's head. But while, irresolute,
She doubted of the end, yet farther down
A slender ray of lamplight fell away
Along the stair, as from a door ajar:
To this again she felt her way, and stepped
Adown the hollow stair, and reached the light;
But fear fell on her, fear; and she forbore
Entrance, and listened. Ay! 't was even so,—
A sigh; the breathing as of one who slept
And was disturbed. So she drew back awhile,
And trembled; then her doubting hand she laid
Against the door, and pushed it; but the light
Waned, faded, sank; and as she came within—
Hark, hark! A spirit was it, and asleep!
A spirit doth not breathe like clay. There hung
A cresset from the roof, and thence appeared
A flickering speck of light, and disappeared;
Then dropped along the floor its elfish flakes,
That fell on some one resting, in the gloom,—
Somewhat, a spectral shadow, then a shape

That loomed. It was a heifer, ay, and white,
Breathing and languid through prolonged repose.

Was it a heifer? all the marble floor
Was milk-white also, and the cresset paled,
And straight their whiteness grew confused and mixed.

But when the cresset, taking heart, bloomed out—
The whiteness—and asleep again! but now
It was a woman, robed, and with a face
Lovely and dim. And Gladys while she gazed
Murmured, "O terrible! I am afraid
To breathe among these intermittent lives,
That fluctuate in mystic solitude,
And change and fade. Lo! where the goddess sits
Dreaming on her dim throne; a crescent moon
She wears upon her forehead. Ah! her frown
Is mournful, and her slumber is not sweet.
What dost thou hold, Isis, to thy cold breast?
A baby god with finger on his lips,
Asleep, and dreaming of departed sway?
Thy son. Hush, hush; he knoweth all the lore
And sorcery of old Egypt; but his mouth
He shuts; the secret shall be lost with him,
He will not tell."

The woman coming down!
"Child, what art doing here?" the woman said;
"What wilt thou of Dame Isis and her bairn?"
*(Ay, ay, we see thee breathing in thy shroud,—
Thy pretty shroud, all frilled and furbelowed.)*
The air is dim with dust of spicéd bones.
I mark a crypt down there. Tier upon tier
Of painted coffers fills it. What if we,
Passing, should slip, and crash into their midst,—
Break the frail ancientry, and smothered lie,
Tumbled among the ribs of queens and kings,
And all the gear they took to bed with them!
Horrible? let us hence.

And Gladys said,
"O they are rough to mount those stairs"; but she
Took her and laughed, and up the mighty flight
Shot like a meteor with her. "There," said she;
"The light is sweet when one has smelled of graves,
Down in unholy heathen gloom; farewell."
She pointed to a gateway, strong and high,
Reared of hewn stones; but, look! in lieu of gate,
There was a glittering cobweb drawn across,
And on the lintel there were writ these words:
"Ho, every one that cometh, I divide
What hath been from what might be, and the line
Hangeth before thee as a spider's web;
Yet, wouldst thou enter, thou must break the line
Or else forbear the hill."

The maiden said,
"So, cobweb, I will break thee." And she passed
Among some oak-trees on the farther side,
And waded through the bracken round their bolls,
Until she saw the open, and drew on
Toward the edge o' the wood, where it was mixed
With pines and heathery places wild and fresh.
Here she put up a creature, that ran on
Before her, crying, "Tint, tint, tint," and turned,
Sat up, and stared at her with elfish eyes,
Jabbering of gramarye, one Michael Scott,
The wizard that wonned somewhere underground,
With other talk enough to make one fear
To walk in lonely places. After passed
A man-at-arms, William of Deloraine;
He shook his head, "An' if I list to tell,"
Quoth he, "I know, but how it matters not;"
Then crossed himself, and muttered of a clap
Of thunder, and a shape in Amice gray,
But still it mouthed at him, and whimpered, "Tint,
Tint, tint." "There shall be wild work some day soon,"
Quoth he, "thou limb of darkness: he will come,
Thy master, push a hand up, catch thee, imp,
And so good Christians shall have peace, perdie."

Then Gladys was so frightened that she ran,
And got away, towards a grassy down,
Where sheep and lambs were feeding, with a boy
To tend them. 'Twas the boy who wears that herb
Called heart's-ease in his bosom, and he sang
So sweetly to his flock, that she stole on
Nearer to listen. "O Content, Content,
Give me," sang he, "thy tender company.
I feed my flock among the myrtles; all
My lambs are twins, and they have laid them down
Along the slopes of Beulah. Come, fair love,
From the other side the river, where their harps
Thou hast been helping them to tune. O come,
And pitch thy tent by mine; let me behold
Thy mouth,—that even in slumber talks of peace,—
Thy well-set locks, and dove-like countenance."

And Gladys hearkened, couched upon the grass,
Till she had rested; then did ask the boy,
For it was afternoon, and she was fain
To reach the shore, "Which is the path, I pray,
That leads one to the water?" But he said,
"Dear lass, I only know the narrow way,

The path that leads one to the golden gate
Across the river." So she wandered on;
And presently her feet grew cool, the grass
Standing so high, and thyme being thick and
soft.
The air was full of voices, and the scent
Of mountain blossom loaded all its wafts;
For she was on the slopes of a goodly mount,
And reared in such a sort that it looked down
Into the deepest valleys, darkest glades,
And richest plains o' the island. It was set
Midway between the snows majestical
And a wide level, such as men would choose
For growing wheat; and some one said to her,
"It is the hill Parnassus." So she walked
Yet on its lower slope, and she could hear
The calling of an unseen multitude
To some upon the mountain, "Give us more;"
And others said, "We are tired of this old
  world:
Make it look new again." Then there were
  some
Who answered lovingly—(the dead yet speak
From that high mountain, as the living do);
But others sang desponding, "We have kept
The vision for a chosen few: we love
Fit audience better than a rough huzza
From the unreasoning crowd."

         Then words came up:
"There was a time, you poets, was a time
When all the poetry was ours, and made
By some who climbed the mountain from our
  midst,
We loved it then, we sang it in our streets.
O, it grows obsolete! Be you as they:
Our heroes die and drop away from us;
Oblivion folds them 'neath her dusky wing,
Fair copies wasted to the hungering world.
Save them. We fall so low for lack of them,
That many of us think scorn of honest trade,
And take no pride in our own shops; who
  care
Only to quit a calling, will not make
The calling what it might be; who despise
Their work, Fate laughs at, and doth let the
  work
Dull, and degrade them."

         Then did Gladys smile;
"Heroes!" quoth she; "yet, now I think on
  it,
There was the jolly goldsmith, brave Sir Hugh,
Certes, a hero ready-made. Methinks
I see him burnishing of golden gear,
Tankard and charger, and a-muttering low,
'London is thirsty'—(then he weighs a chain):
''Tis an ill thing, my masters. I would give
The worth of this, and many such as this,
To bring it water.'

         Ay, and after him
There came up Guy of London, lettered son
O' the honest lighterman. I'll think on him,
Leaning upon the bridge on summer eves,
After his shop was closed: a still, grave man,
With melancholy eyes. 'While these are
  hale,'
He saith, when he looks down and marks the
  crowd
Cheerily working; where the river marge
Is blocked with ships and boats; and all the
  wharves
Swarm, and the cranes swing in with mer-
  chandise,—
'While these are hale, 'tis well, 'tis very well.
But, O good Lord,' saith he, 'when these are
  sick,—
I fear me, Lord, this excellent workmanship
Of Thine is counted for a cumbrance then.
Ay, ay, my hearties! many a man of you,
Struck down, or maimed, or fevered, shrinks
  away,
And, mastered in that fight for lack of aid,
Creeps shivering to a corner, and there dies.'
Well we have heard the rest.

         Ah, next I think
Upon the merchant captain, stout of heart
To dare and to endure. 'Robert,' saith he,
(The navigator Knox to his manful son,)
'I sit a captive from the ship detained;
This heathenry doth let thee visit her.
Remember, son, if thou, alas! shouldst fail
To ransom thy poor father, they are free
As yet, the mariners; have wives at home,
As I have: ay, and liberty is sweet
To all men. For the ship, she is not ours,
Therefore, beseech thee, son, lay on the mate
This my command, to leave me, and set sail.
As for thyself—' 'Good father,' saith the son;
'I will not father, ask your blessing now,
Because, for fair, or else for evil, fate,
We two shall meet again.' And so they did.
The dusky men, peeling off cinnamon,
And beating nutmeg clusters from the tree,
Ransom and bribe contemned. The good ship
  sailed,—
The son returned to share his father's cell.

"O, there are many such. Would I had wit
Their worth to sing!" With that, she turned
  her feet.

"I am tired now," said Gladys "of their talk
Around this hill Parnassus." And, behold,
A piteous sight,—an old, blind, graybeard king
Led by a fool with bells. Now this was loved
Of the crowd below the hill; and when he
  called
For his lost kingdom, and bewailed his age,
And plained on his unkind daughters, they
  were known
To say, that if the best of gold and gear
Could have bought him back his kingdom,
  and made kind
The hard hearts which had broken his erewhile,
They would have gladly paid it from their
  store,
Many times over. What is done is done,
No help. The ruined majesty passed on.

And, look you! one who met her as she walked
Showed her a mountain nymph lovely as light.
Her name Œnone; and she mourned and mourned,
"O Mother Ida," and she could not cease,
No, nor be comforted.

And after this,
Soon there came by, arrayed in Norman cap
And kirtle, an Arcadian villager,
Who said, "I pray you, have you chanced to meet
One Gabriel?" and she sighed; but Gladys took
And kissed her hand; she could not answer her,
Because she guessed the end.

With that it drew
To evening; and as Gladys wandered on
In the calm weather, she beheld the wave,
And she ran down to set her feet again
On the sea-margin, which was covered thick
With white shell-skeletons. The sky was red
As wine. The water played among bare ribs
Of many wrecks, that lay half buried there
In the sand. She saw a cave, and moved thereto
To ask her way, and one so innocent
Came out to meet her, that, with marvelling mute,
She gazed and gazed into her sea-blue eyes,
For in them beamed the untaught ecstasy
Of childhood, that lives on though youth be come,
And love just born.

She could not choose but name her shipwrecked Prince,
All blushing. She told Gladys many things
That are not in the story,—things in sooth,
That Prospero her father knew. But now
'Twas evening, and the sun dropped; purple stripes
In the sea were copied from some clouds that lay
Out in the west. And lo! the boat, and more,
The freakish thing to take fair Gladys home
She mowed at her, but Gladys took the helm:
"Peace, Peace!" she said; "be good, you shall not steer,
For I am your liege lady." Then she sang
The sweetest songs she knew all the way home.

So Gladys set her feet upon the sand;
While in the sunset glory died away
The peaks of that blest island.

"Fare you well,
My country, my own kingdom," then she said,
"Till I go visit you again, farewell.

She looked toward their house with whom she dwelt,—
The carriages were coming. Hastening up,
She was in time to meet them at the door,
And lead the sleepy little ones within;
And some were cross and shivered, and her dames
Were weary and right hard to please; but she
Felt like a beggar suddenly endowed
With a warm cloak to 'fend her from the cold.
"For, come what will," she said, "I had *to-day*
There is an island."

The Moral.

What is the moral? Let us think awhile,
Taking the editorial WE to help,
It sounds respectable.

The moral; yes,
We always read, when any fable ends,
"Hence we may learn." A moral must be found.
What do you think of this: "Hence we may learn
That dolphins swim about the coast of Wales,
And Admiralty maps should now be drawn
By teacher-girls, because their sight is keen,
And they can spy out islands." Will that do?
No, that is far too plain—too evident.

Perhaps a general moralizing vein—
(We know we have a happy knack that way.
We have observed, moreover, that young men
Are fond of good advice, and so are girls;
Especially of that meandering kind
Which, winding on so sweetly, treats of all
They ought to be and do and think and wear,
As one may say, from creeds to comforters.
Indeed, we much prefer that sort ourselves,
So soothing.) Good, a moralizing vein:
That is the thing; but how to manage it?
"*Hence we may learn*," if we be so inclined,
That life goes best with those who take it best;
That wit can spin from work a golden robe
To queen it in; that who can paint at will
A private picture-gallery, should not cry
For shillings that will let him in to look
At some by others painted. Furthermore,
Hence we may learn, you poets—*(and we count
For poets all who ever felt that such
They were, and all who secretly have known
That such they could be; ay, moreover, all
Who wind the robes of ideality
About the bareness of their lives, and hang
Comforting curtains, knit of fancy's yarn,
Nightly betwixt them and the frosty world)*—
Hence we may learn, you poets, that of all
We should be most content. The earth is given
To us: we reign by virtue of a sense
Which lets us hear the rhythm of that old verse,
The ring of that old tune whereto she spins.
Humanity is given to us: we reign

By virtue of a sense which lets us in
To know its troubles ere they have been told,
And take them home and lull them into rest
With mournfullest music. Time is given to us,—
Time past, time future. Who, good sooth, beside
Have seen it well, have walked this empty world
When she went steaming, and from pulpy hills
Have marked the spurting of their flamy crowns?

Have not we seen the tabernacle pitched,
And peered between the linen curtains, blue,
Purple, and scarlet, at the dimness there,
And, frighted, have not dared to look again?
But, quaint antiquity! beheld, we thought,
A chest that might have held the manna pot,
And Aaron's rod that budded. Ay, we leaned
Over the edge of Britain, while the fleet
Of Cæsar loomed and neared; then, afterwards,
We saw fair Venice looking at herself
In the glass below her, while her Doge went forth
In all his bravery to the wedding.

This,
However, counts for nothing to the grace
We wot of in time future:—therefore add,
And afterwards have done: "*Hence we may learn,*"
That though it be a grand and comely thing
To be unhappy—(and we think it is,
Because so many grand and clever folk
Have found out reasons for unhappiness,
And talked about uncomfortable things,—
Low motives, bores, and shams, and hollowness,
The hollowness o' the world, till we at last
Have scarcely dared to jump or stamp, for fear,
Being so hollow, it should break some day,
And let us in)—yet, since we are not grand,
O, not at all, and as for cleverness,
That may be or may not be—it is well
For us to be as happy as we can!

Agreed; and with a word to the nobler sex,
As thus, we pray you carry not your guns
On the full cock; we pray you set your pride
In its proper place, and never be ashamed
Of any honest calling,—let us add,
And end; for all the rest, hold up your heads
And mind your English.

SONGS WITH PRELUDES.

WEDLOCK.

THE sun was streaming in: I woke
     and said,
"Where is my wife, that has been
     made my wife
Only this year?" The casement
     stood ajar:
I did but lift my head: The pear-
     tree dropped,
The great white pear-tree dropped
     with dew from leaves
And blossom, under heavens of happy blue.

My wife had wakened first, and had gone down
Into the orchard. All the air was calm;
Audible humming filled it. At the roots
Of peony bushes lay in rose-red heaps,
Or snowy, fallen bloom. The crag-like hills
Were tossing down their silver messengers,
And two brown foreigners, called cuckoo-
     birds,
Gave them good answer; all things else were
     mute;
An idle world lay listening to their talk,
They had it to themselves.

                    What ails my wife?
I know not if aught ails her; though her step
Tell of a conscious quiet, lest I wake.
She moves atween the almond-boughs, and
     bends
One thick with bloom to look on it. "O love!
A little while thou hast withdrawn thyself,
As unaware to think thy thoughts alone;
How sweet, and yet pathetic to my heart
The reason. Ah! thou art no more thine own.
Mine, mine, O love! Tears gather 'neath my
     lids,—
Sorrowful tears for thy lost liberty,
Because it was so sweet. Thy liberty,
That yet, O love, thou wouldst not have again.
No; all is right. But who can give, or bless,
Or take a blessing, but there comes withal
Some pain?"

             She walks beside the lily bed,
And holds apart her gown; she would not hurt
The leaf-enfolded buds, that have not looked
Yet on the daylight. O, thy locks are brown,
Fairest of colors!—and a darker brown
The beautiful, dear, veilèd, modest eyes.
A bloom as of blush-roses covers her
Forehead, and throat, and cheek. Health
     breathes with her,
And graceful vigor. Fair and wondrous soul!
To think that thou art mine!

                    My wife came in,
And moved into the chamber. As for me,
I heard, but lay as one that nothing hears,
And feigned to be asleep.

I.

The racing river leaped and sang
   Full blithely in the perfect weather,
All round the mountains echoes rang,
   For blue and green were glad together.

II.

This rained out light from every part,
   And that with songs of joy was thrilling;
But, in the hollow of my heart,
   There ached a place that wanted filling.

III.

Before the road and river meet,
   And stepping-stones are wet and glisten,
I heard a sound of laughter sweet,
   And paused to like it, and to listen.

IV.

I heard the chanting waters flow,
   The cushat's note, the bee's low hum-
     ming,—
Then turned the hedge, and did not know—
   How could I?—that my time was coming.

V.

A girl upon the nighest stone,
   Half doubtful of the deed, was standing,
So far the shallow flood had flown
   Beyond the 'customed leap of landing.

VI.

She knew not any need of me,
   Yet me she waited all unweeting;
We thought not I had crossed the sea,
   And half the sphere to give her greeting.

VII.

I waded out, her eyes I met,
   I wished the moments had been hours;
I took her in my arms, and set
   Her dainty feet among the flowers.

VIII.

Her fellow-maids in copse and lane,
   Ah! still, methinks, I hear them calling;

The wind's soft whisper in the plain,
The cushat's coo, the water's falling.

IX.

But now it is a year ago,
  But now possession crowns endeavor;
I took her in my heart, to grow
And fill the hollow place for ever.

REGRET.

O THAT word REGRET!
There have been nights and morns when we
  have sighed,
"Let us alone, Regret! We are content
To throw thee all our past, so thou wilt sleep
For aye." But it is patient, and it wakes;
It hath not learned to cry itself to sleep,
But plaineth on the bed that it is hard.
We did amiss when we did wish it gone
And over; sorrows humanize our race;
Tears are the showers that fertilize this world;
And memory of things precious keepeth warm
The heart that once did hold them.

                    They are poor
That have lost nothing; they are poorer far
Who, losing, have forgotten; they most poor
Of all, who lose and wish they MIGHT forget.
For life is one, and in its warp and woof
There runs a thread of gold that glitters fair,
And sometimes in the pattern shows most
  sweet
Where there are sombre colors. It is true
That we have wept. But O! this thread of
  gold,
We would not have it tarnish; let us turn
Oft and look back upon the wondrous web,
And when it shineth sometimes we shall know
That memory is possession.

I.

When I remember something which I had,
  But which is gone, and I must do without,
I sometimes wonder how I can be glad,
  Even in cowslip time when hedges sprout;
It makes me sigh to think on it,—but yet
My days will not be better days, should I forget.

II.

When I remember something promised me,
  But which I never had, nor can have now,
Because the promiser we no more see
  In countries that accord with mortal vow;
When I remember this, I mourn,—but yet
My happier days are not the days when I forget.

LAMENTATION.

I READ upon that book,
Which down the golden gulf doth let us look
On the sweet days of pastoral majesty;
  I read upon that book
    How, when the Shepherd Prince did flee
    (Red Esau's twin), he desolate took
The stone for a pillow: then he fell on sleep.
And lo! there was a ladder. Lo! there hung
A ladder from the star-place, and it clung
To the earth; it tied her so to heaven; and O!
    There fluttered wings;
Then were ascending and descending things
  That stepped to him where he lay low;
Then up the ladder would a-drifting go
(This feathered brood of heaven), and show
Small as white flakes in winter that are blown
Together, underneath the great white throne.

    When I had shut the book, I said:
"Now, as for me, my dreams upon my bed
    Are not like Jacob's dream;
Yet I have got it in my life; yes, I,
And many more: it doth not us beseem,
    Therefore, to sigh.
Is there not hung a ladder in our sky?
Yea; and, moreover, all the way up on high
Is thickly peopled with the prayers of men.
  We have no dream! What then?
Like wingéd wayfarers the height they scale,
(By Him that offers them they shall prevail)—
    The prayers of men.
  But where is found a prayer for me;
    How should I pray?
My heart is sick and full of strife.
I heard one whisper with departing breath,
'Suffer us not, for any pains of death
    To fall from Thee.'
But O, the pains of life! the pains of life!
  There is no comfort now, and naught to
    win,
    But yet—I will begin."

I.

"Preserve to me my wealth," I do not say,
    For that is wasted away;
And much of it was cankered ere it went.
"Preserve to me my health," I cannot say,
    For that, upon a day,
Went after other delights to banishment.

II.

What can I pray? "Give me forgetfulness?"
    No, I would still possess
Past away smiles, though present fronts be
    stern.
"Give me again my kindred?" Nay; not so,
    Not idle prayers. We know
They that have crossed the river cannot return.

III.

I do not pray, "Comfort me! comfort me!"
    For how should comfort be?
O—O that cooing mouth,—that little white
    head!
No; but I pray, "If it be not too late,
    Open to me the gate,
That I may find my babe when I am dead.

IV.

"Show me the path. I had forgotten Thee,
    When I was happy and free,
Walking down here in the gladsome light o'
    the sun;
But now I come and mourn; O set my feet
    In the road to Thy blest seat,
And for the rest, O God, Thy will be done."

DOMINION.

When found the rose delight in her fair hue?
Color is nothing to this world; 't is I
That see it. Farther, I discover soul,
That trees are nothing to their fellow-trees;
It is but I that love their stateliness,
And I that, comforting my heart, do sit,
At noon beneath their shadow. I will step
On the ledges of this world, for it is mine;
But the other world ye wot of shall go too;
I will carry it in my bosom. O my world,
That was not built with clay!

                      Consider it
(This outer world we tread on) as a harp,—
A gracious instrument on whose fair strings
We learn those airs we shall be set to play
When mortal hours are ended. Let the wings,
Man, of thy spirit move on it as wind,
And draw forth melody. Why shouldst thou
    yet
Lie grovelling? More is won than e'er was lost:
Inherit. Let thy day be to thy night
A teller of good tidings. Let thy praise
Go up as birds go up that, when they wake,
Shake off the dew and soar.

                    So take Joy home,
And make a place in thy great heart for her,
And give her time to grow, and cherish her;
Then will she come, and oft will sing to thee,
When thou art working in the furrows; ay,
Or weeding in the sacred hour of dawn.
It is a comely fashion to be glad,—
Joy is the grace we say to God.

                        Art tired?
There is a rest remaining. Hast thou sinned?
There is a Sacrifice. Lift up thy head,
The lovely world, and the over-world alike,
Ring with a song eterne, a happy rede,
"THY FATHER LOVES THEE."

I.

Yon moorèd mackerel fleet
    Hangs thick as a swarm of bees,
Or a clustering village street
    Foundationless built on the seas.

II.

The mariners ply their craft,
    Each set in his castle frail;
His care is all for the draught,
    And he dries the rain-beaten sail.

III.

For rain came down in the night,
    And thunder muttered full oft,
But now the azure is bright,
    And hawks are wheeling aloft.

IV.

I take the land to my breast,
    In her coat with daisies fine;
For me are the hills in their best,
    And all that's made is mine.

V.

Sing high! "Though the red sun dip,
    There yet is a day for me;
Nor youth I count for a ship
    That long ago foundered at sea.

VI.

"Did the lost love die and depart?
    Many times since we have met;
For I hold the years in my heart,
    And all that was—is yet.

VII.

"I grant to the king his reign;
    Let us yield him homage due;
But over the lands there are twain,
    O king, I must rule as you.

VIII.

"I grant to the wise his meed,
    But his yoke I will not brook,
For God taught ME to read—
    He lent me the world for a book."

FRIENDSHIP.

ON A SUN-PORTRAIT OF HER HUSBAND, SENT
BY HIS WIFE TO THEIR FRIEND.

BEAUTIFUL eyes—and shall I see no more
The living thought when it would leap from
    them,
And play in all its sweetness 'neath their lids?

Here was a man familiar with fair heights
That poets climb. Upon his peace the tears
And troubles of our race deep inroads made,
Yet life was sweet to him; he kept his heart
At home. Who saw his wife might well have
    thought—
"God loves this man. He chose a wife for
    him—
The true one!" O sweet eyes, that seem to live,
I know so much of you, tell me the rest!
Eyes full of fatherhood and tender care
For small, young children. Is a message here
That you would fain have sent, but had not time?
If such there be, I promise, by long love
And perfect friendship, by all trust that comes
Of understanding, that I will not fail,
No, not delay to find it.

      O, my heart
Will often pain me as for some strange fault—
Some grave defect in nature—when I think
How I, delighted, 'neath those olive-trees,
Moved to the music of the tideless main,
While, with sore weeping, in an island home
They laid that much-loved head beneath the
    sod,
And I did not know.

I.

I stand on the bridge where last we stood
 When delicate leaves were young;
The children called us from yonder wood,
 While a mated blackbird sung.

II.

Ah, yet you call,—in your gladness call,—
 And I hear your pattering feet;
It does not matter, matter at all,
 You fatherless children sweet,—

III.

It does not matter at all to you,
 Young hearts that pleasure besets;
The father sleeps, but the world is new,
 The child of his love forgets.

IV.

I too, it may be, before they drop,
 The leaves that flicker to-day,
Ere bountiful gleams make ripe the crop,
 Shall pass from my place away:

V.

Ere yon grey cygnet puts on her white,
 Or snow lies soft on the wold,
Shall shut these eyes on the lovely light,
 And leave the story untold.

VI.

Shall I tell it there? Ah, let that be,
 For the warm pulse beats so high;
To love to-day, and to breathe and see—
 To-morrow perhaps to die—

VII.

Leave it with God. But this I have known,
 That sorrow is over soon;
Some in dark nights, sore weeping alone,
 Forget by full of the moon.

VIII.

But if all loved, as a few can love,
 This world would seldom be well;
And who need wish, if he dwells above,
 For a deep, a long death-knell.

IX

There are four or five, who, passing this place,
 While they live will name me yet;
And when I am gone will think on my face,
 And I feel a kind of regret.

WINSTANLEY.

THE APOLOGY.

QUOTH the cedar to the reeds and
    rushes,
"Water-grass, you know not
    what I do ;
Know not of my storms, nor of my
    hushes,
    And—I know not you."

Quoth the reeds and rushes, "Wind!
    O waken !
Breathe, O wind, and set our answer free,
For we have no voice, of you forsaken,
    For the cedar-tree."

Quoth the earth at midnight to the ocean,
    "Wilderness of water, lost to view,
Naught you are to me but sounds of motion ;
    I am naught to you."

Quoth the ocean, " Dawn ! O fairest, clearest,
    Touch me with thy golden fingers bland ;
For I have no smile till thou appearest
    For the lovely land."

Quoth the hero dying, whelmed in glory,
    "Many blame me, few have understood ;
Ah, my folk, to you I leave a story,—
    Make its meaning good."

Quoth the folk, " Sing poet ! teach us, prove
    us ;
Surely we shall learn the meaning then ;
Wound us with a pain divine, O move us,
    For this man of men."

WINSTANLEY'S deed, you kindly folk,
    With it I fill my lay,
And a nobler man ne'er walked the world,
    Let his name be what it may.

The good ship "Snowdrop" tarried long,
    Up at the vane looked he ;
"Belike," he said, for the wind had dropped,
    "She lieth becalmed at sea."

The lovely ladies flocked within,
    And still would each one say,
" Good mercer, be the ships come up ? "
    But still he answered, " Nay."

Then stepped two mariners down the street,
    With looks of grief and fear :
"Now, if Winstanley be your name,
    We bring you evil cheer !

"For the good ship 'Snowdrop' struck,—she
    struck
On the rock,—the Eddystone,
And down she went with threescore men,
    We two being left alone.

"Down in the deep, with freight and crew,
    Past any help she lies,
And never a bale has come to shore
    Of all thy merchandise."

"For cloth o' gold and comely frieze,"
    Winstanley said, and sighed,
"For velvet coif, or costly coat,
    They fathoms deep may bide.

"O thou brave skipper, blithe and kind,
    O mariners bold and true,
Sorry at heart, right sorry am I,
    A thinking of yours and you.

"Many long days Winstanley's breast
    Shall feel a weight within,
For a waft of wind he shall be 'feared,
    And trading count but sin.

" To him no more it shall be joy
    To pace the cheerful town,
And see the lovely ladies gay
    Step on in velvet gown."

The " Snowdrop " sank at Lammas-tide,
    All under the yeasty spray ;
On Christmas Eve the brig " Content "
    Was also cast away.

He little thought o' New Year's night,
    So jolly as he sat then,
While drank the toast and praised the roast
    The round-faced Aldermen,—

While serving-lads ran to and fro,
    Pouring the ruby wine,
And jellies trembled on the board,
    And towering pasties fine,—

While loud huzzas ran up the roof
    Till the lamps did rock o'erhead,
And holly-boughs from rafters hung
    Dropped down their berries red,—

He little thought on Plymouth Hoe,
  With every rising tide,
How the wave washed in his sailor lads,
  And laid them side by side.

There stepped a stranger to the board :
  "Now, stranger, who be ye?"
He looked to right, he looked to left,
  And "Rest you merry," quoth he;

"For you did not see the brig go down,
  Or ever a storm had blown;
For you did not see the white wave rear
  At the rock,—the Eddystone.

"She drave at the rock with sternsails set;
  Crash went the masts in twain;
She staggered back with her mortal blow,
  Then leaped at it again.

"There rose a great cry, bitter and strong,
  The misty moon looked out !
And the water swarmed with seamen's heads,
  And the wreck was strewed about.

"I saw her mainsail lash the sea
  As I clung to the rock alone;
Then she heeled over, and down she went,
  And sank like any stone.

"She was a fair ship, but all's one !
  For naught could bide the shock."
"I will take horse," Winstanley said,
  "And see this deadly rock."

"For never again shall bark o' mine
  Sail over the windy sea,—
Unless, by the blessing of God, for this
  Be found a remedy."

Winstanley rode to Plymouth town,
  All in the sleet and the snow,
And he looked around on shore and sound
  As he stood on Plymouth Hoe.

Till a pillar of spray rose far away,
  And shot up its stately head,
Reared and fell over, and reared again :
  "'Tis the rock ! the rock !" he said.

Straight to the Mayor he took his way,
  "Good Master Mayor," quoth he,
"I am a mercer of London town,
  And owner of vessels three,—

"But for your rock of dark renown,
  I had five to track the main."
"You are one of many," the old Mayor said,
  "That on the rock complain.

"An ill rock, mercer ! your words ring right,
  Well with my thoughts they chime,
For my two sons to the world to come
  It sent before their time."

"Lend me a lighter, good Master Mayor,
  And a score of shipwrights free,
For I think to raise a lantern tower
  On this rock o' destiny."

The old Mayor laughed, but sighed also ;
  "Ah, youth," quoth he, "is rash ;
Sooner, young man, thou'lt root it out
  From the sea that doth it lash.

"Who sails too near its jagged teeth,
  He shall have evil lot ;
For the calmest seas that tumble there
  Froth like a boiling pot.

"And the heavier seas few look on nigh,
  But straight they lay him dead;
A seventy-gun-ship, sir !—they'll shoot
  Higher than her mast-head.

"O, beacons sighted in the dark,
  They are right welcome things,
And pitchpots flaming on the shore
  Show fair as angel wings.

"Hast gold in hand ? then light the land,
  It 'longs to thee and me ;
But let alone the deadly rock
  In God Almighty's sea."

Yet, said he, "Nay,—I must away,
  On the rock to set my feet ;
My debts are paid, my will I made,
  Or ever I did thee greet.

"If I must die, then let me die
  By the rock and not elsewhere;
If I may live, O let me live
  To mount my lighthouse stair."

The old Mayor looked him in the face,
  And answered : "Have thy way ;
Thy heart is stout, as if round about
  It was braced with an iron stay :

"Have thy will, mercer ! choose thy men,
  Put off from the storm-rid shore;
God with thee be, or I shall see
  Thy face and theirs no more."

Heavily plunged the breaking wave,
  And foam flew up the lea,
Morning and even the drifted snow
  Fell into the dark gray sea.

Winstanley chose him men and gear ;
  He said, "my time I waste,"
For the seas ran seething up the shore,
  And the wrack drave on in haste.

But twenty days he waited and more
  Pacing the strand alone,
Or ever he set his manly foot
  On the rock,—the Eddystone.

Then he and the sea began their strife,
  And worked with power and might:
Whatever the man reared up by day
  The sea broke down by night.

He wrought at ebb with bar and beam,
  He sailed to shore at flow;
And at his side by that same tide,
  Came bar and beam also.

"Give in, give in," the old Mayor cried,
  "Or thou wilt rue the day."
"Yonder he goes," the townsfolk sighed,
  "But the rock will have its way.

"For all his looks that are so stout,
  And his speeches brave and fair,
He may wait on the wind, wait on the wave,
  But he'll build no lighthouse there."

In fine weather and foul weather
  The rock his arts did flout,
Through the long days and the short days,
  Till all that year ran out.

With fine weather and foul weather
  Another year came in:
"To take his wage," the workmen said,
  "We almost count a sin."

Now March was gone, came April in,
  And a sea-fog settled down,
And forth sailed he on a glassy sea,
  He sailed from Plymouth town.

With men and stores he put to sea,
  As he was wont to do;
They showed in the fog like ghosts full faint,—
  A ghostly craft and crew.

And the sea-fog lay and waxed alway,
  For a long eight days and more;
"God help our men," quoth the women then;
  "For they bide long from shore."

They paced the Hoe in doubt and dread:
  "Where may our mariners be?"
But the brooding fog lay soft as down
  Over the quiet sea.

A Scottish schooner made the port,
  The thirteenth day at e'en:
"As I am a man," the captain cried,
  "A strange sight I have seen:

"And a strange sound heard, my masters all,
  At sea, in the fog and the rain,
Like shipwrights' hammers tapping low,
  Then loud, then low again.

"And a stately house one instant showed,
  Through a rift on the vessel's lee;
What manner of creatures may be those
  That build upon the sea?"

Then sighed the folk, "The Lord be praised!"
  And they flocked to the shore again;
All over the Hoe that livelong night,
  Many stood out in the rain.

It ceased, and the red sun reared his head,
  And the rolling fog did flee;
And, lo! in the offing faint and far
  Winstanley's house at sea!

In fair weather with mirth and cheer
  The stately tower uprose;
In foul weather, with hunger and cold,
  They were content to close;

Till up the stair Winstanley went,
  To fire the wick afar;
And Plymouth in the silent night
  Looked out, and saw her star.

Winstanley set his foot ashore:
  Said he, "my work is done;
I hold it strong to last as long
  As aught beneath the sun.

"But if it fail, as fail it may,
  Borne down with ruin and rout,
Another than I shall rear it high,
  And brace the girders stout.

"A better than I shall rear it high,
  For now the way is plain,
And though I were dead," Winstanley said,
  "The light would shine again.

"Yet, were I fain still to remain,
  Watch in my tower to keep,
And tend my light in the stormiest night
  That ever did move the deep;

"And if it stood, why, then 'twere good,
  Amid their tremulous stirs,
To count each stroke, when the mad waves broke,
  For cheers of mariners.

"But if it fell, then this were well,
  That I should with it fall;
Since, for my part, I have built my heart
  In the courses of its wall.

"Ay! I were fain, long to remain,
  Watch in my tower to keep,
And tend my light in the stormiest night
  That ever did move the deep."

With that Winstanley went his way,
   And left the rock renowned,
And summer and winter his pilot star
   Hung bright o'er Plymouth Sound.

But it fell out, fell out at last,
   That he would put to sea,
To scan once more his lighthouse tower
   On the rock o' destiny.

And the winds woke and the storm broke,
   And wrecks came plunging in ;
None in the town that night lay down
   Or sleep or rest to win.

The great mad waves were rolling graves,
   And each flung up its dead ;
The seething flow was white below,
   And black the sky o'erhead.

And when the dawn, the dull, gray dawn,
   Broke on the trembling town,
The men looked south to the harbor mouth,
   The lighthouse tower was down.

Down in the deep where he doth sleep
   Who made it shine afar,
And then in the night that drowned its light,
   Set, with his pilot star.

Many fair tombs in the glorious glooms
   At Westminster they show:
The brave and the great lie there in state:
   Winstanley lieth low.

THE Monitions of the Unseen,

AND

POEMS OF LOVE AND CHILDHOOD.

THE MONITIONS OF THE UNSEEN.

THERE are who give themselves to work for men,—
To raise the lost, to gather orphaned babes
And teach them, pitying of their mean estate,
To feel for misery, and to look on crime
With ruth, till they forget that they themselves
Are of the race, themselves among the crowd
Under the sentence and outside the gate,
And of the family and in the doom.
Cold is the world; they feel how cold it is,
And wish that they could warm it. Hard is life
For some. They would that they could soften it;
And, in the doing of their work they sigh
As if it was their choice and not their lot;
And, in the raising of their prayer to God,
They crave his kindness for the world he made,
Till they, at last, forget that he, not they,
Is the true lover of man.

Now, in an ancient town, that had sunk low,—
Trade having drifted from it, while there stayed
Too many, that it erst had fed, behind,—
There walked a curate once at early day.

It was the summer-time; but summer air
Came never, in its sweetness, down that dark
And crowded alley,—never reached the door,
Whereat he stopped,—the sordid, shattered door.

He paused, and, looking right and left, beheld
Dirt and decay, the lowering tenements
That leaned toward each other; broken panes
Bulging with rags, and grim with old neglect;
And reeking hills of formless refuse, heaped
To fade and fester in a stagnant air.
But he thought nothing of it: he had learned
To take all wretchedness for granted,—he,
Reared in a stainless home, and radiant yet
With the clear hues of healthful English youth,
Had learned to kneel by beds forlorn, and stoop
Under foul lintels. He could touch, with hand
Unshrinking, fevered fingers; he could hear
The language of the lost, in haunt and den,—
So dismal, that the coldest passer-by
Must needs be sorry for them, and, albeit
They cursed, would dare to speak no harder words
Than these,—"God help them!"

Ay! a learned man
The curate in all woes that plague mankind,—
Too learned, for he was but young. His heart
Had yearned till it was overstrained, and now
He—plunged into a narrow slough unblest,
Had struggled with its deadly waters, till
His own head had gone under, and he took
Small joy in work he could not look to aid
Its cleansing.

Yet, by one right tender tie,
Hope held him yet. The fathers coarse and dull,
Vile mothers hard, and boys and girls profane,
His soul drew back from. He had worked for them,—
Work without joy: but, in his heart of hearts,
He loved the little children; and, whene'er
He heard their prattle innocent, and heard
Their tender voices lisping sacred words
That he had taught them,—in the cleanly calm
Of decent school, by decent matron held,—
Then would he say, "I shall have pleasure yet,
In these."

But now, when he pushed back that door
And mounted up a flight of ruined stairs,
He said not that. He said, "Oh! once I thought
The little children would make bright for me
The crown they wear who have won many souls
For righteousness; but oh, this evil place!
Hard lines it gives them, cold and dirt abhorred,—
Hunger and nakedness, in lieu of love,
And blows instead of care.

And so they die,
The little children that I love,—they die,—
And turn their wistful faces to the wall,
And slip away to God."

With that, his hand
He laid upon a latch and lifted it.
Looked in full quietly, and entered straight.

What saw he there? He saw a three-years child,
That lay a-dying on a wisp of straw
Swept up into a corner. O'er its brow
The damps of death were gathering: all alone,
Uncared for, save that by its side was set

A cup, it waited. And the eyes had ceased
To look on things at hand. He thought they
gazed
In wistful wonder, or some faint surmise
Of coming change,—As though they saw the
gate
Of that fair land that seems to most of us
Very far off.

When he beheld the look,
He said, "I knew, I knew how this would be!
Another! Ay, and but for drunken blows
And dull forgetfulness of infant need,
This little one had lived." And thereupon
The misery of it wrought upon him so,
That, unaware, he wept. O! then it was
That, in the bending of his manly head,
It came between the child and that whereon
He gazed, and, when the curate glanced again,
Those dying eyes, drawn back to earth once
more,
Looked up into his own, and smiled.

He drew
More near, and kneeled beside the small frail
thing,
Because the lips were moving; and it raised
Its baby hand, and stroked away his tears,
And whispered, "Master! Master!" and so
died.
Now, in that town there was an ancient church,
A minster of old days which these had turned
To parish uses: there the curate served.
It stood within a quiet swarded Close,
Sunny and still, and, though it was not far
From those dark courts where poor humanity
Struggled and swarmed, it seemed to wear its
own
Still atmosphere about it and to hold
That old-world calm within its precincts pure
And that grave rest which modern life foregoes.

When the sad curate, rising from his knees,
Looked from the dead to heaven,—as, unaware,
Men do when they would track departed life,—
He heard the deep tone of the minster-bell
Sounding for service, and he turned away
So heavy at heart, that, when he left behind
That dismal habitation, and came out
In the clear sunshine of the minster-yard,
He never marked it. Up the aisle he moved,
With his own gloom about him; then came
forth,
And read before the folk grand words and
calm,—
Words full of hope; but into his dull heart
Hope came not. As one talketh in a dream,
And doth not mark the sense of his own words,
He read; and, as one walketh in a dream,
He after walked toward the vestment-room,
And never marked the way he went by,—no,
Nor the grey verger that before him stood,
The great church-keys depending from his hand,
Ready to follow him out and lock the door.

At length, aroused to present things, but not
Content to break the sequence of his thought,
Nor ready for the working day that held
Its busy course without, he said, "Good friend,
Leave me the keys: I would remain awhile."
And, when the verger gave, he moved with
him
Toward the door distraught, then shut him out,
And locked himself within the church alone.
The minster-church was like a great brown cave,
Fluted and fine with pillars, and all dim
With glorious gloom; but as the curate turned,
Suddenly shone the sun,—and roof and walls,
Also the clustering shafts from end to end,
Were thickly sown all over, as it were,
With seedling rainbows. And it went and
came
And went, that sunny beam, and drifted up
Ethereal bloom to flush the open wings
And craven cheeks of dimpled cherubim,
And dropped upon the curate as he passed,
And covered his white raiment and his hair.

Then did look down upon him from their place,
High in the upper lights, grave mitred priests,
And grand old monarchs in their flowered
gowns
And capes of miniver; and therewithal
(A veiling cloud gone by) the naked sun
Smote with his burning splendor all the pile,
And in there rushed, through half translucent
panes,
A sombre glory as of rusted gold,
Deep ruby stains, and tender blue and green,
That made the floor a beauty and delight,
Strewed as with phantom blossoms, sweet
enough
To have been wafted there the day they dropt
On the flower-beds in heaven.

The curate passed
Adown the long south aisle, and did not think
Upon this beauty, nor that he himself—
Excellent in the strength of youth, and fair
With all the majesty that noble work
And stainless manners give—did add his part
To make it fairer.

In among the knights
That lay with hands uplifted, by the lute
And palm of many a saint,—'neath capitals
Whereon our fathers had been bold to carve
With earthly tools their ancient childlike dream
Concerning heavenly fruit and living bowers,
And glad full-throated birds that sing up there
Among the branches of the tree of life—
Through all the ordered forests of the shafts,
Shooting on high to enter into light,
That swam aloft,—he took his silent way,
And in the southern transept sat him down,
Covered his face, and thought.

He said, "No pain,
No passion, and no aching, heart o' mine,
Doth stir within thee. Oh! I would there did:

Thou art so dull, so tired. I have lost
I know not what. I see the heavens as lead:
They tend no whither. Ah! the world is
  bared
Of her enchantment now: she is but earth
And water. And, though much hath passed
  away.
There may be more to go. I may forget
The joy and fear that have been: there may
  live
No more for me the fervency of hope
Nor the arrest of wonder.

                       "Once I said,
'Content will wait on work, though work appear
Unfruitful.' Now I say, 'Where is the good?
What is the good?' A lamp when it is lit
Must needs give light; but I am like a man
Holding his lamp in some deserted place
Where no foot passeth. Must I trim my lamp,
And ever painfully toil to keep it bright,
When use for it is none? I must, I will.
Though God withhold my wages, I must work,
And watch the bringing of my work to nought—
Weed in the vineyard through the heat o' the
  day,
And, overtasked, behold the weedy place
Grow ranker yet in spite of me.

                          "Oh! yet
My meditated words are trodden down
Like a little wayside grass. Castaway shells
Lifted and tossed aside by a plunging wave,
Have no more force against it than have I
Against the sweeping, weltering wave of life,
That, lifting and dislodging me, drives on,
And notes not mine endeavor."

                         Afterward,
He added more words like to these; to wit,
That it was hard to see the world so sad:
He would that it were happier. It was hard
To see the blameless overborne; and hard
To know that God, who loves the world, should
  yet
Let it lie down in sorrow, when a smile
From him would make it laugh and sing,—a
  word
From him transform it to a heaven. He said,
Moreover, "When will this be done? My life
Hath not yet reached the noon, and I am tired;
And oh! it may be that, uncomforted
By foolish hope of doing good and vain
Conceit of being useful, I may live,
And it may be my duty to go on
Working for years and years, for years and
  years."

But, while the words were uttered, in his heart
There dawned a vague alarm. He was aware
That somewhat touched him and he lifted up
His face. "I am alone," the curate said,—
"I think I am alone. What is it, then?
I am ashamed! my raiment is not clean.
My lips,—I am afraid they are not clean.

My heart is darkened and unclean. Ah me,
To be a man, and yet to tremble so!
Strange, strange!"
                  And there was sitting at his feet—
He could not see it plainly—at his feet
A very little child. And while the blood
Drave to his heart, he set his eye on it,
Gazing, and, lo! the loveliness from heaven
Took clearer form and color. He beheld
The strange, wise sweetness of a dimpled
  mouth,
The deep serene of eyes at home with bliss,
And perfect in possession. So it spoke,
"My master!" but he answered not a word;
And it went on: "I had a name, a name.
He knew my name; but here they can forget."
The curate answered: "Nay, I know thee well.
I love thee. Wherefore art thou come?" It
  said,
"They sent me;" and he faltered, "Fold thy
  hand,
O most dear little one! for on it gleams
A gem that is so bright I cannot look
Thereon." It said, "When I did leave this
  world,
That was a tear. But that was long ago;
For I have lived among the happy folk,
You wot of, ages, ages." Then said he,
"Do they forget us, while beneath the palms
They take their infinite leisure?" and with eyes
That seemed to muse upon him, looking up
In peace the little child made answer, "Nay;"
And murmured in the language that he loved,
"How is it that this hair is not yet white;
For I and all the others have been long
Waiting for him to come."

                    "And was it long?"
The curate answered, pondering. "Time
  being done,
Shall life indeed expand, and give the sense,
In our to-come, of infinite extension?"
Then said the child, "In heaven we children
  talk
Of the great matters, and our lips are wise;
But here I can but talk with thee in words
That here I knew." And therewithal arisen,
It said, "I pray you take me in your arms."
Then, being afraid, but willing, so he did;
And partly drew about the radiant child,
For better covering his dread purity,
The foldings of his gown. And he beheld
Its beauty, and the tremulous woven light
That hung upon its hair; withal the robe,
'Whiter than fuller of this world can white,'
That clothed its immortality. And so
The trembling came again, and he was dumb,
Repenting his uncleanness: and he lift
His eyes, and all the holy place was full
Of living things; and some were faint and dim,
As if they bore an intermittent life,
Waxing and waning; and they had no form,
But drifted on like slowly trailèd clouds,
Or moving spots of darkness, with an eye
Apiece. And some, in guise of evil birds,

Came in by troops, and stretched their naked necks,
And some were men-like, but their heads hung down ;
And he said, "O my God! let me find grace
Not to behold their faces, for I know
They must be wicked and right terrible."
But while he prayed, lo! whispers ; and there moved
Two shadows on the wall. He could not see
The forms of them that cast them: he could see
Only the shadows as of two that sat
Upon the floor, where, clad in women's weeds,
They lisped together. And he shuddered much :
There was a rustling near him, and he feared
Lest they should touch him, and he feel their touch.

"It is not great," quoth one, "the work achieved.
We do, and we delight to do, our best :
But that is little; for, my dear," quoth she,
"This tower and town have been infested long
With angels."—"Ay," the other made reply,
"I had a little evil one, of late,
That I picked up as it was crawling out
O' the pit, and took and cherished it in my breast.
It would divine for me, and oft would moan,
'Pray thee, no churches,' and it spake of this.
But I was harried once,—thou knowest by whom,—
And fled in here ; and, when he followed me,
I crouching by this pillar, he let down
His hand,—being all too proud to send his eyes
In its wake,—and, plucking forth my tender imp,
Flung it behind him. It went yelping forth ;
And, as for me, I never saw it more.
Much is against us,—very much : the times
Are hard." She paused : her fellow took the word,
Plaining on such as preach and them that plead.
"Even such as haunt the yawning mouths of hell,"
Quoth she, "and pluck them back that run thereto."
Then, like a sudden blow, there fell on him
The utterance of his name. "There is no soul
That I loathe more, and oftener curse. Woe's me,
That cursing should be vain ! Ay, he will go
Gather the sucking children, that are yet
Too young for us, and watch and shelter them
Till the strong Angels—pitiless and stern,
But to them loving ever—sweep them in,
By armsful, to the unapproachable fold.

"We strew his path with gold : it will not lie.
'Deal softly with him,' was the master's word.
We brought him all delights : his angel came
And stood between them and his eyes. They spend

Much pains upon him,—keep him poor and low
And unbeloved ; and thus he gives his mind
To fill the faithful, the impregnable
Child-fold, and sow on earth the seed of stars.

"Oh! hard is serving against love,—the love
Of the unspeakable ; for if we soil
The souls He openeth out a washing-place ;
And if we grudge, and snatch away the bread,
Then will He save by poverty, and gain
By early giving up of blameless life ;
And if we shed out gold, He even will save
In spite of gold,—of twice-refined gold."

With that the curate set his daunted eyes
To look upon the shadows of the fiends.
He was made sure they could not see the child
That nestled in his arms ; he also knew
They were unconscious that his mortal ears
Had new intelligence, which gave their speech
Possible entrance through his garb of clay.

He was afraid, yet awful gladness reached
His soul : the testimony of the lost
Upbraided him; but while he trembled yet,
The heavenly child had lifted up its head
And left his arms, and on the marble floor
Stood beckoning.

And, its touch withdrawn, the place
Was silent, empty ; all that swarming tribe
Of evil ones concealed behind the veil,
And shut into their separate world, were closed
From his observance. He arose, and paced
After the little child,—as half in fear
That it would leave him,—till they reached a door ;
And then said he,—but much distraught he spoke,
Laying his hand across the lock,—"This door
Shuts in the stairs whereby men mount the tower.
Wouldst thou go up, and so withdraw to heaven?"
It answered, "I will mount them." Then said he,
"And I will follow."—"So thou shalt do well,"
The radiant thing replied, and it went up,
And he, amazed, went after ; for the stairs,
Otherwhile dark, were lightened by the rays
Shed out of raiment woven in high heaven,
And hair whereon had smiled the light of God.

With that, they, pacing on, came out at last
Into a dim, weird place,—a chamber formed
Betwixt the roofs : for you shall know that all
The vaulting of the nave, fretted and fine,
Was covered with the dust of ages, laid
Thick with those chips of stone which they had left
Who wrought it ; but a high-pitched roof was reared
Above it, and the western gable pierced

With three long narrow lights.   Great tie
  beams loomed
Across, and many daws frequented there
The starling and the sparrow littered it
With straw, and peeped from many a shady
  nook;
And there was lifting up of wings, and there
Was hasty exit when the curate came.
But sitting on a beam and moving not
For him, he saw two fair gray turtle-doves
Bowing their heads, and cooing; and the child
Put forth a hand to touch his own, but straight
He, startled, drew it back, because, forsooth,
A stirring fancy smote him, and he thought
That language trembled on their innocent
  tongues,
And floated forth in speech that man could
  hear.
Then said the child, "Yet touch, my master
  dear."
And he let down his hand, and touched again;
And so it was. "But if they had their way,"
One turtle cooed, "how should this world go
  on?"

Then he looked well upon them, as he stood
Upright before them. They were feathered
  doves,
And sitting close together; and their eyes
Were rounded with the rim that marks their
  kind.
Their tender crimson feet did pat the beam,—
No phantoms they; and soon the fellow-dove
Made answer, "Nay, they count themselves
  so wise,
There is no task they shall be set to do
But they will ask God why. What mean they
  so?
The glory is not in the task, but in
The doing it for him. What should he think,
Brother, this man that must, forsooth, be set
Such noble work, and suffered to behold
Its fruit, if he knew more of us and ours?"
With that the other leaned as if attent:
"I am not perfect, brother, in his thought."
The mystic bird replied, "Brother, he saith,
'But it is nought: the work is overhard.'
Whose fault is that? God sets not overwork.
He saith the world is sorrowful, and he
Is therefore sorrowful. He cannot set
The crooked straight;—but who demands of
  him,
O brother, that he should? What! thinks he,
  then,
His work is God's advantage, and his will
More bent to aid the world than its dread
  Lord's.
Nay, yet there live amongst us legions fair,
Millions on millions, who could do right well
What he must fail in; and 'twas whispered me,
That chiefly for himself the task is given,—
His little daily task." With that he paused.

Then said the other, preening its fair wing,
"Men have discovered all God's islands now,

And given them names; whereof they are as
  proud,
And deem themselves as great, as if their hands
Had made them. Strange is man, and strange
  his pride.
Now, as for us, it matters not to learn
What and from whence we be. How should
  we tell?
Our world is undiscovered in these skies
Our names not whispered. Yet, for us and
  ours,
What joy it is,—permission to come down,
Not souls, as he, to the bosom of their God,
To guide, but to their goal the wingèd fowls,
His lovely lower-fashioned lives to help
To take their forms by legions, fly, and draw
With us the sweet, obedient, flocking things
That ever hear our message reverently,
And follow us far. How should they know
  their way,
Forsooth, alone? Men say they fly alone;
Yet some have set on record and averred,
That they, among the flocks, had duly marked
A leader."

      Then his fellow made reply:
"They might divine the Maker's heart. Come
  forth,
Fair dove, to find the flocks, and guide their
  wings,
For Him that loveth them."

      With that, the child
Withdrew his hand, and all their speech was
  done.
He moved toward them, but they fluttered
  forth
And fled into the sunshine.

      "I would fain,"
Said he, "have heard some more. And wilt
  thou go?"
He added to the child, for this had turned.
"Ay," quoth he, gently, "to the beggar's
  place;
For I would see the beggar in his porch."

So they went down together to the door,
Which, when the curate opened, lo! without
The beggar sat; and he saluted him:
"Good morrow, master." "Wherefore art thou
  here?"
The curate asked: "it is not service time,
And none will enter now to give thee alms."
Then said the beggar, "I have hope at heart
That I shall go to my poor house no more."
"Art thou so sick that thou dost think to die?"
The curate said. With that the beggar laughed,
And under his dim eyelids gathered tears,
And he was all a-tremble with a strange
And moving exaltation. "Ay," quoth he,
And set his face toward high heaven: "I
  think
The blessing that I wait on must be near."
Then said the curate, "God be good to thee."

And, straight, the little child put forth his
  hand,
And touched him. "Master, master, hush!
You should not, master, speak so carelessly
In this great presence."

　　　　　　　．　But the touch so wrought,
That, lo! the dazzled curate staggered back,
For dread effulgence from the beggar's eyes
Smote him, and from the crippled limbs shot
  forth
Terrible lights, as pure long blades of fire.
"Withdraw thy touch! withdraw thy touch!"
  he cried,
"Or else shall I be blinded:" Then the child
Stood back from him; and he sat down apart,
Recovering of his manhood: and he heard
The beggar and the child discourse of things
Dreadful for glory, till his spirits came
Anew; and, when the beggar looked on him,
He said, "If I offend not, pray you tell
Who and what are you—I behold a face
Marred with old age, sickness and poverty,—
A cripple with a staff, who long hath sat
Begging, and oftimes moaning, in the porch,
For pain and for the wind's inclemency.
What are you?" Then the beggar made reply,
"I was a delegate, a living power;
My work was bliss, for seeds were in my hand
To plant a new-made world. O happy work!
It grew and blossomed; but my dwelling-place
Was far remote from heaven. I have not seen;
I knew no wish to enter there. But, lo!
There went forth rumors, running out like rays,
How some, that were of power like even to
  mine,
Had made request to come and find a place
Within its walls. And these were satisfied
With promises, and sent to this far world
To take the weeds of your mortality,
And minister, and suffer grief and pain,
And die like men. Then were they gathered
  in.
They saw a face, and were accounted kin
To Whom thou knowest, for he is kin to men.

"Then I did wait; and oft, at work, I sang,
'To minister! oh, joy, to minister!'
And, it being known, a message came to me:
'Whether is best, thou forest-planter wise,
To minister to others, or that they
Should minister to thee?' Then, on my face
Low lying, I made answer: 'It is best,
Most High, to minister;' and thus came back
The answer,—'Choose not for thyself the best:
Go down, and, lo! my poor shall minister,
Out of their poverty, to thee; shall learn
Compassion by thy frailty; and shall oft
Turn back, when speeding home from work,
  to help
Thee, weak and crippled, home. My little
  ones,
Thou shalt importune for their slender mite,
And pray, and move them that they give it up
For love of Me.'"

　　　　　　The curate answered him,
"Art thou content, O great one from afar!
If I may ask, and not offend?" He said,
"I am. Behold! I stand not all alone,
That I should think to do a perfect work.
I may not wish to give; for I have heard
'Tis best for me that I receive. For me,
God is the only giver, and His gift
Is one." With that, the little child sighed out,
"O master! master! I am out of heaven
Since noonday, and I hear them calling me.
If you be ready, great one, let us go:—
Hark! hark! they call."

　　　　　　　Then did the beggar lift
His face to heaven, and utter forth a cry
As of the pangs of death, and every tree
Moved as if shaken by a sudden wind.
He cried again, and there came forth a hand
From some invisible form, which, being laid
A little moment on the curate's eyes,
It dazzled him with light that brake from it,
So that he saw no more.
　　　　　　　　　"What shall I do?"
The curate murmured, when he came again
To himself and looked about him. "This is
  strange!
My thoughts are all astray; and yet, methinks,
A weight is taken from my heart. Lo! lo!
There lieth at my feet, frail, white, and dead,
The sometime beggar. He is happy now.
There was a child; but he is gone, and he
Is also happy. I am glad to think
I am not bound to make the wrong go right;
But only to discover, and to do,
With cheerful heart, the work that God ap-
  points."

With that, he did compose, with reverent care,
The dead; continuing, "I will trust in Him,
THAT HE CAN HOLD HIS OWN; and I will take
His will, above the work He sendeth me,
To be my chiefest good."

　　　　　　　　Then went he forth,
"I shall die early," thinking: "I am warned,
By this fair vision, that I have not long
To live." Yet he lived on to good old age;—
Ay, he lives yet, and he is working still.

It may be there are many in like case:
They give themselves, and are in misery
Because the gift is small, and doth not make
The world by so much better as they fain
Would have it. 'Tis a fault; but, as for us,
Let us not blame them. Maybe, 'tis a fault
More kindly looked on by The Majesty
Than our best virtues are. Why, what are we!
What have we given, and what have we desired
To give, the world?

　　　　　　There must be something wrong.
Look to it: let us mend our ways.　Farewell.

A BIRTHDAY WALK.

WRITTEN FOR A FRIEND'S BIRTHDAY.

"The days of our life are threescore years and ten."

A BIRTHDAY:—and now a day
    that rose
    With much of hope, with
      meaning rife—
    A thoughtful day from dawn to
      close :
    The middle day of human life.

In sloping fields on narrow plains,
  The sheep were feeding on their knees,
As we went through the winding lanes,
  Strewed with red buds of alder-trees.

So warm the day—its influence lent
  To flagging thought a stronger wing ;
So utterly was winter spent,
  So sudden was the birth of spring.

Wild crocus flowers in copse and hedge—
  In sunlight, clustering thick below,
Sighed for the firwood's shaded ledge,
  Where sparkled yet a line of snow.

And crowded snowdrops faintly hung
  Their fair heads lower for the heat,
While in still air all branches flung
  Their shadowy doubles at our feet.

And through the hedge the sunbeams crept,
  Dropped through the maple and the birch ;
And lost in airy distance slept
  On the broad tower of Tamworth Church.

Then, lingering on the downward way,
  A little space we resting stood,
To watch the golden haze that lay
  Adown that river by the wood.

A distance vague, the bloom of sleep
  The constant sun had lent the scene,
A veiling charm on dingles deep
  Lay soft those pastoral hills between.

There are some days that die not out,
  Nor alter by reflection's power,
Whose converse calm, whose words devout,
  For ever rest, the spirit's dower.

And they are days when drops a veil—
  A mist upon the distance past ;
And while we say to peace—"All hail !"
  We hope that always it shall last.

Times when the troubles of the heart
  Are hushed—as winds were hushed that
    day—
And budding hopes begin to start,
  Like those green hedgerows on our way :

When all within and all around,
  Like hues on that sweet landscape blend,
And Nature's hand has made to sound
  The heartstrings that her touch attend :

When there are rays within, like those
  That streamed through maple and through
    birch,
And rested in such calm repose
  On the broad tower of Tamworth Church.

NOT IN VAIN I WAITED.

SHE was but a child, a child,
    And I a man grown ;
  Sweet she was, and fresh, and wild,
    And I thought my own.
What could I do ? The long grass groweth,
  The long wave floweth with a murmur on :
The why and the wherefore of it all who
    knoweth ?
Ere I thought to lose her she was grown—
    and gone.
This day or that day in warm spring weather,
  The lamb that was tame will yearn to break
    its tether.
"But if the world wound thee," I said, "come
    back to me,
Down in the dell wishing—wishing, wishing
    for thee."

  The dews hang on the white may,
    Like a ghost it stands,
  All in the dusk before day
    That folds the dim lands :
Dark fell the skies when once belated,
  Sad, and sorrow-fated, I missed the sun ;
But wake, heart, and sing, for not in vain I
    waited.
  O clear, O solemn dawning, lo, the maid is
    won !
Sweet dews, dry early on the grass and clover,
  Lest the bride wet her feet while she walks
    over ;
Shine to-day, sunbeams, and make all fair to see:
Down the dell she's coming—coming, coming
    with me.

A GLEANING SONG.

"WHITHER away, thou little careless rover?
  (Kind Roger's true)
Whither away, across yon bents and clover,
  Wet, wet with dew?"
    "Roger here, Roger there—
    Roger—O, he sighed,
  Yet let me glean among the wheat,
    Nor sit kind Roger's bride."

"What wilt thou do when all the gleaning's
    ended,
  What wilt thou do?
The cold will come, and fog and frost-work
    blended
    (Kind Roger's true)."
  "Sleet and rain, cloud and storm,
    When they cease to frown
  I'll bind me primrose bunches sweet,
    And cry them up the town."

"What if at last thy careless heart awaking
    This day thou rue?"
"I'll cry my flowers, and think for all its
    breaking,
    Kind Roger's true;
  Roger here, Roger there,
    O, my true love sighed,
  Sigh once, once more, I'll stay my feet
    And rest kind Roger's bride."

WITH A DIAMOND.

WHILE Time a grim old lion gnawing lay,
  And mumbled with his teeth yon regal tomb,
Like some immortal tear undimmed for aye,
  This gem was dropped among the dust of
    doom.

Dropped, haply, by a sad forgotten queen,
  A tear to outlast name, and fame, and
    tongue:
Her other tears, and ours, all tears terrene,
  For great new griefs to be hereafter sung.

Take it,—a goddess might have wept such
    tears,
  Or Dame Electra changed into a star,
That waxed so dim because her children's
    years
  In leaguered Troy were bitter through long
    war.

Not till the end to end grow dull or waste,—
  Ah, what a little while the light we share!
Hand after hand shall yet with this be graced,
  Signing the Will that leaves it to an heir.

FANCY.

O FANCY, if thou flyest, come back anon,
  Thy fluttering wings are soft as love's first
    word,
  And fragrant as the feathers of that bird,
Which feeds upon the budded cinnamon.
I ask thee not to work, or sigh—play on,
  From nought that was not, was, or is, de-
    terred;
  The flax that Old Fate spun thy flights have
    stirred,
And waved memorial grass of Marathon.
Play, but be gentle, not as on that day
  I saw thee running down the rims of doom
With stars thou hadst been stealing—while
    they lay
  Smothered in light and blue—clasped to thy
    breast;
Bring rather to me in the firelit room
  A netted halcyon bird to sing of rest.

COMPENSATION.

ONE launched a ship, but she was wrecked at
    sea;
  He built a bridge, but floods have borne it
    down;
He meant much good, none came: strange
    destiny,
  His corn lies sunk, his bridge bears none to
    town,
  Yet good he had not meant became his
    crown;
For once at work, when even as nature free,
  From thought of good he was, or of renown,
God took the work for good and let good be.
So wakened with a trembling after sleep,
  Dread Mona Roa yields her fateful store;
All gleaming hot the scarlet rivers creep,
  And fanned of great-leaved palms slip to the
    shore,
Then stolen to unplumbed wastes of that far
    deep,
  Lay the foundations for one island more.

LOOKING DOWN.

MOUNTAINS of sorrow, I have heard your
    moans,
  And the moving of your pines; but we sit
    high
On your green shoulders, nearer stoops the sky,
  And pure airs visit us from all the zones.
Sweet world beneath, too happy far to sigh,
  Dost thou look thus beheld from heavenly
    thrones?
No; not for all the love that counts thy stones,
  While sleepy with great light the valleys lie.
Strange, rapturous peace! its sunshine doth
    enfold

My heart; I have escaped to the days divine,
It seemeth as bygone ages back had rolled,
   And all the eldest past was now was mine;
Nay, even as if Melchizedec of old
   Might here come forth to us with bread and
     wine.

MARRIED LOVERS.

Come away, the clouds are high,
Put the flashing needles by.
Many days are not to spare,
Or to waste, my fairest fair!
All is ready. Come to-day,
For the nightingale her lay,
When she findeth that the whole
Of her love, and all her soul,
Cannot forth of her sweet throat,
Sobs the while she draws her breath,
And the bravery of her note
In a few days altereth.

Come, ere she despond, and see
In a silent ecstacy
Chestnuts heave for hours and hours
All the glory of their flowers
To the melting blue above,
That broods over them like love.
Leave the garden walls, where blow
Apple-blossoms pink, and low
Ordered beds of tulips fine.
Seek the blossoms made divine
With a scent that is their soul.
These are soulless. Bring the white
Of thy gown to bathe in light
Walls for narrow hearts. The whole
Earth is found, and air and sea,
Not too wide for thee and me.

Not too wide, and yet thy face
Gives the meaning of all space;
And thine eyes with starbeams fraught,
Hold the measure of all thought;
For of them my soul besought,
And was shown a glimpse of thine—
A veiled vestal, with divine
Solace, in sweet love's despair,
For that life is brief as fair.
Who hath most, he yearneth most,
Sure, as seldom heretofore,
Somewhere of the gracious more.
Deepest joy the least shall boast,
Asking with new-opened eyes
The remainder; that which lies
O, so fair! but not all conned—
O, so near! and yet beyond.

Come, and in the woodland sit,
Seem a wonted part of it.
Then, while moves the delicate air,
And the glories of thy hair
Little flickering sun-rays strike,
Let me see what thou art like;
For great love enthrals me so,

That, in sooth, I scarcely know.
Show me, in a house all green,
Save for long gold wedges' sheen,
Where the flies, white sparks of fire,
Dart and hover and aspire,
And the leaves, air-stirred on high,
Feel such joy they needs must sigh,
And the untracked grass makes sweet
All fair flowers to touch thy feet,
And the bees about them hum.
All the world is waiting. Come!

A WINTER SONG.

Came the dread Archer up yonder lawn—
   Night is the time for the old to die—
But woe for an arrow that smote the fawn,
   When the hind that was sick unscathed went
     by.

Father lay moaning, "Her fault was sore
   (Night is the time when the old must die),
Yet, ah to bless her, my child, once more,
   For heart is failing: the end is nigh."

"Daughter, my daughter, my girl," I cried
   (Night is the time for the old to die)
"Woe for the wish if till morn ye bide"—
   Dark was the welkin and wild the sky.

Heavily plunged from the roof the snow—
   (Night is the time when the old will die),
She answered, "My mother, 'tis well, I go."
   Sparkled the north star, the wrack flew high.

First at his head, and last at his feet
   (Night is the time when the old should die),
Kneeling I watched till his soul did fleet,
   None else that loved him, none else were
     nigh.

I wept in the night as the desolate weep
   (Night is the time for the old to die),
Cometh my daughter? the drifts are deep,
   Across the cold hollows how white they lie.

I sought her afar through the spectral trees
   (Night is the time when the old must die),
The fells were all muffled, the floods did freeze,
   And a wrathful moon hung red in the sky.

By night I found her where pent waves steal
   (Night is the time when the old should die),
But she lay stiff by the locked mill wheel,
   And the old stars lived in their homes on high.

BINDING SHEAVES.

Hark! a lover binding sheaves
   To his maiden sings,
Flutter, flutter go the leaves,

Larks drop their wings.
Little brooks for all their mirth
Are not blythe as he.
"Give me what the love is worth
That I give thee.

"Speech that cannot be forborne
Tells the story through:
I sowed my love in with the corn,
And they both grew.
Count the world full wide of girth,
And hived honey sweet,
But count the love of more worth
Laid at thy feet.

"Money's worth is house and land,
Velvet coat and vest.
Work's worth is bread in hand,
Ay, and sweet rest.
Wilt thou learn what love is worth?
Ah! she sits above,
Sighing, 'Weigh me not with earth,
Love's worth is love.'"

WORK.

LIKE coral insects multitudinous
The minutes are whereof our life is made.
They build it up as in the deep's blue shade
It grows, it comes to light, and then, and thus
For both there is an end. The populous
Sea-blossoms close, our minutes that have paid
Life's debt of work are spent; the work is laid
Before our feet that shall come after us.
We may not stay to watch if it will speed,
The bard if on some luter's string his song
Live sweetly yet; the hero if his star
Doth shine. Work is its own best earthly meed,
Else have we none more than the sea-born throng
Who wrought those marvellous isles that bloom afar.

WISHING.

WHEN I reflect now little I have done,
And add to that how little I have seen,
Then furthermore how little I have won
Of joy, or good, how little known, or been:
I long for other life more full, more keen,
And yearn to change with such as well have run—
Yet reason mocks me—nay, the soul, I ween,
Granted her choice would dare to change with none;
No,—not to feel, as Blondel when his lay
Pierced the strong tower, and Richard answered it—
No, not to do, as Eustace on the day
He left fair Calais to her weeping fit—
No, not to be,—Columbus, waked from sleep
When his new world rose from the charmèd deep.

TO ———.

STRANGE was the doom of Heracles, whose shade
Had dwelling in dim Hades the unblest,
While yet his form and presence sat a guest
With the old immortals when the feast was made.
Thine like, thus differs; form and presence laid
In this dim chamber of enforcèd rest,
It is the unseen "shade" which, risen hath pressed
Above all heights where feet Olympian strayed.
My soul admires to hear thee speak; thy thought
Falls from a high place like an August star,
Or some great eagle from his air hung rings—
When swooping past a snow-cold mountain scar—
Down the steep slope of a long sunbeam brought,
He stirs the wheat with the steerage of his wings.

ON THE BORDERS OF CANNOCK CHASE.

A COTTAGER leaned whispering by her hives,
Telling the bees some news as they lit down,
And entered one by one their waxen town.
Larks passioning hung o'er their brooding wives,
And all the sunny hills where heather thrives
Lay satisfied with peace. A stately crown
Of trees enringed the upper headland brown,
And reedy pools, wherein the moor-hen dives,
Glittered and gleamed.

A resting-place for light,
They that were bred here love it; but they say,
"We shall not have it long; in three years' time
A hundred pits will cast out fires by night,
Down yon still glen their smoke shall trail its way,
And the white ash lie thick in lieu of rime."

THE MARINER'S CAVE.

ONCE on a time there walked a mariner,
That had been shipwrecked;—on a lonely shore,
And the green water made a restless stir,
And a great flock of mews sped on before.
He had nor food nor shelter, for the tide
Rose on the one, and cliffs on the other side.

Brown cliffs they were; they seemed to pierce
    the sky,
That was an awful deep of empty blue,
Save that the wind was in it, and on high
    A wavering skein of wild-fowl tracked it
    through.
He marked them not, but went with move-
    ment slow,
Because his thoughts were sad, his courage low.

His heart was numb, he neither wept nor
    sighed,
But wearifully lingered by the wave;
Until at length it chanced that he espied,
    Far up, an opening in the cliff, a cave,
A shelter where to sleep in his distress,
And lose his sorrow in forgetfulness.

With that he clambered up the rugged face
    Of that steep cliff that all in shadow lay,
And, lo, there was a dry and homelike place,
    Comforting refuge for the castaway;
And he laid down his weary, weary head,
And took his fill of sleep till dawn waxed red.

When he awoke, warm stirring from the south
    Of delicate summer air did sough and flow;
He rose, and, wending to the cavern's mouth,
    He cast his eyes a little way below
Where on the narrow ledges, sharp and rude,
    Preening their wings the blue rock-pigeons
    cooed.

Then he looked lower and saw the lavender
    And sea-thrift blooming in long crevices,
And the brown wallflower—April's messenger,
    The wallflower marshalled in her companies.
Then lower yet he looked adown the steep,
And sheer beneath him lapped the lovely deep,

The laughing deep;—and it was pacified
    As if it had not raged that other day.
And it went murmuring in the morningtide
    Innumerable flatteries on its way,
Kissing the cliffs and whispering at their feet
With exquisite advancement and retreat.

This when the mariner beheld he sighed,
    And thought on his companions lying low.
But while he gazed with eyes unsatisfied
    On the fair reaches of their overthrow,
Thinking it strange he only lived of all,
But on returning thanks, he heard a call!

A soft sweet call, a voice of tender ruth,
    He thought it came from out the cave. And
    lo!
It whispered, "Man, look up!" But he,
    forsooth,
    Answered, "I cannot, for the long waves
    flow
Across my gallant ship where sunk she lies
With all my riches and my merchandise.

"Moreover, I am heavy for the fate
    Of these my mariners drowned in the deep;
I must lament me for their sad estate
    Now they are gathered in their last long sleep.
O! the unpitying heavens upon me frown,
Then how should I look up?—I must look
    down."

And he stood yet watching the fair green sea
    Till hunger reached him; then he made a
    fire,
A driftwood fire, and wandered listlessly
    And gathered many eggs at his desire,
And dressed them for his meal, and then he lay
And slept, and woke upon the second day.

When as he said, "The cave shall be my home;
    None will molest me, for the brown cliffs rise
Like castles of defence behind,—the foam
    Of the remorseless sea beneath me lies;
'Tis easy from the cliff my food to win—
The nations of the rock-dove breed therein.

" For fuel, at the ebb yon fair expanse
    Is strewed with driftwood by the breaking
    wave,
And in the sea is fish for sustenance.
    I will build up the entrance of the cave,
And leave therein a window and a door,
And here will dwell and leave it nevermore."

Then even so he did; and when his task,
    Many long days being over, was complete;
When he had eaten, as he sat to bask
    In the red firelight glowing at his feet,
He was right glad of shelter, and he said,
"Now for my comrades am I comforted."

Then did the voice awake and speak again;
    It murmured, "Man look up!" But he
    replied,
"I cannot. O, mine eyes, mine eyes are fain
    Down on the red wood-ashes to abide
Because they warm me." Then the voice was
    still,
And left the lonely mariner to his will.

And soon it came to pass that he got gain.
    He had great flocks of pigeons which he fed,
And drew great store of fish from out the main,
    And down from eiderducks; and then he
    said,
" It is not good that I should lead my life
In silence, I will take to me a wife."

He took a wife, and brought her home to him;
    And he was good to her and cherished her
So that she loved him; then when light waxed
    dim
    Gloom came no more; and she would min-
    ister
To all his wants; while he, being well content,
Counted her company right excellent.

But once as on the lintel of the door
  She leaned to watch him while he put to sea,
This happy wife, down-gazing at the shore,
  Said sweetly, "It is better now with me
Than it was lately when I used to spin
In my old father's house beside the lin.

And then the soft voice of the cave awoke—
  The soft voice which had haunted it erewhile—
And gently to the wife it also spoke,
  "Woman, look up!" But she, with tender guile,
Gave it denial, answering, "Nay, not so,
For all that I should look on lieth below.

"The great sky overhead is not so good
  For my two eyes as yonder stainless sea,
The source and yielder of our livelihood,
  Where rocks his little boat that loveth me."
This when the wife had said she moved away,
And looked no higher than the wave all day.

Now when the year ran out a child she bore,
  And there was such rejoicing in the cave
As surely never had there been before
  Since God first made it. Then full, sweet, and grave,
The voice, "God's utmost blessing brims thy cup,
O, father of this child, look up, look up!"

"Speak to my wife," the mariner replied.
  "I have much work—right welcome work, 'tis true—
Another mouth to feed." And then it sighed,
  "Woman, look up!" She said, "Make no ado,
For I must needs look down on anywise,
My heaven is in the blue of these dear eyes."

The seasons of the year did swiftly whirl,
  They measured time by one small life alone;
On such a day the pretty pushing pearl
  That mouth they loved to kiss had sweetly shown,
That smiling mouth, and it had made essay
To give them names on such another day.

And afterward his infant history,
  Whether he played with baubles on the floor,
Or crept to pat the rock-doves pecking nigh,
  And feeding on the threshold of the door,
They loved to mark, and all his marvellings dim,
The mysteries that beguiled and baffled him.

He was so sweet, that oft his mother said,
  "O, child, how was it that I dwelt content
Before thou camest? Blessings on thy head,
  Thy pretty talk it is so innocent,
That oft for all my joy, though it be deep,
When thou art prattling, I am like to weep."

Summer and winter spent themselves again,
  The rock-doves in their season bred, the cliff
Grew sweet, for every cleft would entertain
Its tuft of blossom, and the mariner's skiff,
Early and late, would linger in the bay,
Because the sea was calm and winds away.

The little child about that rocky height,
  Led by her loving hand who gave him birth,
Might wander in the clear unclouded light,
  And take his pastime in the beauteous earth;
Smell the fair flowers in stony cradles swung,
And see God's happy creatures feed their young.

And once it came to pass, at eventide,
  His mother set him in the cavern door,
And filled his lap with grain, and stood aside
  To watch the circling rock-doves soar, and soar,
Then dip, alight, and run in circling bands,
To take the barley from his open hands.

And even while she stood and gazed at him,
  And his grave father's eyes upon him dwelt,
They heard the tender voice and it was dim,
  And seemed full softly in the air to melt;
"Father," it murmured, "Mother," dying away,
"Look up, while yet the hours are called to-day."

"I will," the father answered, "but not now;"
  The mother said, "Sweet voice, O speak to me
At a convenient season." And the brow
  Of the cliff began to quake right fearfully,
There was a rending crash, and there did leap
A riven rock and plunge into the deep.

They said, "A storm is coming;" but they slept
  That night in peace, and thought the storm had passed,
For there was not a cloud to intercept
  The sacred moonlight on the cradle cast;
And to his rocking boat at dawn of day,
With joy of heart the mariner took his way.

But when he mounted up the path at night,
  Foreboding not of trouble or mischance,
His wife came out into the fading light,
  And met him with a serious countenance;
And she broke out in tears and sobbing thick,
"The child is sick, my little child is sick."

They knelt beside him in the sultry dark,
  And when the moon looked in his face was pale,
And when the red sun, like a burning barque,
  Rose in a fog at sea, his tender wail
Sank deep into their hearts, and piteously
They fell to chiding of their destiny.

The doves unheeded cooed that livelong day,
  Their pretty playmate cared for them no more;
The sea-thrift nodded, wet with glistening spray,

None gathered it; the long wave washed
    the shore;
He did not know, nor lift his eyes to trace,
The new fallen shadow in his dwelling-place.

The sultry sun beat on the cliffs all day,
    And hot calm airs slept on the polished sea,
The mournful mother wore her time away,
    Bemoaning of her helpless misery,
Pleading and plaining, till the day was done,
"O, look on me, my love, my little one.

"What aileth thee, that thou dost lie and
    moan?
    Ah would that I might bear it in thy stead."
The father made not his forebodings known,
    But gazed, and in his secret soul he said,
"I may have sinned, on sin waits punishment,
But as for him, sweet blameless innocent,

"What has he done that he is stricken down?
    O it is hard to see him sink and fade,
When I, that counted him my dear life's crown,
    So willingly have worked while he has
    played;
That he might sleep, have risen, come storm,
    come heat,
And thankfully would fast that he might eat."

My God, how short our happy days appear!
    How long the sorrowful! They thought it
    long,
The sultry morn that brought such evil cheer,
    And sat, and wished, and sighed for even-
    song;
It came, and cooling wafts about him stirred,
Yet when they spoke he answered not a word.

"Take heart," they cried, but their sad hearts
    sank low
    When he would moan and turn his restless
    head,
And wearily the lagging morns would go,
    And nights, while they sat watching by his
    bed,
Until a storm came up with wind and rain,
And lightning ran along the troubled main.

Over their heads the mighty thunders brake,
    Leaping and tumbling down from rock to
    rock;
Then burst anew and made the cliffs to quake
    As they were living things and felt the shock;
The waiting sea to sob as if in pain,
And all the midnight vault to ring again.

A lamp was burning in the mariner's cave,
    But the blue lightning flashes made it dim;
    And when the mother heard those thunders
    rave,
    She took her little child to cherish him;
She took him in her arms, and on her breast
Full wearily she courted him to rest,

And soothed him long until the storm was
    spent,
    And the last thunder peal had died away,
And stars were out in all the firmament.
    Then did he cease to moan, and slumbering
    lay,
While in the welcome silence, pure and deep,
The care-worn parents sweetly fell asleep.

And in a dream enwrought with fancies thick,
    The mother thought she heard the rock-
    doves coo
(She had forgotten that her child was sick),
    And she went forth their morning meal to
    strew;
Then over all the cliff with earnest care
She sought her child, and lo, he was not there!

But she was not afraid, though long she sought
    And climbed the cliff, and set her feet in
    grass,
Then reached a river, broad and full, she
    thought,
    And at its brink he sat. Alas! alas!
For one stood near him, fair and undefiled,
An innocent, a marvellous man-child.

In garments white as wool, and O, most fair,
    A rainbow covered him with mystic light;
Upon the warmèd grass his feet were bare,
    And as he breathed, the rainbow in her sight
In passions of clear crimson trembling lay,
With gold and violet mist made fair the day.

Her little life! she thought, his little hands
    Were full of flowers that he did play withal;
But when he saw the boy o' the golden lands,
    And looked him in the face, he let them fall,
Held through a rapturous pause in wistful wise
To the sweet strangeness of those keen child-
    eyes.

"Ah, dear and awful God, who chasteneth me,
    How shall my soul to this be reconciled.
It is the Saviour of the world," quoth she,
    "And to my child He cometh as a child."
Then on her knees she fell by that vast stream—
Oh, it was sorrowful, this woman's dream!

For lo, that Elder Child drew nearer now,
    Fair as the light, and purer than the sun,
The calms of heaven were brooding on his brow,
    And in his arms He took her little one,
Her child, that knew her, but with sweet demur
Drew back, nor held his hands to come to her.

With that in mother misery sore she wept—
    "O Lamb of God, I love my child so MUCH!
He stole away to Thee while we two slept,
    But give him back, for thou hast many such;
And as for me I have but one. O deign,
Dear Pity of God, to give him me again."

His feet were on the river. Oh, his feet
    Had touched the river now, and it was great;

And yet He hearkened when she did entreat,
  And turned in quietness as He would wait—
Wait till she looked upon Him, and behold,
There lay a long way off a city of gold.

Like to a jasper and a sardine stone,
  Whelmed in the rainbow stood that fair man-child,
Mighty and innocent, that held her own,
  And as might be his manner at home he smiled,
Then while she looked and looked, the vision brake,
And all amazed she started up awake.

And lo, her little child was gone indeed!
  The sleep that knows no waking he had slept,
Folded to heaven's own heart; in rainbow brede
  Clothed and made glad, while they two mourned and wept,
But in the drinking of their bitter cup
The sweet voice spoke once more, and sighed, "Look up!"

They heard, and straightway answered, "Even so:
  For what abides that we should look on here?
The heavens are better than this earth below,
  They are of more account and far more dear.
We will look up for all most sweet and fair,
Most pure, most excellent, is garnered there."

A REVERIE.

When I do sit apart
  And commune with my heart,
She brings me forth the treasures once my own ;
  Shows me a happy place
  Where leaf-buds swelled apace,
And wasting rims of snow in sunlight shone,

  Rock, in a mossy glade,
  The larch-trees lend thee shade,
That just begin to feather with their leaves ;
  From out thy crevice deep
  White tufts of snow-drops peep,
And melted rime drips softly from thine eaves.

  Ah, rock, I know, I know
  That yet thy snowdrops grow,
And yet doth sunshine fleck them through the tree,
  Whose sheltering branches hide
  The cottage at its side,
That nevermore will shade or shelter me.

  I know the stockdove's note
  Athwart the glen doth float ;
With sweet foreknowledge of her twins oppressed,
  And longings onward sent,
  She broods before the event,
While leisurely she mends her shallow nest.

  Once to that cottage door,
  In happy days of yore,
My little love made footprints in the snow.
  She was so glad of spring,
  She helped the birds to sing,
I know she dwells there yet—the rest I do not know.

  They sang, and would not stop,
  While drop, and drop, and drop,
I heard the melted rime in sunshine fall ;
  And narrow wandering rills,
  Where leaned the daffodils,
Murmured and murmured on, and that was all.

  I think, but cannot tell,
  I think she loved me well,
And some dear fancy with my future twined.
  But I shall never know,
  Hope faints, and lets it go,
That passionate want forbid to speak its mind.

DEFTON WOOD.

I held my way through Defton Wood,
  And on to Wandor Hall ;
The dancing leaf let down the light,
  In hovering spots to fall,
"O young, young leaves, you match me well,"
  My heart was merry, and sung—
"Now wish me joy of my sweet youth ;
  My love—she, too, is young !
    O so many, many, many
    Little homes above my head !
    O so many, many, many
    Dancing blossoms round me spread !
    O so many, many, many
    Maidens sighing yet for none !
  Speed, ye wooers, speed with any—
  Speed with all but one."

I took my leave of Wandor Hall,
  And trod the woodland ways.
"What shall I do so long to bear
  The burden of my days ?"
I sighed my heart into the boughs
  Whereby the culvers cooed ;
For only I between them went
  Unwooing and unwooed.
    "O so many, many, many
    Lilies bending stately heads !
    O so many, many, many
    Strawberries ripened on their beds !
    O so many, many, many
    Maids, and yet my heart undone !
  What to me are all, are any—
  I have lost my—one."

THE SNOWDROP MONUMENT (IN LICHFIELD CATHEDRAL).

MARVELS of sleep, grown cold!
  Who hath not longed to fold
With pitying ruth, forgetful of their bliss,
  Those cherub forms that lie,
  With none to watch them nigh,
Or touch the silent lips with one warm human kiss?

  What! they are left alone
  All night with graven stone,
Pillars and arches that above them meet;
  While through those windows high
  The journeying stars can spy,
And dim blue moonbeams drop on their uncovered feet?

  O cold! yet look again,
  There is a wandering vein
Traced in the hand where those white snowdrops lie.
  Let her rapt dreamy smile
  The wondering heart beguile,
That almost thinks to hear a calm, contented sigh.

  What silence dwells between
  Those severed lips serene!
The rapture of sweet waiting breathes and grows.
  What trance-like peace is shed
  On her reclining head,
And e'en on listless feet what languor of repose!

  Angels of joy and love
  Lean softly from above
And whisper to her sweet and marvellous things;
  Tell of the golden gate
  That opened wide doth wait,
And shadow her dim sleep with their celestial wings.

  Hearing of that blest shore
  She thinks on earth no more,
Contented to forego this wintry land.
  She has nor thought nor care
  But to rest calmly there,
And hold the snowdrops pale that blossom in her hand.

  But on the other face
  Broodeth a mournful grace,
This had foreboding thoughts beyond her years,
  While sinking thus to sleep
  She saw her mother weep,
And could not lift her hand to dry those heart-sick tears.

  Could not—but failing lay,
  Sighed her young life away,
And let her arm drop down in listless rest,
  Too weary on that bed
  To turn her dying head,
Or fold the little sister nearer to her breast.

  Yet this is faintly told
  On features fair and cold,
A look of calm surprise, of meek regret,
  As if with life oppressed
  She turned her to her rest,
But felt her mother's love and looked not to forget.

  How wistfully they close,
  Sweet eyes to their repose!
How quietly declines the placid brow!
  The young lips seem to say,
  "I have wept much to-day,
And felt some bitter pains, but they are over now."

  Sleep! there are left below
  Many who pine to go,
Many who lay it to their chastened souls,
  That gloomy days draw nigh,
  And they are blest who die,
For this green world grows worse the longer that she rolls.

  And as for me I know
  A little of her woe,
Her yearning want doth in my soul abide,
  And sighs of them that weep,
  "O put us soon to sleep,
For when we wake—with Thee—we shall be satisfied."

AN ANCIENT CHESS KING.

HAPLY some Rajah first in the ages gone
  Amid his languid ladies fingered thee,
  While a black nightingale, sun-swart as he,
Sang his one wife, love's passionate oraison;
Haply thou may'st have pleased Old Prester John
  Among his pastures, when full royally
  He sat in tent, grave shepherds at his knee,
While lamps of balsam winked and glimmered on.
What doest thou here? Thy masters are all dead;
  My heart is full of ruth and yearning pain
At sight of thee; O king that hast a crown
  Outlasting theirs, and tell'st of greatness fled
Through cloud-hung nights of unabated rain
And murmurs of the dark majestic town.

COMFORT IN THE NIGHT.

SHE thought by heaven's high wall that she did stray
  Till she beheld the everlasting gate:
And she climbed up to it to long, and wait,

Feel with her hands (for it was night), and lay
Her lips to it with kisses ; thus to pray
  That it might open to her desolate.
  And lo ! it trembled, lo ! her passionate
Crying prevailed. A little little way
It opened : there fell out a thread of light,
  And she saw wingèd wonders move within ;
Also she heard sweet talking as they meant
To comfort her. They said, "Who comes to-night
Shall one day certainly an entrance win ;"
Then the gate closed and she awoke content.

THOUGH ALL GREAT DEEDS.

Though all great deeds were proved but fables fine,
  Though earth's old story could be told anew,
  Though the sweet fashions loved of them that sue
Were empty as the ruined Delphian shrine—
Though God did never man, in words benign,
  With sense of His great Fatherhood endue,
  Though life immortal were a dream untrue,
And he that promised it were not divine—
Though soul, though spirit were not, and all hope
  Reaching beyond the bourne, melted away ;
Though virtue had no goal and good no scope,
  But both were doomed to end with this our clay—
Though all these were not,—to the ungraced heir
Would this remain,—to live, as though they were.

THE LONG WHITE SEAM.

As I came round the harbor buoy,
  The lights began to gleam,
No wave the land-locked water stirred,
  The crags were white as cream ;
And I marked my love by candle-light
  Sewing her long white seam.
    It's aye sewing ashore, my dear,
      Watch and steer at sea,
    It's reef and furl, and haul the line,
      Set sail and think of thee.

I climbed to reach her cottage door ;
  O sweetly my love sings !
Like a shaft of light her voice breaks forth,
  My soul to meet it springs
As the shining water leaped of old,
  When stirred by angel wings.
    Aye longing to list anew,
      Awake and in my dream,
    But never a song she sang like this,
      Sewing her long white seam.

Fair fall the lights, the harbor lights,
  That brought me in to thee,
And peace drop down on that low roof
  For the sight that I did see,
And the voice, my dear, that rang so clear
  All for the love of me.
    For O, for O, with brows bent low
      By the candle's flickering gleam,
    Her wedding gown it was she wrought,
      Sewing the long white seam.

AN OLD WIFE'S SONG.

And what will ye hear, my daughters dear ?—
  Oh, what will ye hear this night ?
Shall I sing you a song of the yuletide cheer,
  Or of lovers and ladies bright ?

"Thou shalt sing," they say (for we dwell far away
  From the land where fain would we be),
"Thou shalt sing us again some old-world strain
  That is sung in our own countrie.

"Thou shalt mind us so of the times long ago,
  When we walked on the upland lea,
While the old harbor light waxed faint in the white,
  Long rays shooting out from the sea ;

"While lambs were yet asleep, and the dew lay deep
  On the grass, and their fleeces clean and fair.
Never grass was seen so thick nor so green
  As the grass that grew up there !

"In the town was no smoke, for none there awoke—
  At our feet it lay still as still could be ;
And we saw far below the long river flow,
  And the schooners a-warping out to sea.

"Sing us now a strain shall make us feel again
  As we felt in that sacred peace of morn,
When we had the first view of the wet sparkling dew,
  In the shyness of a day just born."

So I sang an old song—it was plain and not long—
  I had sung it very oft when they were small;
And long ere it was done they wept every one:
  Yet this was all the song—this was all :—

The snow lies white, and the moon gives light,
  I'll out to the freezing mere,
And ease my heart with one little song,
  For none will be nigh to hear.
And it's O my love, my love !
  And it's O my dear, my dear !
It's of her that I'll sing till the wild woods ring,
  When nobody's nigh to hear.

My love is young, she is young, is young;
  When she laughs the dimple dips.
We walked in the wind, and her long locks blew
  Till sweetly they touched my lips.
And I'll out to the freezing mere,
  Where the stiff reeds whistle so low,
And I'll tell my mind to the friendly wind,
  Because I have loved her so.

Ay, and she's true, my lady is true!
  And that's the best of it all;
And when she blushes my heart so yearns
  That tears are ready to fall.
And it's O my love, my love!
  And it's O my dear, my dear!
It's of her that I'll sing till the wild woods ring,
  When nobody's nigh to hear.

COLD AND QUIET.

COLD, my dear,—cold and quiet.
  In their cups on yonder lea,
Cowslips fold the brown bee's diet;
  So the moss enfoldeth thee.
"Plant me, plant me, O love, a lily flower—
  Plant at my head, I pray you, a green tree;
And when our children sleep," she sighed "at the dusk hour,
  And when the lily blossoms, O come out to me!"

Lost, my dear? Lost! nay, deepest
  Love is that which loseth least;
Through the night-time while thou sleepest,
  Still I watch the shrouded east.
Near thee, near thee, my wife that aye liveth,
  "Lost" is no word for such a love as mine;
Love from her past to me a present giveth,
  And love itself doth comfort, making pain divine.

Rest, my dear, rest. Fair showeth
  That which was, and not in vain
Sacred have I kept, God knoweth,
  Love's last words atween us twain.
"Hold by our past, my only love, my lover;
  Fall not, but rise, O love, by loss of me!"
Boughs from our garden, white with bloom hang over.
  Love, now the children slumber, I come out to thee.

A SNOW MOUNTAIN.

CAN I make white enough my thought for thee,
  Or wash my words in light? Thou hast no mate
To sit aloft in the silence silently
  And twin those matchless heights undesecrate.
Reverend as Lear, when, lorn of shelter, he
  Stood, with his old white head, surprised at fate;
Alone as Galileo, when, set free,
  Before the stars he mused disconsolate.
Ay, and remote, as the dead lords of song,
  Great masters who have made us what we are,
For thou and they have taught us how to long
  And feel a sacred want of the fair and far:
Reign, and keep life in this our deep desire—
Our only greatness is that we aspire.

SLEEP.

(A WOMAN SPEAKS.)

O SLEEP, we are beholden to thee, sleep,
  Thou bearest angels to us in the night,
Saints out of heaven with palms. Seen by thy light
Sorrow is some old tale that goeth not deep;
Love is a pouting child. Once I did sweep
  Through space with thee, and lo, a dazzling sight—
Stars! They came on, I felt their drawing and might;
And some had dark companions. Once (I weep
When I remember that) we sailed the tide,
And found fair isles, where no isles used to bide,
  And met there my lost love, who said to me,
That 'twas a long mistake: he had not died.
Sleep, in the world to come how strange 'twill be
Never to want, never to wish for thee!

PROMISING.

(A MAN SPEAKS.)

ONCE, a new world, the sunswart marinere,
  Columbus, promised, and was sore withstood,
Ungraced, unhelped, unheard for many a year;
  But let at last to make his promise good.
Promised and promising I go, most dear,
  To better my dull heart with love's sweet feud,
My life with its most reverent hope and fear,
  And my religion, with fair gratitude.
O we must part; the stars for me contend,
  And all the winds that blow on all the seas.
Through wonderful waste places I must wend,
  And with a promise my sad soul appease.
Promise then, promise much of far-off bliss;
But—ah, for present joy, give me one kiss.

LOVE.

Who veileth love should first have vanquished fate.
 She folded up the dream in her deep heart,
 Her fair full lips were silent on that smart,
Thick fringèd eyes did on the grasses wait.
What good? one eloquent blush, but one, and straight
The meaning of a life was known; for art
Is often foiled in playing nature's part,
And time holds nothing long inviolate.
Earth's buried seed springs up—slowly, or fast:
The ring came home, that one in ages past
 Flung to the keeping of unfathomed seas:
 And golden apples on the mystic trees
Were sought and found, and borne away at last,
 Though watched of the divine Hesperides.

POEMS.

Written on the Deaths of Three Lovely Children who were taken from their Parents within a Month of one another.

HENRY,

AGED EIGHT YEARS.

YELLOW leaves, how fast they
    flutter — woodland hollows
    thickly strewing,
    Where the wan October sun-
    beams scantly in the mid-day
    win,
    While the dim gray clouds are
    drifting, and in saddened
    hues imbuing
All without and all within !

All within ! but winds of autumn, little Henry,
    round their dwelling
Did not load your father's spirit with those
    deep and burdened sighs ;—
Only echoed thoughts of sadness, in your
    mother's bosom swelling,
    Fast as tears that dim her eyes.

Life is fraught with many changes, checked
    with sorrow and mutation,
But no grief it ever lightened such a truth
    before to know:—
I behold them—father, mother—as they seemed
    to contemplation,
    Only three short weeks ago !

Saddened for the morrow's parting—up the
    stairs at midnight stealing—
As with cautious foot we glided past the child-
    ren's open door,—
"Come in here," they said, the lamplight dim-
    pled forms at last revealing,
    "Kiss them in their sleep once more."

You were sleeping, little Henry, with your eye-
    lids scarcely closing,
Two sweet faces near together, with their
    rounded arms entwined :—
And the rose-bud lips were moving, as if stirred
    in their reposing
    By the movements of the mind !

And your mother smoothed the pillow, and her
    sleeping treasures numbered,
    Whispering fondly—"He is dreaming"—as
    you turned upon your bed—

And your father stooped to kiss you, happy
    dreamer, as you slumbered,
    With his hand upon your head !
Did he know the true deep meaning of his
    blessing? No ! he never
Heard afar the summons uttered—"Come
    up hither"—Never knew
How the awful Angel faces kept his sleeping
    boy for ever,
    And for ever in their view.

Awful Faces, unimpassioned, silent Presences
    were by us
Shrouding wings—majestic beings—hidden
    by this earthly veil—
Such as we have called on, saying, "Praise
    the Lord, O Ananias,
    Azarias and Misael !"

But we saw not, and who knoweth, what the
    missioned Spirits taught him,
To that one small bed drawn nearer, when
    we left him to their will?
While he slumbered, who can answer for what
    dreams they may have brought him,
    When at midnight all was still ?

Father ! Mother ! must you leave him on his
    bed, but not to slumber?
Are the small hands meekly folded on his
    breast, but not to pray?
When you count your children over, must you
    tell a different number,
    Since that happier yesterday?

Father ! Mother ! weep if need be, since this
    is a "time" for weeping,
    Comfort comes not for the calling, grief is
    never argued down—
Coldly sounds the admonition, "Why lament?
    in better keeping
    Rests the child than in your own."

"Truth indeed ! but, oh ! compassion ! Have
    you sought to scan my sorrow ? "
(Mother you shall meekly ponder, list'ning
    to that common tale)
"Does your heart repeat its echo. or by fellow-
    feeling borrow
    Even a tone that might avail?

'Might avail to steal it from me, by its deep
  heart-warm affection?
 Might perceive by strength of loving how the
  fond words to combine?
Surely no! I will be silent, in your soul is no
  reflection
    Of the care that burdens mine!"

When the winter twilight gathers, Father, and
  your thoughts shall wander,
 Sitting lonely you shall blend him with your
  listless reveries,
Half forgetful what division holds the form
  whereon you ponder
    From its place upon your knees—

With a start of recollection, with a half-
  reproachful wonder,
 Of itself the heart shall question, "Art thou
  then no longer here?
Is it so, my little Henry? Are we set so far
  asunder
    Who were wont to be so near?"

While the fire-light dimly flickers, and the
  lengthened shades are meeting,
 To itself the heart shall answer, "He shall
  come to me no more :
I shall never hear his footsteps nor the child's
  sweet voice entreating
    For admission at my door."

But upon *your* fair, fair forehead, no regrets
  nor griefs are dwelling,
 Neither sorrow nor disquiet do the peaceful
  features know ;
Nor that look, whose wistful beauty seemed
  their sad hearts to be telling,
    "Daylight breaketh, let me go!"

Daylight breaketh, little Henry; in its beams
  your soul awaketh—
 What though night should close around us,
  dim and dreary to the view—
Though *our* souls should walk in darkness, far
  away that morning breaketh
    Into endless day for you!

SAMUEL,

AGED NINE YEARS.

They have left you, little Henry, but they
  have not left you lonely—
 Brothers' hearts so knit together could not,
  might not separate dwell,
Fain to seek you in the mansions far away—
  One lingered only
    To bid those behind farewell!

Gentle Boy!—His childlike nature in most
  guileless form was moulded,
 And it may be that his spirit woke in glory
  unaware,

Since so calmly he resigned it, with his hands
  still meekly folded,
    Having said his evening prayer.

Or—if conscious of that summons—"Speak,
  O Lord, Thy servant heareth"—
 As one said, whose name they gave him,
  might his willing answer be,
"Here am I"—like him replying—"At Thy
  gates my soul appeareth,
    For behold thou calledst me!"

A deep silence—utter silence, on his earthly
  home descendeth:—
 Reading, playing, sleeping, waking—he is
  gone, and few remain !
"O the loss!"—they utter, weeping—every
  voice its echo lendeth—
    "O the loss!"—But, O the gain!

On that tranquil shore his spirit was vouchsafed
  an early landing,
 Lest the toils of crime should stain it, or the
  thrall of guilt control—
Lest that "wickedness should alter the yet
  simple understanding,
    Or deceit beguile his soul!"

"Lay not up on earth thy treasure"—they have
  read that sentence duly,
 Moth and rust shall fret thy riches—earthly
  good hath swift decay—
"Even so," each heart replieth—"As for me,
  my riches truly
    Make them wings and flee away!"

"O my riches!—O my children!—dearest part
  of life and being,
 Treasures looked to for the solace of this
  life's declining years,—
Were our voices cold to hearing—or our faces
  cold to seeing,
    That ye left us to our tears?"

"We inherit conscious silence, ceasing of some
  merry laughter,
 And the hush of two sweet voices—(healing
  sounds for spirits bruised!)
Of the tread of joyous footsteps in the pathway
  following after,
    Of two names no longer used!"

Question for them, little Sister, in your sweet
  and childish fashion—
 Search and seek them, Baby Brother, with
  your calm and asking eyes—
Dimpled lips that fail to utter fond appeal or
  sad compassion,
    Mild regret or dim surprise!

There are two tall trees above you, by the high
  east window growing,
 Underneath them, slumber sweetly, lapt in
  silence deep, serene ;

Save, when pealing in the distance, organ notes
    towards you flowing
        Echo—with a pause between !

And that pause ?—a voice shall fill it—tones
    that blessed you daily, nightly,
    Well beloved, but not sufficing, Sleepers, to
        awake you now,
Though so near he stand, that shadows from
    your trees may tremble lightly
        On his book and on his brow !

Sleep then ever! Neither singing of sweet
    birds shall break your slumber,
    Neither fall of dew, nor sunshine, dance of
        leaves, nor drift of snow,
Charm those dropt lids more to open, nor the
    tranquil bosom cumber
        With one care for things below !

It is something, the assurance, that *you* ne'er
    shall feel like sorrow,
    Weep no past and dread no future—know
        not sighing, feel not pain—
Nor a day that looketh forward to a mournfuller to-morrow—
        " Clouds returning after rain !"

No, far off, the daylight breaketh, in its beams
    each soul awaketh :
    "What though clouds," they sigh, "be gathered dark and stormy to the view,
Though the light our eyes forsaketh, fresh and
    sweet behold it breaketh
        Into endless day for you !"

KATIE, AGED FIVE YEARS.

(ASLEEP IN THE DAYTIME.)

ALL rough winds are hushed and silent, golden
    light the meadow steepeth,
And the last October roses daily wax more
    pale and fair;
They have laid a gathered blossom on the breast
    of one who sleepeth
        With a sunbeam on her hair.

Calm, and draped in snowy raiment she lies
    still, as one that dreameth,
And a grave sweet smile hath parted dimpled
    lips that may not speak ;
Slanting down that narrow sunbeam like a ray
    of glory gleameth
        On the sainted brow and cheek.

There is silence ! They who watch her, speak
    no word of grief or wailing,
In a strange unwonted calmness they gaze
    on and cannot cease,
Though the pulse of life beat faintly, thought
    shrink back, and hope be failing,
        They, like Aaron, "hold their peace."

While they gaze on her, the deep bell with its
    long slow pauses soundeth ;
Long they hearken—father—mother—love
    has nothing more to say :
Beating time to feet of Angels leading her where
    love aboundeth
        Tolls the heavy bell this day.

Still in silence to its tolling they count over all
    her meetness
To lie near their hearts and soothe them in
    all sorrows and all fears ;
Her short life lies spread before them, but they
    cannot tell her sweetness,
        Easily as tell her years.

Only daughter—Ah ! how fondly Thought
    around that lost name lingers,
Oft when lone your mother sitteth, she shall
    weep and droop her head,
She shall mourn her baby-sempstress, with
    those imitative fingers,
        Drawing out her aimless thread.

In your father's Future cometh many a sad uncheered to-morrow,
But in sleep shall three fair faces heavenly-calm towards him lean—
Like a threefold cord shall draw him through
    the weariness of sorrow,
        Nearer to the things unseen.

With the closing of your eyelids close the
    dreams of expectation,
And so ends the fairest chapter in the records
    of their way :
Therefore—O thou God most holy—God of
    rest and consolation,
        Be thou near to them this day !

Be Thou near, when they shall nightly, by the
    bed of infant brothers,
Hear their soft and gentle breathing, and
    shall bless them on their knees ;
And shall think how coldly falleth the white
    moonlight on the others,
        In their bed beneath the trees.

Be thou near, when they, they *only*, bear those
    faces in remembrance,
And the number of their children strangers
    ask them with a smile :
And when other childlike faces touch them by
    the strong resemblance
        To those turned to them erewhile.

Be thou near, each chastened Spirit for its
    course and conflict nerving,
Let Thy voice say. "Father—mother—lo !
    thy treasures live above !
Now be strong, be strong, no longer cumbered
    overmuch with serving
        At the shrine of human love."

Let them sleep!   In course of ages e'en the
    Holy House shall crumble,
  And the broad and stately steeple one day
    bend to its decline,
And high arches, ancient arches bowed and
    decked in clothing humble,
    Creeping moss shall round them twine.

Ancient arches, old and hoary, sunny beams
    shall glimmer through them,
  And invest them with a beauty we would
    fain they should not share,
And the moonlight slanting down them, the
    white moonlight shall imbue them
    With a sadness dim and fair.

Then the soft green moss shall wrap you, and
    the world shall all forget you,
  Life, and stir, and toil, and tumult unawares
    shall pass you by ;
Generations come and vanish : but it shall not
    grieve nor fret you,
    That they sin, or that they sigh.

And the world, grown old in sinning, shall
    deny her first beginning,
  And think scorn of words which whisper
    how that all must pass away ;
Time's arrest and intermission shall account
    a vain tradition,
    And a dream, the reckoning day !

Till His blast, a blast of terror, shall awake in
    shame and sadness
  Faithless millions to a vision of the failing
    earth and skies,
And more sweet than song of Angels, in their
    shout of joy and gladness,
    Call the dead in Christ to rise!

Then, by One Man's intercession, standing
    clear from their transgression,
  Father—mother—you shall meet them fairer
    than they were before,
And have joy with the Redeemèd, joy ear hath
    not heard—heart dreamèd,
    Ay for ever—evermore !

THE TWO MARGARETS.

I.

MARGARET BY THE MERE SIDE.

LYING imbedded in the green champaigne
  That gives no shadow to thy silvery face,
  Open to all the heavens, and all their train,
  The marshalled clouds that cross with stately pace,
  No steadfast hills on thee reflected rest,
Nor waver with the dimpling of thy breast.

O, silent Mere! about whose marges spring
  Thick bulrushes to hide the reed-bird's nest;
Where the shy ousel dips her glossy wing,
  And balanced in the water takes her rest:
While under bending leaves, all gem-arrayed,
Blue dragon-flies sit panting in the shade:

Warm, stilly place, the sundew loves thee well,
  And the green sward comes creeping to thy brink,
And golden saxifrage and pimpernel
  Lean down to thee their perfumed heads to drink;
And heavy with the weight of bees doth bend
White clover, and beneath thy waves descend:

While the sweet scent of bean-fields, floated wide
  On a long eddy of the lightsome air
Over the level mead to thy lone side,
  Doth lose itself among thy zephyrs rare,
With wafts from hawthorn bowers and new-cut hay,
And blooming orchards lying far away.

Thou hast thy Sabbaths, when a deeper calm
  Descends upon thee, quiet Mere, and then
There is a sound of bells, a far-off psalm
  From gray church-towers, that swims across the fen;
And the light sigh where grass and waters meet,
Is thy meek welcome to the visit sweet.

Thou hast thy lovers. Though the angler's rod
  Dimple thy surface seldom; though the oar
Fill not with silvery globes thy fringing sod,
  Nor send long ripples to thy lonely shore;
Though few, as in a glass, have cared to trace
The smile of nature moving on thy face;

Thou hast thy lovers truly, 'Mid the cold
  Of northern tarns the wild-fowl dream of thee,
And, keeping thee in mind, their wings unfold,
  And shape their course, high soaring, till they see
Down in the world, like molten silver, rest
Their goal, and screaming plunge them in thy breast.

Fair Margaret, who sittest all day long
  On the gray stone beneath the sycamore,
The bowering tree with branches lithe and strong,
  The only one to grace the level shore,
Why dost thou wait? for whom with patient cheer
Gaze yet so wistfully adown the Mere?

Thou canst not tell, thou dost not know, alas!
  Long watchings leave behind them little trace;
And yet how sweetly must the mornings pass,
  That bring that dreamy calmness to thy face!
How quickly must the evenings come that find
Thee still regret to leave the Mere behind!

Thy cheek is resting on thy hand; thine eyes
  Are like twin violets but half unclosed,
And quiet as the deeps in yonder skies.
  Never more peacefully in love reposed
A mother's gaze upon her offspring dear,
Than thine upon the long far-stretching Mere.

Sweet innocent! Thy yellow hair floats low
  In rippling undulations on thy breast,
Then stealing down the parted love-locks flow,
  Bathed in a sunbeam on thy knees to rest,
And touch those idle hands that folded lie,
Having from sport and toil a like immunity.

Through thy life's dream with what a touching
grace
Childhood attends thee, nearly woman grown;
Her dimples linger yet upon thy face,
Like dews upon a lily this day blown;
Thy sighs are born of peace, unruffled, deep;
So the babe sighs on mother's breast asleep.

It sighs, and wakes,—but thou! thy dream is
all,
And thou wert born for it, and it for thee;
Morn doth not take thy heart, nor evenfall
Charm out its sorrowful fidelity,
Nor noon beguile thee from the pastoral shore,
And thy long watch beneath the sycamore.

No, down the Mere as far as eye can see,
Where its long reaches fade into the sky,
Thy constant gaze, fair child, rests lovingly;
But neither thou nor any can descry
Aught but the grassy banks, the rustling sedge,
And flocks of wild-fowl splashing at their edge.

And yet 'tis not with expectation hushed
That thy mute rosy mouth doth pouting close;
No fluttering hope to thy young heart e'er
rushed,
Nor disappointment troubled its repose;
All satisfied with gazing evermore
Along the sunny Mere and reedy shore.

The brooding wren flies pertly near thy seat,
Thou wilt not move to mark her glancing
wing;
The timid sheep browse close before thy feet,
And heedless at thy side do thrushes sing.
So long amongst them thou hast spent thy days,
They know that harmless hand thou wilt not
raise.

Thou wilt not lift it up—not e'en to take
The foxglove bells that flourish in the shade,
And put them in thy bosom; not to make
A posy of wild hyacinth inlaid
Like bright mosaic in the mossy grass,
With freckled orchis and pale sassafras.

Gaze on; take in the voices of the Mere,
The break of shallow water at thy feet,
Its plash among long weeds and grasses sere,
And its weird sobbing,—hollow music meet
For ears like thine; listen and take thy fill,
And dream on it by night, when all is still.

Full sixteen years have slowly passed away,
Young Margaret since thy fond mother here
Came down, a six months' wife, one April day,
To see her husband's boat go down the Mere,
And track its course, till, lost in distance blue,
In mellow light it faded from her view.

It faded, and she never saw it more;—
Nor any human eye;—oh, grief! oh, woe!
It faded,—and returned not to the shore;
But far above it still the waters flow—

And none beheld it sink, and none could tell
Where coldly slept the form she loved so well!

But that sad day, unknowing of her fate,
She homeward turn'd her still reluctant feet;
And at her wheel she spun, till dark and late,
The evening fell; the time when they should
meet;—
Till the stars paled that at deep midnight
burned—
And morning dawned, and he was not returned.

And the bright sun came up—she thought too
soon,
And shed its ruddy light along the Mere;
And day wore on too quickly, and at noon
She came and wept beside the waters clear.
"How could he be so late?"—and then hope
fled;
And disappointment darkened into dread.

He NEVER came, and she with weepings sore
Peered in the water-flags unceasingly;
Through all the undulations of the shore,
Looking for that which most she feared to
see.
And then she took home sorrow to her heart,
And brooded over its cold cruel smart.

And after, desolate she sat alone
And mourned, refusing to be comforted,
On the gray stone, the moss-embroidered stone,
With the great sycamore above her head;
Till after many days a broken oar
Hard by her seat was drifted to the shore.

It came,—a token of his fate,—the whole,
The sum of her misfortune to reveal;
As if sent up in pity to her soul,
The tidings of her widowhood to seal;
And put away the pining hope forlorn,
That made her grief more bitter to be borne.

And she was patient; through the weary day
She toiled; though none was there her work
to bless,
And did not wear the sullen months away,
Nor call on death to end her wretchedness,
But lest the grief should overflow her breast,
She toiled as heretofore and would not rest.

But, her work done, what time the evening
star
Rose over the cool water, then she came
To the gray stone, and saw its light from far
Drop down the misty Mere white lengths of
flame,
And wondered whether there might be the
place
Where the soft ripple wandered o'er HIS face.

Unfortunate! In solitude forlorn
She dwelt, and thought upon her husband's
grave,
Till when the days grew short a child was born

To the dead father underneath the wave;
And it brought back a remnant of delight,
A little sunshine to its mother's sight;

A little wonder to her heart grown numb,
   And a sweet yearning pitiful and keen:
She took it as from that poor father come,
Her and the misery to stand between;
Her little maiden babe, who day by day
Sucked at her breast and charmed her woes away.

But years flew on; the child was still the same,
   Nor human language she had learned to speak:
Her lips were mute, and seasons went and came,
   And brought fresh beauty to her tender cheek;
And all the day upon the sunny shore
She sat and mused beneath the sycamore.

Strange sympathy! she watched and wearied not,
   Haply unconscious what it was she sought;
Her mother's tale she easily forgot,
   And if she listened no warm tears it brought;
Though surely in the yearnings of her heart
The unknown voyager must have had his part.

Unknown to her; like all she saw unknown,
   All sights were fresh as when they first began,
All sounds were new; each murmur and each tone
   And cause and consequence she could not scan,
Forgot that night brought darkness in its train,
Nor reasoned that the day would come again.

There is a happiness in past regret;
   And echoes of the harshest sound are sweet.
The mother's soul was struck with grief, and yet,
   Repeated in her child, 'twas not unmeet
That echo-like the grief a tone should take
Painless, but ever pensive for her sake,

For her dear sake, whose patient soul was linked
   By ties so many to the babe unborn:
Whose hope, by slow degrees become extinct,
   For evermore had left her child forlorn,
Yet left no consciousness of want or woe,
Nor wonder vague that these things should be so.

Truly her joys were limited and few,
   But they sufficed a life to satisfy,
That neither fret nor dim foreboding knew,
But breathed the air in a great harmony
With its own place and part, and was at one
With all it knew of earth and moon and sun.

For all of them were worked into the dream,
   The husky sighs of wheat-fields in it wrought;
All the land-miles belong to it; the stream
   That fed the Mere ran through it like a thought.
It was a passion of peace, and loved to wait
'Neath boughs with fair green light illuminate.

To wait with her alone; always alone;
   For any that drew near she heeded not,
Wanting them little as the lily grown
   Apart from others in a shady plot,
Wants fellow-lilies of like fair degree,
In her still glen to bear her company.

Always alone; and yet there was a child
   Who loved this child, and from his turret towers,
Across the lea would roam to where, inisled
   And fenced in rapturous silence went her hours,
And, with slow footsteps drawn anear the place
Where mute she sat, would ponder on her face,

And wonder at her with a childish awe,
   And come again to look, and yet again,
Till the sweet rippling of the Mere would draw
   His longing to itself; while in her train
The water-hen, come forth, would bring her brood
From slumbering in the rushy solitude;

Or to their young would curlews call and clang
   Their homeless young that down the furrows creep;
Or the wind-hover in the blue would hang,
   Still as a rock set in the watery deep.
Then from her presence he would break away,
Unmarked, ungreeted yet, from day to day.

But older grown, the Mere he haunted yet,
   And a strange joy from its sweet wildness caught;
Whilst careless sat alone maid Margaret,
   And "shut the gates" of silence on her thought,
All through spring mornings gemmed with melted rime,
All through hay-harvest and through gleaning time.

O pleasure for itself that boyhood makes,
   O happiness to roam the sighing shore,
Plough up with elfin craft the water-flakes,
   And track the nested rail with cautious oar;
Then floating lie and look with wonder new
Straight up in the great dome of light and blue.

O pleasure! yet they took him from the wold,
   The reedy Mere, and all his pastime there,
The place where he was born, and would grow old
   If God his life so many years should spare;
From the loved haunts of childhood and the plain
And pasture-lands of his own broad domain.

And he came down when wheat was in the sheaf,
  And with her fruit the apple-branch bent low,
While yet in August glory hung the leaf.
  And flowerless aftermath began to grow;
He came from his gray turrets to the shore,
And sought the maid beneath the sycamore.

He sought her, not because her tender eyes
  Would brighten at his coming, for he knew
Full seldom any thought of him would rise
  In her fair breast when he had passed from view;
But for his own love's sake, that unbeguiled
Drew him in spirit to the silent child.

For boyhood in its better hour is prone
  To reverence what it hath not understood;
And he had thought that some heavenly meaning shone
  From her clear eyes, that made their watchings good;
While a great peacefulness of shade was shed
Like oil of consecration on her head.

A fishing wallet from his shoulder slung,
  With bounding foot he reached the mossy place,
A little moment gently o'er her hung,
  Put back her hair and looked upon her face,
Then fain from that deep dream to wake her yet,
He "Margaret!" low murmured, "Margaret!

"Look at me once before I leave the land,
  For I am going,—going, Margaret."
And then she sighed, and, lifting up her hand,
  Laid it along his young fresh cheek, and set
Upon his face those blue twin-deeps, her eyes,
And moved it back from her in troubled wise,

Because he came between her and her fate,
  The Mere. She sighed again as one oppressed;
The waters, shining clear, with delicate
  Reflections wavered on her blameless breast;
And through the branches dropt, like flickerings fair,
And played upon her hands and on her hair.

And he, withdrawn a little space to see,
  Murmured in tender ruth that was not pain,
"Farewell, I go; but sometimes think of me,
  Maid Margaret;" and there came by again
A whispering in the reed-beds and the sway
Of waters: then he turned and went his way.

And wilt thou think on him now he is gone?
  No; thou wilt gaze: though thy young eyes grow dim,
And thy soft cheek become so pale and wan,
  Still thou wilt gaze, and spend no thought on him;
There is no sweetness in his laugh for thee—
No beauty in his fresh heart's gayety.

But wherefore linger in deserted haunts?
  Why of the past, as if yet present, sing?
The yellow iris on the margin flaunts,
  With hyacinth the banks are blue in spring,
And under dappled clouds the lark afloat
Pours all the April-tide from her sweet throat

But Margaret—ah! thou art there no more,
  And thick dank moss creeps over thy gray stone;
Thy path is lost that skirted the low shore,
  With willow-grass and speedwell overgrown;
Thine eye has closed for ever, and thine ear
Drinks in no more the music of the Mere.

The boy shall come—shall come again in spring,
  Well pleased that pastoral solitude to share,
And some kind offering in his hand will bring
  To cast into thy lap, O maid most fair—
Some clasping gem about thy neck to rest,
Or heave and glimmer on thy guileless breast.

And he shall wonder why thou art not here
  The solitude with "smiles to entertain,"
And gaze along the reaches of the Mere;
  But he shall never see thy face again—
Shall never see upon the reedy shore
Maid Margaret beneath her sycamore.

II.

MARGARET IN THE XEBEC.

[Concerning this man (Robert Delacour) little further is known than that he served in the king's army, and was wounded in the battle of Marston Moor, being then about twenty-seven years of age. After the battle of Nazeby, finding himself a marked man, he quitted the country, taking with him the child whom he had adopted; and he made many voyages between the different ports of the Mediterranean and Levant."]

RESTING within his tent at turn of day,
    A wailing voice his scanty sleep beset;
He started up—it did not flee away—
    'Twas no part of his dream, but still did fret
And pine into his heart, "Ah me! ah me!"
Broken with heaving sobs right mournfully.

Then he arose, and, troubled at this thing,
    All wearily toward the voice he went
Over the down-trod bracken and the ling,
    Until it brought him to a soldier's tent,
Where, with the tears upon her face he found
A little maiden weeping on the ground;

And backward in the tent an aged crone
    Upbraided her full harshly more and more,
But sunk her chiding to an undertone
    When she beheld him standing at the door,
And calmed her voice, and dropped her lifted hand,
And answered him with accent soft and bland.

No, the young child was none of hers, she said,
    But she had found her where the ash lay white
About a smouldering tent; her infant head
    All shelterless, she through the dewy night
Had slumbered on the field,—ungentle fate
For a lone child so soft and delicate.

"And I," quoth she, "have tended her with care,
    And thought to be rewarded of her kin,
For by her rich attire and features fair
    I know her birth is gentle: yet within
The tent unclaimed she doth but pine and weep,
A burden I would fain no longer keep."

Still while she spoke the little creature wept,
    Till painful pity touched him for the flow
Of all those tears, and to his heart there crept
    A yearning as of fatherhood, and lo!
Reaching his arms to her, "My sweet," quoth he,
"Dear little madam, wilt thou come with me?"

Then she left off her crying, and a look
    Of wistful wonder stole into her eyes.
The sullen frown her dimpled face forsook,
    She let him take her, and forgot her sighs,
Contented in his alien arms to rest,
And lay her baby head upon his breast.

Ah, sure a stranger trust was never sought
    By any soldier on a battle-plain.
He brought her to his tent, and soothed his voice,
    Rough with command; and asked, but all in vain,
Her story, while her prattling tongue rang sweet,
She playing, as one at home, about his feet.

Of race, of country, or of parentage,
    Her lisping accents nothing could unfold;—
No questioning could win to read the page
    Of her short life;—she left her tale untold,
And home and kin thus early to forget,
She only knew,—her name was—Margaret.

Then in the dusk upon his arm it chanced
    That night that suddenly she fell as'eep;
And he looked down on her like one entranced,
    And listened to her breathing still and deep,
As if a little child, when daylight closed,
With half-shut lids had ne'er before reposed.

Softly he laid her down from off his arm,
    With earnest care and new-born tenderness:
Her infancy, a wonder-working charm,
    Laid hold upon his love; he stayed to bless
The small sweet head, then went he forth that night
And sought a nurse to tend his new delight.

And day by day his heart she wrought upon,
    And won her way into its inmost fold—

A heart which, but for lack of that whereon
  To fix itself, would never have been cold;
And, opening wide, now let her come to dwell
  Within its strong unguarded citadel.

She, like a dream, unlocked the hidden springs
  Of his past thoughts, and set their currents free
To talk with him of half-forgotten things—
  The pureness and the peace of infancy,
"Thou also, thou," to sigh, "wert undefiled
(O God, the change!) once as this little child."

The baby-mistress of a soldier's heart,
  She had but friendlessness to stand her friend,
And her own orphanhood to plead her part,
  When he, a wayfarer, did pause, and bend,
And bear with him the starry blossom sweet
Out of its jeopardy from trampling feet.

A gleam of light upon a rainy day,
  A new-tied knot that must be severed soon,
At sunrise once before his tent at play,
  And hurried from the battle-field at noon,
While face to face in hostile ranks they stood,
Who should have dwelt in peace and brotherhood.

But ere the fight, when higher rose the sun,
  And yet were distant far the rebel bands,
She heard at intervals a booming gun,
  And she was pleased, and laughing clapped her hands;
Till he came in with troubled look and tone,
Who chose her desolate to be his own.

And he said, "Little madam, now farewell,
  For there will be a battle fought ere night.
God be thy shield, for He alone can tell
  Which way may fall the fortune of the fight.
To fitter hands the care of thee pertain,
My dear, if we two never meet again,"

Then he gave money shortly to her nurse,
  And charged her straitly to depart in haste,
And leave the plain whereon the deadly curse
  Of war should light with ruin, death and waste,
And all the ills that must its presence blight,
E'en if proud victory should bless the right.

"But if the rebel cause should prosper, then
  It were not good among the hills to wend;
But journey through to Boston in the fen,
  And wait for peace, if peace our God shall send;
And if my life is spared, I will essay,"
Quoth he, "to join you there as best I may."

So then he kissed the child, and went his way;
  But many troubles rolled above his head;
The sun arose on many an evil day,
  And cruel deeds were done, and tears were shed;
And hope was lost, and loyal hearts were fain
In dust to hide,—ere they two met again.

So passed the little child from thought, from view—
  (The snowdrop blossoms, and then is not there,
Forgotten till men welcome it anew),
  He found her in his heavy days of care,
And with her dimples was again beguiled,
As on her nurse's knee she sat and smiled.

And he became a voyager by sea,
  And took the child to share his wandering state;
Since from his native land compelled to flee,
  And hopeless to avert her monarch's fate;
For all was lost that might have made him pause,
And, past a soldier's help, the royal cause.

And thus rolled on long days, long months, and years,
  And Margaret within the Xebec sailed;
The lulling wind made music in her ears,
  And nothing to her life's completeness failed.
Her pastime 'twas to see the dolphins spring,
And wonderful live rainbows glimmering.

The gay sea-plants familiar were to her,
  As daisies to the children of the land;
Red wavy dulse the sunburnt mariner
  Raised from its bed to glisten in her hand;
The vessel and the sea were her life's stage—
Her house, her garden, and her hermitage.

Also she had a cabin of her own,
  For beauty like an elfin palace bright,
With Venice glass adorned and crystal stone,
  That trembled with a many-colored light;
And therewith two caged ringdoves she did play,
And feed them carefully from day to day.

Her bed with silken curtains was enclosed,
  White as the snowy rose of Guelderland;
On Turkish pillows her young head reposed,
  And love had gathered with a careful hand
Fair playthings to the little maiden's side,
From distant ports, and cities parted wide.

She had two myrtle plants that she did tend,
  And think all trees were like to them that grew:
For things on land she did confuse and blend,
  And chiefly from the deck the land she knew,
And in her heart she pitied more and more
The steadfast dwellers on the changeless shore.

Green fields and inland meadows faded out
  Of mind, or with sea images were linked;
And yet she had her childish thoughts about
  The country she had left—though indistinct
And faint as mist the mountain-head that shrouds,
Or dim through distance as Magellan's clouds,

And when to frame a forest scene she tried,
  The ever-present sea would yet intrude,
And all her towns were by the water's side,
  It murmured in all moorland solitude,
Where rocks and the ribbed sand would intervene,
And waves would edge her fancied village green;

Because her heart was like an ocean shell,
  That holds (men say) a message from the deep;
And yet the land was strong, she knew its spell,
  And harbor lights could draw her in her sleep;
And minster chimes from piercèd towers that swim,
Were the land angels making God a hymn.

So she grew on, the idol of one heart,
  And the delight of many—and her face,
Thus dwelling chiefly from her sex apart,
  Was touched with a most deep and tender grace—
A look that never aught but nature gave,
Artless, yet thoughtful; innocent, yet grave.

Strange her adornings were, and strangely blent:
  A golden net confined her nut-brown hair;
Quaint were the robes that divers lands had lent,
  And quaint her aged nurse's skill and care;
Yet did they well on the sea-maiden meet,
Circle her neck, and grace her dimpled feet.

The sailor folk were glad because of her,
  And deemed good fortune followed in her wake;
She was their guardian saint, they did aver—
  Prosperous winds were sent them for her sake;
And strange rough vows, strange prayers, they nightly made,
While, storm or calm, she slept, in nought afraid.

Clear were her eyes, that daughter of the sea,
Sweet, when uplifted to her aged nurse,
She sat, and communed what the world could be;
And rambling stories caused her to rehearse
How Yule was kept, how maidens tossed the hay,
And how bells rang upon a wedding day.

But they grew brighter when the evening star
  First trembled over the still glowing wave,
That bathed in ruddy light, mast, sail, and spar;
  For then, reclined in rest that twilight gave,
With him who served for father, friend and guide,
She sat upon the deck at eventide.

Then turned towards the west, that on her hair
  And her young cheek shed down its tender glow,
He taught her many things with earnest care
  That he thought fitting a young maid should know,
Told of the good deeds of the worthy dead,
And prayers devout, by faithful martyrs said.

And many psalms he caused her to repeat
  And sing them, at his knees reclined the while,
And spoke with her of all things good and meet,
  And told the story of her native isle,
Till at the end he made her tears to flow,
Rehearsing of his royal master's woe.

And of the stars he taught her, and their names,
  And how the chartless mariner they guide:
Of quivering light that in the zenith flames,
  Of monsters in the deep sea caves that hide;
Then changed the theme to fairy records wild,
Enchanted moor, elf dame, or changeling child.

To her the Eastern lands their strangeness spread,
  The dark-faced Arab in his long blue gown,
The camel thrusting down a snake-like head
  To browse on thorns outside a walled white town,
Where palmy clusters rank by rank upright
Float as in quivering lakes of ribbèd light.

And when the ship sat like a broad-winged bird
  Becalmed, lo, lions answered in the night
Their fellows, all the hollow dark was stirred
  To echo on that tremulous thunder's flight,
Dying in weird faint moans;—till look! the sun
And night, and all the things of night, were done.

And'they, toward the waste as morning brake,
  Turned, where, inisled in the green watered land,
The Lybian Zeus lay couched of old, and spake,
  Hemmed in with leagues of furrow-facèd sand—
Then saw the moon (like Joseph's golden cup
Come back) behind some ruined roof swim up.

But blooming childhood will not always last,
  And storms will rise e'en on the tideless sea;
His guardian love took fright, she grew so fast,
  And he began to think how sad 'twould be
If he should die, and pirate hordes should get
By sword or shipwreck his fair Margaret.

It was a sudden thought; but he gave way,
  For it assailed him with unwonted force;
And, with no more than one short week's delay,
  For English shores he shaped the vessel's course;

And ten years absent saw her landed now,
With thirteen summers on her maiden brow.

And so he journeyed with her, far inland,
  Down quiet lanes, by hedges gemmed with dew,
Where wonders met her eye on every hand,
  And all was beautiful and strange and new—
All, from the forest trees in stately ranks,
To yellow cowslips trembling on the banks.

All new—the long drawn slope of evening shades,
  The sweet solemnities of waxing light,
The white-haired boys, the blushing rustic maids,
  The ruddy gleam through cottage casements bright.
The green of pastures, bloom of garden nooks,
And endless bubbling of the water-brooks.

So far he took them on through this green land,
  The maiden and her nurse, till journeying
They saw at last a peaceful city stand
  On a steep mount, and heard its clear bells ring.
High were the towers' and rich with ancient state,
In its old wall enclosed and massive gate.

There dwelt a worthy matron whom he knew,
  To whom in time of war he gave good aid,
Shielding her household from the plundering crew
  When neither law could bind nor worth persuade;
And to her house he brought his care and pride,
Aweary with the way and sleepy-eyed.

And he, the man whom she was fain to serve,
  Delayed not shortly his request to make,
Which was, if aught of her he did deserve,
  To take the maid, and rear her for his sake,
To guard her youth, and let her breeding be
In womanly reserve and modesty.

And that same night into the house he brought
  The costly fruits of all his voyages—
Rich Indian gems of wandering craftsmen wrought,
  Long ropes of pearls from Persian palaces,
With ingots pure and coins of Venice mould,
And silver bars and bags of Spanish gold;

And costly merchandise of far-off lands,
  And golden stuffs and shawls of Eastern dye,
He gave them over to the matron's hands,
  With jewelled gauds, and toys of ivory,
To be her dower on whom his love was set,—
His dearest child, fair Madam Margaret.

Then he entreated, that if he should die,
  She would not cease her guardian mission mild,
Awhile, as undecided, lingered nigh,

Beside the pillow of the sleeping child,
Severed one wandering lock of wavy hair,
Took horse that night, and left her unaware.

And it was long before he came again—
  So long that Margaret was woman grown;
And oft she wished for his return in vain,
  Calling him softly in an undertone;
Repeating words that he had said the while,
And striving to recall his look and smile.

If she had known—oh, if she could have known—
  The toils, the hardships of those absent years—
How bitter thraldom forced the unwilling groan—
  How slavery wrung out subduing tears,
Not calmly had she passed her hours away,
Chiding half pettishly the long delay.

But she was spared. She knew no sense of harm,
  While the red flames ascended from the deck;
Saw not the pirate band the crew disarm.
  Mourned not the floating spars, the smoking wreck.
She did not dream, and there was none to tell,
That fetters bound the hands she loved so well.

Sweet Margaret—withdrawn from human view,
  She spent long hours beneath the cedar shade,
The stately trees that in the garden grew,
  And, overtwined, a towering shelter made;
She mused among the flowers, and birds, and bees,
In winding walks, and bowering canopies;

Or wandered slowly through the ancient rooms,
  Where oriel windows shed their rainbow gleams;
And tapestried hangings, wrought in Flemish looms,
  Displayed the story of King Pharaoh's dreams;
And, come at noon because the well was deep,
Beautiful Rachel leading down her sheep.

At last she reached the bloom of womanhood,
  After five summers spent in growing fair;
Her face betokened all things dear and good,
  The light of somewhat yet to come was there
Asleep, and waiting for the opening day,
When childish thoughts, like flowers, would drift away.

O! we are far too happy while they last;
  We have our good things first, and they cost naught;
Then the new splendor comes unfathomed, vast,
  A costly trouble, ay, a sumptuous thought,
And will not wait, and cannot be possessed,
Though infinite yearnings fold it to the breast.

And time, that seemed so long, is fleeting by,
    And life is more than life; love more than love;
We have not found the whole—and we must die—
    And still the unclasped glory floats above.
The inmost and the utmost faint from sight,
For ever secret in their veil of light.

Be not too hasty in your flow, you rhymes,
    For Margaret is in her garden bower;
Delay to ring, you soft cathedral chimes,
    And tell not out too soon the noontide hour:
For one draws nearer to your ancient town,
On the green mount down settled like a crown.

He journeyed on, and, as he neared the gate,
    He met with one to whom he named the maid,
Inquiring of her welfare, and her state,
    And of the matron in whose house she stayed.
"The maiden dwelt there yet," the townsman said;
"But, for the ancient lady,—she was dead."

He further said, she was but little known,
    Although reputed to be very fair,
And little seen (so much she dwelt alone)
    But with her nurse at stated morning prayer;
So seldom passed her sheltering garden wall,
Or left the gate at quiet evening fall.

Flow softly, rhymes—his hand is on the door;
    Ring out ye noonday bells, his welcoming—
"He went out rich, but he returneth poor;"
    And strong—now something bowed with suffering.
And on his brow are traced long furrowed lines,
Earned in the fight with pirate Algerines.

Her aged nurse comes hobbling at his call:
    Lifts up her withered hand in dull surprise,
And, tottering, leads him through the pillared hall;
    "What! come at last to bless my lady's eyes!
Dear heart, sweet heart, she's grown a likesome maid—
Go, seek her where she sitteth in the shade."

The noonday chime had ceased—she did not know
    Who watched her, while her ringdoves fluttered near;
While, under the green boughs, in accents low
    She sang unto herself. She did not hear
His footstep till she turned, then rose to meet
Her guest with guileless blush and wonder sweet.

But soon she knew him, came with quickened pace,
    And put her gentle hands about his neck;
And leaned her fair cheek to his sun-burned face,
    As long ago upon the vessel's deck:
As long ago she did in twilight deep,
When heaving waters lulled her infant sleep.

So then he kissed her, as men kiss their own,
    And, proudly parting her unbraided hair,
He said: "I did not think to see thee grown
    So fair a woman,"—but a touch of care
The deep-toned voice through its caressing kept,
And hearing it, she turned away and wept.

Wept,—for an impress on the face she viewed—
    The stamp of feelings she remembered not;
His voice was calmer now, but more subdued,
    Not like the voice long loved and unforgot!
She felt strange sorrow and delightful pain—
Grief for the change, joy that he came again.

O pleasant days, that followed his return,
    That made his captive years pass out of mind;
If life had yet new pains for him to learn,
    Not in the maid's clear eyes he saw it shrined;
And three full weeks he stayed with her, content
To find her beautiful and innocent.

It was all one in his contented sight
    As though she were a child, till suddenly,
Waked of the chimes in the dead time of the night,
    He fell to thinking how the urgency
Of Fate had dealt with him, and could but sigh
For those best things wherein she passed him by.

Down the long river of life how, cast adrift,
    She urged him on, still on, to sink or swim;
And all at once, as if a veil did lift,
    In the dead time of the night, and bare to him
The want in his deep soul, he looked, was dumb,
And knew himself, and knew his time was come.

In the dead time of the night his soul did sound
    The dark sea of a trouble unforeseen,
For that one sweet that to his life was bound
    Had turned into a want—a misery keen:
Was born, was grown, and wounded sorely cried
All 'twixt the midnight and the morning tide.

He was a brave man, and he took this thing
    And cast it from him with a man's strong hand;
And that next morn, with no sweet altering
    Of mien, beside the maid he took his stand,
And copied his past self till ebbing day
Paled its deep western blush, and died away.

And then he told her that he must depart
  Upon the morrow, with the earliest light ;
And it displeased and pained her at the heart.
  And she went out to hide her from his sight
Aneath the cedar trees, where dusk was deep,
  And be apart from him awhile to weep

And to lament, till, suddenly aware
  Of steps, she started up as fain to flee,
And met him in the moonlight pacing there,
  Who questioned with her why her tears might be,
Till she did answer him, all red for shame,
  "Kind sir, I weep—the wanting of a name."

"A name!" quoth he, and sighed. "I never knew
  Thy father's name ; but many a stalwart youth,
Would give thee his, dear child, and his love too,
  And count himself a happy man forsooth.
Is there none here who thy kind thought hath won?"
  But she did falter, and made answer, "None."

Then, as in father-like and kindly mood,
  He said, "Dear daughter, it would please me well
To see thee wed ; for know it is not good
  That a fair woman thus alone should dwell."
She said, "I am content it should be so,
  If when you journey I may with you go."

This when he heard, he thought, right sick at heart,
  Must I withstand myself and also thee?
Thou, also thou ! must nobly do thy part ;
  That honor leads thee on which holds back me.
No, thou sweet woman ; by love's great increase,
  I will reject thee for thy truer peace,

Then said he, "Lady !—look upon my face,
  Consider well this scar upon my brow ;
I have had all misfortune but disgrace ;
  I do not look for marriage blessings now,
Be not thy gratitude deceived. I know
  Thou think'st it is thy duty—I will go !

"I read thy meaning, and I go from hence,
  Skilled in the reason ; though my heart be rude,
I will not wrong thy gentle innocence,
  Nor take advantage of thy gratitude.
But think, while yet the light these eyes shall bless,
  The more for thee—of woman's nobleness."

Faultless and fair, all in the moony light,
  As one ashamed she looked upon the ground,
And her white raiment glistened in his sight.
  And, hark ! the vesper chimes began to sound,
Then lower yet she drooped her young, pure cheek,
  And still she was ashamed, and could not speak.

A swarm of bells from that old tower o'erhead,
  They sent their message sifting through the boughs
Of cedars ; when they ceased his lady said,
  "Pray you forgive me," and her lovely brows
She lifted, standing in her moonlit place,
  And one short moment looked him in the face.

Then straight he cried, "O sweetheart, think all one
  As no word yet were said between us twain,
And know thou that in this I yield to none—
  I love thee, sweetheart, love thee ! So full fain,
While she did leave to silence all her part,
  He took the gleaming whiteness to his heart—

The white-robed maiden with the warm white throat,
  The sweet white brow, and locks of umber flow,
Whose murmuring voice was soft as rock-dove's note,
  Entreating him, and saying. "Do not go!"
"I will not, sweetheart ; nay, not now," quoth he,
  "By faith and troth, I think thou art for me!"

And so she won a name that eventide,
  Which he gave gladly, but would ne'er bespeak,
And she became the rough sea-captain's bride,
  Matching her dimples to his sunburnt cheek ;
And chasing from his voice the touch of care,
  That made her weep when first she heard it there.

One year there was, fulfilled of happiness,
  But O ! it went so fast, too fast away.
Then came that trouble which full oft doth bless—
  It was the evening of a sultry day,
There was no wind the thread-hung flowers to stir,
  Or float abroad the filmy gossamer.

Toward the trees his steps the mariner bent,
  Pacing the grassy walks with restless feet ;
And he recalled, and pondered as he went,
  All her most duteous love and converse sweet,
Till summer darkness settled deep and dim,
  And dew from bending leaves dropt down on him.

The flowers sent forth their nightly odors faint—
  Thick leaves shut out the starlight overhead ;
While he told over, as by strong constraint
  Drawn on, her childish life on shipboard led,

And beauteous youth, since first low kneeling there,
With folded hands she lisped her evening prayer.

Then he remembered how, beneath the shade,
She wooed him to her with her lovely words,
While flowers were closing, leaves in moonlight played,
And in dark nooks withdrew the silent birds.
So pondered he that night in twilight dim,
While dew from bending leaves dropt down on him.

The flowers sent forth their nightly odors faint—
When in the darkness waiting, he saw one
To whom he said—"How fareth my sweet saint?"
Who answered—"She hath borne to you a son;"
Then, turning, left him,—and the father said,
"God rain down blessings on his welcome head!"

But Margaret!—*she* never saw the child,
Nor heard about her bed love's mournful wails;
But to the last, with ocean dreams beguiled,
Murmured of troubled seas and swelling sails -
Of weary voyages, and rocks unseen,
And distant hills in sight, all calm and green. .

Woe and alas!—the times of sorrow come,
And make us doubt if we were ever glad!
So utterly that inner voice is dumb.
Whose music through our happy days we had!
So, at the touch of grief, without our will,
The sweet voice drops from us, and all is still.

Woe and alas! for the sea captain's wife—
That Margaret who in the Xebec played—
She spent upon his knee her baby life;
Her slumbering head upon his breast she laid.
How shall he learn alone his years to pass?
How in the empty house?—woe and alas!

She died, and in the aisle, the minster aisle,
They made her grave; and there, with fond intent,
Her husband raised, his sorrow to beguile,
A very fair and stately monument:
Her tomb (the careless vergers show it yet),
The mariner's wife, his love, his Margaret.

A woman's figure, with the eyelids closed,
The quiet head declined in slumber sweet;
Upon an anchor one fair hand reposed,
And a long ensign folded at her feet,
And carved upon the bordering of her vest
The motto of her house—"𝔖𝔢 𝔤𝔦𝔟𝔢𝔱𝔥 𝔯𝔢𝔰𝔱."

There is an ancient window richly fraught
And fretted with all hues most rich, most bright,
And in its upper tracery enwrought
An olive-branch and dove wide-winged and white,
An emblem meet for her, the tender dove,
Her heavenly peace, her duteous earthly love.

Amid heraldic shields and banners set,
In twisted knots and wildly-tangled bands,
Crimson and green, and gold and violet,
Fall softly on the snowy sculptured hands;
And, when the sunshine comes, full sweetly rest
The dove and olive-branch upon her breast.

NOTES.

PAGE I.

THIS story I first wrote in prose, and it was published some years ago.

PAGE 102.

The name of the patriarch's wife is intended to be pronounced Nigh-loi-ya.

Of the three sons of Noah—Shem, Ham, and Japhet—I have called Japhet the youngest (because he is always named last), and have supposed that, in the genealogies where he is called "Japhet the elder," he may have received the epithet because by that time there were younger Japhets.

PAGE 119.

The quivering butterflies in companies,
That slowly crept adown the sandy marge,
Like *living crocus beds*.

This beautiful comparison is taken from "The Naturalist on the River Amazon." "Vast numbers of orange-colored butterflies congregated on the moist sands. They assembled in densely-packed masses, sometimes two or three yards in circumference, their wings all held in an upright position, so that the sands looked as though variegated with *beds of crocuses*."

"GLADYS AND HER ISLAND."

The woman is Imagination; she is brooding over what she brought forth.
The two purple peaks represent the domains of Poetry and of History.
The girl is Fancy.

"WINSTANLEY."

This ballad was intended to be one of a set, and was read to the children of the National Schools at Sherborne, Dorsetshire, in order to discover whether, if the actions of a hero were simply and plainly narrated, English children would like to learn the verses recording them by heart as their forefathers did.

www.ingramcontent.com/pod-product-compliance
Lightning Source LLC
Chambersburg PA
CBHW020239170426
43202CB00008B/149